THE STATE OF FOOD AND AGRICULTURE 1994

FAO Agriculture Series   No. 27

ISSN 0081-4539

THE STATE
OF FOOD
AND
AGRICULTURE
1994

FOOD AND AGRICULTURE ORGANIZATION OF THE UNITED NATIONS

Rome, 1994

The statistical material in this publication has been prepared from the information available to FAO up to August 1994.

The designations employed and the presentation do not imply the expression of any opinion whatsoever on the part of the Food and Agriculture Organization of the United Nations concerning the legal status of any country, territory, city or area, or of its authorities, or concerning the delimitation of its frontiers or boundaries. In some tables, the designations "developed" and "developing" economies are intended for statistical convenience and do not necessarily express a judgement about the stage reached by a particular country or area in the development process.

David Lubin Memorial Library
Cataloguing in Publication Data

FAO, Rome (Italy)
The state of food and agriculture 1994.
(FAO Agriculture Series, no. 27)
ISBN 92-5-103550-4

1. Agriculture.   2. Forestry development.
3. Food production.   4. Trade.

I. Title   II. Series

FAO code: 70   AGRIS: E16 E70 K01

Printed in Italy

Foreword

"Agriculture is the mother and nourisher of all other arts: when
agriculture is well conducted, all other arts prosper; when agriculture is
neglected, all other arts decay, on the land and on the sea."

(Xenophon, *Economico*, V)

More than two millennia after it was written, this statement still contains
much truth. In modern times, for many countries agriculture remains, if not
the cornerstone of their economy, a crucial source of income, employment
and foreign exchange. Even those countries that have reduced their
economic dependence on primary agriculture to a minimum tend to
consider the sector important enough to warrant special attention.

Whether or not agriculture remains a nourisher of the "other arts", it
will always be the source of our daily nourishment. Its role in food
security alone justifies priority attention from policy-makers, and calls
for a "well-conducted" agriculture with the same urgency as in
Xenophon's time.

However well trained to sophism and paradox, an ancient Greek mind
would surely find many aspects of our agricultural order strange, including
the policies that have contributed to its configuration. For instance, that
agriculture should often be neglected where it matters most and yet, in
other countries where its economic and social role is relatively minor,
supported to the point of creating worldwide market distortions. It would
be equally difficult to explain the existence of 800 million malnourished
people in a world of abundance and with societies capable of admirable
scientific and technological feats; our inability to counter the depletion
of more than 15 million ha of tropical forest each year during the past
decade; or the fact that rich countries and societies have tended
to become richer and needy ones needier, while external assistance,
particularly to agriculture, has shown a decline in real terms in
recent years.

The State of Food and Agriculture 1994 examines these issues in the
light of recent trends and developments, with a particular focus on the way
policy-makers "conduct agriculture". As a special feature, it discusses the
difficult policy dilemmas involved in managing our forest resources in a
way that ensures equilibrium between economic and social demands,
sustainability of production and consumption patterns and environmental
stability.

This publication reports the accentuation of anomalies and obstacles to
economic progress and food security in many parts of the world, but it also
reviews a number of positive recent developments in the global political,
economic and institutional fields that raise optimistic expectations for
the future.

Among the positive features, the recent past has seen remarkable economic dynamism in much of the developing world, despite the global recessionary conditions that have prevailed since the beginning of the 1990s. Recent signs of economic recovery in the industrial world augur well for the continuation of this process.

Even more solid grounds for optimism are provided by events within the developing countries themselves. Together with the consolidation of democracy there has been a strengthening of the economic liberalization process in much of the developing world, and this has extended to agriculture. Many developing countries, including some of the largest and most populous, have benefited from this process and made further inroads into the longstanding problems of hunger and malnutrition.

The 1993-1994 period also saw a number of major market and institutional developments affecting agricultural trade. Foremost among these was the signing in Marrakesh of the Final Act concluding the Uruguay Round of GATT negotiations and the agreement to create a World Trade Organization. These important events bear the promise of global welfare benefits as well as clearer, more orderly and enforceable "rules of the game" for trade, including in agriculture. Nevertheless, the Uruguay Round's outcome in terms of market access and reductions in domestic support and export subsidization fell short of what could be expected from the importance of the issues at stake and the seven years of strenuous negotiations involved. Protectionism remains intense and is likely to remain so in the future, and major efforts still have to be made to improve market access for and the competitiveness of developing countries' agricultural exports. While recent months have witnessed a welcome strengthening in prices for commodities of crucial importance to many developing country economies, this cannot be taken as the sign of a fundamental improvement in the distortions and weaknesses of the global agricultural market. Moreover, different groups of countries will be affected by trade liberalization in different ways. In particular, many low-income net food importers risk seeing their import bill increase and their food security situation deteriorate, at least initially. This calls for generous and farsighted efforts to help food-deficit countries overcome the negative impact of the new trade environment while maximizing any market opportunities that may be offered to them.

Another major process under way is the strengthening of regional trade and economic integration agreements. The consolidation and broadening of economic integration in Europe and the establishment of the North American Free Trade Agreement have been milestones in this process. I must, however, emphasize the importance of extending the benefits of integration schemes to all countries, particularly the least advantaged, and of allowing participation in such schemes by all countries willing to join.

The 1993-1994 period has also seen its share of distressing events and human tragedies, which have directly or indirectly affected global food security. Among the developed countries, the European region has seen the continuation of the devastating conflict in Bosnia and Herzegovina, severe and mounting unemployment and problems of fiscal and monetary consolidation that cast doubts on the extent and timing of the current recovery. In Central and Eastern Europe, several countries have strengthened the pace and depth of market-oriented reform and seem set to enter an expansionary phase. Others, however, particularly in the former USSR, are still struggling to break a vicious circle: deep recession and related political and social problems render reform increasingly difficult to pursue, yet extensive and systematic reform constitute a precondition for recovery.

Agriculture, a central element in the process of reform in the economies in transition, has been fully exposed to the disruptions and initial recessionary effects associated with the breakdown of the old organizational structures. Sharp drops in production have resulted in declines in per caput food consumption, and large population groups are actually facing the problem of malnutrition.

Turning to the situation in Africa, I should first refer to what is perhaps the most momentous political event of 1994 – the demise of apartheid and the introduction of majority rule in South Africa. Also welcome is the cessation of a number of armed conflicts that had long afflicted various parts of the region. Against such positive developments, however, the recent past has seen the tragedy of civil war in Rwanda, with a dramatic sequel of human suffering, large-scale refugee problems and famine; the disappointing turn of events in Somalia, where civil conflicts have stalled the process of national reconciliation; the continuation of a seemingly unstoppable process of economic and social regression in much of the region; the emergence or aggravation of food emergency situations in numerous countries, chiefly in East Africa; and, as discussed in this publication, the alarming spread of AIDS throughout the world which, particularly in sub-Saharan Africa, has come to represent not only a major health problem with long-term demographic and economic implications, but also an additional threat to food security.

A few indicators suffice to illustrate the explosive nature of the food security problem in the sub-Saharan Africa region and point to the direction of policy action required. With per caput food production falling by more than 20 percent over the past two decades, sub-Saharan Africa has progressively become a net importer of food. The region's per caput calorie intake two decades ago was above the average for developing countries as a whole, whereas it is now 18 percent lower. It appears obvious, therefore, that the achievement of food security in Africa is to be realized first and foremost through a revival of food production in the years ahead. This task, which involves huge investments in key areas such as irrigation, productivity-enhancing technology, environmental protection and the formation of a skilled, highly productive labour force, requires decisive and immediate action by African countries themselves. The establishment and preservation of a policy environment that is conducive to agricultural growth is a prerequisite for achieving this task. However, it also requires the international donor and development community's awareness that the food problem in sub-Saharan Africa is arguably the most pressing problem for the contemporary world. Humankind would suffer an incalculable cost in allowing Africa to be further marginalized in the areas of trade, development assistance and international capital flows.

Jacques Diouf
DIRECTOR-GENERAL

Contents

Foreword   v
Glossary   xviii
Explanatory note   xxi

PART I
WORLD REVIEW

I. CURRENT AGRICULTURAL
SITUATION – FACTS AND
FIGURES   3

1. Crop and livestock production
    in 1993   3

2. Per caput food production   6

3. Food shortages and emergencies   11

4. Current cereal supply, utilization
    and stocks   14

5. External assistance to agriculture   16

6. Food aid flows in 1993/94   18

7. International agricultural prices   20

8. Agricultural terms of trade   22

9. Fisheries: catch, disposition
    and trade   24

10. Forestry production and trade   26

II. OVERALL ECONOMIC
ENVIRONMENT AND
AGRICULTURE   29

Economic overview   29

Economic outlook for developing
countries' agriculture   31

Outlook for developing countries
highly dependent on agricultural
exports   37

III. SELECTED ISSUES   45

AIDS – the price of an epidemic   45

The economic impact of AIDS   46

A note on statistics   48

Regional overviews   50

Patterns of transmission and
risk factors   51

Interventions   53

A global greenhouse   55

Global warming linkages to
agriculture, forestry and fisheries   56

Contribution to GHGs from
agriculture, forestry and fisheries   58

The overall policy approach   58

Short-term responses and no-regrets
policies   58

Policy linkages to agriculture,
forestry and fisheries   60

Longer-term responses   61

Summary   61

**Uruguay Round of multilateral
trade negotiations** 62

Provisions of the Final Act 62

Effects on agricultural markets 68

Policy implications 73

**North American Free Trade
Agreement** 74

Canada-Mexico-United States
linkages 75

An enlarged NAFTA? 80

Current issues in fisheries 83

Food security and economic
development in small island
countries 83

Compliance with international
conservation and management on
the high seas 84

PART II
REGIONAL REVIEW

**I. DEVELOPING COUNTRY
REGIONS** 89

SUB-SAHARAN AFRICA 89

Regional overview 89

Changes in the international
economic environment 89

Political events and intraregional
cooperation 91

The GATT agreement and Africa 92

Regional cooperation 93

Country policies 96

Devaluation of the CFA franc 98

Effects on agriculture 100

Ghana 104

General characteristics and
economic setting 104

Macroeconomic policies before
1983 105

Policies for the agricultural sector 107

Overall and agriculture-specific
effects of pre-1983 policies 109

Economic decline: the critical role
of agriculture 110

Post-1983 policies 112

From adjustment to growth:
constraints, prospects and the role
of agriculture 116

Conclusions 124

ASIA AND THE PACIFIC 126

Regional overview 126

Public and private sector roles
under policy reforms 129

Growing importance of intraregional
trade, investment flows and growth
triangles 131

Implications of the Uruguay Round
Agreement for Asian agriculture 132

Growth, poverty alleviation and
regional development 133

China 135

Economic overview 135

China's agricultural sector in
transition 137

Rural reforms and agricultural
development 141

Rural enterprise development and
agriculture 143

Future directions in farm
organization and agriculture 145

LATIN AMERICA AND
THE CARIBBEAN 150

Regional overview 150

The agricultural sector 152

Trade arrangements in Latin
America and the Caribbean 156

Brazil 162

The economy 162

Stabilization and adjustment
programmes since the 1980s 162

Role and performance of agriculture 165

Sectoral policies in the context of
macroeconomic adjustment 168

Government intervention in
marketing 174

Foreign exchange policies and
agricultural markets 175

Financial markets, inflation and
agriculture 178

Conclusions 181

NEAR EAST AND NORTH AFRICA 183

Regional overview 183

Economic and agricultural
performance in 1993 183

Policy reforms and issues 187

Water issues 188

Turkey 190

Agriculture's role in the economy 190

Government intervention 190

Changes in rural and urban
consumer demand 195

Production outlook 196

Resource and environmental issues 198

**II. DEVELOPED COUNTRY
REGIONS** 203

CENTRAL AND EASTERN EUROPE 203

Regional overview 203

Estonia, Latvia and Lithuania 208

The agricultural sector 208

Economic reforms 209

Main policy issues and outlook 217

Ukraine 220

The agricultural sector 220

Economic reforms 222

Prospects for food and agriculture 226

OECD COUNTRIES 229

**Agricultural policy developments
in Canada** 229

Slow-growth high-deficit economy 229

Structural adjustment in the
primary sector 230

Agriculture is highly dependent on
world trade 231

High levels of government
assistance for the sector 232

Policy process 233

Current policy issues 233

Impact of policies 238

Conclusion 243

The European Union 244

PART III
FOREST DEVELOPMENT AND POLICY DILEMMAS

I. FORESTS IN TRANSITION 251

Introduction 251

The policy challenge 254

Purpose and scope 256

The state of forest resources 258

Temperate and boreal forests:
resources and issues 259

The tropical forest zone 264

Plantations 267

II. FORESTS AND NATIONAL DEVELOPMENT 270

Forests in early development strategies 271

Forests in national economies 273

Forests as a source of national development 278

Forests as a consequence of national development 285

The economic contributions of forests 287

III. FORESTS IN NATIONAL POLICY 292

Policy choices and forests 292

Domestic policies and forest management 297

Forestry policies and management practices 305

IV. FORESTS, TRADE AND THE ENVIRONMENT 315

World trade patterns in forest products 316

Trade policies and forest management 318

Export restrictions 318

Import restrictions 319

Tropical timber import bans 319

Forest trade and environmental policies 323

Trade liberalization and the environment 325

Environmental labelling, certification and sustainable management 326

Balancing trade and the environment 328

Summary 330

V. FORESTS AND FUTURE DIRECTIONS 333

Community forestry 335

Capacity development 339

The international dimensions 344

EXHIBITS

1. Changes in agricultural
   production, 1990-1993   5

2. Changes in per caput food
   production, 1988-1993   7

3. Food supply shortfalls requiring
   exceptional assistance   13

4. Supply/utilization trends
   in cereals   15

5. Commitments of external
   assistance to agriculture   17

6. Shipments of food aid in cereals   19

7. Export prices of selected
   commodities, 1990-1994   21

8. Terms of trade of agricultural
   exports for manufactured
   goods and crude petroleum   23

9. World fish catch, disposition
   and trade   25

10. Output and export value
    of main forest products   27

BOXES

1. External debt situation of
   developing countries   33

2. Economies highly dependent on
   agricultural exports: export
   performance and growth   41

3. AIDS   49

4. Key NAFTA provisions   76

5. Reform and rural poverty in
   Ghana   121

6. Recent development issues in
   the Pacific Islands   146

7. Selected trading blocs in
   Latin America and
   the Caribbean   157

8. Emergency Agrarian
   Reform Programme   166

9. Social problems in Brazil   179

10. Baltic fisheries   214

11. Temperate forests' values:
    carbon storage and biodiversity   262

12. Malaysia's compensatory
    plantation programme   268

13. Environmental trade:
    debt-for-nature swaps   277

14. The role of forests in five
    domains of human welfare   279

15. Minor forest products in
    West Africa   281

16. Changing forest conditions: India, Thailand and the United States   283

17. Economic services provided by forest ecosystems   288

18. Landscape formation models and forests   294

19. Economic policy and potential impacts on timber management   302

20. Concession pricing and licensing   306

21. Clear-felling practices   313

22. Northern influences on tropical forest policies   321

23. Country certification   330

24. Joint forest management in India   337

25. Canada's forests and the Model Forest concept   340

26. Forestry-related conventions at UNCED   343

27. International organizations and forests   345

TABLES

1. Economies highly dependent on agricultural exports   39

2. Agricultural greenhouse gases and trends   59

3. Simulated effects of Uruguay Round trade liberalization on world prices   70

4. Growth rates in agricultural GDP   128

5. Aggregate production of main agricultural commodities in the four new member countries as a percentage of production in EC-12   245

6. Net exports of major agricultural commodities from the four new EC member countries   245

7. The top ten most forested countries, 1990   260

8. Area of tropical forest formation, 1990   265

9. Forest cover and deforestation in the tropical zone   266

10. Economic value of Swedish forests   289

11. Production of forest products, 1992   289

12. Fuelwood in world energy consumption   290

13. Tropical timber rent capture   310

14. World trade in forest products   316

FIGURES

1. World economic output   30

2. World output and volume
of world trade   31

3. Composition of debt   32

4. Growth in total GDP and
value added in agriculture,
developing country regions   36

5. Sub-Saharan Africa   90

6. Asia and the Pacific   127

7. Latin America and
the Caribbean   151

8. Near East and North Africa   184

9. The world forest cover, 1990   259

10. World wood consumption,
1961-1992   287

11. Composition of biofuels in
energy supply of selected
countries   290

12. The largest importers and
exporters of forest
products, 1992   317

Acknowledgements

The State of Food and Agriculture 1994 has been prepared by a team from the Policy Analysis Division led by F.L. Zegarra and comprising P.L. Iacoacci, G.E. Rossmiller, J. Skoet, K. Stamoulis and R. Stringer. Secretarial support was provided by S. di Lorenzo and P. Di Santo; computer and statistical support was provided by T. Sadek, G. Arena and Z. Pinna.

Contributions and background papers for the World review were prepared by B.J. Brindley, J. Greenfield, S. Langley, M. Palmieri, M. Spinedi, S. Teodosijevic, P. Wardle, R. Wingle and G. Zanias.

Background papers for the Regional review were prepared by A. Buainain, O. Cismondi, H.B. Huff, M. Kurtzig, D.J. Sedik, S.S. Sheffield and F. Zhong.

The special chapter, Forest development and policy dilemmas, was prepared by R. Stringer with assistance from P. Wardle and I.J. Bourke. It was based on contributions from J. Romm, E.B. Barbier, R. Mohamed Ali, R. Turner, U. Banerjee, W. Stewart and J. Carvalho. Many officers from the World Bank, World Resources Institute, Worldwatch Institute and the World Wide Fund for Nature provided helpful comments and suggestions.

The State of Food and Agriculture 1994 was edited by R. Tucker. The graphics were prepared by M. Cappucci and the layout by M. Criscuolo with C. Ciarlantini. The cover and illustrations were produced by Studio Page.

Glossary

ACP
African, Caribbean and Pacific States
AfDB
African Development Bank
AGF
Federal Government Acquisition
AIDS
Acquired immune deficiency syndrome
ALADI (LAIA)
Latin America Integration Association
AMS
Aggregate Measurement of Support
AsDB
Asian Development Bank
ASEAN
Association of Southeast Asian Nations
ATO
African Timber Organization

BEAC
Bank of Central African States

CACM
Central America Common Market
CAP
Common Agricultural Policy
CARICOM
Caribbean Community and Common Market
CBI
Caribbean Basin Initiative
CGIAR
Consultative Group on International
Agricultural Research
c.i.f.
Cost, insurance and freight
CIFOR
Centre for International Forestry Research
CINTRAFOR
Center for International Trade of Forest
Products
CIS
Commonwealth of Independent States

CMB
Cocoa Marketing Board
COCOBOD
Ghana Cocoa Board
CUSTA
Canada-US Free Trade Agreement

EAI
Enterprise for the Americas Initiative
EAP
Economically active population
EC
European Community
EGF
Federal Government Loans
EHDAEs
Economies highly dependent on agricultural
exports
ERP
Economic recovery programme
ERS
Economic Research Service
EU
European Union

FAPRI
Food and Agricultural Policy Research
Institute
FDI
Foreign direct investment
f.o.b.
Free on board
FSC
Forest Stewardship Council
FTA
Free trade agreement

GATT
General Agreement on Tariffs and Trade
GDP
Gross domestic product

GEF
Global Environmental Facility
GHG
Greenhouse gas
GNP
Gross national product
GRIP
Gross Revenue Insurance Plan
GSP
Generalized System of Preferences

HIV
Human immunodeficiency virus
HRS
Household responsibility system
HYV
High-yielding varieties

IBRD
International Bank for Reconstruction and Development
ICCO
International Cocoa Organization
ICO
International Coffee Organization
ICRAF
International Center for Research in Agroforestry
IDA
International Development Association
IEFR
International Emergency Food Reserve
IFPRI
International Food Policy Research Institute
IIED
International Institute for Environment and Development
IMF
International Monetary Fund
IPCC
Intergovernmental Panel on Climate Change
IPGRI
International Plant Genetic Resources Institute
IPPC
International Plant Protection Convention

ISA
International Sugar Agreement
ITTA
International Tropical Timber Agreement
ITTO
International Tropical Timber Organization
IUCN
World Conservation Union

LAFTA
Latin American Free Trade Area
LDC
Least-developed country

MERCOSUR
Southern Common Market
MFA
Multifibre Arrangement
MFN
Most favoured nation
MMA
Multilateral Monetary Area
MPP
Minimum price programme
MTNs
Multilateral trade negotiations

NAFTA
North American Free Trade Agreement
NCPB
National Cereals and Produce Board
NGO
Non-governmental organization
NISA
Net Income Stabilization Account
NMP
Net material product
NTB
Non-tariff barrier
NTSP
National Tripartite Stabilization Programme

ODI
Overseas Development Institute

OECD
Organisation for Economic Co-operation
and Development
OPEC
Organization of the Petroleum Exporting
Countries

PSE
Producer subsidy equivalent

SAARC
South Asian Association for Regional
Cooperation
SACU
Southern Africa Customs Union
SADC
Southern African Development Community
SAFTA
South Asian Free Trade Agreement
SAL
Structural adjustment loan
SAP
Structural adjustment programme
SNCR
National Rural Credit System
SPDC
Special Programme for Developing
Countries

TFAP
Tropical Forests Action Programme
TRIM
Trade-related investment measure
TRQ
Tariff-rate quota
TVE
Township and village enterprise

UEMOA
West African Economic and Monetary
Union
UMOA
West African Monetary Union
UNCED
United Nations Conference on Environment
and Development

UNCTAD
United Nations Conference on Trade and
Development
UNDP
United Nations Development Programme
UNEP
United Nations Environment Programme
URV
Unit reference value
USDA
United States Department of Agriculture

VAT
Value added tax

WFP
World Food Programme
WGTA
Western Grain Transportation Act
WHFTA
Western Hemisphere Free Trade Agreement
WHO
World Health Organization
WIDER
World Institute for Development Economics
Research
WRI
World Resources Institute
WTO
World Trade Organization
WWF
World Wide Fund for Nature

Explanatory note

The following symbols are used in the tables:

- = none or negligible
... = not available
1991/92 = a crop, marketing or fiscal year running from one calendar year to the next
1990-92 = average for three calendar years

Figures in statistical tables may not add up because of rounding. Annual changes and rates of change have been calculated from unrounded figures. Unless otherwise indicated, the metric system is used.

The dollar sign ($) refers to US dollars. "Billion" is equal to 1 000 million.

Production index numbers
FAO index numbers have *1972-81* as the base period. The production data refer to primary commodities (e.g. sugar cane and sugar beet instead of sugar) and national average producer prices are used as weights. The indices for food products exclude tobacco, coffee, tea, inedible oilseeds, animal and vegetable fibres and rubber. They are based on production data presented on a calendar-year basis.[1]

Trade index numbers
The indices of trade in agricultural products also are based on *1979-81*. They include all the commodities and countries shown in the *FAO Trade Yearbook*. Indices of total food products include those edible products generally classified as "food".

All indices represent changes in current values of exports (f.o.b.) and imports (c.i.f.), all expressed in US dollars. When countries report imports valued at f.o.b. (free on board), these are adjusted to approximate c.i.f. (cost, insurance, freight) values. This method of estimation shows a discrepancy whenever the trend of insurance and freight diverges from that of the commodity unit values.

Volumes and unit value indices represent the changes in the price-weighted sum of quantities and of the quantity-weighted unit values of products traded between countries. The weights are, respectively, the price and quantity averages of *1979-81*, which is the base reference period used for all the index number series currently computed by FAO. The Laspeyres formula is used in the construction of the index numbers.[2]

Definitions of "narrow" and "broad"
The OECD definitions of agriculture are generally used in reporting on external assistance to agriculture. The *narrow* definition of agriculture, now referred to as "directly to the sector" includes the following items:
- Appraisal of natural resources
- Development and management of natural resources
- Research
- Supply of production inputs
- Fertilizers
- Agricultural services
- Training and extension
- Crop production
- Livestock development
- Fisheries
- Agriculture (subsector unallocated)

---

[1] For full details, see *FAO Production Yearbook 1993*.

[2] For full details, see *FAO Trade Yearbook 1992*.

The *broad* definition includes, in addition to the above items, activities that are defined as "indirectly to the sector". These activities are:
- Forestry
- Manufacturing of inputs
- Agro-industries
- Rural infrastructure
- Rural development
- Regional development
- River development

Regional coverage

Developing countries include sub-Saharan Africa, Latin America and the Caribbean, the Near East and North Africa[3] and Asia and the Pacific.[4]

Developed countries include: the industrial countries and economies in transition.[5]

---

[3] The Near East and North Africa includes: Afghanistan, Algeria, Bahrain, Cyprus, Egypt, Islamic Republic of Iran, Iraq, Jordan, Kuwait, Lebanon, Libyan Arab Jamahiriya, Morocco, Oman, Qatar, Kingdom of Saudi Arabia, the Sudan, Syrian Arab Republic, Tunisia, Turkey, United Arab Emirates and Yemen.

[4] Asia and the Pacific also includes the former Asian centrally planned economies: Cambodia, China, Democratic People's Republic of Korea, Mongolia and Viet Nam.

[5] The "industrial countries" include: Australia, Austria, Belgium, Canada, Denmark, Finland, France, Germany, Greece, Iceland, Ireland, Italy, Japan, Luxembourg, the Netherlands, New Zealand, Norway, Portugal, Spain, Sweden, Switzerland, United Kingdom and United States. The "economies in transition" include: Albania, Bosnia and Herzegovina, Bulgaria, Croatia, Czech Republic, the former Yugoslav Republic of Macedonia, Hungary, Poland, Romania, Slovakia, Slovenia, Yugoslavia, SFR and the former Soviet republics.

PART I
WORLD REVIEW

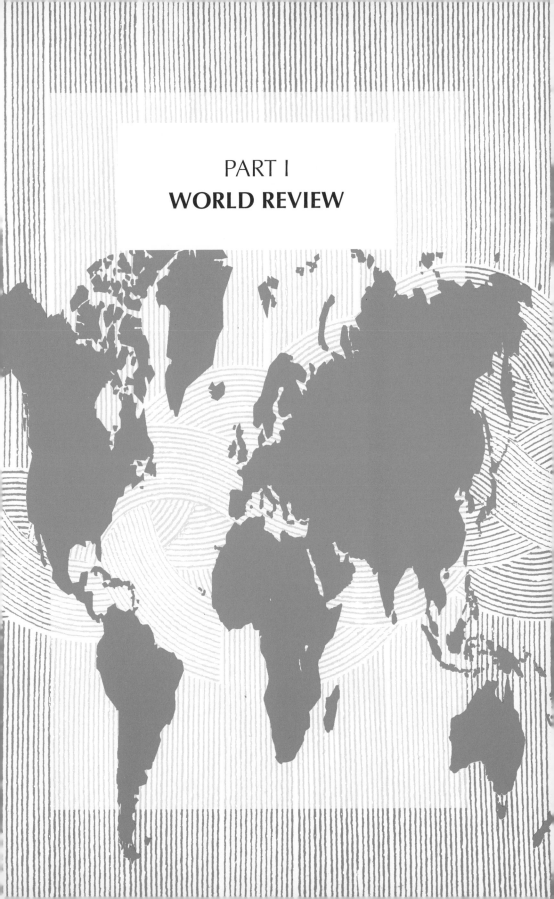

WORLD REVIEW
I. Current agricultural situation – facts and figures

1. CROP AND LIVESTOCK PRODUCTION IN 1993

- At the global level, 1993 was an unfavourable agricultural year. Global agricultural production declined by 1.2 percent, following the 2.8 percent expansion recorded in 1992. Performance, however, was uneven among regions and between developing and developed countries.

- The global contraction was largely accounted for by a significant drop in developed country production, which declined by 5.2 percent after the expansion of 2.9 percent recorded in 1992.

- Agricultural output declined in 1993 in most developed country regions, but particularly so in North America, where production dropped by no less than 10 percent. Crop production in the United States fell by almost 17 percent, as adverse weather conditions sharply reduced major crops. A reduction of 3.3 percent was recorded in the EC, while in Oceania the estimated contraction was of 2.1 percent.

- In Eastern Europe, agricultural production increased for the first time since 1989, by 2.1 percent, as crop production in major producing countries picked up after the drought-affected 1992 crop. Reliable aggregate indices of overall agricultural production in the former Soviet republics do not exist at present, but agricultural production appears to have declined in 1993 in most of the republics.

- Developing country production in 1993 expanded by an estimated 1.7 percent, slightly below population growth, representing a further deceleration from the rates of 2.7 percent recorded in 1992, 3 percent in 1991 and 4.1 percent in 1990.

- Among the developing country regions, the most favourable performance in 1993 was recorded by sub-Saharan Africa with an estimated expansion of 3.4 percent. This increase was, however, only marginally above the rate of population growth of 3.2 percent and followed a virtual stagnation in production the previous year, characterized by severe drought in southern Africa.

- An increase in agricultural production of about 2.4 percent was recorded in the Far East (0.5 percent per caput), which nevertheless constituted a slow-down from the production growth of the previous three years.

• After three years of mediocre agricultural performances, when output barely kept pace with population growth, Latin America and the Caribbean experienced a severe production shortfall in 1993. The 1990-93 average growth in agricultural production – 1.2 percent – was about half the already low average growth rate of the 1980s.

• The Near East and North Africa saw a marked deceleration in agricultural output growth after the bumper 1990 crop year. In 1993 regional output declined slightly, largely as a result of damaging droughts in Morocco, for the second consecutive year, as well as in Algeria.

Exhibit 1

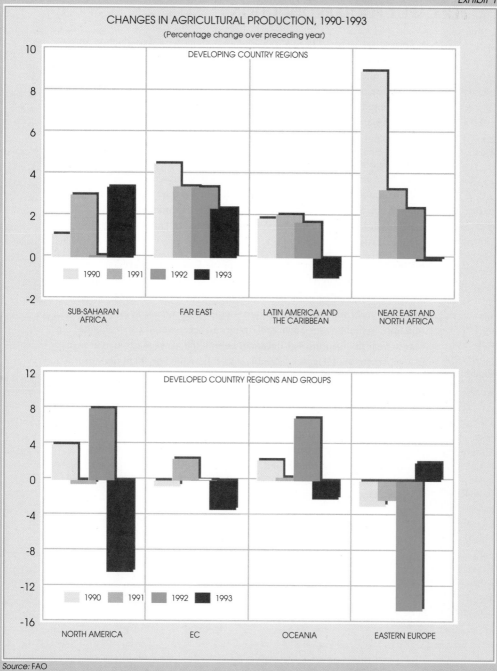

CHANGES IN AGRICULTURAL PRODUCTION, 1990-1993
(Percentage change over preceding year)

DEVELOPING COUNTRY REGIONS

1990   1991   1992   1993

SUB-SAHARAN AFRICA   FAR EAST   LATIN AMERICA AND THE CARIBBEAN   NEAR EAST AND NORTH AFRICA

DEVELOPED COUNTRY REGIONS AND GROUPS

1990   1991   1992   1993

NORTH AMERICA   EC   OCEANIA   EASTERN EUROPE

Source: FAO

2. PER CAPUT FOOD PRODUCTION

• The period 1988-1993 saw a decline in per caput food production levels in approximately 60 percent of the total number of developing countries. Nevertheless, regional differences were significant. In sub-Saharan Africa about three-quarters of all countries recorded stagnating or falling levels of per caput food production. By contrast, in Latin America and the Caribbean, the Near East and North Africa and continental Asia, roughly the same number of countries recorded gains and losses.

• A more positive picture emerges when considering the populations involved. Several of the largest and most densely populated countries in each region achieved gains in per caput food production: Nigeria and Zaire in sub-Saharan Africa; China, India, Pakistan, Indonesia and Bangladesh in Asia; Brazil, Mexico and Colombia in Latin America; and Egypt and Algeria in North Africa.

• Exhibit 2 clearly points to a grave domestic food supply problem in much of sub-Saharan Africa. No less than 33 countries have seen their production lag behind population growth – in several cases dramatically so. Problems of supply instability have compounded the gravity of the situation. In many cases, favourable performances overall conceal wide year-to-year fluctuations. For instance, behind the average positive growth in Zimbabwe, Mali, Uganda, Zambia and Togo were very high rates of increase in 1993, a year of recovery from the severe shortfall the previous year.

• All countries in transition in Eastern Europe and the former USSR except Poland suffered a dramatic contraction in per caput food production. The year 1993 saw a continuation of negative trends for the former Soviet republics, former Yugoslavia, SFR, former Czechoslovakia, Bulgaria and Hungary. For Romania and Poland, however, 1993 saw a recovery in food production following the drought-reduced harvest of 1992.

Exhibit 2

CHANGES IN PER CAPUT FOOD PRODUCTION BY DEVELOPING COUNTRIES, 1988-1993
(Average percentage rate of change)

%	Sub-Saharan Africa	Asia and the Pacific	Latin America and the Caribbean	Near East and North Africa
More than 5				Lebanon Libyan Arab Jamahiriya Tunisia
3.01 to 5		China Malaysia Viet Nam		Algeria Iran, Islamic Rep.
1.01 to 3	Nigeria Togo Uganda	Fiji Indonesia Myanmar Pakistan	Chile Costa Rica Ecuador Guyana Jamaica Nicaragua Uruguay	Jordan
0.01 to 1	Benin Guinea Guinea-Bissau Malawi Zaire Zambia Zimbabwe	Bangladesh India Laos	Belize Bolivia Brazil Colombia El Salvador Mexico Trinidad and Tobago Venezuela	Egypt

Source: FAO

Exhibit 2

CHANGES IN PER CAPUT FOOD PRODUCTION BY DEVELOPING COUNTRIES, 1988-1993
(Average percentage rate of change)

%	Sub-Saharan Africa	Asia and the Pacific	Latin America and the Caribbean	Near East and North Africa
0 to -1	Burkina Faso Chad Namibia Senegal	Bhutan Korea, Rep. Nepal Papua New Guinea Philippines Vanuatu	Argentina Dominican Rep. Guatemala Martinique Paraguay	Cyprus Saudi Arabia
-1.01 to -2	Burundi Comoros Ghana Madagascar Mali Mauritius Mozambique Niger Reunion	Cambodia Maldives Sri Lanka Thailand Tonga	Barbados Guadeloupe Honduras Panama Suriname	Iraq Sudan Syrian Arab Rep. Turkey
-2.01 to -4	Angola Botswana Cameroon Central African Rep. Congo Côte d'Ivoire Gabon Mauritania Rwanda Sierra Leone Swaziland Tanzania, United Rep.	Samoa Solomon Islands	Peru Puerto Rico	Morocco Yemen
-4.01 to -10	Cape Verde Gambia Kenya Lesotho Sao Tome and Principe	Brunei Darussalam Korea, Dem. People's Rep. Mongolia	Bahamas Cuba Haiti	Afghanistan
More than -10	Ethiopia Liberia Somalia			

Source: FAO

Exhibit 2

CHANGES IN PER CAPUT FOOD PRODUCTION BY INDUSTRIAL COUNTRIES AND ECONOMIES IN TRANSITION, 1988-1993
(Average percentage rate of change)

%	Industrial countries	Economies in transition
More than 5	Portugal	
3.01 to 5	Belgium/Luxembourg Canada Ireland	
1.01 to 3	Australia Denmark Greece Malta Netherlands United States	
0.01 to 1	Finland Italy Norway Sweden	Poland

Source: FAO

Exhibit 2

CHANGES IN PER CAPUT FOOD PRODUCTION BY INDUSTRIAL COUNTRIES AND ECONOMIES IN TRANSITION, 1988-1993
(Average percentage rate of change)

%	Industrial countries	Economies in transition
0 to -1	France Spain Switzerland United Kingdom	
-1.01 to -2	Austria Iceland Japan New Zealand South Africa	
-2.01 to -4	Germany Israel	Romania
-4.01 to -10		Albania Bulgaria Hungary
More than -10		Former Czechoslovakia Former Yugoslavia, SFR Former USSR

Source: FAO

3. FOOD SHORTAGES AND EMERGENCIES

• Africa is still the continent most seriously affected by food shortages requiring exceptional and/or emergency assistance. The situation is most critical in East Africa, where severe food shortages are emerging and deaths from starvation-related causes and acute malnutrition are increasingly reported from several areas. Fifteen countries in the region are currently facing exceptional food emergencies and half of these countries are also being affected by civil strife.

• In *Rwanda*, the civil strife has had disastrous consequences for national food security. The strife has seriously disrupted farming activities. Massive international support for the provision of relief food and the rehabilitation of the agricultural sector will be needed to avert suffering and further losses of lives.

• In *Burundi*, agricultural activities were seriously affected by ethnic conflicts in October 1993. The food deficit in 1994 is estimated to be 1 million tonnes. In addition to emergency food assistance, donor support and the implementation of a massive agricultural rehabilitation programme are needed to restore domestic food production to its pre-crisis levels.

• Famine conditions are emerging in several parts of the *Horn of Africa*. Substantial relief assistance is required by *Ethiopia, Eritrea, Kenya, Somalia* and *the Sudan*. In the *United Republic of Tanzania*, the food supply situation is critical for a large number of subsistence farmers who lost their short rains crops. The already tight food supply situation in *Uganda* has been further aggravated by the influx of refugees from Rwanda and the Sudan.

• Grave food shortages persist in *Angola*. The food supply outlook for 1994 is extremely bleak owing to a sharp reduction in the output of cereals and cassava. There is a serious threat of widespread famine unless arrangements for large-scale food assistance and its distribution are made to feed the affected population.

• Despite some recovery of cereal production, the food supply situation will remain tight in *Mozambique*, as the 1994 cassava output is forecast to be down by 6 percent from last year. Some 1.5 million people will need emergency food aid in 1994/95. A poor harvest in *Malawi* points to a substantial increase in cereal import requirements in 1994/95.

• Other African countries facing shortfalls in food supplies and requiring exceptional or emergency assistance include *Chad, Liberia* and *Zaire*.

• In *Afghanistan*, the already tight food supply situation has deteriorated further as a result of renewed fighting, and large numbers of returnees and internally displaced people need international food aid. In *Iraq*, the food and nutrition situation remains grave in all parts of the country. The latest

FAO Nutrition Status Assessment Mission stressed that the food supply problems cannot be solved by the provision of food aid alone and that a more constructive solution should be sought for the country to produce and/or import its food needs. In *Laos*, following a reduced paddy output in 1993, some 10 percent of the total population is in need of exceptional emergency food assistance. The food supply situation is also tight in *Cambodia* and *Mongolia*.

• In *Bosnia and Herzegovina*, the tight food situation has eased somewhat with the improved food aid distribution to central parts, particularly Sarajevo, following the opening of the roads from the Adriatic coast and the increasing commercial traffic in the past two months.

• The already difficult food supply situation in *Haiti* is deteriorating rapidly owing to the tightening of the UN embargo. Prices of basic foods and essential consumer goods have increased sharply and conditions in all sectors of the economy continue to worsen.

• Other countries facing shortfalls in food supplies and requiring exceptional and/or emergency assistance are *Armenia, Azerbaijan, Georgia* and *Tajikistan*.

Exhibit 3

FOOD SUPPLY SHORTFALLS* REQUIRING EXCEPTIONAL ASSISTANCE

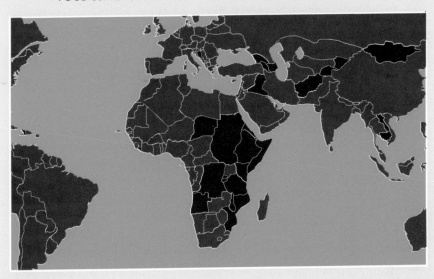

Source: FAO, Global Information and Early Warning System, July 1994

* In current marketing year

4. CURRENT CEREAL SUPPLY, UTILIZATION AND STOCKS

• Global cereal production fell in 1993 by 3.8 percent to 1 890 million tonnes, mainly as a result of a significant decline in maize output in the United States. With rice converted from paddy to a milled basis, this corresponds to 1 705 million tonnes, as shown in Exhibit 4. Reflecting this, world cereal supplies in 1993/94 dropped to 2 088 million tonnes, or 33 million tonnes less than in 1992/93.

• As a result of smaller crops, global cereal carryover stocks were drawn down sharply during the 1993/94 seasons to 326 million tonnes, i.e. some 12 percent or 46 million tonnes below their opening level. However, the ratio of global cereal stocks at the end of the 1993/94 seasons to the trend utilization in 1994/95 remained within the 17 to 18 percent range, which is considered by FAO to be the minimum necessary to safeguard world food security.

• FAO's first forecast of 1994 global cereal output is 1 947 million tonnes, 3 percent above the reduced crop in 1993, but still below the trend. Most of the rise in production in 1994 is expected to occur in the developed countries and should be confined to coarse grains, although some advance in rice production in developing countries may take place, provided weather is normal. Cereal output in the developing countries is currently forecast to rise by 0.8 percent only, partly owing to sharp production falls anticipated for wheat in Turkey and Saudi Arabia. Nevertheless, the 1994 cereal production increase in other developing countries as a group will probably still remain below population growth.

• If current production forecasts materialize, total global cereal availabilities in 1994/95 will be sufficient to meet the expected rise in consumption, although a drawdown of wheat stocks is likely. In aggregate, however, the global carryover of cereals at the close of the national crop years ending in 1995 would remain close to the minimum safety level as determined by FAO.

15

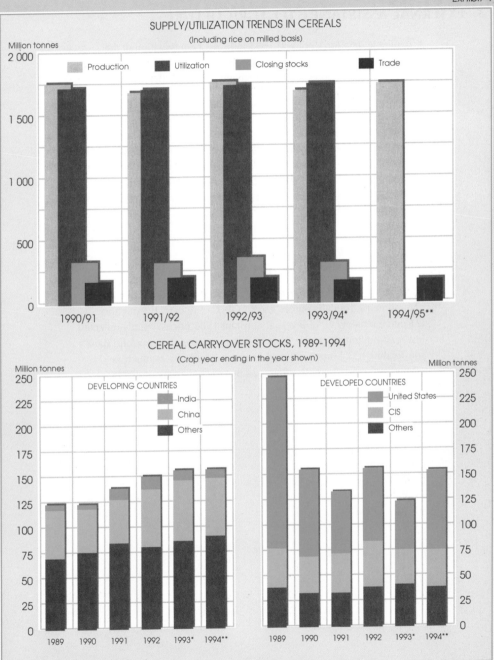

Exhibit 4

SUPPLY/UTILIZATION TRENDS IN CEREALS
(Including rice on milled basis)

CEREAL CARRYOVER STOCKS, 1989-1994
(Crop year ending in the year shown)

Source: FAO

*Estimate   **Forecast

5. EXTERNAL ASSISTANCE TO AGRICULTURE

• Available data for 1992 and 1993 indicate a continuation of the downward trend in commitments of external assistance to agriculture. After fluctuating around $11 billion yearly during 1980-1985, commitments in real terms peaked at about $12 billion in 1986 and have declined steadily since.

• For 1992, the latest year for which complete information is available, total commitments in *current* prices amounted to $11.3 billion, 6.6 percent less than in 1991. At *constant* 1985 prices, commitments in 1992 reached approximately $7 billion, representing a 9 percent decline from the previous year in real terms and a 42 percent decline in real terms from the peak levels of 1986.

• The concessional component of external assistance commitments to agriculture represented 70 percent of the total in 1992, close to the levels of 1989 and 1990 but above the 64 percent recorded in 1991.

• Preliminary data for 1993 indicate a further reduction in multilateral commitments from all sources except OPEC. The overall reduction (21 percent below 1992 levels at constant 1985 prices) mainly reflected lower commitments by the World Bank (-17 percent). The World Bank's soft-lending IDA branch reduced its commitments by as much as 60 percent, more than offsetting a 24 percent expansion in IBRD commitments.

Exhibit 5

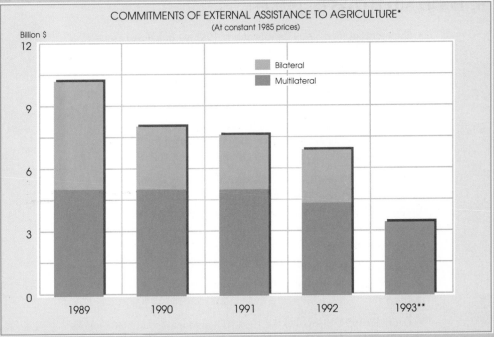

COMMITMENTS OF EXTERNAL ASSISTANCE TO AGRICULTURE*
(At constant 1985 prices)

Billion $

Bilateral
Multilateral

Source: FAO and OECD

* Broad definition   ** Preliminary

6. FOOD AID FLOWS IN 1993/94

• Shipments of food aid in cereals during 1993/94 (July/June) are estimated to be 12.2 million tonnes (21 percent below the previous year's level of 15.1 million tonnes), mainly owing to the reduced level of budgetary allocations.

• Of the total cereal food aid in 1993/94, 7.5 million tonnes were destined for developing countries compared with 10.8 million tonnes in 1992/93. In fact, the level of cereal food aid provided in 1993/94 to developing countries was the lowest observed since 1975/76.

• Most of the decline is expected to occur in Africa, where food aid is projected to fall from the 6.7 million tonnes recorded in 1992/93 to about 3.5 million tonnes. Although food aid requirements have declined considerably after the southern African drought emergency, requirements of many countries still remain unmet.

• Shipments of food aid to the CIS and East European countries in 1993/94 are estimated to be 4.7 million tonnes, compared with 4.4 million shipped in 1992/93.

• As of July 1994, pledges to the 1994 IEFR amounted to 808 365 tonnes of food commodities, of which 635 798 tonnes were in the form of cereals and 172 567 tonnes in the form of other foodstuffs, about the same level as the previous year.

• In addition to IEFR contributions, as of late July 1994, 534 000 tonnes of cereals and other commodities had been pledged under the subset of WFP regular resources for meeting the requirements of Protracted Refugee Operations, compared with 830 000 tonnes pledged in 1993.

• As of March 1994, total pledges to WFP's regular resources for the biennium 1993-1994 stood at $912 million, representing 61 percent of the pledging target of $1.5 billion. In the previous biennium 1991-1992, total contributions amounted to $1.14 billion, representing 76 percent of the pledging target of $1.5 billion.

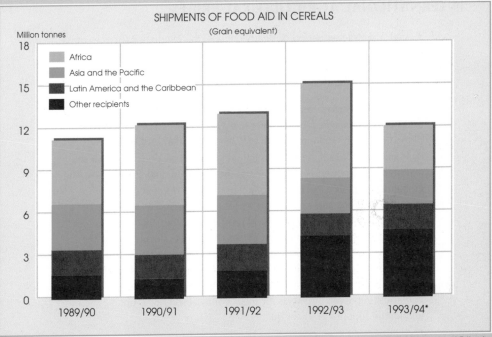

Note: Years refer to the 12-month period July/June   * Estimate

7. INTERNATIONAL AGRICULTURAL PRICES

• After a protracted period of steady decline, the international prices of several major traded agricultural commodities strengthened during the fourth quarter of 1993. The tendency continued, or even accentuated, for some commodities in the first half of 1994.

• Most *cereal* prices strengthened during the fourth quarter of 1993. The upward trend for *wheat* halted in January and prices generally weakened in the first half of 1994 as a result of slack import demand, stiff competition for available markets among the major exporters and mostly favourable prospects for 1994 crops in the major producing countries. The global decline in *coarse grain* production in 1993 resulted in tighter market conditions and stronger prices for these commodities in late 1993 and early 1994; however, with good prospects for the 1994 crops, prices have weakened in recent months. Prices of *rice* rose steeply during the second half of 1993 following an unusually poor harvest and strong demand for high-quality rice in Japan. Prices weakened subsequently, reflecting expectations of increased area in several major producing countries, improved prospects for the second-season rice crop in Thailand and ample supplies of lower-quality rice.

• Prices of *oilseeds, oils* and *oilmeals* increased significantly during the second half of 1993, reflecting expectations of supply shortfalls. A downward movement was recorded in more recent months owing to increased harvests in South America and depressed demand for oilmeals. In July 1994 price increases relative to mid-1993 were 14 percent for sunflower seeds and 35 percent for rapeseed.

• *Coffee* prices increased steeply in recent months reflecting tight supplies, caused in particular by the worst frost in Brazil since 1961 and a production decline in Colombia. By late May, prices had increased to the highest levels in seven years. After a second frost in Brazil in June, coffee prices rose through July to more than three times the levels of July 1993. Stock retention by ACP members also contributed to tighter supplies.

• *Cocoa* prices also rose markedly, mainly because of an increase in demand from the Russian Federation, European countries and North America, and this may cause consumption to exceed production in 1993/94 for the third year in a row.

• World *tea* prices fell to record lows during the first nine months of 1993, following a recovery in supply in all the main tea-producing countries. Prices have recovered somewhat since October 1993, mainly owing to a severe drought that reduced Kenya's output.

• *Cotton* prices soared during the first quarter of 1994, as a massive shortfall in world production in 1993/94 reduced exportable supplies.

Exhibit 7

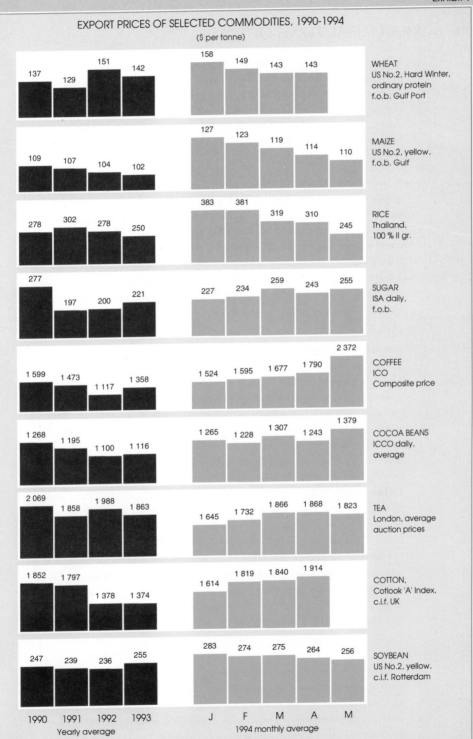

EXPORT PRICES OF SELECTED COMMODITIES, 1990-1994
($ per tonne)

WHEAT
US No.2, Hard Winter,
ordinary protein
f.o.b. Gulf Port

137 — 129 — 151 — 142   158 — 149 — 143 — 143

MAIZE
US No.2, yellow,
f.o.b. Gulf

109 — 107 — 104 — 102   127 — 123 — 119 — 114 — 110

RICE
Thailand,
100 % II gr.

278 — 302 — 278 — 250   383 — 381 — 319 — 310 — 245

SUGAR
ISA daily,
f.o.b.

277 — 197 — 200 — 221   227 — 234 — 259 — 243 — 255

COFFEE
ICO
Composite price

1 599 — 1 473 — 1 117 — 1 358   1 524 — 1 595 — 1 677 — 1 790 — 2 372

COCOA BEANS
ICCO daily,
average

1 268 — 1 195 — 1 100 — 1 116   1 265 — 1 228 — 1 307 — 1 243 — 1 379

TEA
London, average
auction prices

2 069 — 1 858 — 1 988 — 1 863   1 645 — 1 732 — 1 866 — 1 868 — 1 823

COTTON,
Cotlook 'A' Index,
c.i.f. UK

1 852 — 1 797 — 1 378 — 1 374   1 614 — 1 819 — 1 840 — 1 914

SOYBEAN
US No.2, yellow,
c.i.f. Rotterdam

247 — 239 — 236 — 255   283 — 274 — 275 — 264 — 256

1990   1991   1992   1993   J   F   M   A   M
Yearly average   1994 monthly average

Source: FAO

8. AGRICULTURAL TERMS OF TRADE

• The recent increase in international prices of several commodities of economic importance to many developing countries must be seen in the context of earlier trends. The 1980s and early 1990s had seen a steady deterioration in both the terms of trade and the purchasing capacity of agricultural exports. By 1992 the net barter terms of trade (or real prices) of developing countries' agricultural exports had fallen to less than 60 percent of the levels of the early 1980s.

• The deteriorating trend continued in 1993, as the general commodity price increase only manifested itself by the fourth quarter of the year. For the year as a whole, the UN index of agricultural export dollar prices indicated a 6 percent decline from 1992 levels. For the developing countries, the decline was 3 percent. On the other hand, the combined price index of manufactured goods and crude petroleum declined by 3 percent. This implies a 3 percent deterioration in agricultural real export prices overall and a levelling off of agricultural real export prices for developing countries.

• The economic importance of terms of trade is best appreciated when considering trends in both prices and volumes of agricultural exports. The index of income terms of trade – or purchasing capacity of agricultural exports – takes both variables into account.[1] The general picture presented by the income terms of trade is also unfavourable for the developing countries, although it is subject to important qualifications. First, purchasing capacity deteriorated far less than net barter terms of trade after the early 1980s, implying that developing countries were able to compensate for falling agricultural real prices through larger volumes of exports. Second, regional trends varied widely. The Far East and the Near East and North Africa regions actually expanded the purchasing capacity of agricultural exports from the levels of the early 1980s despite adverse real price trends. The Latin America and Caribbean region was less successful, as the expansion in export volumes was insufficient to compensate for declining real prices. In sub-Saharan Africa real prices and purchasing capacity of agricultural exports deteriorated *pari passu*. In 1992 sub-Saharan African agricultural exports could theoretically finance approximately 40 percent less of manufactured goods and crude petroleum than they did in 1979-81.

---

[1] It should be noted that the index considers changes in the quantity and not the quality of the goods that agricultural export earnings are able to finance. In other words, the same volume of agricultural exports may have enabled the purchasing of fewer and fewer cars and capital goods, less electronic equipment, etc. However, technological improvements in the goods purchased may have provided at least partial compensation.

Exhibit 8

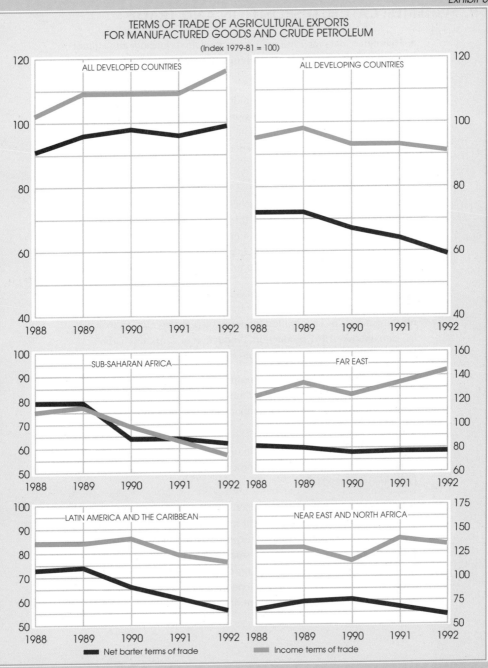

TERMS OF TRADE OF AGRICULTURAL EXPORTS
FOR MANUFACTURED GOODS AND CRUDE PETROLEUM
(Index 1979-81 = 100)

ALL DEVELOPED COUNTRIES

ALL DEVELOPING COUNTRIES

SUB-SAHARAN AFRICA

FAR EAST

LATIN AMERICA AND THE CARIBBEAN

NEAR EAST AND NORTH AFRICA

■ Net barter terms of trade   ■ Income terms of trade

Source: FAO

9. FISHERIES: CATCH, DISPOSITION AND TRADE

• Preliminary data for 1993 indicate that total *world catch and culture* of fish and shellfish reached about 98 million tonnes, thus remaining at the level of 1992.

• Peru expanded its production rapidly from 6.8 million tonnes in 1992 to 8.4 million tonnes in 1993. China's production is also expected to have increased substantially over the same period. Among other large producer countries, Chile and the Russian Federation reported declining production in 1993.

• *World marine fish production* in 1992 has been confirmed at 82.5 million tonnes, about the level reached in 1991. The decline in production of clupeoids continued; however, they remained the largest group of marine species, accounting for 20.4 million tonnes of catch. As a result of decreased catches of wild salmon, total production of salmon from catch and culture fell back by 12 percent to 1.4 million tonnes, the level reached in 1989 and 1990.

• *World inland fish production* continued to grow rapidly in 1992, reaching a total of 15.6 million tonnes, which represented an increase of 5.5 percent over 1991 production. Production of carps and barbels expanded by 11 percent to just more than 7 million tonnes.

• Preliminary estimates of the *disposition of world catch* in 1993 indicate a 2 percent decline in fish used for human consumption to 69.2 million tonnes, following an increase of about twice that magnitude in 1992.

• In 1992, international *trade in fishery products* grew slightly in value, as exports increased from $38.9 billion in 1991 to $40.3 billion in 1992. Volume was 17 million tonnes of processed product, a negligible decrease compared with 1991.

• Developing country exports in 1992 represented 32 percent of their total catch, as compared with 47 percent for developed countries. Developing countries as a group recorded an increasingly positive trade balance in fishery products, which reached a surplus of $11.7 billion in 1992, as developed country imports of fish products continued to grow strongly. Indeed, in 1992 the value of developed country fish exports was equivalent to only about 56 percent of their imports.

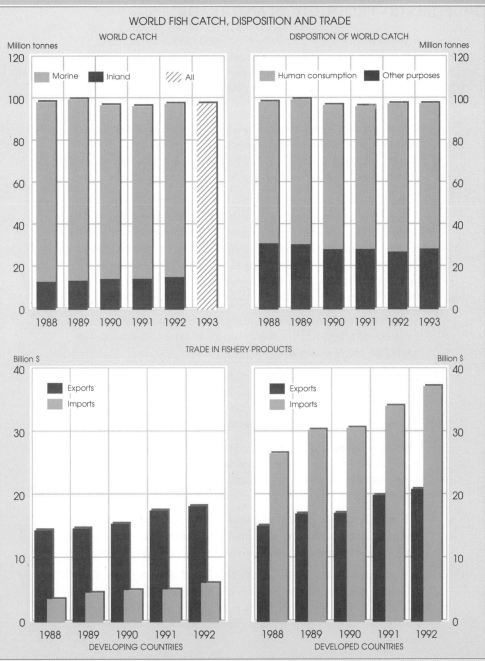

Exhibit 9

WORLD FISH CATCH, DISPOSITION AND TRADE

WORLD CATCH

DISPOSITION OF WORLD CATCH

TRADE IN FISHERY PRODUCTS

Source: FAO

10. FORESTRY PRODUCTION AND TRADE

• World production of *roundwood* continued to increase in 1993, reflecting a significant expansion of fuelwood and industrial roundwood output in the developing countries. On the other hand, removals of roundwood in the developed economies declined, remaining well below the peak level reached in 1990.

• As demand for roundwood products by the processing industries in Western Europe and Japan remained weak in 1993, there was a further fall of roundwood removals in most East European countries and particularly in the former USSR. By contrast, North American markets continued to recover strongly.

• Environmental concern for wildlife habitat protection resulted in a strong reduction in timber supplies from the federal forests on the Pacific Northwest of the United States (from 20 million m^3 in 1990 to 2 million m^3 in 1993) and a sharp increase in prices. International markets were significantly affected, the United States being the main supplier of coniferous logs and sawnwood to the large Asian timber market.

• The reduced temperate timber supply in Asia led to an unprecedented escalation of prices, which favoured exports of plantation forest timber from Chile and New Zealand.

• An additional supply constraint resulted from further restrictions on the harvesting of tropical logs in Malaysia, Indonesia, Myanmar and Papua New Guinea. This led to sharp increases in prices of tropical logs, sawnwood and plywood in the Asian market.

• By mid-1994, a United States federal court ruled that logging in the protected public forests of the Pacific Northwest may be partially resumed. The resulting harvest increase, to a forecast 5 million m^3 in 1996, may help stabilize prices in the United States domestic and international markets.

• Production of *sawnwood* declined to slightly below the already low 1992 levels, with a recovery in North America being more than offset by declines in other markets, particularly in the former Soviet republics.

• With improved markets for *wood-based panels*, the Indonesian and Malaysian tropical plywood industry continued to expand. In the temperate area, there was a sizeable expansion in North American output coupled with a slight recovery of the particle board industry in Western Europe.

• Production of *paper and paperboard* in 1993 increased marginally, mainly reflecting continuing output growth in Southeast Asia, North America and the Scandinavian countries.

Exhibit 10

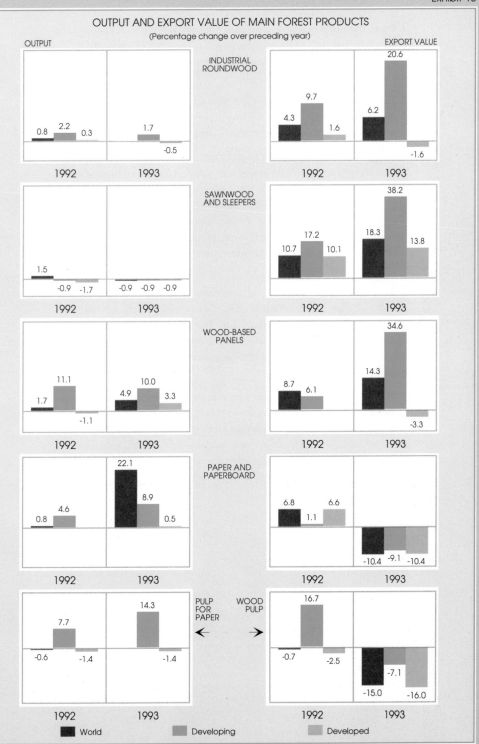

OUTPUT AND EXPORT VALUE OF MAIN FOREST PRODUCTS

(Percentage change over preceding year)

OUTPUT

EXPORT VALUE

INDUSTRIAL ROUNDWOOD

SAWNWOOD AND SLEEPERS

WOOD-BASED PANELS

PAPER AND PAPERBOARD

PULP FOR PAPER ← → WOOD PULP

■ World   ■ Developing   ■ Developed

Source: FAO

• Production of *wood pulp* remained stagnant, despite rising paper production, because of the increasing use of recycled fibres by the industry. Both industries continued to suffer from low profitability and utilization rates.

• The value of world *trade* in forest products is estimated to have declined marginally in 1993, mainly reflecting depressed prices for pulp and paper. Trade in the other main forest products expanded, however.

• Larger export earnings from tropical logs in Asian countries resulted from a sharp increase in the export unit value of logs more than offsetting reduced volumes of shipments. Sawnwood and plywood export values also rose in these countries. Government policies, particularly in Malaysia and Indonesia, continued to encourage exports of processed wood products such as sawnwood, plywood, mouldings, furniture and furniture parts. African countries continued to expand their tropical sawnwood exports in lieu of logs.

• Trade in coniferous sawnwood continued to increase, although at a slower rate than in 1992. Canadian lumber exports into the United States grew further in both volume and value. The Scandinavian countries continued to increase their exports to Western Europe vigourously, benefiting from a devaluation of their currencies and the fall of exports from the former USSR.

• The volume of world trade in pulp and paper products is estimated to have increased by about 3 percent in 1993, mainly as a result of expanded shipments by North America and developing countries of the Far East. However, the value of trade in these products declined by approximately 11 percent, reflecting depressed international prices – with the prices of some wood pulp grades falling to around 50 percent of their 1989 peak levels.

WORLD REVIEW

II. Overall economic environment and agriculture

ECONOMIC OVERVIEW

In 1994 the world economy entered the fourth consecutive year of depressed growth, reflecting continuing weak economic activity in the industrial countries – which account for over 70 percent of world output – and to a lesser extent the deep recession in Central and Eastern Europe and the former USSR. In the *industrial countries*, however, increasing indications of a solid resumption of growth in North America as well as converging, if still incipient, signs of recovery in other countries suggest that the trough may have been reached. Underlying such improved prospects are low inflation rates, which for many countries have fallen to the lowest levels in three decades; relatively low interest rates, despite mounting upward pressure in some countries; renewed efforts towards fiscal consolidation and deficit reduction – a key economic challenge in many countries; greater monetary stability within the European Monetary System; and the conclusion of the Uruguay Round of GATT negotiations which, beyond its expected benefits for trade, has generated more optimistic business expectations worldwide.

Against such positive features, mounting unemployment has reached worrisome proportions in many countries, particularly in Europe. A resumption of sustained growth could reverse the rise in cyclical unemployment; however, the risk of persistently high structural unemployment in many industrial countries points to the need for reforms to reduce rigidity in labour markets.

Several *economies in transition* in Central and Eastern Europe and the Baltic states have pursued or even accelerated the pace of economic reform and some have achieved encouraging progress in growth and stabilization. By contrast, the process of reform has continued to be sluggish and uneven in most former Soviet republics, which have seen their economic performances deteriorate further – in turn undermining popular and political support for pursuing reform.

Economic growth in 1993 in the *developing countries* again substantially outpaced that of industrial countries. A number of factors contributed to improving the economic outlook significantly for the developing countries: the ongoing process of recovery in the

Figure

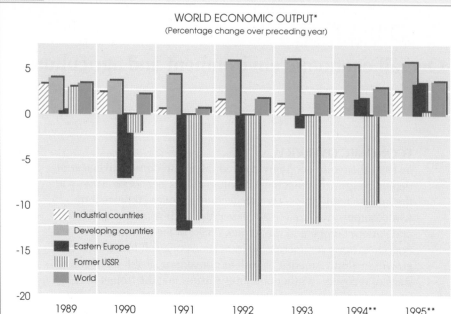

WORLD ECONOMIC OUTPUT*
(Percentage change over preceding year)

Industrial countries
Developing countries
Eastern Europe
Former USSR
World

1989   1990   1991   1992   1993   1994**   1995**

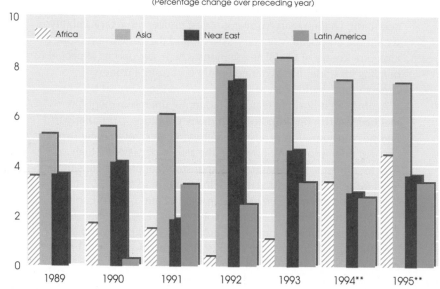

ECONOMIC GROWTH, DEVELOPING COUNTRY REGIONS
(Percentage change over preceding year)

Africa   Asia   Near East   Latin America

1989   1990   1991   1992   1993   1994**   1995**

Source: IMF

* Real GDP or real NMP   ** Projection

industrial world; generally lower interest rates, an important factor in the context of external debt servicing; the consolidation of economic reform and stabilization in many countries; the improved prospects for trade with the completion of the Uruguay Round, the North American Free Trade Agreement (NAFTA) and the revival of other regional arrangements; the recent strengthening in commodity prices; the massive inflow of private capital, particularly to Asia and Latin America and the Caribbean (which, nevertheless, has created its own set of problems, as discussed in the Regional review); reduced levels of civil strife in sub-Saharan Africa (the dramatic events in Rwanda reminding us, however, that peace and stability remain elusive targets in much of the region); and positive spillover effects of developments in South Africa.

Clearly, these factors have benefited developing countries to varying degrees and, indeed, performances and prospects widely differ among regions and countries (see Regional review). Nevertheless, the continuation of current economic trends seems set to evolve into the best environment in many years for developing countries' economic and agricultural development.

Economic outlook for developing countries' agriculture
Current Project LINK economic forecasts for the short and medium term (1994-1997) suggest annual growth rates in the order of 2.5 to

Figure 2

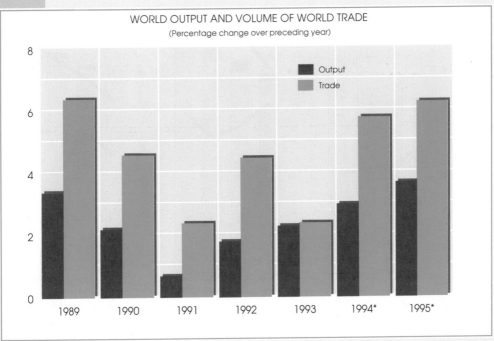

WORLD OUTPUT AND VOLUME OF WORLD TRADE
(Percentage change over preceding year)

Source: IMF

* Projections

Figure

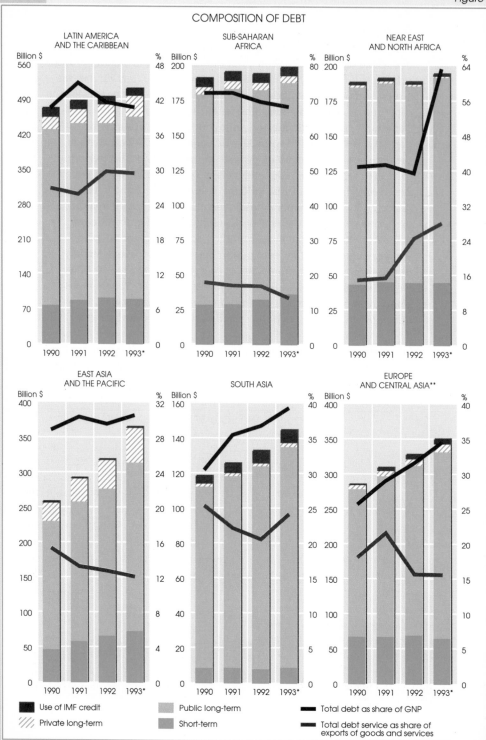

COMPOSITION OF DEBT

LATIN AMERICA
AND THE CARIBBEAN

SUB-SAHARAN
AFRICA

NEAR EAST
AND NORTH AFRICA

EAST ASIA
AND THE PACIFIC

SOUTH ASIA

EUROPE
AND CENTRAL ASIA**

■ Use of IMF credit

/// Private long-term

Public long-term

Short-term

━━ Total debt as share of GNP

━━ Total debt service as share of
exports of goods and services

Source: World Bank, World Debt Tables, 1992-93

* Projections   **Including former USS

BOX 1
EXTERNAL DEBT SITUATION OF DEVELOPING COUNTRIES

The total external debt stock of all developing countries, which totalled $1 662 billion at the end of 1992, is projected to reach $1 770 billion in 1993, up by 6.5 percent from the end of the previous year. The projected increase of $108 billion is due to: i) a substantial increase in positive net flows, which reached almost $90 billion in 1993 and were composed of long-term and short-term net flows and the use of IMF credits; ii) the capitalization of interest through debt rescheduling, totalling $15 billion; and iii) the effect of cross-currency valuation change which is projected to add another $23 billion. Debt forgiveness and voluntary debt reductions, on the other hand, reduced the debt stock by $9 billion, while decreases in interest arrears accounted for a reduction of a further $10 billion. The largest growth in external debt liabilities was shown by East Asia and the Pacific, mainly as the result of easy access by many countries in the region to the capital markets.

Agricultural external debt in 1992 reached $73.4 billion, almost unchanged from the previous year. The share therein of official debt (bilateral and multilateral) is gradually increasing, having risen from 87 percent in 1988 to 93 percent in 1992.

During 1993, 11 countries reached restructuring agreements on a total of $4 billion of official bilateral debt with Paris Club member countries. Further, the Russian Federation rescheduled a total of $15 billion of its official debt outside the Paris Club framework.

Total debt-service payments of all the developing countries increased to $182 900 million in 1993 from $178 500 million the previous year. The debt-to-exports ratio, which reached 174 percent in 1992, is projected to increase to 180 percent in 1993. The projected debt-service ratio (the ratio between total debt service and export earnings) for 1993 should stabilize at 19 percent, remaining unchanged since 1990. However, for the 29 severely indebted low-income countries, with an outstanding debt stock of almost $208 billion in 1993, the debt-to-exports ratio is expected to increase from 413 percent in 1992 to 432 percent in 1993. Debt forgiveness, mainly by official bilateral creditors, which in 1991 reduced the debt stock of severely indebted low-income countries by some $22 billion, was largely offset by the capitalization of interest and accumulated interest arrears totalling $19 billion.

Total net flows on debt (disbursements less principal repayments of short- and long-term debt and IMF credits) are estimated to be $89 700 million in 1993, a 2.5 percent increase over 1992. In 1992 net transfers on debt (net flows minus interest payments) turned positive, at $13 billion, for the first time since the outburst of the debt crisis in early 1980. For 1993 they are estimated to be $11 400 million.

Net long-term resource flows[1] (which

_____

[1] Includes net flows on long-term debt, grants (excluding technical assistance) and net flows on equity investment.

include both debt-creating and non-debt-creating flows) to developing countries increased further from $156 600 million in 1992 to a projected $176 660 million in 1993, reflecting improved access to international capital markets by the developing countries. For some regions, especially Latin America, the increase in net flows is to a large extent attributable to repatriated capital flight.

In 1993, aggregate net long-term resource flows from private sources reached more than $113 200 million ($102 000 million in 1992), the highest in a decade, and for the second consecutive year they exceeded official flows (loans and grants), which accounted for $54 580 million in 1992 and are projected to be $63 450 million in 1993. The expansion of private capital flows is driven by a strong surge in foreign direct investment (FDI), estimated to be $56 300 million in 1993, more than double the level recorded in 1990. The increase in equity investments and bonds is also remarkable, having gone from $3.8 billion in 1990 to 13.2 billion in 1993. The main beneficiaries of the expansion of private resource flows have been middle-income countries undergoing strong economic policy and market-oriented reforms and the countries that have avoided a commercial bank debt overhang. Most low-income countries, on the other hand, have not benefited from the rapidly rising private capital flows, except China which is the largest single recipient of FDI among developing countries.

Sources: World Bank. 1993. World Debt Tables, 1993-94; and The World Bank Annual Report 1993.

3 percent in the industrial countries; 5.2 to 5.8 percent in the developing countries; 2.5 to 4 percent in the transitional economies in Eastern and Central Europe; and a continuing stagnation or even further contraction in output in most countries of the former Soviet republics which, in the aggregate, may not resume positive rates of growth before 1997.

The overall acceleration in output growth is expected to be accompanied by an expansion in the value of world trade of about 6 percent in 1994, 6.6 percent in 1995 and close to 6 percent the following two years.

Trade is expected to gather considerable buoyancy in the developing countries, with both exports and imports rising at annual rates of approximately 10 percent throughout the period 1994-1997. Developed countries' trade should also gain momentum, the rate of change in their imports rising from a depressed -5 percent in 1993 to 3.8 percent in 1994 and 7 to 9 percent in 1995-97.

The revival of growth and trade is also forecast to extend to agriculture. Stronger economic activity in the industrial countries is expected to activate international demand for agricultural products. A strengthening in the prices of several key commodities is already under way, and this tendency may be accentuated moderately. While sluggish demand from major grain-importing countries should keep grain prices generally depressed, prices of sugar and coffee are expected to strengthen in the short to medium term, reflecting supply shortages and to a certain extent the effects of producer countries' export retention schemes. An early 1994 forecast from the International Cocoa Organization (ICCO) points to three more years of production deficits, which may push up cocoa prices and perhaps reverse the rise in world consumption. Beef prices may also strengthen, owing in particular to increased demand for beef in Asia and a sharp reduction in stocks in the EC. Thus, after many years of steady deterioration, the terms of trade and purchasing power of agricultural exports may improve somewhat.

Overall, mid-term forecasts for total and agricultural output are summarized in Figure 4. The data underlying the Figure suggest the following developments:

- Developing countries are expected to accelerate their total and agricultural output growth but performances will remain uneven across regions.
- A certain convergence of growth rates relative to past trends is likely, but less than would be necessary to reduce regional polarization. In particular, differentials in per caput income

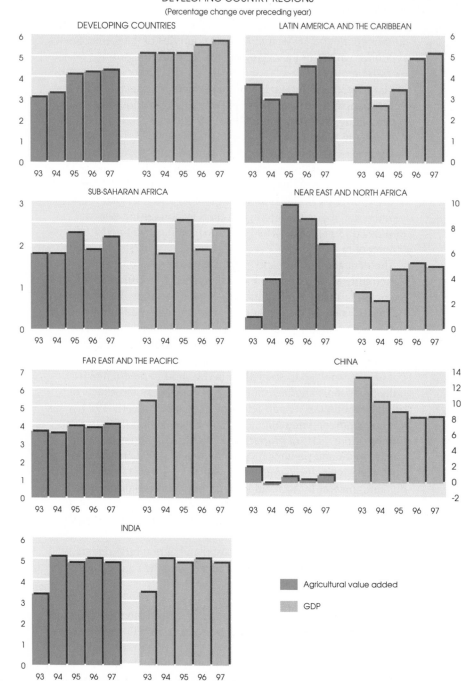

Figure

GROWTH IN TOTAL GDP AND VALUE ADDED IN AGRICULTURE,
DEVELOPING COUNTRY REGIONS
(Percentage change over preceding year)

DEVELOPING COUNTRIES

LATIN AMERICA AND THE CARIBBEAN

SUB-SAHARAN AFRICA

NEAR EAST AND NORTH AFRICA

FAR EAST AND THE PACIFIC

CHINA

INDIA

■ Agricultural value added

■ GDP

Source: Project LINK and FAO

Note: 1993 - estimates; 1994-1997 - projections

levels between Africa and the other regions are expected to widen.

- Fast-growing economies, particularly in East Asia, are expected to expand less dramatically than in the recent past, reflecting in particular the overheating of the economy in China and resource and infrastructural constraints. Regional agriculture is forecast to continue lagging behind other sectors, its share in GDP falling from 20 percent in 1991 to 16 percent in 1997. However, agricultural and food output would continue expanding significantly faster than population.

- Sub-Saharan Africa is forecast to improve its economic performance somewhat, thanks to better prices for several of the region's key export commodities; competitive gains in several countries, particularly in the CFA area consecutive to its currency devaluation; progress in stabilization in some countries; and reduced civil and political strife. Agricultural growth is likely to follow closely that of output overall, reflecting the still large agricultural base of the region's economy. Nevertheless, growth in total and agricultural output in particular is still likely to lag behind population growth, implying further losses in per caput terms.

- A continuation of relatively high output growth is forecast in Latin America and the Caribbean on the assumption of a consolidation of reform and stabilization and of continuing capital inflows. Although agriculture accounts for a relatively small share of total GDP in the region (about 9 percent compared with 15 percent for developing countries as a whole), the sector is expected to contribute significantly to the overall improvement.

- Economies in the Near East and North Africa should greatly benefit from the abatement of political tensions, some strengthening in petroleum prices and economic reform. The agricultural sector is forecast to play a major role in the economic upsurge, with its growth significantly outpacing that of other sectors.

Outlook for developing country economies highly dependent on agricultural exports

The effects of the changing economic and trade environment are examined here from the perspective of a selected group of developing countries for which agricultural exports account for a high proportion of total exports and imports (see definition and list of economies highly dependent on agricultural exports [EHDAEs] in Table 1). Box 2 on p. 41 summarizes the results of a study on structural characteristics and past export and growth performances of these countries. As regards their economic and agricultural prospects for the short term (1994 and 1995), IMF and Project LINK forecasts point to the following:[1]

- Real GDP of EHDAEs is expected to rise by approximately 4.4 percent in both 1994 and 1995, somewhat below the high rate recorded in 1993 but above past trends (3.5 percent average during the 1980s and 3.3 percent in 1990-93).
- GDP growth for these countries will converge to the average of their respective regions in 1994 and 1995. This would be a discontinuation of past trends, when EHDAEs' growth rates had been generally lower than that of economies with a more diversified export base. Agricultural GDP growth, expected to be slightly above 3 percent in 1994-95, should accelerate in the following years, mainly reflecting improved production prospects and dynamic trade in Latin America and the Caribbean. On the other hand, no improvement in agricultural GDP per caput is foreseen for the African group.
- Underlying the improved economic prospects are higher forecast levels of gross capital formation (around 23 percent of GDP, up from about 19 percent since the mid-1980s). Asian countries in the group, where savings and investment rates were already much higher than in other regions, are expected to be those where gross capital formation rates will increase most.
- Except for most countries in Africa, EHDAEs are forecast to achieve significant progress in restraining expenditure and consolidating fiscal balances – suggesting that the private rather than public sector will play the main role in generating accelerated growth. Central government fiscal deficits are expected to decline from an equivalent of 4 to 5 percent of GDP during most of the 1980s to about 1 percent in 1994-95. Fiscal balances are actually forecast to turn positive in Latin American countries in the group.
- The growth of exports is forecast to accelerate markedly, to 10 percent in 1994 and 12.3 percent in 1995 (current US dollar terms). The increase would stem from a firming in prices and, to a greater extent, from larger shipment volumes. Agricultural export growth should accelerate from a yearly average of

---

[1] The economic estimates and forecasts for EHDAEs are drawn from material elaborated for FAO by the IMF's World Economic Studies Division on the basis of IMF. *World Economic Outlook*, May 1994. Forecasts for agricultural value added, agricultural exports and agricultural terms of trade have been elaborated for FAO by Project LINK.

TABLE 1

Economies highly dependent on agricultural exports[1]

Latin America and the Caribbean	Far East and the Pacific	Sub-Saharan Africa
Argentina	Sri Lanka	Côte d'Ivoire
Paraguay	Thailand	Malawi
Honduras	Afghanistan	Zimbabwe
Cuba	Viet Nam	Mali
Uruguay	Malaysia	Sudan
Brazil		Madagascar
Guatemala		Burundi
Costa Rica		Cameroon
Colombia		Ghana
Saint Vincent and		Liberia
the Grenadines		Uganda
Ecuador		Kenya
Guyana		Ethiopia
Belize		Rwanda
Dominica		Swaziland
Nicaragua		Mauritius
El Salvador		Central African Rep.
Dominican Rep.		Tanzania, United Rep.
Sao Tome and Principe		Chad
		Burkina Faso
		Somalia
		Benin
		Guinea-Bissau
		Gambia

[1] Countries for which agricultural, fishery and forestry exports were equivalent to 20 percent or more of their total export earnings, or 20 percent or more of their total imports, in 1988-90.

2 percent during the 1980s to 4 percent in 1990-93 and a forecast 7 percent in 1994-95. Agricultural exports are expected to increase even faster in 1996-97, more significantly in Latin America and the Caribbean.
• Reflecting the above, the terms of trade and, more pronouncedly, the purchasing power of exports are forecast to improve, thereby reversing the negative trend since the early 1980s. Moderate gains (from 1 to 3 percent per annum) are expected in the purchasing power of agricultural exports in the short and medium term.
• With imports increasing even faster than exports, the merchandise trade balances are expected to show growing

deficits or – in the case of Latin American countries in the group – smaller surpluses. As the balance of services is also forecast to turn increasingly negative, EHDAEs are likely to face pronounced current account deficits in 1994-95. Such deficits would be relatively moderate in African countries, which would benefit from larger unrequited transfers (mainly official intragovernmental financing).

• Unlike total merchandise trade, trade in agricultural products is forecast to show increasing surpluses.

• The debt burden, already significant in these countries, is likely to accentuate sharply in terms both of the overall volume of debt and debt-service obligations. While over half of the current and projected debt is in Latin America and the Caribbean, it is African countries that face the worst debt-servicing difficulties. The debt service-to-exports ratio for African EHDAEs is projected to increase to around 42 percent in 1994-95 (from around 25 percent in the 1980s) compared with approximately 33 percent in EHDAEs in Latin America and the Caribbean and 8.5 percent in Asia and the Pacific.

The above forecasts generally indicate a marked improvement in the economic and trade outlook of developing countries, including those that are more oriented towards agricultural exports. The tentative nature of these forecasts must, however, be underlined. Many remaining impediments to a strong and sustained recovery in both developing and developed countries suggest that projections are subject to a considerable downside risk. Uncertainties particularly concern: the pace and speed of recovery in OECD countries (mainly in Europe and Japan) and, more generally, the ability of industrial countries to maintain growth-conducive monetary policies, absorb unemployment significantly and reduce fiscal deficits; the economic collapse, political instability and ethnic and regional tension in the former USSR and other transitional economies; emerging excess demand pressure in China where major efforts also remain to be made to broaden the benefits of rapid growth, particularly into rural areas; the unwelcome side-effects of capital inflows, particularly into Latin American and Caribbean countries and – on the other hand – fears that a reversal of such inflows would involve severe economic and financial imbalances and disruptive monetary and exchange rate adjustments; the still vulnerable adjustment and recovery process in many developing countries; the unevenness of economic recovery among and within regions – the dismal economic situation and prospects in many African countries being a major reason for concern; and the likelihood that the international trading

BOX 2
ECONOMIES HIGHLY DEPENDENT ON AGRICULTURAL EXPORTS: EXPORT PERFORMANCE AND GROWTH

A number of background studies are under way for the preparation of the 1995 issue of *The State of Food and Agriculture*, which will feature a special chapter on agricultural trade and development. One of these studies[1] analyses the structural characteristics and past export performances of EHDAEs and explores some of the main factors behind successes and failures in expanding agricultural exports and economic growth. Highlights of the findings are as follows:

• Although these economies share the characteristic of being strongly agriculture-based, their dependence on agricultural exports tends to decline over time, amid wide intracountry variations.
• On average, the share of food and agricultural raw materials in total export earnings declined from 83 percent in 1970 to 64 percent in 1990. Asian countries achieved the most significant diversification of exports away from agriculture, the average share falling from 77 to 35 percent. For Latin American countries, the share fell from 88 to 61 percent (reflecting, *inter alia*, the rapid industrialization process in Brazil and other countries and the emergence of petroleum as a major export earner in

Ecuador and Colombia); African countries' share declined from 85 to 71 percent on average but the share remained constant or actually increased in a number of countries, including Liberia, Uganda and Somalia.
• Thus, while for Asian and Latin American EHDAEs, manufactures were an increasingly important component of export earnings (becoming the main source for Asian countries in recent years), exports remained heavily agriculture-based for the African countries in the group.
• Along with dependence on agricultural exports, these countries have faced a pronounced and persistent dependence on developed country markets for their exports. Again, however, regional differences are important. Asian and Latin American countries have tended to intensify intraregional exchanges. Developed countries absorb around 70 to 80 percent of Africa's total agricultural exports. All EHDAEs have lost important markets in Eastern Europe and the former USSR in recent years.
• A distinction with significant policy implications should be made between commodities that compete with commodities produced in the developed countries and those that do not. "Noncompeting" products (cocoa, coffee, tea, bananas, spices, palm and coconut oil, jute, etc.) accounted for a declining share of total agricultural exports by EHDAEs – from 79 percent in 1961 to 34 percent in 1990. In Africa, however, unlike the

[1] *Export performance and GDP growth in EHDAEs – an empirical study.* Prepared for FAO by G. Zanias, Agricultural University of Athens, and M. Spinedi, Nomisma, Bologna.

general trend, the share of "non-competing" products increased between 1961 and 1975 and has only declined slightly since then. The overall declining relative importance of non-competing products generally reflected the slow growth in demand for many of these products and the intense market competition on the part of producers. Conversely, the movement towards the relatively more dynamic markets for "competing" products was largely influenced by changes in Latin American countries' trade patterns – in particular, their entry into the interrelated soybean and meat markets (most forcefully Brazil since the early 1970s). For Argentina and Brazil, the fact that competing products account for, respectively, 98 and 73 percent of their total agricultural exports explains their keen participation in the recently concluded GATT negotiations and in the Cairns Group.

• Income growth in trading partners (mainly developed countries) was an important factor behind the EHDAEs' agricultural export growth. This was more so for countries exporting a large proportion of non-competing products.

• The dependence on one or few export commodities, which has characterized many EHDAEs, has tended to attenuate somewhat over the past decades. However, the largest single agricultural export item still accounts for half of the total agricultural export earnings of these countries. Moreover, "monodependence" has actually been accentuated in African EHDAEs.

• Agricultural export and economic growth performances have varied widely among countries and within periods but, by and large, EHDAEs' performances have lagged behind those of countries with a more diversified export base. For the EHDAEs, the theory of a link between exports and growth is generally supported under specific conditions. Regression analysis indicates a positive and statistically significant relationship between exports and GDP growth *only* for countries above a given level of per caput GDP ($400 or more was used as a benchmark); or countries with a sizeable share (10 percent or more) of manufactures in total exports.

• There is a positive correlation between changes in real agricultural exports and real exchange rates. In other words, devaluations were found to be associated with increases in real exports and vice versa. Such a correlation was particularly significant in a number of countries such as Brazil, Colombia, Ecuador and Thailand. However, in others, including Guyana, Kenya and Côte d'Ivoire, the two variables did not appear to be significantly correlated, suggesting the predominant role of other structural, market and policy factors in determining agricultural export performance. A common pattern was that of currencies being allowed to appreciate during periods of favourable agricultural market conditions such as the late 1970s. Conversely, many countries devalued their currency during periods of depressed commodity prices.

Further research is under way to explore the main questions and issues arising from the study, for example: By what means did some countries reduce their dependence on a few products and markets? What are the policy options for countries that produce and trade a narrow range of commodities if they face unpromising markets and intense competition among themselves? Should they aim primarily at improving productivity and competitiveness in their traditional exports or pursue alternatives? What are their alternatives – forging closer links with upstream (inputs) and downstream (food processing) industrial activities and promoting non-traditional agricultural exports, or accelerating the process of "de-agriculturization" in favour of industry? What are the options for those low-income countries that do not appear to have developed to a point of "critical mass" for their exports to be translated into growth?

environment following the Uruguay Round Agreement, particularly for agricultural products, will remain subject to intense competition and protectionist pressure.[2]

However welcome, the recent upsurge in commodity prices should also be subject to cautious interpretation. The prices of several of these commodities had fallen for so long and to such depressed levels that the recent upturn provides only meagre compensation for commodity exporters. Moreover, the strengthening in commodity prices can hardly be seen as a sign either of an emerging new trend or of any significant reduction of the structural weaknesses and inherent instability of commodity markets.

---

[2] Increased protectionism is a well-known consequence of depressed economic conditions. Despite its obvious spuriousness, a common argument in recent years has been that imports from countries with low labour costs may aggravate industrial countries' unemployment. This ignores the fact that giving developing countries the opportunity to raise their incomes results in better market and employment opportunities for the richer economies themselves.

WORLD REVIEW
III. Selected issues

AIDS – THE PRICE OF AN EPIDEMIC

Until recently, policy-makers have viewed the human immunodeficiency virus (HIV), the cause of acquired immune deficiency syndrome (AIDS), as a health problem but, as the pandemic progresses, it appears that its effects are reverberating through all sectors of the economy, creating soaring health and social welfare costs, labour shortages and lowered productivity. The impacts on national economies, the agricultural sector and food security will be significant. Although available data are limited, they provide sufficient evidence that the profound demographic effects of AIDS will seriously hamper, if not reverse, economic growth in certain regions. There are at least three compelling reasons for urgent policy discussions of the effects of AIDS on developing country economies.

First, unlike most epidemics, AIDS is primarily transmitted by sexual contact; the sexually active sector of society is also the most economically productive – roughly 15 to 45 years of age. The survivors, children and the elderly, are least able to create a livelihood for themselves.

Second, although at present AIDS accounts for far fewer deaths than malaria, tuberculosis, heart disease or cancer, its rate of transmission is rapid. This is exacerbated by the fact that sexual behaviour is a private, even taboo, subject in many societies, which limits possibilities of intervention to arrest the spread of the disease. Infection rates are estimated to be doubling in as little as six months in some countries.[3]

Finally, although AIDS is always fatal, in developing countries it can take as long as two years before infection results in death. This delay between cause and effect, the so-called "silent phase", does not encourage people to give up high-risk behaviour such as unsafe sex or intravenous drug use. It also means that the infected population can multiply rapidly before any symptoms appear to warn of its presence.

The World Health Organization (WHO) estimates that 14 million

---

[3] *Panos WorldAIDS*, May 1994.

to 15 million people have been infected with HIV worldwide and that, during the next five years, this figure will rise to 40 million to 50 million, including millions of children; 90 percent of these cases will be in developing countries.

The economic impacts of AIDS

The unchecked spread of AIDS has the potential to create shortages among skilled and unskilled workers. Lengthy and recurrent bouts of illness seriously hamper workers' productivity; deaths rob children and elderly family members of their only means of support. Although skilled workers represent a smaller proportion of the population in developing countries, the cost of replacing their contributions presents a heavy burden.

Health care costs for treating AIDS patients, already very high, are expected to spiral. In several African cities, more than 50 percent of hospital beds are now occupied by AIDS patients. In the United Republic of Tanzania, clinicians estimate that, on average, HIV-infected adults suffer 17 episodes of HIV-related illness prior to death while children suffer from six to seven. The average health care costs per death from AIDS in developing countries is about 150 percent of per caput income. The excessive demand for health care created by HIV jeopardizes a nation's ability to deal with other pressing health problems and diverts resources from productive investments in other sectors.

Far more alarming are the indirect costs of AIDS – including loss of earnings of those affected – estimated to be at least ten times the direct health care costs. To give an idea of the magnitude, Thailand has estimated that the direct health care costs alone will run in the neighbourhood of $65 million by the year 2000.[4] A UNDP study states that, in Asia, these costs will be borne primarily by individuals and their families (unlike Western economies where costs are usually covered by state or private insurance). This is likely to be the pattern in other developing regions, since public health care resources will be rapidly exhausted.

Scarce resources force governments to choose between investment in long-term growth and urgent short-term demands for health care. In developing countries, state-supported palliative care for AIDS victims is a relatively high short-term cost which provides no long-term benefit for society, since the disease is always fatal. In Kenya, for example, a 60-day hospital stay costs $938, three times the per caput GNP.

In the developing world, particularly in countries where

---

[4] UNDP. *Choices*, September 1993.

agriculture constitutes a significant portion of the GDP, a reduced agricultural labour force as a result of AIDS deaths requires substantial capital investment to counteract declines in agricultural production.

Decreased food production endangers household and national food security. In six out of ten countries in sub-Saharan Africa, nutritional intake is already below minimum standards; a lowered nutritional status increases vulnerability to illness and death while leading to further declines in productivity. Furthermore, an unmet food demand increases dependency on imports and food aid.

The effects of AIDS on agricultural production have already been observed in Uganda, Tanzania and Zambia, where detailed surveys reveal that farmers cope with reduced labour by adopting practices that jeopardize immediate and future productivity. For example, delays and the inadequate execution or cessation of routine farming operations such as tilling, weeding, planting and mulching lead to poorer harvests; they also perpetuate or enlarge the perils of crop pests and diseases, thus creating hazards for individual households and entire communities.

Furthermore, labour shortages force farmers to reduce the land area under cultivation; if the land reverts to bush, it is difficult to reclaim, and usufruct rights may be lost owing to a lack of continuous cultivation. Crops may be chosen for their low-labour input rather than their nutritional value or marketability. As more labour-intensive crops are dropped, the range of crops declines and crop failures take on more significance because there is less to fall back on. Crop substitution may also reduce or eliminate cash crops destined for export, thereby worsening foreign exchange earning potential.

In addition to labour shortages, deaths of productive farmers erode agricultural knowledge, built up over centuries, regarding local cultivars and specialized cultivation skills and techniques. As a result, genetic diversity of adapted local crop varieties, the backbone of subsistence farming, may decline and some traditional varieties may become extinct.

Maintaining productivity levels with a depleted agricultural labour force requires capital investment to increase the productivity of remaining farmers or to attract labour from other sectors. In some countries, the barriers to achieving this are substantial.

For example, in Uganda agriculture currently accounts for 70 percent of GDP, 95 percent of export earnings and 90 percent of all employment. It is estimated that 20 percent of the population over 15 years of age is HIV-positive. As the death toll mounts, each productive person becomes responsible for a higher number of dependants; there will be about one million orphaned children in the next five years. Coping with illness and death is a constant drain on individual and community resources, making it increasingly difficult to maintain, much less increase, productivity. Since other sectors account for only 10 percent of the labour force in Uganda, and given the grim circumstances, the prospects of attracting additional labour to agriculture appear to be rather dim.

Labour can be substituted by other inputs such as expanded mechanization, increased access to credit, agrochemicals, improved seeds and extension education. Losses in productivity could be balanced by international aid and government investment for modernizing production methods. Since resources are scarce and the effects of AIDS are expected to have dramatic geographic variations, accurate local assessments are essential before interventions are undertaken.

A note on statistics

Global AIDS statistics are based on scant research and are subject to rapid change as research reveals new information about the disease. For example, in 1993 the Center for Disease Control in the United States expanded the definition of AIDS to include three new indicator diseases (pulmonary tuberculosis, recurrent bacterial pneumonia and invasive cervical cancer). These new diagnostics more than doubled the number of AIDS cases merely by changing the definition.[5] If this phenomenon is observed in a country with one of the most developed AIDS programmes in the world, the difficulty of accurate global numbers can be grasped.

Furthermore, a lack of testing and diagnostic facilities makes estimates unreliably low. Low recorded and estimated numbers of both AIDS- and HIV-positive persons in developing countries are due to various factors, including: insufficient funds for testing; low rates of diagnosis because few AIDS victims are seen by doctors; misdiagnoses through lack of training and the prevalence of other concomitant ailments such as tuberculosis; and a lack of funds for keeping accurate records.

Many national HIV/AIDS estimates are based on back-calculations from diagnosed AIDS cases. This is misleading because such cases include only those who have fallen ill or died; as many as ten times that number may be HIV-positive. This estimate rises to 100 times in South and Southeast Asia where the pandemic is thought to be in its early stages. Despite this weakness, patterns that are useful to planners and policy-makers are beginning to emerge.

---

[5] *The Lancet,* 7 November 1992.

BOX 3
AIDS

Acquired immune deficiency syndrome (AIDS) is the name of the fatal clinical condition that results from infection with the *human immunodeficiency virus (HIV)*, which progressively damages the body's ability to protect itself from disease organisms. Thus, many AIDS deaths result from pneumonia, tuberculosis or diarrhoea; death is not caused by HIV itself but by one or more of these infections.

HIV-1 and *HIV-2* are two similar viruses, both of which gradually erode the body's immune system. HIV-1 is found throughout the world; it has higher infection rates, currently doubling in about 5.7 years. WHO estimates that, in five years from now (in the year 2000), 30 million to 40 million people will be infected with HIV-1, half of whom will be in sub-Saharan Africa. The incidence of mother-infant transmission is 10 to 30

percent and many infants develop symptoms after four months. HIV-2 is found primarily, although not exclusively, in West Africa and has a doubling rate of 31 years; it is rarely passed on from mother to infant.

High-risk behaviour describes sexual intercourse (either male/female or male/male) without using a condom, or the sharing of needles to inject drugs. *High-risk groups* comprise, in epidemiological terms, people whose behaviour places them repeatedly at high risk, for example intravenous drug users, prostitutes, those who have several sex partners without using condoms. *High-risk situations* comprise inadequate health resources, low levels of education, poverty, rapid urbanization, social upheaval and social and economic marginalization and high levels of preventable diseases.

Source: British Medical Journal, 1991.

Regional overviews

At the end of 1993, two-thirds of all HIV carriers worldwide were estimated to be in *sub-Saharan Africa*, a region which accounts for only 10 percent of the global population. About 50 percent of the total population in this region is in the high-risk and economically productive age cohort of 15 to 45 years of age; the birth rate is the highest, with a 3.2 percent population growth in the last decade, and per caput production also the lowest in the world. A recent study estimates that the GDP growth rate in sub-Saharan Africa will be halved in the next five years through deaths from AIDS.[6]

For example, in the largest study of its kind in sub-Saharan Africa, the mortality among inhabitants in 15 villages in the Masaka District of Southwestern Uganda, mainly subsistence farmers, was observed over two years. More than 80 percent of deaths in the 13- to 44-year-old group were due to HIV-1. The highest mortality occurred in males from 25 to 34 years old and in females from 13 to 34 years old. A substantial number of these deaths occurred less than *six months* after the first symptoms appeared. The prevalence of HIV-1 is lower in Masaka than it is in many urban centres in Africa.[7]

Furthermore, in sub-Saharan Africa the more rapidly infective HIV-1 is more common than HIV-2 and has activated outbreaks of tuberculosis, now the leading cause of death in HIV-positive people. Unlike HIV, tuberculosis is easily transmitted through routine household and casual contact, thus endangering family members and entire communities.

These factors alone are sufficient to set the scene for disaster. When other characteristics about the region are added – low crop yields and declining per caput production – it is clear that sub-Saharan Africa may be the global epicentre of death from AIDS, both from the disease itself and from its effects on livelihoods.

In *Latin America and the Caribbean*, transmission patterns have changed markedly in the last decade; male/female intercourse now accounts for 75 percent of infections and the number of perinatally infected children has risen dramatically. Between 1.5 million and two million people are thought to be infected, primarily in urban centres. Large numbers of tourists and business travellers, along with migrant workers, further the spread of infection. Brazil has the fourth highest reported number of AIDS cases in the world, and the

---

[6] G. Kambou, S. Deverjan and M. Over. 1993. The economic impacts of AIDS in an African country: simulations with a computable general equilibrium model of Cameroon. *Journal of African Economies,* 1(1).

[7] *The Lancet,* 23 April 1994.

number quadrupled from 1990 to 1992. On average, health care for an AIDS patient is estimated to be more than 800 percent of the per caput GNP.[8]

In *Asia*, HIV infection is spreading more rapidly than anywhere else in the world. In Thailand, for example, the number of HIV-infected people doubled in 1990, has more than doubled again since then, and is expected to reach up to four million within five years.[9] In 1992, the government implemented education, awareness and comprehensive monitoring programmes aimed at reducing rates of infection.

In India, in late 1992 HIV was estimated to be present in between 600 000 and three million people.

In the *Near East and North Africa*, little information is available on AIDS and numbers of reported cases are very low. In Lebanon there is some concern that foreign-donated blood used for transfusions during the 15-year civil war may have been a source of infection. Also, many Lebanese who went to Africa during the war are now returning, some with AIDS. Despite the low numbers, the health ministry has already launched a strong public information programme to promote the use of condoms against infection.

Patterns of transmission and risk factors
At present, there is a high correlation between poverty and the rapid growth of AIDS. Where poverty is endemic, greater proportions of the population are both at a higher risk of infection and less able to mitigate against its effects. Other poverty-related health risks, such as poor nutrition and a lack of medicine and health infrastructure, ensure that the disease proceeds more rapidly from its onset to death. In sub-Saharan Africa, for example, the time from infection to death averages between six months and two years, whereas in developed countries it is ten years.

Epidemiological research has also revealed that high mobility elevates the risk of HIV infection. For example, high levels of seasonal or permanent migration, a flourishing tourist industry or a developed transportation infrastructure can all facilitate the rapid spread of the virus.

Sexual intercourse accounts for between 75 and 85 percent of HIV transmission; this includes male/female intercourse (70 to 75 percent) and male/male intercourse (5 to 10 percent). Other means of transmission are injecting drugs (5 to 10 percent), mother to

---

[8] Atlantic Information Services. 1994. *AIDS reference guide: a sourcebook for planners and decision makers.* Washington, DC.

[9] UNDP, op. cit., footnote 4, p. 46.

infant (5 to 10 percent) and medical use of contaminated blood or blood products (3 to 5 percent). However, the averages mask important differences both between and within regions and countries.

In the early 1980s, AIDS was primarily an urban phenomenon, a feature now associated with the early stages of the pandemic. As we approach the middle of the second decade of AIDS, infection rates are mounting in rural areas.[10] In a somewhat parallel movement, national epidemics appear to start in the highest socio-economic stratum and move downwards. Similarly, in the early 1980s AIDS primarily affected the wealthier classes and this pattern can still be observed in countries where prevalence of the disease is low.[11] If the transmission rate remains stable, the absolute number of HIV-affected people will increase simply because there are more people who are poor and live in rural areas.

As the disease moves down the socio-economic scale, it strengthens the grip of poverty. Poor people have less access to health care and education. Illiterate people are more economically vulnerable and their vulnerability is compounded because information on AIDS prevention rarely reaches them. In any case, condoms are often unavailable and unaffordable for poor people.

Poverty induces people to migrate in search of employment; this social dislocation often leads to high-risk behaviour such as drug abuse or involvement in the sex industry, either as a supplier or purchaser. Returning migrant workers are frequently a source of HIV infection. Poverty also influences attitudes towards risk; immediate needs for food and shelter may propel individuals to work in the sex industry to support themselves and their families in rural areas. Even outside the commercial sex industry, trading sex for material gains is common if other options for livelihood are not available.

AIDS has profound differential effects on women and men. Women's lack of equity is a leading risk factor in the spread of AIDS. First, a potent combination of biological and social reasons means that women are 2.5 times more likely to be infected by men than the reverse. Second, all other risk factors are compounded for women. They are more likely to be illiterate; more likely to be saddled with the care of the sick and dying, in addition to carrying

---

[10] Atlantić Information Services, op. cit., footnote 8, p. 51. *Note:* No figures are given to support this statement.

[11] WHO points out that "the well-educated élites ... were the first to change their lifestyles as information became available about the disease and its prevention".

heavier paid and unpaid workloads in the home, in agriculture and in other sectors. Poverty among women tends to limit all of their choices, including when and with whom to have sexual relations. They are the least likely to have knowledge of, access to, the means to purchase or the power to enforce the use of condoms.

In Africa and parts of Asia and Latin America, women contribute the bulk of agricultural labour. The loss of their contributions through family illness – their own or others' – therefore creates a substantial drop in productivity. Also, in many African countries, women have few legal rights, particularly property rights. A wife whose husband dies of AIDS is likely to be stripped of assets by her husband's family and sent home where she and her children become a burden on her own relatives. Alternatively, she may be taken on as a wife by one of her husband's brothers in which case, if she is HIV-infected, she will proceed to infect him and his other wives and any subsequent children. WHO predicts a 50 percent increase in infant mortality in sub-Saharan Africa during this decade as a result of AIDS.

Furthermore, in many developing countries, a woman's value and status in society are directly linked to her fertility. Failure to produce children can lead to social disgrace and humiliation, if not divorce and displacement in the marriage. This situation promotes the spread of AIDS because societal prohibition of contraception deters condom use.

Interventions
AIDS is more than a health problem. It has significant, long-term socio-economic implications on food security, agricultural productivity and national economies.

Current annual worldwide expenditure on prevention of the disease is about $1.5 billion. Less than $200 million of this is spent in developing countries, where some 85 percent of infections occur. A recent study for WHO's Global Programme on AIDS suggested that comprehensive prevention of AIDS and sexually transmitted diseases could cost up to $2.9 billion per year in developing countries – ten to 15 times current spending levels. However, the study estimates that 9.5 million adult HIV infections could be averted from now until the year 2000. Early intervention aimed at high-risk, high-transmission groups is the most cost-effective means of bringing the spread of the virus under control. Because of the high numbers of sexual contacts in these groups, each infection avoided prevents an estimated ten times as many infections in the general population.

Crucial elements of AIDS prevention include providing information on how to avoid infection, promoting condom use, treating other sexually transmitted diseases and reducing blood-borne transmission.

Strong political will is essential to the fight against AIDS. However, interventions offer little political benefit and may be highly controversial because they pertain to sexual behaviour.

WHO cautions that no single strategy will meet the needs of every country. Therefore, policy-makers should perhaps view the AIDS pandemic as a series of "subepidemics" in countries and regions which have different characteristics such as their percentage of HIV prevalence, rates of transmission and numbers of AIDS cases. For example, Uganda has high numbers of AIDS cases while Thailand has high rates of HIV infection but, as yet, few cases of AIDS; each country will require a different approach.

The impacts of AIDS underline the need for policy measures to alleviate poverty and increase equity, particularly for women, who suffer the greatest consequences of AIDS. Removing discrimination against women – in the labour market, in access to credit and education and in property law, for example – will increase female income. It is well documented that higher levels of income and education among women are directly linked to improved child and family health. It is clear that AIDS will create a lower standard of living for everyone, not just those afflicted by the disease.

Finally, the issue must be raised regarding the involvement of agricultural policy-makers in dealing with AIDS and its consequences. The problem transcends agriculture and has wide economic, social and demographic implications. Nevertheless, to the extent of its impact on food security, agricultural public services need to formulate and implement measures to complement those related to education and information, health care and prevention and social assistance. However, the effectiveness of such measures hinges crucially on adequate knowledge. Not only is the disease not yet well understood but also its dynamics – current and prospective effects on urban and rural areas – are inadequately researched and documented.

Agricultural policy-makers require more information about the likely effects of the disease on food supply and demand, i.e. how the balance between net food buyers (chiefly urban populations) and net food sellers is likely to evolve; and the extent to which AIDS and related effects may affect levels and patterns of agricultural output. On the demand side, research is needed on changes in levels and patterns of food consumption in the light of population and per caput income reductions. Policy action will then have to address such specific problems as: i) compensating for the loss of 15- to 45-year-old able-bodied farm workers by introducing labour-saving technology and creating incentives for farming; ii) consolidating farm holdings so that they remain in operation after the death of farmers – land tenure rules should be adjusted to give maximum flexibility for renting, selling or other arrangements and, if buying land is a viable option, credit may be needed; iii) compensating for reduced domestic supplies through food imports or food aid.

A GLOBAL GREENHOUSE

Global warming refers to the process whereby increasing atmospheric concentrations of "greenhouse gases" (GHGs) contribute to warming of the earth. In brief, while gases such as carbon dioxide, methane and water vapour are transparent to the sun's short-wave rays, they trap the radiant long-wave energy and reflect it back to the earth's surface. Many scientists believe that higher concentrations of these gases will cause an increase in global average temperatures.

Carbon dioxide (CO_2), which is generated by burning fossil fuels and biomass, accounts for about 50 percent of the "radiative forcing" attributable to humans. Other important GHGs are methane (CH_4), produced by marshes, landfills, livestock and wetland crops such as rice; and nitrous oxide (N_2O), produced by nitrification and denitrification processes in soils, nitrogen fertilizer application and land-use changes. Current agricultural practices and land-use changes account for about one-third of anticipated greenhouse effects.

Although there is debate about whether or not global warming has already begun, many scientists agree that a slow rise will take place in the future. The main impacts of rising concentrations of GHGs are: increases in average temperatures, especially night-time temperatures in temperate regions; local changes in rainfall-evaporation ratios and associated shifts in agro-ecological zones; and increases in sea level by up to 40 cm by the year 2100 (as a result of thermal expansion of the ocean and possibly the melting of polar ice).[12] Over the past century, the earth's annual near-surface temperature has risen by 0.3 to 0.6°C, while the global sea level has risen by about 12 cm. These changes have already had some effects on agriculture as well as on local climates and other conditions of interest to agriculture.

FAO considers that there is still too much conjecture about

---

[12] There seems to be most agreement about the broadest category of impacts (global average temperature rises, for example); there is progressively less agreement about the pattern and nature of impacts as the geographical area is more refined.

certain features of climate change and national-level impacts on agriculture to warrant specific investment responses by developing countries, given their heavy financial requirements to meet more immediate food and agricultural needs. On the other hand, there is a degree of scientific consensus that the greenhouse effect is real, that concentrations of GHGs have been rising at unprecedented rates in the past decades,[13] that global warming will slowly occur and that such changes will affect crop, animal, forest and fisheries sectors. Moreover, certain agricultural policy measures that make sense in any scenario and can be justified in benefit-cost terms could help slow the negative impacts of climate change.

An important theme linking the effects of global warming on agriculture, forestry and fisheries is that the most significant impacts may be the hardest to predict. Further, the broad trends in worldwide averages mask crucial differences in the incidence of warming-related damages. These differences are made more acute because countries likely to suffer most from warming may be the least able to respond.

Global warming linkages to agriculture, forestry and fisheries

It is difficult to predict how agricultural productivity will be affected by the higher temperatures associated with global warming, as many of the expected changes will have both positive and negative effects on production. For example, higher temperatures are likely to increase yields in higher-latitude countries but decrease yields in countries closer to the equator – the worst affected would be developing countries. Another expected change, increased CO_2 concentrations, may increase plant growth – but this is likely to benefit both crop plants and weeds, heightening the competition between them for water and nutrients. Other experiments have shown higher water-use efficiency by plants at increased CO_2 levels – which may become very important for semi-arid areas.

Similarly, global warming will have mixed effects on livestock production. In some locations, higher temperatures may encourage poleward migration of animal pests, promote herd growth or reduce feed requirements. Equally likely is that livestock numbers will be reduced in other locations. The effects on fisheries would be similarly mixed. Complex interactions between surface warming, warm and cold ocean currents and interrelated marine species make it difficult to predict the impacts on populations of specific commercial fish species.

---

[13] In the past few years, however, the increases have slowed down (see Table 2, notes 3 and 4).

A possible sea level rise of several hundred millimetres would not only affect the coastline and the structures along it, but also the hydrology, soils and natural or cultivated vegetation over an appreciable distance inland. The nature and extent of these changes depends on the length of the dry season, the sediment supply from rivers and the incidence of storms and cyclones.[14]

The natural ranges of many tree species could advance to higher latitudes or higher altitudes as temperatures increase. Forests stressed by climate change would become more susceptible to damage by fire, insects, pollution and disease. Genetic diversity could be reduced, leaving only the more resistant genotypes, and areas and many tree and undergrowth species could be lost.

Some researchers draw an important distinction between the effects of global warming on worldwide production and on consumption and producer gains. For instance, warming could lower yields in one region by 5 percent but increase world prices by 10 percent, thereby reducing the negative impact on agriculture. Therefore, the regional impacts are expected to differ greatly. As a result, the attractive locations for many agricultural activities may move, often across national or regulatory boundaries.

In the absence of large-scale field experiments, no clear-cut conclusions can be reached on the geographic distribution of the impacts, on the interaction between environmental and socio-economic factors or on the agricultural sectors most likely to be affected. Indications, however, suggest that: i) in the absence of stress conditions, many annual crops could benefit from the CO_2 fertilization effect and improved water-use efficiency; ii) natural vegetation and some perennial crops are less likely to benefit and may actually suffer to an extent that is largely unknown; iii) the quality of agricultural products and their nutritional value, soils, crop and forest interaction with pests and diseases, and water availability may be affected; iv) climate change impacts between developed and developing countries are likely to be uneven; v) interseasonal and interannual variabilities of climate are likely to increase, resulting in higher risks of crop failures and food shortages.

These indications are, however, largely uncertain owing to the lack of confidence in global circulation models and to the insufficient knowledge of the biophysical responses of crops and ecosystems to elevated levels of CO_2.

---

[14] S. Jelgersma, M. van der Zijp and R. Brinkman. 1993. Sea level rise and the coastal lowlands in the developing world. *Journal of Coastal Research*, 9(4): 958-972.

Contribution to GHGs from agriculture, forestry and fisheries

The agricultural, forestry and fisheries activities that contribute to GHG emissions are relatively few. Deforestation is the most important source of CO_2 emissions from agriculture and forestry. Livestock and irrigated and wetland crop production account for 70 percent of total CH_4 emissions (see Table 2); emissions of N_2O are mostly associated with changing soil management practices (which modify natural nitrification and denitrification processes), wood burning and, to a small extent, the use of nitrogen fertilizers.

The overall policy approach

Global warming is similar to ozone depletion in the stratosphere in that the emissions in one country have almost the same impact as those released in another. However, the emissions of ozone-depleting chemicals are concentrated in a relatively small number of countries and their production is dominated by relatively few firms. These factors make it easier to arrive at a series of agreements that progressively restrict the production and release of such chemicals.

By contrast, emissions of GHGs are spread throughout the world and are attributable to almost every firm and household. This feature requires wide-scale international coordination and complicates the task of monitoring and enforcing emerging policies.

The time lapse between cause and effect presents problems for a worldwide response to global warming. For example, while the local effects of some industrial emissions are dramatically reduced within days of cessation, the most significant effects of GHG emissions are expected to occur over the next century. Thus, given the scientific uncertainties about global warming and its effects, together with the expected costs of cutting emissions, agreements to reduce GHGs are difficult to achieve.

Given these complications and uncertainties, the emerging policy approach has two stages at the international level. In the first (short-term) stage, the focus would be on research and a "no-regrets" policy approach. The second (longer-term) stage would involve tough commitments to deal with warming which would follow only if further research shows that global warming must be avoided.

Short-term responses and no-regrets policies

A no-regrets response to global warming would include technological and economic policies that are justifiable even if global warming does not become a problem. These responses include using existing technologies that are economically feasible.

TABLE 2

Agricultural greenhouse gases and trends			
	CO_2	CH_4	N_2O
TOTAL			
Atmospheric lifetime	120 yrs	10.5 yrs	132 yrs
Global warming potential, direct[1]	1	11	70
Global warming potential, indirect[2]	0	$\pm$10	...
Pre-industrial levels (1750-1800)	280 ppmv	0.80 ppmv	288 ppbv
Present-day levels (1990)	353 ppmv	1.72 ppmv	310 ppbv
Average yearly increase (%)	0.5[3]	0.9[4]	0.25
Reduction in emissions required for stabilization at current levels (%)	> 60	15-20	70-80
AGRICULTURE			
Emissions from agriculture (%)	30	70	90
Main agricultural sources	Deforestation	Irrigated and wetland crops; ruminant digestion	Soil management practices; nitrogen fertilizer use
Trend 1900/1990-2100	Decreasing	10-30% increase	5-10% increase

[1] In relation to CO_2 at a 100-year time horizon.
[2] Through chemical transformation.
[3] Increase much less than linear since 1990.
[4] Increase less than linear since 1980; at present nearly stable.
Note: Concentrations specified as: ppmv = parts per 10^6 by volume; ppbv = parts per 10^9 by volume.
Sources: IPCC Second Assessment Report 1992; and R. Brinkman and W.G. Sombroek. The effects of global climatic change on soil conditions in relation to plant growth and food production. *In* D. Norse and W.G. Sombroek, eds. *Global climatic change and agricultural production. Direct and indirect effects of changing hydrological, soil and plant physiological processes.* Chichester, UK, Wiley. (in press)

For example, existing and affordable energy-efficient lighting technologies would reduce fossil fuel consumption. Greater use of such technologies would require public education. Similarly, current techniques that make more efficient use of nitrogen fertilizers are already justified by decreased costs and increased productivity, but they will also reduce emissions of N_2O.

The no-regrets approach involves policy changes that are already justifiable and desirable for improving economic efficiency but that would also have important direct or indirect impacts on GHG emissions – such policy changes include addressing market systems and policies that distort economic costs and underprice resources – such policy reforms generally have the characteristics of no-regrets actions in that they are desirable, even without global warming.

Policy linkages to agriculture, forestry and fisheries

Some important agricultural policies that may be encouraged because they contribute to GHG abatement include reforestation, soil organic matter conservation and improved efficiency of irrigation systems and fertilizer application. Many argue that actions to reduce deforestation in some developing countries should be described as no-regrets responses, partly since many other serious problems are associated with deforestation (loss of biodiversity and diminished watershed protection). CO_2 abatement also includes improving energy efficiency and reducing or eliminating fuel subsidies for agricultural users. Measures to improve fertilizer formulations and to decrease fertilizer waste could reduce N_2O emissions; measures that improve the quality of livestock feeds may reduce CH_4 and N_2O emissions. If global warming is deemed to be a serious enough threat, taxes on fertilizer use or restrictions on energy inputs may have to be considered. The latter policy options will not be viable in many developing countries with actual or impending food shortages. Ongoing research may identify other ways of reducing the emissions concerned.

Although CH_4 is an important component of agriculture's contribution to global warming, there is currently little discussion of using taxes or quantity restrictions to reduce these emissions. Alternatives to taxes or quotas could include different cropping practices (in the case of rice, for example), or the production and provision of higher-quality feeds (in the case of livestock). In the longer term, however, if warming becomes an acute problem, more binding policies (such as taxes on goods with high CH_4 emissions or quotas on these outputs) may have to be considered. In addition, there is a need for expanded research and education about other techniques for reducing CH_4 emissions, such as better management of landfills and livestock wastes.

In the case of forestry, two longer-term responses are being discussed. First, further attention should be paid to counteracting deforestation. Governments should be encouraged to eliminate policies that contribute to deforestation and to promote reforestation in some cases. The real returns to agriculture from forest clearing in many parts of the world are very low, and reducing deforestation may be an efficient way of reducing current levels of CO_2 emissions by up to 10 percent. International loans may provide gap funding for those countries seeking to stop unwanted deforestation.

Second, reforestation involving planting trees on previously cropped land or the expansion of existing forests would sequester additional carbon. However, recent research questions its cost-effectiveness on a large scale. These studies argue that there is a limited supply of land suitable for growing trees as an economically viable alternative. In the simplest terms, the land that tends to be best for "carbon forestry" also tends to be reasonably good for crops, thus increasing the opportunity cost of the land. Further, reforestation absorbs carbon only as long as the forest is growing, since once it achieves maturity, carbon losses through decomposition and fires offset the carbon taken up by new growth. In contrast, the extra storage of carbon in soil organic matter, already two to three times that of standing biomass, offers more possibilities while also improving soil quality.

Research into the effects of warming, reducing emissions and mitigating the consequences is likely to be expanded in a number of directions. Among the many areas of great interest to agriculture, forestry and fisheries is that of research into the effects of changes in water levels on wetland crops and the local changes in rainfall-evaporation ratios, including the consequences for local plant growth and water for downstream irrigation. More generally, ongoing research may reduce uncertainties for policy formulation. However, lack of research should not be an excuse for inaction in crucial areas, particularly where projects or policies under consideration have no-regrets justifications.

Longer-term responses
If global warming is "confirmed", policy-makers must consider another set of longer-term policy options. The most important of these would aim to curtail the burning of fossil fuels. Supplementary policy responses would be directed at agriculture and forestry, as indicated above.

CO_2 emissions can be reduced by: increasing energy efficiency; reducing energy use; changing the mix of fossil fuel use; and substituting biomass for fossil fuels. For example, policies that shift the demand for energy away from high carbon-content fuels such as coal to lower carbon-content fuels such as natural gas will reduce CO_2 emissions because they generate less CO_2 per unit of energy. Even more significant reductions would follow from substituting carbon-free energy such as hydroelectricity, geothermal, solar and wind energy or bio-energy.

Summary
One of the major challenges to policy-makers in the coming decades is the broad range of uncertainty surrounding global warming, its likely climatic and biological effects and its effects on specific sectors of the economy as well as on society at large. These uncertainties are particularly pronounced for agriculture, and they

grow greater the further one looks into the future. Finally, the greatest uncertainty concerns the level of geographic detail necessary for appropriate policy-making. As a result of this uncertainty, there is a pressing need for information on relevant linkages.

Crucial international equity issues must also be addressed in order to evaluate who will bear the cost of greenhouse warming abatement. For the purposes of agricultural policy-making, the issues raised above may help determine which approaches to the abatement of greenhouse warming will be affordable for high- and low-income countries, respectively.

URUGUAY ROUND OF MULTILATERAL TRADE NEGOTIATIONS

The Uruguay Round of GATT multilateral trade negotiations (MTNs) was launched in 1986 at Punta del Este, Uruguay. The Final Act concluding the Round was signed at Marrakesh in April 1994. It includes agreements and decisions that will be of economic significance to the world and to the developing countries. Of greatest direct concern to the agricultural sector are the Agreement on Agriculture, the Agreement on the Application of Sanitary and Phytosanitary Measures and the Decision on Measures Concerning the Possible Negative Effects of the Reform Programme on Least-Developed and Net Food-Importing Developing Countries.

Provisions of the Final Act

Providing it is ratified, the implementation of the Agreement on Agriculture should start in 1995, and developed countries' commitments to reduce support and export subsidies as well as to expand market access should be completed within six years, i.e. by the year 2000. Developing countries' commitments, on the other hand, should be completed within ten years, by the year 2004. The least-developed countries (LDCs) are not required to make any reductions. The commodity coverage of the Agreement on Agriculture includes most of the products normally considered as part of agriculture (i.e. it excludes fishery and forest products) with the exception of rubber, jute, sisal, abaca and coir which are covered by industrial product negotiations. However, domestic support measures for these commodities are completely excluded from reduction commitments, as there are no such commitments for industrial products. Initially, negotiations on tropical products were conducted separately from those on agriculture but in the end they were grouped together.

There are three elements to the commitment on market access: tariffication, tariff reduction and access opportunities. First, members must convert their non-tariff barriers (NTBs) into tariffs. This means that specific NTBs (quotas, variable levies, minimum import prices, discretionary licensing, state trading measures, voluntary restraint agreements and similar border measures) need to be abolished and converted into an equivalent tariff (*ad valorem* or specific). The basic approach is to set a tariff equal to the difference in 1986-88 between the internal price (typically the domestic wholesale price) and the external price (typically the import unit value c.i.f. converted into national currency). Adjustments may be made for quality or variety; however, most developing countries have opted to use a special clause which allows them to set bound ceiling tariffs instead of full tariffication.

Ordinary tariffs, including those resulting from tariffication, should be reduced by 36 percent (as an *average* over all commodities) in the six years starting in 1995, with a minimum rate of reduction of 15 percent for each tariff item (for developing countries the figures are 24 and 10 percent). The tariff reduction will be undertaken in equal annual instalments and all customs duties will be bound.

As existing NTBs have sometimes resulted in zero or negligible imports, there are special provisions concerning *minimum access* opportunities. Where there are no significant imports, a minimum access equal to 3 percent of domestic consumption in 1986-88 will be established for 1995, rising to 5 percent of base year consumption at the end of the implementation period. Minimum access opportunities will be implemented on the basis of a tariff quota at low rates provided on a most favoured nation (MFN) basis. In cases where current access opportunities are more than the minimum, they will be maintained and increased during the implementation process.

The Agreement on Agriculture contains important *special safeguard provisions*, which allow additional duties when there are either import surges or particularly low prices (both compared with 1986-88 levels). In the case of import surges (defined by specified trigger levels above average imports in the previous three years and the most recent change in consumption), additional duties shall not exceed one-third of the ordinary customs duties in effect. In the case of low import prices (in national currency terms), an additional duty can be charged which progressively increases as the price level drops further below the 1986-88 level. Thus, there is a strong stabilizing influence on domestic prices in the case of very large import price falls. However, this effect would aggravate the fall in prices on world markets because the additional duties would curb the increase in import demand which would be necessary to help shore up international prices.

The introduction of reduction commitments on domestic support marks perhaps the greatest single innovation of the Agreement on Agriculture. The general approach adopted has been to divide policies into two groups: i) policies that have a minimal or no effect on production or trade distortion (the Green Box category); and ii) policies subject to reduction commitments. The total support given to agriculture in 1986-88 by the latter policies, measured by the Total Aggregate Measurement of Support (Total AMS), is subject to reduction commitments of 20 percent in developed countries over the period 1995-2000 and 13.3 percent in developing countries in the period 1995-2004. Reduction commitments refer to *total levels of support* and not to individual commodities.

Green Box policies, which are exempt from reduction commitments, are those that do not entail price support to producers and for which support is provided by the government and not by consumers. The list of exempt policies is very long and includes such policies as general services (research, training, extension, inspection, marketing and promotion, infrastructure) food security stocks, domestic food aid and certain direct payments to producers (decoupled income insurance and safety net programmes; disaster relief; producer or resource retirement schemes; investment aids; environmental programmes; and regional assistance).

In addition to the Green Box category, other policies excluded from the AMS include investment subsidies that are generally available to agriculture in developing country members and agricultural input subsidies, generally available to poor farmers of developing country members. Policies that amount to a small percentage transfer value to producers (less than 5 percent of the value of production for developed countries and less than 10 percent for developing countries) are also excluded under the *de minimis* rule. Finally, direct payments to production-limiting programmes have been excluded from the Current Total AMS, provided certain conditions are met (namely that they are decoupled or that payments are made on 85 percent or less of base production).

The Agreement on Agriculture lists the export subsidies that are to be reduced: direct subsidies, sales from stocks by governments at prices lower than the domestic market price, export payments financed by obligatory levies, subsidized export marketing costs and special domestic transport charges. The volume of exports benefiting from such subsidies must be reduced by 21 percent and the expenditure on export subsidies by 36 percent over the 1995-2000 period. Unlike the reduction commitments in domestic support, reductions in export subsidies will be product-specific.

Also, calculations of the commodity-specific final level of subsidized exports are based on average 1986-90 levels. However, in certain cases exporters have been allowed to maintain a higher level of subsidized exports permissible in the years up to 1999, by availing themselves of a special option (the higher of the subsidized levels of 1991-92 and 1986-90) to make reductions to the same final level by the year 2000.

The Final Act also provides some provisions for the *prevention of circumvention* of export subsidy commitments. First, export subsidies not included in the reduction commitment must not be used to circumvent the commitments. Second, members have undertaken to work towards internationally agreed disciplines on the use of export credit and credit guarantees. Third, the onus of proof in contentious cases rests on the exporter to show that there has been no violation of export subsidies. Finally, there are some important provisions on *food aid*, namely that it should not be tied directly or indirectly to commercial exports; that food aid transactions should be carried out in accordance with FAO Principles of Surplus Disposal; and that such aid should be provided to the extent possible in full grant form or on terms no less concessional than those provided for in Article IV of the 1986 Food Aid Convention.

A late addition to the Final Act was Article 12, Disciplines on Export Prohibitions and Restrictions, which concerns limitations on exports of foodstuffs taken under paragraph 2(a) of Article XI of the GATT. This allows such restrictions to be "temporarily applied to prevent or relieve critical shortages of foodstuffs or other products essential to the exporting contracting party". This possibility is now to be tightened up. In future, exporters must consider the effects on importing members' food security and must consult with importing members who have a substantial interest at stake, at their request.

Special and differential treatment for developing countries is an integral part of the Agreement on Agriculture, although it may not be adequate. Special and differential treatment has three basic elements. First, developing countries are given *more time* to adjust and are expected to make *smaller reductions* in support. Thus, the period of implementation is ten years, not six, and reduction commitments in the areas of market access, domestic support and export competition amount to two-thirds of those expected of developed countries. Also, developing countries are allowed a higher *de minimis* level of domestic support (10 percent instead of 5 percent for developed countries). LDCs are exempt from the reduction commitments.

The second area where special and differential treatment applies concerns the various types of policies that are "acceptable" to

GATT. As regards *export subsidies*, developing countries are allowed to provide subsidies to reduce the marketing costs of agricultural products and differential internal transport costs, which developed countries must curtail. Regarding *domestic support*, the Green Box category has a special provision for developing countries in regard to public stockholding for food security and domestic food aid. Moreover, developing countries may exclude the following policies from the calculation of the Total AMS: i) investment subsidies that are generally available to agriculture; ii) domestic support to producers to encourage diversification from illicit narcotic crops; and iii) agricultural input subsidies provided to low-income or resource-poor producers that are available to all producers, providing they meet certain criteria.

Third, there are special provisions for developing countries contained in the Decision on Measures Concerning the Possible Negative Effects of the Reform Programme on Least-Developed and Net Food-Importing Developing Countries. The idea behind the Decision is that agricultural trade liberalization is likely to lead to higher world prices for food, while reduced export subsidies will also raise the effective price paid by importers. There is also some concern that the volume of food aid, which historically has been closely linked to the level of surplus stocks, could decline as the surplus stocks are run down. The Decision promises action to improve food aid by i) reviewing the level of food aid; and ii) providing an increasing share of aid on grant terms. It also promises to consider requests for technical and financial assistance to improve agricultural productivity and infrastructure and, furthermore, that any agreement on export credits would make "appropriate provision" for differential treatment in favour of these countries. Finally, it provides for short-term assistance in financing normal commercial imports from international financial institutions under "existing facilities, or such facilities as may be established, in the context of adjustment programmes".

The Final Act also includes the important Agreement on Sanitary and Phytosanitary Measures. It recognizes that governments have the right to take sanitary and phytosanitary measures but that they should be applied only to the extent necessary to protect human, animal or plant life and should not arbitrarily or unjustifiably discriminate between members where identical or similar conditions prevail. Members are encouraged to base their sanitary and phytosanitary measures on international standards, guidelines and recommendations where they exist, including the Codex Alimentarius and the International Plant Protection Convention (IPPC). However, members may maintain or introduce higher standards if there is scientific justification or an acknowledged risk.

The Agreement spells out procedures and criteria for risk assessment and the determination of adequate levels of protection. It is expected that members will accept the sanitary and phytosanitary measures of others as equivalent if the exporting member demonstrates to the importing member that its measures achieve the importing member's appropriate level of protection. The Agreement provides for control, inspection and approval procedures. It also contains requirements on transparency, including the publication of regulations, the establishment of national inquiry points and notification procedures. It establishes a Committee to provide a forum for consultations, maintain contact with other organizations and monitor the process of international harmonization.

The Final Act also contains texts that refer to technical aspects of trade. These include harmonizing rules of origin (other than those relating to the granting of preferences) and ensuring that such rules do not create unnecessary obstacles to trade. There is also a text on pre-shipment inspection which sets out the obligations of importing and exporting countries. The Agreement on Implementing Article VI (anti-dumping and countervailing duties) strengthens the requirement for an importing country to establish a clear causal relationship between dumped imports and injury to the domestic industry. There are procedures for handling anti-dumping cases. The Agreement on Subsidies and Countervailing Measures builds on the existing Subsidies Code and establishes three categories of subsidy: prohibited, actionable and non-actionable. There is special treatment for developing countries. The Final Act also contains a text that extends and clarifies the Agreement on Technical Barriers to Trade to ensure that technical regulations and standards do not create unnecessary barriers to trade. A Code of Good Practice for the Preparation, Adoption and Application of Standards is included. The new agreement strengthens the disciplines regarding the users of import licensing systems, which are much less widely used than in the past. There are also new texts on Customs Valuation and new accession procedures to the existing Agreement on Government Procurement to facilitate the membership of developing countries. Finally, the Uruguay Round agreements would also tighten up the application of safeguard action taken under Article XIX against unforeseen increases in imports that could cause damage to the industry.

There are also several important agreements in addition to the reduction of tariffs. The Agreement on Trade-Related Investment Measures (TRIMs) prohibits any TRIM that is inconsistent with GATT articles on national treatment (requiring imported goods to be treated in a non-discriminatory way *vis-à-vis* domestic goods) and on quantitative restrictions. Regarding textiles and clothing, the object is to secure the eventual integration of this sector into GATT on the basis of strengthened rules and disciplines. This would lead not only to the phasing out of Multifibre Arrangement (MFA) restrictions but also of non-MFA restrictions. The General Agreement on Trade in Services extends to this sector a basic MFN approach, with exemptions, and other provisions such as transparency and recognition requirements. It establishes the basis for progressive liberalization in services and the institutional arrangements, including dispute settlement and a Council on Services. The Agreement on Trade-Related Aspects of Intellectual Property Rights, Including Trade in Counterfeit Goods (TRIPs), covers such matters as copyright, trademarks and service marks, industrial designs, patents and trade secrets. In addition to the above, there are texts designed to reform the system of dispute settlement, confirm the Trade Policy Review Mechanism and encourage greater transparency in the GATT system.

Finally, there was a decision to set up a World Trade Organization (WTO). Decisions by the WTO will be based on consensus and, if votes are needed, each member will have one vote. The WTO will provide a common institutional framework for conducting trade relations among members in matters related to the Final Act. The WTO will absorb the existing GATT and is expected to cooperate with the relevant UN agencies and the Bretton Woods organizations (the World Bank and the IMF), in order to achieve "greater coherence in global economic policy-making".

The Uruguay Round also established a Committee on Agriculture, which will meet annually to discuss the implementation of the Agreement. Members can discuss the question of market shares, the linked issue of export subsidies and the problem of inflation affecting the level of domestic support. The Committee will discuss follow-up to the Decision relating to the concerns of the least-developed and net food-importing developing countries. It will also be involved in the notification requirements for the use of the safeguard provisions and for export prohibitions and restrictions.

Effects on agricultural markets

Although the Agreement on Agriculture is comprehensive, it represents only a partial liberalization agreement. Overall, a large degree of distortion in the world market of agricultural commodities will still remain even after the complete implementation of the reduction commitments in these three areas.

In general, according to most studies and compared with the

situation without the effect of the Uruguay Round Agreement, moderate increases can be expected in the prices of temperate zone products (5 to 10 percent on average) but smaller increases or even slight declines in the prices of the principal tropical products (Table 3). Developing countries are concerned about the price changes of both temperate and tropical products. Moreover, the expansion in world trade in these commodities, which is projected to be slower than during the 1970s and 1980s, will only be stimulated to a limited extent by the Uruguay Round agreements. Major changes in the global volumes of trade are not expected, although there will be changes in the patterns of trade and scope for the more competitive exporters.

Beyond agriculture *per se*, important changes are expected from trade expansion under the liberalized MFA. A large rise in textile exports to the developed countries is expected, while the upward pressure on price could curtail demand somewhat in the developing countries where the bulk of textile consumption takes place.

On balance, demand for textile fibres could be stimulated, which could be of considerable interest to a number of fibre-exporting developing countries. At the same time, a beneficial effect on the expansion of world agricultural markets could come from the boost to world income through the Uruguay Round. This boost to income, mainly in the developed countries, would presumably increase the demand for higher-valued products as well as for niche market products such as exotic fruit and vegetables, cut flowers and horticultural products.

The price increases that are likely for the main temperate zone food products together with reduced export subsidies could significantly increase import prices paid by the net food-importing developing countries, which are the large majority of developing countries. In this context, the Decision on Measures Concerning the Possible Negative Effects of the Reform Programme on Least-developed and Net Food-Importing Developing Countries could, in principle, help these countries in the event of higher world food prices and import bills.

While it is likely that world agricultural prices may be affected as a result of the Uruguay Round Agreement, there is a question mark over food stocks. The general move towards liberalization and a reduced role of governments in price support activities could lead to a fall in government stockholding of agricultural commodities. The reduction may not be large but there is a question as to whether the private sector would step in to fill the gap. If not, as seems likely, then global food stocks are likely to be reduced. Fortunately, however, support to food security stocks that is

TABLE 3

Simulated effects of Uruguay Round trade liberalization on world prices

Commodity	Sources				
	UNCTAD/ WIDER (1990)	Page, Davenport & Hewit (1991)	FAPRI (1993)	Brandao & Martin (1993)	Goldin, Knudsen & van der Mansbrugghe (1993)
	(.. percentage change ....)				
TEMPERATE ZONE PRODUCTS					
Wheat	7.5	5.0	6.3	6.3	5.9
Coarse grains	3.4[1]	1.8	2.4	4.4	3.6
Rice	18.3	1.2	4.4	4.2	-1.9
Meat	13.0	5.3	0.5	6.1[6]	4.7[8]
Sugar	10.6	5.0	...	10.2	10.2
Soybeans	0.0	...	0.0	4.52[7]	...
Soybean oil	0.1	...	3.8	...	4.1[9]
Dairy products	...	9.3	6.9[5]	10.1	7.2
TROPICAL PRODUCTS					
Coffee	0.4[2]	0.8	...	0.41	-6.1
Cocoa	0.0[3]	1.0	...	0.14	-4.0
Tea	0.5	...	...	2.34	3.0
Tobacco	0.3[4]	...	...	...	...
Cotton	0.9	...	...	2.23	3.7
Groundnuts	1.5	...	...	4.52[7]	...
Groundnut oil	0.6	...	...	...	4.1[9]
Plants and Flowers	...	1.0	...	...	...
Spices	...	0.2	...	...	...

[1] Simple average of maize and sorghum.
[2] Refers to beans: for roasted, 0 percent; for coffee extracts, 1.4 percent.
[3] Refers to beans: for butter, 0.5 percent; for powder, 0.8 percent; for chocolate, 1.8 percent.
[4] Refers to leaves: for cigarettes, 0.1 percent; for cigars, 0.8 percent.
[5] Refers to butter.
[6] Refers to beef, veal and sheep meat; for other meats, 3.1 percent.
[7] Refers to all oilseeds.
[8] Refers to beef, veal and sheep meat.
[9] Refers to all vegetable oils.
Sources: UNCTAD/WIDER. 1990. Agricultural trade liberalization in the Uruguay Round: implications for developing countries. New York, UN; S. Page, M. Davenport and A. Hewit. 1991. The GATT Uruguay Round: effects on developing countries. London, ODI; FAPRI. 1993. World Agricultural Outlook, Staff Report No. 2-93. Iowa State University and University of Missouri-Columbia; A.S.P. Brandao and W.J. Martin. 1993. Implications of agricultural trade liberalization for the developing countries. Agricultural Economics, 8: 313-343; E. Goldin, O. Knudsen and D. van der Mensbrugghe. 1993. Trade liberalisation: global economic implications, Paris, OECD/World Bank.

undertaken in a prescribed fashion has been excluded from reduction targets in the Final Act. As called for by FAO's Intergovernmental Group on Grains, at its 25th session in 1993, it is to be hoped that countries would take advantage of this exemption and build up adequate food security reserves, but developing countries may not be able to make major efforts on this score because holding stocks is an expensive undertaking. The costs and benefits of building and utilizing food reserves or relying on the world market for food supplies need to be carefully weighed.

The impacts on individual developing countries will depend mainly on the pattern of their agricultural commodity trade and their responses to the new trading opportunities.

As regards *Africa*, most countries tend to be food importers, particularly of wheat, rice and dairy products, while exporting tropical products such as cocoa, coffee, fruit and some agricultural raw materials. Most are LDCs (28 out of more than 50) and have some preferential access for a part of their exports under the Generalized System of Preferences (GSP) or the Lomé Convention, the value of which may be eroded by overall trade liberalization. The increase in world market prices foreseen for the temperate zone food commodities, combined with a substantial reduction in export subsidies on these commodities, points to a considerable increase in the prices paid by the importing countries. Thus, Africa is likely to face increased foreign exchange expenditures on imports of cereals, meat and sugar and small gains in tropical products, possibly coffee and cotton. The situation varies from subregion to subregion.

As regards *Latin America and the Caribbean*, only one country is among the least-developed group. The region as a whole is a net importer of cereals, even though several countries in the region are exporters of one or more cereals, particularly Argentina and Uruguay. Hence, on balance, the rise in the price of cereals could lead to a rise in the import bills of most of these countries. For most other agricultural commodities, the region is a net exporter and, if the increase in international prices is passed back to the domestic economy, this net export situation should be improved further.

The *Near East* region is predominantly a net importing region, relying extensively on food imports and producing a variety of horticultural and cotton exports. Only two countries are in the least-developed group. The rise in the prices of basic foodstuffs should give the countries in this region the chance of passing on the higher prices to their farmers and hence giving a fillip to output, but they are likely to remain large net importers. For horticulture, the challenge will be to take advantage of growing markets in the region itself and especially in Europe.

South Asia, where four countries are least-developed, is largely self-sufficient in basic cereals although it is a net exporter of rice and a net importer of wheat. It is also a net importer of oilseeds and dairy products but a major exporter of agricultural commodities such as tea, spices, cotton, jute, tobacco and fruit.

On balance, the region may be a small loser in net trade in the basic foodstuffs except for possible gains in the rice sector, although the concentration of gains in rice would favour the japonica rice exporters more than the indica rice exporters of this subregion. Bigger gains may be expected from textiles with the liberalization of the MFA, which could give a boost to the domestic production of fibres.

Southeast and East Asia, where two countries are least-developed, share a similar pattern to South Asia and could lose from higher world prices of wheat and coarse grains, which would more than offset possible export gains from higher rice prices. With some significant exceptions, most countries in the region will stay relatively close to food self-sufficiency, and the main result of the Uruguay Round price changes would be to reinforce this tendency. The subregion enjoys a wide and diversified range of exports, including rice, oilseeds, fibres, tropical beverages, fruit, sugar, cassava and hides and skins.

Few gains can be expected in the tropical beverages area, while the market for cassava may shrink and rice opportunities will depend partly on the varietal considerations noted above. Fibres may be boosted somewhat by increased demand from the textile sector; oilseeds, fruit and hides and skins could benefit from market expansion.

The *Pacific Islands* include four LDCs and are generally net importers of food and net exporters of sugar (Fiji) and palm and coconut products. Land shortages in most of the countries will presumably limit the possibilities of a major increase in domestic food production so that a careful focus on high-value products and exploitation of the possibilities for diversification where feasible will still be important options.

The Uruguay Round has established a new international trade environment for agriculture. However, the liberalization of trade achieved is only partial; therefore, the question of further reducing the barriers to trade in agriculture may be expected to be high on the agenda of international action in the years ahead. Also rising in the agenda are other trade policy issues that may well complicate rather than ease the path of reform. These include the integration of environmental and trade concerns and the growing attraction of regional economic groupings, free trade areas and preferential schemes.

Policy implications

The main implications for the developing countries are the changed set of policy options that they face in the post-Uruguay Round world. These apply to all developing countries, least-developed or not. The main differences between the two groups is that the LDCs are not expected to reduce support levels but they are expected to embrace the new policy disciplines. *Other developing countries* have to reduce support but, under the special and differential treatment clause, they may cut support by less than the developed countries and spread their reductions over more years. For most developing countries, policy initiatives will take place within the framework of structural adjustment programmes (SAPs). In agricultural and food policy, there is currently a general trend towards more accurate targeting, which is partly due to increasing concern about the administrative difficulties and excessive costs of many current policies and broadly reflects the requirements of SAPs. Therefore, there are two sets of agricultural policies – those that are circumscribed and hence are of restricted use and those that are broadly acceptable but which of course may not always be feasible to employ.

The main implication of the Agraement on Agriculture is that policies that, according to given criteria, "distort" agricultural production or trade are likely to be increasingly untenable. This includes many of the policies employed in the developing countries, such as minimum guaranteed prices, procurement prices and price stabilization schemes, even though some exemptions are made for food security purposes. In cases where administered prices are above world prices, countries may keep administered prices but the total amount spent on these and similar policies must not exceed the 1986-88 level for the LDCs and must be reduced by other developing countries. As the commitment on domestic support is expressed in an AMS, there is flexibility for countries to decide where to make cuts. This flexibility in price policy should be of considerable use to developing countries in deciding on which commodities are given priority in the provision of support. Input subsidies, providing they are widely available to farmers in developing countries, are acceptable as far as the Uruguay Round of MTNs is concerned but are often less acceptable under structural adjustment policies. At the same time, in many developing countries the main thrust of policies has been to tax agricultural producers, particularly those producing export crops. The extent to which agricultural producers and exporters are taxed is not addressed by the Agreement on Agriculture, even though it is likely to form part of domestic reform policies.

The exempt, or Green Box, policies can be defined as those

interventions which imply no, or minimal, "distortions" for domestic production or international trade. To be eligible for inclusion in this category, policies must be government-funded and entail neither i) transfers from consumers to producers through, for example, management of the price structure; nor ii) direct price support. The list of such policies is given in Annex 2 to the Agreement on Agriculture but, while the list of exemptions is long, many of these involve government expenditures that the developing countries cannot afford. The challenge will be to develop low-cost, decoupled methods of support for use in the developing countries that nonetheless give the necessary boost to agricultural productivity and production.

The dual influences of changes in the international trading environment and SAPs generally require governments in developing countries to shift the focus of their interventions away from attempts to influence the price mechanism and towards programmes of investment in the infrastructure of the agricultural economy, in particular programmes to develop the marketing services and appropriate storage facilities accessible to the rural population. In addition, a shift in resources away from direct input subsidies to enhanced credit provision is recommended. Trade policy initiatives witness a shift from the use of quotas to tariffs and a general reduction in the latter.

In conclusion, the implications for the developing countries are significant mainly for future formulation of agricultural policies. Whether the pressure for change comes from the new disciplines of the Final Act or from those deriving from structural adjustment policies, both point in a similar direction – one where influencing prices is no longer the main instrument of agricultural policy. Determining whether agriculture in the developing countries can progress under these circumstances, when the main developed country exports of agricultural products may retain reduced price-distorting policies, will require case-by-case examination.

NORTH AMERICAN FREE TRADE AGREEMENT

The North American Free Trade Agreement (NAFTA) was ratified by the United States, Canada and Mexico, creating a free trade zone with a population of almost 370 million people – the world's biggest trading bloc, with a GDP of $6.5 trillion compared with the EC's $5.5 trillion. The world community saw the NAFTA outcome as a big push for the Uruguay Round of MTNs, which was still in the final stage of negotiation at the time but which was concluded in mid-December 1993. The Latin American and Caribbean countries perceived NAFTA's ratification as a strong endorsement of greater economic integration in the hemisphere.

Canada-Mexico-United States linkages

Even before NAFTA, Canada and Mexico were the second and third largest markets for United States agricultural exports and the first and second largest suppliers of United States agricultural imports. Since the 1989 Canada-US Free Trade Agreement (CUSTA), two-way agricultural trade between the two countries had risen from $5.4 billion to $9.4 billion in 1992, a 74 percent increase. During the same period, Canada's share in world markets of United States agricultural exports and imports also increased. Two-way agricultural trade between the United States and Mexico increased by almost 97 percent from $3.1 billion in 1986 to $6.1 billion in 1992. Mexico's share in world markets of both United States agricultural exports and imports also increased during the period.

Trade among the three countries is projected to increase under NAFTA. For example, the United States is the major exporter of coarse grains to Mexico but, in the past, imports were limited by tariffs and import licences. The Mexico-United States agreement on agriculture calls for the tariffs and licensing to be phased out by 2008. It is also expected that the United States will export more soybeans and livestock products such as pork, beef and poultry. One study has estimated the gain in United States agricultural exports to be from $2 billion to $2.5 billion even without NAFTA. Mexico's main agricultural exports to the United States are coffee, cocoa, bananas, vegetables, fruit and live cattle. NAFTA could increase these exports by $500 million to $600 million annually by the end of the transition period.

After extensive debate on the possible effects of NAFTA on jobs, the environment, food safety and agriculture, the United States Congress ratified the Agreement in November 1993. NAFTA will phase out all tariffs and quotas among the member countries by the end of 2008, the 15th year of the transition period. It establishes a free trade area in accordance with Article XXIV of GATT. The objectives of NAFTA are to: liberalize trade in goods and services; remove barriers to investment; protect and enforce intellectual property rights; and establish a framework for further trilateral, regional and multilateral cooperation to expand and enhance the benefits of the Agreement (see Box 4, p. 76).

NAFTA is a product of four major trade agreements. In addition, three side agreements on labour, the environment and import surges have been signed to deal with issues not specifically covered in the original agreement. As in the Uruguay Round Agreement, agriculture remains a sensitive area for all three countries and is the only area where NAFTA comprises three bilateral agreements. First, the CUSTA agricultural provision has been included in NAFTA, while Mexico has negotiated two independent free trade

BOX 4
KEY NAFTA PROVISIONS

MARKET ACCESS

Article 302 provides for the phased elimination of United States, Canadian and Mexican tariffs on goods traded between the three countries that qualify under the rules of origin. Article 703 includes commitments of the NAFTA countries regarding market access for agricultural goods. Specific market access provisions of CUSTA continue to apply to agricultural trade between Canada and the United States.

Within 15 years of implementation, all tariffs will be eliminated on products traded by NAFTA members. Most products traded between the United States and Canada will be tariff-free by 1998 under CUSTA. Tariff reduction between Mexico and the United States and between Mexico and Canada will be phased out in four stages – immediately, in five, ten and 15 years. Sensitive products, such as sugar for the United States and maize for Mexico, will have a 15-year tariff phase-out period.

In addition to tariffs, NAFTA will eliminate quantitative restrictions such as quotas and import licences for commodities traded between Mexico and the United States. Quotas and import licences will be replaced with either tariff-rate quotas (TRQs) or ordinary tariffs. Lower or no tariffs will be imposed on imports within the TRQ amount. Imports above the TRQs will face tariff levels which will be phased out during the transition period. Non-tariff barriers for dairy, poultry and sugar products remain intact under the Mexico-Canada agricultural trade agreement. The three countries also agreed to phase out customs user fees.

RULES OF ORIGIN

NAFTA will create a "North American Made" standard. Only products that qualify for "North American Made" will receive preferential treatment in the application of NAFTA tariffs. Non-NAFTA products must be transformed or processed significantly in a NAFTA country to qualify for tariff preferences. For example, milk, cream, cheese, yoghurt, ice-cream or milk-based products must be made from NAFTA milk or milk products. Sensitive products for the United States, such as peanuts, peanut products and products containing sugar, receive special treatment.

NAFTA imposes stricter rules of origin than would otherwise be applicable. For example, to qualify for NAFTA benefits, peanuts exported to the United States must be harvested in Mexico and peanut products such as peanut butter must be made from peanuts harvested in Mexico. Similar rules apply to sugar and sugar products.

DUTY DRAWBACK

Current practices of duty drawback, such as in Mexico's *maquiladora* programmes, and other duty waivers are eliminated under NAFTA. In the past, industries participating in Mexico's *maquiladora* programme could import duty-free inputs to produce goods for export out of Mexico. Eliminating duty drawback will be a disincentive for Asian and European countries to establish export platforms in Mexico or Canada.

SPECIAL SAFEGUARD PROVISIONS FOR IMPORT ADJUSTMENT

During the transition period, a specific quantity of a commodity may enter a NAFTA country at NAFTA preferential rates but imports at higher levels will face higher tariff rates.

SANITARY AND PHYTOSANITARY PROTECTION

All NAFTA countries will continue to protect animal and plant health. The Agreement recognizes each country's right to determine the level of protection necessary as long as it is based on scientific evidence. NAFTA encourages trading partners to adopt higher international and regional standards.

SIDE AGREEMENTS

The current United States administration has negotiated three main side agreements on labour, the environment and import surges with Canada and Mexico. These enhance the original Agreement, signed by the previous administration, by strengthening domestic laws; establishing commissions for settling disputes on labour and the environment; safeguarding against import surges; strengthening border clean-up; and encouraging high standards.

agreements for agriculture – one with the United States and the other with Canada.

The Mexico-United States bilateral agricultural trade accord deals with both tariff and non-tariff barriers in all commodities. Sensitive farm products such as maize for Mexico and sugar for the United States have longer phase-out periods (see Box 4).

Mexico has higher tariffs than the United States although, since joining the GATT in 1986, its tariffs and non-tariff barriers have been reduced. For example, Mexico's maximum tariff rates were reduced from 100 to 20 percent.

When NAFTA was ratified, the average import duty on United States products entering Mexico was 10 percent, 2.5 times greater than that levied by the United States (which averaged 4 percent on Mexican products). Mexico's tariffs on all industrial goods will be phased out within ten years and, within 15 years, its tariffs on all products, including agricultural commodities, will be eliminated. Non-NAFTA country products imported into Mexico will face tariffs as high as 20 percent. In addition to tariffs, non-NAFTA countries will continue to face Mexico's import licences for maize, wheat, barley, malt, dry beans, poultry, eggs, non-fat dry milk, table grapes and potatoes. Some other Latin American and Caribbean countries that have bilateral or multilateral trade agreements with Mexico receive preferential tariff treatment at the level stipulated in the agreements (for instance, Chile under the Mexico-Chile FTA and a group of Central American countries under the Central America Common Market [CACM]).

The economic integration that NAFTA achieves will result not only in trade gains but also in increased economic growth through competition-based productivity growth and economies of scale. A number of studies have shown that all three countries – Canada, Mexico and the United States – should gain from the elimination of tariff and non-tariff barriers. In the longer term, the greatest gains are projected for Mexico. According to static studies, Mexican real income should increase from 0.3 percent, assuming constant returns to scale and no capital inflows, to 6.8 percent, allowing for labour migration and for the Mexican capital stock to grow by 7.6 percent. Without new investment, the elimination of border trade measures would result in only slight welfare gains in real income in Mexico and in no changes in real income in the United States. Wage rates, especially for rural workers in Mexico, are expected to decline without capital increases. Assuming capital growth, more positive gains are projected, especially for Mexico. Capital inflows, either from outside Mexico or from intersectoral mobility, should increase investment and productivity and could push real income growth rates much higher than projected increases in either the

United States or Canada. In dynamic studies, Mexico's NAFTA-induced welfare gains or changes in real income growth could reach 8 percent, and agricultural trade should also increase.

In the short term, if capital mobility has not taken place, Mexico is expected to face more adjustment than either the United States or Canada. Estimates of the effects of trade liberalization and domestic policy changes point to an overall rural migration of 500 000 to 700 000 workers by the end of the transition period. Anticipating this, Mexico has imposed a new farm policy, PROCAMPO, which will provide direct income support mainly to subsistence farmers (see Regional review, Latin America and the Caribbean).

Overall NAFTA will have a small effect on the United States economy; as a result, there should be an increase of less than 1 percent in the country's GDP. However, research indicates that United States agriculture is a major beneficiary of NAFTA, which is expected to create nearly 200 000 new export-related jobs, of which 56 000 in agriculture and related industries. Under NAFTA, half of the products that the United States normally exports to Mexico could be sold in Mexico completely duty-free as of 1 January 1994. This proportion is expected to increase to more than two-thirds within five years.

Mexico will send more fruit and winter vegetables to the United States as seasonal tariffs of these commodities in the United States are phased out. Maize producers, especially those entering commercial channels, will switch their production to other commodities under PROCAMPO. As a result, Mexico will import more maize. It is also expected to import more livestock and livestock products under NAFTA as Mexican import tariffs on cattle and beef are eliminated. However, it is expected that Mexico will export more feeder cattle to the United States under NAFTA. In the short term, although Mexico will have to adjust more in agriculture, it should have permanent access to the United States market under NAFTA. The toughest adjustment will be among rural maize producers, who will need to switch to other commodities.

Prior to CUSTA, Canadian tariffs on United States dutiable goods averaged 9.9 percent, while United States tariffs on Canadian goods averaged 3.3 percent. At the end of NAFTA's 15-year transition period, most agricultural trade of NAFTA-originating products among the three countries will be duty-free. The 1989 CUSTA has been incorporated in or amended under NAFTA, except for its agricultural provisions. For example, the tariff phase-out schedules for cars and other goods traded between the United States and Canada will remain the same but, since rules of origin, safeguards and sanitary and phytosanitary standards were negotiated trilaterally, the NAFTA rules of origin, rather than the CUSTA rules, will apply to automobiles, textiles and agricultural products. Since all obligations under CUSTA are amended under NAFTA, the United States and Canada will suspend the operation of CUSTA on NAFTA's entry into force. Although trade between the United States and Canada has increased since CUSTA took effect in 1989, Canada's gains in agriculture under NAFTA will be small.

The bilateral Mexico-Canada trade deal will have a small effect on Canada. More than 85 percent of Canada's agricultural imports from Mexico are already duty-free. NAFTA would allow Mexico to gain access in coffee, orange juice and some meat products. Although all tariffs will be phased out over a ten-year period, most NTBs on sensitive products will remain intact. All trade between Mexico and Canada was only $3.3 billion in 1992, of which $357 million was agricultural trade; this is not expected to increase significantly as a result of NAFTA.

The impact of economic integration such as NAFTA on productivity growth is not only important to the countries directly involved, but it could also provide a stimulus for the rest of the Western Hemisphere. Therefore, larger benefits from NAFTA will result primarily from efficiency and productivity gains through new or increased investment.

An enlarged NAFTA?
Two issues will determine what the future will bring. First, which country or group of countries will be next to join NAFTA (and what are the criteria for joining)? Second, what would be the structure of the proposed Western Hemisphere Free Trade Agreement (WHFTA) and would agriculture be given special treatment? NAFTA has reconfirmed what the Enterprise for the Americas Initiative (EAI) proposed: that there be further economic integration between the United States and the rest of the Western Hemisphere. The United States' implementing legislation for NAFTA indicates that countries wishing to negotiate future FTAs with the United States must meet certain criteria – they must have democratically elected governments and a strong economic base. No later than 1 July 1994 and again by 1 July 1997, the United States President must submit to the Congress a report of his recommendation for free trade negotiations with countries other than Canada and Mexico. The findings of the report will provide one mechanism for further regional economic integration.

A few countries with substantive economic and trade reforms under way would meet the criteria outlined in the NAFTA implementing legislation. Chile has a strong, stable economy and a high economic growth rate and is expected to be the next country either to join NAFTA or negotiate a bilateral FTA with the United States. An FTA with Chile would have little effect on the United States economy whereas Chile would gain substantially.

It is still early for other countries in the process of restructuring their economies. It may be several years before they reach the levels of fundamental reform and restructuring found in Mexico and Chile. Some countries – Argentina, Colombia and Venezuela – may not be too far behind Chile. However, other countries in Central America and the Caribbean have much to accomplish to meet the criteria. Also, both groups already receive preferential treatment from the United States under the Caribbean Basin Initiative (CBI), the GSP and special import duty treatment for exports from export-processing zones.

Experience from NAFTA indicates that market access is not the only criterion for negotiating an FTA with the United States. Other issues such as intellectual property rights, the environment and food safety are among the chief concerns of the United States. Furthermore, the potential increase in United States grain exports to Latin American and Caribbean countries would put pressure on farmers in these countries, while the potential increase in trade of lower-cost labour-intensive goods would also create some concern in the United States.

For many countries the magnitude of long-term economic gains from regional free trade will depend on how the trade area is formed and structured. Access to the larger United States market seems to be a primary objective of many countries seeking to negotiate a free trade pact.

A true free trade area consists of member countries that adhere to the same trade pact and reduce or eliminate trade barriers equally among themselves. A regional free trade area built around a series of separate bilateral or trilateral agreements limits the potential for full economic gains from trade. The current integration arrangements in the Western Hemisphere are cross-memberships and, in some cases, small integration arrangements within larger ones. For example, all five members of the ANDEAN Pact are also members of the larger Latin America Integration Association (ALADI), as are members of the Southern Common Market (MERCOSUR) and the Chile-Mexico FTA. In addition to its agreement with Mexico, Chile also signed an FTA with two other ALADI members, Bolivia and Venezuela. Mexico, in addition to its membership of ALADI, the Chile-Mexico FTA and NAFTA, has also negotiated another FTA with Colombia and Venezuela, which are also ALADI members. Similar cross-memberships of integration arrangements occurred within the CACM. This proliferation of economic integration and multiple memberships must be sorted out because each arrangement has its own rules, which may not be consistent with the others. Consequently, the current pattern of integration arrangements is overly complex and prevents a more coherent process of negotiating the proposed WHFTA.

Chile, for example, is quite interested in a bilateral trade pact with the United States but has also expressed an interest to negotiate accession to NAFTA. Such an approach spread across a large number of countries in the region would lead to a series of separate trade pacts. Economists refer to this structure as a hub-and-spoke system. The spoke countries are not directly linked to each other; instead, they are linked only through the hub country. Countries (spokes) in a hub-and-spoke system may not gain fully from free trade, since greater opportunities for specialization and trade through the lowering of market access barriers are not realized.

The United States' approach to regional free trade – through the CBI, CUSTA, NAFTA and a series of "framework" agreements with ten other Latin American countries to negotiate a free trade pact at some future date – resembles a hub-and-spoke system. Its approach to regionalism appears to have changed, however. The United States' implementing legislation for NAFTA allows countries to negotiate entry into NAFTA. In addition, some Latin American countries have expressed interest in negotiating a Latin American Free Trade Area (LAFTA) and then, on the basis of a stronger bargaining position, negotiating a WHFTA with the United States. With either approach – through NAFTA or a larger LAFTA to include the United States and Canada – it appears now that a WHFTA would emerge more as a true free trade area, with members removing barriers to market access for all other member countries.

A second "structural" issue has to do with agriculture and how this sector would be handled as membership in NAFTA or a WHFTA grows. Agriculture was negotiated separately in both CUSTA and NAFTA, for much the same reasoning that was behind the differential treatment afforded agriculture in the Uruguay Round of GATT negotiations. Border measures for food and agricultural products are often key elements in a country's domestic agricultural support system. Eliminating or changing those border measures would require placing the respective country's agricultural policies on the negotiating table.

For CUSTA and NAFTA, the United States, Canada and Mexico were not willing to make their basic agricultural policies the subject of negotiation. Besides, the removal of trade-distorting support for agriculture was to be a major element in the recent

GATT agreement. The Uruguay Round Agreement on Agriculture will not, of course, result in the removal of all trade-distorting policies inherent in a country's agricultural support system. The interesting question is: how far can membership in NAFTA or a WHFTA be expanded before member countries' domestic agricultural policies become subject to negotiation? For full economic gains to be realized from a regional trade pact, free trade in food and agricultural products must be included.

CURRENT ISSUES IN FISHERIES
Food security and economic development in small island countries
Fish and fishery products play a special role in the food security equation of small island developing states, most of which have limited opportunities for land-based development and are crucially dependent on their marine fisheries resources both for food and socio-economic development.

Most small island developing states can only support the production of a limited range of agricultural crops. Moreover, there is generally little scope for extensive animal production, although the production of small animals and poultry is often promoted by their governments. Consequently, the total and per caput amount of food available from land-based sources is severely restricted in many of these states, particularly in those that consist of largely infertile atolls. In addition, food shortages resulting from devastation by natural disasters, which appear to be occurring with greater frequency, further increase the islanders' dependence on their fisheries resources for food.

Small island developing states have among the highest annual per caput rates of fish consumption in the world. In 1990 per caput consumption in many of these states exceeded 50 kg, compared with an average of 9 kg in other developing countries and 27 kg in developed countries. Indeed, in some small island developing states, fish account for as much as 95 percent of the population's total animal protein intake. In view of this extreme dependence on fish for food, the rational utilization of fisheries resources, and in particular inshore fisheries resources, must be promoted vigorously and existing management mechanisms strengthened as a means of ensuring sustainable resource use and avoiding food insecurity.

The restricted opportunities that many small island developing states face for industrial development require them to pursue economic development strategies closely linked to the use of their fisheries resources. Indeed, revenue that some earn from the exploitation and processing of their fisheries resources accounts for more than 50 percent of public sector revenue. This means that, in these states, the fisheries sector represents the national engine of growth, supporting broader social and economic programmes such as health and education.

Effective fisheries management in small island developing states is of critical importance in ensuring that resources are utilized and, where possible, developed in a sustainable manner. In many of these states, inshore fisheries resources, especially those near urban or peri-urban areas, are subject to heavy fishing pressure; this situation will continue, as most have high rates of population increase.

A key consideration for enhancing fisheries management in small island developing states is the need to strengthen national institutional capacity. Characteristically, these countries' fisheries administrations are small and fragile and lack a range of technical expertise. Programmes to strengthen fisheries administration are thus important for improved fisheries management and development practices.

In those island states where fisheries have traditionally been managed by resource-owning groups, the importance of this approach to management should be recognized and ways should be explored in which traditional management practices may be used successfully today to enhance the management of inshore resources.

Aware of their individual physical and economic vulnerability and the importance of fish to the lives of all islanders, small island developing states have formed different regional fishery bodies to coordinate fisheries management and development activities. These bodies have played a notable role in helping the states implement the provisions of the 1982 UN Convention on the Law of the Sea and the recommendations and policies agreed at the 1984 FAO World Conference on Fisheries Management and Development.

Compliance with international conservation and management on the high seas

For centuries, ship operators have found it convenient to fly the flags of certain states. In recent years, the so-called "flags of convenience" have offered low taxes and other benefits to shipowners. Some flag states have not demanded high standards of ship maintenance, and crew standards have been well below the requirements of the recognized "national registers".

The issue of reflagging fishing vessels only became prominent in the mid-1980s, as more vessels operating on the high seas sought to avoid the regulatory systems set up by international agreements to manage fisheries.

In 1992, the International Conference on Responsible Fishing, held in Cancún, Mexico, condemned the practice of reflagging and called for early action. Later, in November 1992 the 105th Session of the FAO Council proposed that an agreement to deter reflagging should be elaborated as a matter of priority.

A series of consultations were held by FAO, starting with a small group of experts in February 1993. It soon became clear that the competent authority for matters relating to the allocation of a flag by a state to a fishing vessel rarely was the same as for fisheries management. Thus, it was held that, in order to deter reflagging of fishing vessels, the authority for flag allocation should be transferred to fisheries managers. Therefore, when the 20th Session of the Committee on Fisheries (COFI) met in March 1993, it established an open-ended working group to develop further the concept of authorizing vessels to fish on the high seas and of tying conditions to be set by fisheries managers to this authorization.

The Agreement to Promote Compliance with International Conservation and Management Measures by Fishing Vessels on the High Seas was adopted by the 27th Session of the FAO Conference in November 1993 and will enter into force when the 25th letter of ratification is deposited with the Director-General of FAO.

The Agreement provides for flag states to take measures as may be necessary to ensure that vessels flying their flags do not engage in any activity that undermines the effectiveness of international conservation and management measures. They must not allow any of their flag vessels to be used for fishing on the high seas without authorization by the appropriate national authorities. Furthermore, the flag states must not grant authorizations to fish on the high seas unless they are satisfied that they are able, taking into account the links that exist between themselves and the vessels concerned, to exercise their responsibilities in the agreement effectively in respect of those fishing vessels. The Agreement also seeks to limit the freedom of vessels that have a bad compliance record from changing flag and obtaining a new authorization to fish on the high seas (unless it can be shown, without any doubt, that there has been a true change of ownership).

The Agreement provides for flag states to inform FAO of the technical details of vessels they authorize to fish and to ensure that there is an adequate flow of information between FAO and all parties. Similarly, FAO should be informed of action taken by flag states against offending vessels.

In general, the Agreement applies to all vessels operating on the high seas. For vessels of less than 24 m in length, however, there are exemptions from some provisions of the Agreement, but not from the main obligation undertaken by the state to ensure that the vessels concerned do not undermine the effectiveness of international conservation and management measures.

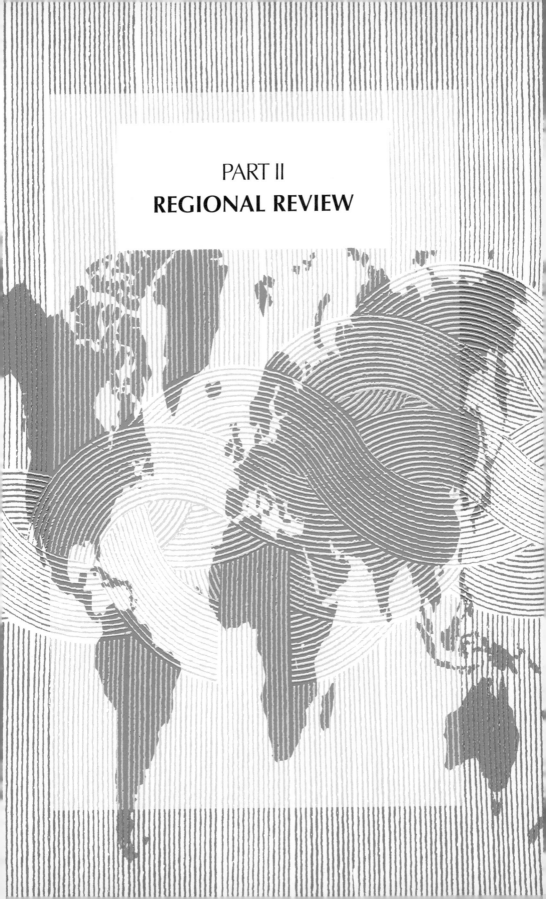

PART II
REGIONAL REVIEW

REGIONAL REVIEW
I. Developing country regions

Recent economic and agricultural performances in the four developing country regions are examined and the main policy developments affecting their agricultural sectors during 1993 to mid-1994 are highlighted in this section. The review then focuses more specifically on the experience of selected countries in each region: Ghana in Africa; China in Asia; Brazil in Latin America and the Caribbean; and Turkey in the Near East and North Africa.

SUB-SAHARAN AFRICA

REGIONAL OVERVIEW
Five major factors have affected, and will continue to affect, overall economic and agricultural performance in the region: i) the world economic environment; ii) political events, including intracountry, civil and ethnic confrontations; iii) international and intraregional economic cooperation; iv) individual country policies; v) agroclimatic conditions and natural disasters. Another factor with significant economic and agricultural consequences for several countries in the region has been the devaluation of the CFA franc.

Changes in the international economic environment
The world economic environment in the last few years had been dominated by slow growth in developed countries which, through trade and capital flows as well as other financial links, created a negative environment for growth in developing countries.[1]

The implications for developing countries of the slowdown in industrial countries was not uniform across regions. While many Asian and Latin America and Caribbean economies expanded significantly in recent years, sub-Saharan Africa's per caput GDP declined again in 1992 and 1993, continuing a long-term

---

[1] The IMF has estimated that a 1 percent increase in the real GDP of industrial countries increases the purchasing power of developing countries' exports by 3.4 percent.

Figure 5

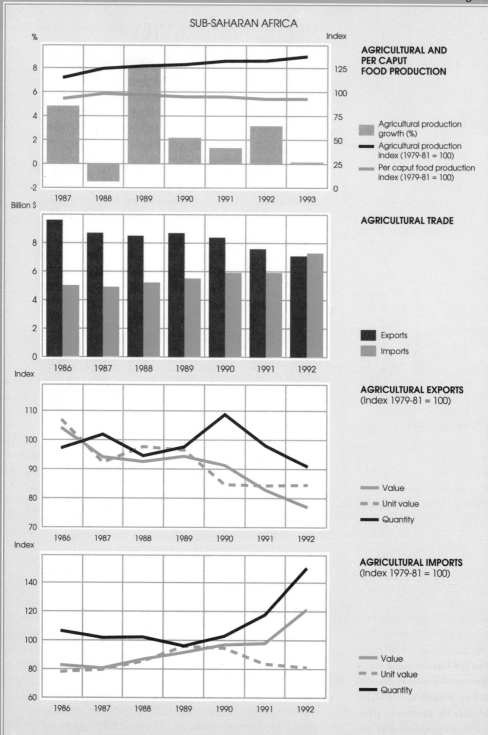

SUB-SAHARAN AFRICA

AGRICULTURAL AND PER CAPUT FOOD PRODUCTION

- Agricultural production growth (%)
- Agricultural production index (1979-81 = 100)
- Per caput food production index (1979-81 = 100)

AGRICULTURAL TRADE

- Exports
- Imports

AGRICULTURAL EXPORTS
(Index 1979-81 = 100)

- Value
- Unit value
- Quantity

AGRICULTURAL IMPORTS
(Index 1979-81 = 100)

- Value
- Unit value
- Quantity

Source: FAO

SUB-SAHARAN AFRICA

negative trend.[2] One factor behind such poor growth performance was the fact that a big proportion (at least 80 percent) of the region's exports went to developed (mostly West European) countries which were themselves experiencing economic downturns. An additional but partly interrelated factor was the continuing fall in the region's terms of trade which declined by 6.3 percent in 1992 and by 7.6 percent in 1993.[3] Although most developing country regions (with the exception of East and South Asia and the Pacific) experienced falls in their terms of trade, the decline was by far the steepest in sub-Saharan Africa.

This drastic terms of trade deterioration for the region occurred against a background of mixed directions in real overall commodity prices.[4] While petroleum prices fell by 12.1 percent, the overall index of non-petroleum commodity prices increased by 1 percent, reflecting the balance of increases in food, beverage and raw material prices (0.2, 5.7 and 22.5 percent, respectively) and decreases in prices of metals and minerals (-15 percent). The unit value index for manufactures decreased slightly (-0.5 percent). Thus, the overall decline in the terms of trade for sub-Saharan Africa mostly reflects the large decreases in petroleum export prices. Petroleum exports, mostly from West and Central Africa, account for about 40 percent of the region's total exports (including South Africa). The aggregate index is heavily influenced by Nigeria which has the largest weight in the overall index. Other countries affected by the decline in petroleum prices include Cameroon, Angola, the Congo and Gabon. The negative overall index also reflects negative terms of trade of metal and mineral exporters such as Zambia, for which copper accounts for 75 percent of export earnings.

Increases in the overall non-petroleum commodity price index in late 1993 and early 1994 reflect the firming of timber and beverage (coffee and cocoa) prices.[5] Increases in coffee prices benefited in particular Uganda, Ethiopia and the United Republic of Tanzania where the average share of coffee exports in total export earnings is 80, 50 and 32 percent, respectively.

Political events and intraregional cooperation

In 1993, the sub-Saharan Africa region witnessed the ending of several conflicts and civil strife as well as the beginning of others.

[2] Sub-Saharan countries have recorded declines in per caput GDP in ten out of 12 years since 1982. High population growth rates (in the order of 3 percent per year during the 1980s) have prevented even relatively high aggregate growth rates in some years from being translated into positive per caput growth rates.

[3] See World Bank. 1994. *Global Outlook and the Developing Countries: a World Bank Quarterly*. Trial series (January and April). Real commodity prices were calculated as commodity prices in current prices divided by the manufactures unit value index.

[4] Ibid. (April).

[5] See World review in this publication.

SUB-SAHARAN AFRICA

Civil strife continued in *Somalia*, requiring the intervention of the major world powers and the UN. Although the security situation in the country has improved somewhat, permitting the partial resumption of farming and market activity, the overall economic environment remains fragile and uncertain.

In the *Sudan*, the effects of recurring droughts (three in the last decade alone) have been exacerbated by the continuing war. In 1993, agricultural production, marketing and food aid have been severely disrupted.

The disruption of production, transportation and marketing of agricultural commodities and localized famines continued in *Angola* where the civil war recommenced in 1993, interrupting two continuous years of good harvests.

Zaire achieved a record cereal crop in 1993, but the breakdown of central government authority has caused the disruption of marketing activities in the urban areas which are, consequently, facing a serious risk of food shortages.

In *Liberia*, parties in conflict burnt rubber plantations, causing a drop in rubber production from 106 000 tonnes in 1989 to 10 000 tonnes in 1993.

The conflict in *Rwanda*, where more than 500 000 people are estimated to have been killed, is the largest – and possibly the most catastrophic – addition to the long list of civil confrontations that have lacerated the African continent.

On the positive side, the civil war in *Mozambique* has ended and the country is slowly heading towards normality. This will positively affect neighbouring countries (such as Malawi and Zimbabwe) which provided shelter for displaced refugees. Furthermore, cereal production in the country is recovering from the devastating drought of 1992.

The GATT agreement and Africa

The conclusion of the Uruguay Round of GATT negotiations and the subsequent signing of the Uruguay Round Agreement was a major event in 1993, with short-term and long-term consequences for all developing countries. The effects of trade liberalization will have an impact on developing countries through access to markets, terms of trade, direct effects on growth from efficiency gains and indirect efficiency effects through growth in other liberalizing countries.

SUB-SAHARAN AFRICA

The partial liberalization of grain trade is expected to increase world grain prices (assuming other factors to be constant). This will have negative effects on those sub-Saharan African countries that have a high ratio of food to overall imports or exports (Burkina Faso, Guinea-Bissau, Sierra Leone, Togo) as well as for countries that are prone to natural disasters, such as drought (e.g. Botswana and Ethiopia), and rely on food imports and/or emergency food aid.

An important aspect of the Uruguay Round Agreement for Africa is the reduction in the value of the numerous trade preferences that Africa currently receives from developed countries (i.e. the Generalized System of Preferences [GSP], the Lomé Convention and, when applicable, least-developed country [LDC] preferences). By reducing non-preferential rates, the agreement reduces the advantage of countries enjoying preferential treatment. Nearly four-fifths of sub-Saharan Africa's exports go to developed countries, with the European Community (EC) absorbing 60 percent and North America about 30 percent of the region's total exports to developed countries. Ninety-seven percent of African exports enter the EC duty-free, while the average tariff on sub-Saharan African exports to the EC ranges from zero to three-tenths of 1 percent. Such preferences give sub-Saharan African countries a 2 to 4 percentage point "preference margin".[6]

A reduction of most favoured nation (MFN) tariffs by 30 percent by the EC alone is expected to cause a loss of (non-fuel) export revenues of $70 million per year to sub-Saharan African countries. Some of this loss could be compensated by the reduction in non-tariff barriers (NTBs) for products such as textiles, clothing and temperate zone agricultural products, but the overall effect is expected to be negative.[7] This is in contrast to the projected overall positive effects of agricultural trade liberalization on other developing regions.

Regional cooperation

The process of democratization and integration of South Africa in the world, regional and subregional economic systems following the abolition of the apartheid system was intensified in 1993. A historic benchmark in this process was the free participation of all citizens in the 1994 presidential elections.

[6] Material from ECA. 1994. *Economic Report on Africa, 1994;* ERS/USDA. 1994. *International Agriculture and Trade Reports: Sub-Saharan Africa.* Unpublished report. Washington, DC.

[7] See A. Yeats. 1994. *What are OECD trade preferences worth to sub-Saharan Africa?* Policy Research Working Paper 1254. Washington, DC, World Bank. The negative effects of GATT may be overestimated, as the potential income expansion and productivity increases that will be created as a result of liberalization are not taken into account.

The sheer size of the country and its advanced stage of economic and technological development means that its moving away from isolation may have a significant economic impact on the economies of the subregion. While South Africa accounts for 17.6 percent of the total area occupied by the ten Southern African Development Community (SADC) countries plus South Africa itself, its population is about 30 percent of the total and its GNP about 4.8 times that of all SADC countries[8] combined. With a per caput GDP of about $2 500, South Africa and Botswana ($2 888) are by far the richest countries in the subregion. In addition, South Africa's natural resource deposits (diamonds, gold, coal and non-ferrous metals) are among the richest in the world.

These features have imparted new momentum to the issue of economic cooperation among the countries in the region – and the related issue of South Africa's possible role as a "locomotive" for enhancing regional growth potential and welfare.

Currently, South Africa is a signatory to few economic cooperation agreements in the area. Examples include the Southern Africa Customs Union (SACU) and the Multilateral Monetary Area (MMA).[9] The 1992 transformation of the Southern African Development Coordination Conference, whose objectives included reduced dependence on South Africa, into the Southern Africa Development Community was, in part, in anticipation of South Africa's likely accession to the community.

The ongoing efforts aimed at trade liberalization are likely to change the modalities and institutions of economic cooperation in the subregion. Currently, a host of trade policies as well as more or less effective multilateral and bilateral trade agreements exist in the area, often complemented (or subverted) by informal cross-border arrangements. Trade in the area is dominated by South Africa. According to the African Development Bank (AfDB) the total merchandise trade involving the ten SADC countries plus South Africa in 1990 was $54.5 billion. Of that total, $3.2 billion only was accounted for by intraregional flows and only $0.9 billion by intra-SADC trade.

Intra-SADC trade is constrained by the similar patterns of competitive advantage of the countries in the region. With the exception of South Africa,

[8] Angola, Botswana, Lesotho, Malawi, Mozambique, Namibia, Swaziland, Tanzania, Zambia and Zimbabwe. These countries constitute the "core" countries of an AfDB study, *Economic integration in southern Africa*, published in 1993, which served as a basis for some of the data and facts reported in this subsection.

[9] SACU is a century-old customs union between South Africa and its smaller neighbours while the MMA is a multilateral monetary framework among four of the SACU countries (South Africa, Namibia, Lesotho and Swaziland). See AfDB, ibid.

Zimbabwe and Mauritius (which have significant manufacturing activities), countries in the region produce similar primary agricultural commodities and minerals and export them largely unprocessed.

Under the existing patterns of trade, domestic trade policies and regional institutions, the incorporation of South Africa in a regional trading arrangement in southern Africa will not have a large impact. However, liberal domestic and trade policies, including a shift from self-sufficiency to more open policies in South Africa, may result in significant changes in competitiveness with South Africa exporting more manufactured goods to the countries in the region and importing more agricultural products. In such a case, a form of a welfare-increasing, net trade-creating arrangement may emerge. Moreover, South Africa is expected to phase out cereal production subsidies, resulting in diminishing exportable surpluses unless corresponding improvements in productivity are achieved.

Several other forms of cooperation, short of full economic integration, are possible. In its study (see footnote 8), the AfDB identified a number of areas of fruitful regional cooperation in southern Africa with the participation of South Africa. The successful cooperation between maritime and landlocked countries of the subregion in dealing with the 1991/92 drought showed the benefits of having a coordinating mechanism for transport and information activities.

In agriculture, opportunities exist for the coordination of research on plant and animal disease control. As South Africa is the country with the most advanced agricultural research system, it could become the centre of agricultural research and training activity for the area. A regional agency could be established to coordinate the research carried out by national research centres and universities. Another area of fruitful cooperation in the region is farm investment. The ongoing land reform in Zimbabwe and the one that will inevitably occur in South Africa means that a large number of experienced farmers will probably move out of Zimbabwe and South Africa. A successful subregional land swap or resettlement programme would retain those farmers in the subregion and encourage them to invest in agriculture in countries with a relative abundance of good-quality land reserves, such as Angola,

SUB-SAHARAN AFRICA

Mozambique, Tanzania and Zambia. Steps have already been taken in that direction by some SADC countries.[10]

Country policies

Macroeconomic policies of the countries of the region continued to pursue stabilization of their economies, the achievement of internal and external balances, low inflation and price stability and undistorted exchange rates. Such policies continue to have a profound impact on the agricultural sector.

In addition, a number of sector-specific reforms are being undertaken, aimed at liberalizing market institutions, enhancing private sector activity and reducing direct state involvement in production and distribution.

Adherence to these general principles characterized a number of recent policy interventions affecting agriculture. Thus, pursuing its agricultural sector reform programme, in February 1993 the Government of *Kenya* abolished all restrictions on wheat trade by drastically reducing the role of the National Cereals and Produce Board (NCPB). In the future, the functions of the NCPB are expected to be limited to market stabilization and maintenance of the strategic reserve.

In *Tanzania*, liberalization of the grain trade has been pursued, raising the private sector's participation in this trade to 90 percent in 1993, while leaving prices to be determined by market forces. As in Kenya, the government's role was restricted to the maintenance of a strategic reserve. Input distribution has also been liberalized. United States Department of Agriculture (USDA) estimates of producer subsidy equivalents (PSEs) show that, in 1992, both Tanzanian and Kenyan agricultural producers were actually subsidized, reversing a longstanding trend of overall (direct and indirect) taxation of the sector.

In *Zambia*, increased transport costs and mixed signals on the part of the public sector regarding its role in maize marketing resulted in the private sector purchasing and transporting less than the available quantity of maize. The government had to resume grain marketing through agents. In an effort to redress the poor performance of the agricultural sector, the Zambian Government, in cooperation with donor agencies, has initiated (November 1992) an ambitious Agricultural Sector Investment Programme (ASIP) which

---

[10] AfDB, Vol. 3, Chap. 3 (Agriculture), op. cit., footnote 8, p. 94.

SUB-SAHARAN AFRICA

will establish agricultural sector objectives, strategies and policies and a detailed investment programme for each subsector. It will also harmonize and coordinate donor-funded agricultural projects to optimize the utilization of financial and material resources.[11]

In *Uganda*, price decontrol coupled with the liberalization of agricultural trade has increased private sector participation in agricultural marketing and reduced the role of the public sector in those activities. Coffee procurement for export by private traders increased from nil in 1990/91 to 3 percent in 1991/92 and 44 percent in 1992/93. Private traders exported lint cotton for the first time (8 percent of total exports) and handled 11 percent of tea exports. There has also been an enhanced role of the private sector in the importation of agricultural inputs, while the government's role is mostly regulatory. Meanwhile, the liberalization of the investment code and the abolition of export taxes have resulted in a large increase in the applications and proposals for investments in the country.[12]

A mixed set of policies were followed in *Nigeria*. On the one hand, the free float of the naira (₦) was stopped and the currency was pegged at ₦22 to the US dollar, reversing the floating currency policy that was followed in the last few years. Interest rates were also fixed. On the other hand, the ban on wheat imports, enacted with the onset of the structural adjustment programme in 1986, was largely relaxed.

Seed production and marketing were liberalized in *Malawi* as part of the government's effort to encourage private participation in those activities.

Zimbabwe and *Botswana* are taking measures to accelerate recovery from the recent drought and prepare for eventual future droughts. In Zimbabwe, high priority is given to the agricultural and water sectors (the construction of dams and irrigation schemes), while labour-intensive rural projects are being set up in Botswana to provide employment and income opportunities for the victims of the last drought.

[11] N. Mukutu. *The Zambian Agricultural Sector Investment Programme: an example of an ongoing programme that can be used as a pilot study.* Paper presented at the UNDP-sponsored Workshop on New Forms of Programme Aid, Harare, Zimbabwe, 30 January-1 February 1994.

[12] See *The effects of agricultural sector policies on agricultural growth – Uganda's experience.* Country paper presented at the UNDP-sponsored Workshop on New Forms of Programme Aid, Harare, Zimbabwe, 30 January-1 February 1994.

DEVALUATION OF THE CFA FRANC

On 11 January 1994, at the end of a two-day summit in Dakar, Senegal, the 14 African countries of the franc zone announced a devaluation of the CFA franc, to take effect from 12 January 1994. The fixed exchange rate with the French franc went from a rate of CFAF 50 per French franc, which had remained unchanged since 1948, to CFAF 100 per French franc. At the same time, the Comorian franc was devalued from CF 50 to CF 75 per French franc. The devaluation in no way affects the institutional framework or mechanisms of the franc zone, which remain in place.

The African franc zone comprises 13 countries (excluding the Comoros which has its own central bank) which are grouped into two separate monetary unions, each with its own central bank. The West African Monetary Union (UMOA) – now the West African Economic and Monetary Union – comprises Benin, Burkina Faso, Côte d'Ivoire, Mali, the Niger, Senegal and Togo. The second group constitutes the Bank of Central African States (BEAC), the members of which are Cameroon, the Central African Republic, Chad, the Congo, Equatorial Guinea and Gabon.

Each of the two groups has its own separate currency, issued by the central bank. Both currencies are commonly referred to as the CFA franc.[13] The functioning of the African franc zone is based on the free convertibility of the CFA franc into French francs at a fixed rate guaranteed by the French Treasury. Each of the two central banks, as well as the Banque centrale des Comores, runs a so-called operations account with the French Treasury, into which they are obliged to deposit 65 percent of their foreign exchange reserves. The convertibility of the CFA franc into French francs is supported by the possibility of overdrafts on the operations accounts. Interest is charged on overdrafts and paid on credit balances. In addition, the rules call for the central banks to implement restrictive monetary policies in the case of the operations account balances falling below a certain level. There are also limits on credit that can be accorded by the central banks to governments.

The franc zone arrangements have provided the African member countries with a stable framework for macroeconomic policies. They have secured low rates of inflation, comparable to industrial country inflation

---

[13]The CFA franc, however, has a different meaning in the two areas: in the UMOA (now UEMOA) the official name of the currency is the "franc de la Communauté financière africaine" whereas, in the BEAC zone, it is the "franc de la coopération financière en Afrique centrale".

SUB-SAHARAN AFRICA

rates and significantly below the levels experienced on average by the non-CFA African countries. Until the mid-1980s the CFA countries also enjoyed sustained economic growth, with the average annual rate of GDP growth calculated by the International Monetary Fund (IMF) to be 4.6 percent in the period 1975-85. In the following years, however, their economic growth stagnated. Average annual changes in GDP in the CFA countries for the period 1986-93 is indeed estimated by the IMF to be only 0.1 percent, compared with a non-CFA average in Africa of 2.5 percent.

The problems confronted by the area since the mid-1980s had their inception in two major external shocks. From 1985 onwards, the member countries suffered a sharp deterioration in terms of trade. This was due to sharp declines in world market prices for main CFA commodity exports such as cocoa, coffee, cotton and petroleum. Indeed, during the second half of the 1980s, according to IMF estimates, the external terms of trade of the CFA countries worsened by almost 50 percent. Problems were exacerbated by a concomitant appreciation of the real effective exchange rate of the CFA franc, as the dollar depreciated significantly and developing country competitors in Asia, Latin America and Africa devalued their real effective exchange rates in response to the deterioration in their terms of trade. The result was a sharp worsening in the external competitiveness of the franc zone countries.

The period since the mid-1980s has seen the CFA countries engaged in efforts of internal adjustment, relying on domestic macroeconomic and structural policies only, and not a nominal devaluation. Although country experiences differ to some extent, on the whole these efforts have not been successful. The period has been characterized by a long and protracted stagnation of economic growth and a consequent sharp decline in per caput GDP. Government balances have also suffered as fiscal revenues, traditionally heavily dependent on the export sector, have declined. The social impact of the prolonged stagnation has been extremely harsh.

The Bretton Woods institutions (along with many other analysts) estimated that the CFA franc was significantly overvalued and that, although not sufficient, a devaluation was a necessary element in any adjustment effort with prospects of success. Still, the

SUB-SAHARAN AFRICA

extent and durability of any benefit from the devaluation will depend on supporting domestic policy measures. In particular, tight monetary, fiscal and wage policies are critical to control inflationary pressures following the devaluation.

For the UMOA countries, the devaluation was accompanied by the signing of a treaty which transformed the monetary union into the West African Economic and Monetary Union (UEMOA). The treaty was signed on 10 January 1994 and provides a new institutional framework for promoting the regional integration and coordination of economic and sectoral policies. In the BEAC zone, a similar project has been under study since 1991.

As for any devaluation, that of the CFA will increase the relative prices of tradables *vis-à-vis* non-tradables. Thus, prices of imports will increase in CFA francs, as will export prices, while there will be no initial impact on CFA prices of non-tradables. The effect will be an expansion of domestic production of tradables, owing to the improved relative price structure, accompanied by a compression of domestic demand for tradables. The trade balance will thus be positively affected both on the export and the import side.

The effectiveness of the devaluation in bringing about the described changes will depend on accompanying policy measures. First, as already mentioned, tight macroeconomic policies are essential to prevent the initial increase in prices of imported goods from starting off an inflationary spiral. Further, structural policies can contribute to enhancing the foreseen supply response and ease the factor reallocation process. Such policies would include domestic liberalization of labour, capital and product markets and the removal of constraints to competition on such markets. These would be combined with trade policy reform aimed at liberalizing export and import regimes. Other measures would be legal reforms, tax reforms and other reforms aimed at stimulating private investment in the medium term, along with increased public investment to provide supporting infrastructure and services.

Effects on agriculture
Generally, countries depending on agricultural exports should be able to increase export earnings through an expansion of export volumes resulting from the

increased domestic producer prices. If the full effect of the CFA devaluation were to be passed on to producers, CFA prices would theoretically double. One major issue is, however, the extent to which the absence of effective competition in marketing and transport services may cause the CFA price increases to be largely absorbed by private intermediaries or parastatals rather than feeding through to primary producers. Also, the less crop production is dependent on internationally traded inputs, the stronger the incentive for an expansion of volumes will be.

For a number of products, such an expansion of African franc zone exports could be achieved without a significant impact on world market prices, owing to the small market share attained by the CFA countries. For products in which CFA countries have a significant share of the world market, the situation is different. This is the case for cocoa, of which Côte d'Ivoire is the world's largest producer, with almost one-third of total world production, and which is also among the most important export items of Benin, Cameroon and Togo.

For food crops, the devaluation could lead to increased import substitution as domestic production expands. This would be, in particular, the case for rice in West Africa. Currently, rice production in the seven UEMOA countries covers close to half of domestic consumption. Annual imports are roughly in the magnitude of about 1 million tonnes, corresponding to an annual import bill in the order of $250 million. There are, however, significant differences between the rice sectors of the various countries and in production systems across the area as well as in their dependence on imported inputs. Prospects for expanding production consequently differ. Generally, prospects appear favourable for rain-fed rice production, which is less dependent on imported inputs and for which cultivated areas can be relatively easily expanded, while the possibilities of expansion for irrigated rice are limited in the short term. Higher costs of imported food could also induce changes in consumption habits, for example the substitution of millet and sorghum for rice. Consumption of roots and tubers may likewise increase in coastal West African or Central African countries.

Two other sectors that are liable to receive a stimulus to production are forestry and fisheries. Timber is a major export in several of the CFA countries

(Cameroon, the Central African Republic, the Congo, Côte d'Ivoire, Gabon) and the devaluation will provide enhanced incentives for commercial timber production. Fisheries are particularly important for Senegal, for which fresh, frozen and processed fish account for a sizeable portion of export earnings.

The devaluation will have major distributional and social implications and will affect the various geographic areas, economic sectors and social groups in different ways. Sectors of the economy and production systems, making limited or no use of internationally traded inputs and services, will be relatively advantaged in terms of costs of production. Also, the devaluation may affect urban and rural incomes differently. Generally, for countries that are highly dependent on agricultural exports, rural real incomes should be positively affected by the increased profitability of cash crop production. Urban dwellers, on the other hand, will tend to see their real incomes negatively affected by the increase in prices of imported goods (including foodstuffs), consumed mostly in urban areas. The short-term social implications could thus be highly negative on the urban poor. Consequently, social safety nets and the improvement of basic social services would appear to be necessary accompanying measures to the devaluation.

Finally, the devaluation of the CFA franc may have a certain environmental impact. The improved profitability resulting from the devaluation may lead to the intensification of crop and livestock production, with possible detrimental environmental effects, although the increased cost of imported inputs could limit somewhat the scope for crop intensification. The enhanced profitability of agricultural production might also represent an increased incentive for the conversion of forest land to agriculture. The improved incentives for commercial wood production could also increase the pressure on forests, while the same could be the case for fish resources. The devaluation would thus appear to strengthen the need for appropriate resource management policies in both sectors.

In conclusion, rather than being a solution in itself to the serious economic problems of the African franc zone, the devaluation of the CFA franc represents an opportunity which, if accompanied by appropriate macroeconomic, structural and social policies and by

SUB-SAHARAN AFRICA

adequate assistance from the international community, could help put the CFA countries back on the path of economic growth.

SUB-SAHARAN AFRICA

GHANA

Ghana has been for some time the centre of attention of the development and donor community, since it has implemented stabilization and structural adjustment more consistently than any other country in sub-Saharan Africa. This report follows the evolution of the economy since independence, analysing the factors that led to the economic crisis, the reform measures and their effects and the economy's future prospects. Particular emphasis is given to the role of macroeconomic policies in shaping the environment for agricultural growth. It is shown that, although macroeconomic and exchange rate policies were determining factors in the decline of the agricultural sector, a reversal of such policies may not be sufficient in itself to revive agricultural growth.

General characteristics and economic setting

Ghana spans an area of 238 537 km² and has a population of about 16 million, according to the mid-1991 UN estimates. Population growth was estimated to be 2.6 percent between 1961 and 1992.

Agriculture's share in GDP, about 42.4 percent, is declining, as other sectors have grown faster in recent years.[14] About 13.6 million ha or 57 percent of total land area is classified as suitable for cultivation; approximately one-third is actually cultivated. There are big regional differences in soil quality and rainfall patterns.

Agriculture employs about 49.1 percent of the economically active population (EAP) (1991 data). The EAP's share in agriculture is declining, although it is increasing in absolute numbers (from 2.3 million in 1980 to 2.8 million in 1991).

Although cocoa is the dominant commodity, its share in agricultural GDP has been halved in the last ten years (from 30 to about 15 percent) while the share of food crops has been increasing. FAO's index of food production in Ghana shows increases from 100 in 1979-81, to 125 in 1988 and to 160 in 1992. Ghana is self-sufficient, or nearly so, in roots and tubers, plantain, fresh fruit, vegetables and eggs. Its main imports are wheat (not produced in the country), rice, maize, dairy, fish, edible oils and sugar.

Agriculture accounts for approximately 35 percent of total exports; cocoa beans and cocoa butter make up

[14] Ghana Statistical Service. 1993. *Quarterly Digest of Statistics* (March). 1992 data.

some 70 percent of total agricultural exports. Since 1992, gold has become the top foreign exchange earner (40 percent), overtaking agriculture. Forestry products account for about 12 percent of total merchandise exports. A number of agricultural commodities (about 50) are classified as non-traditional exports (cola nuts, pineapples, cotton seed, natural rubber, yams, palm kernels, etc.). Their contribution to overall exports averaged 3 percent between 1988 and 1992. Agriculture now contributes about 11 percent to government revenue, down from 26 percent in 1987.

Ghanaian agriculture is mainly rain-fed and dominated by smallholders using traditional production methods. Traditional farming systems using the hoe and the cutlass prevail, while bullock farming, although still rare, is increasingly practised. Only about 0.2 percent of all cultivated land is under irrigation. There are some large farms and plantations producing rubber, coconuts and oil-palm, while a few produce rice, maize and pineapples.

The roots of economic crisis. When Ghana became independent in 1957, it was one of the richest countries in Africa. It had an established manufactured goods sector, it exported minerals (especially gold) and it was the world's leading exporter of cocoa, which provided about 60 percent of the country's export earnings. A combination of negative exogenous shocks and ill-focused and/or badly implemented economic policies caused a turnaround of the country's economic fortunes and prospects. In the ensuing economic crisis, macroeconomic policies were crucial and their effects on agriculture were critical. As a result, by the early 1980s the country was on the verge of economic collapse and drastic policy reform measures had to be taken to turn the economy around.

Macroeconomic policies before 1983
Following independence, Ghana adopted a development model which emphasized import substitution and rapid industrialization supported by the erection of high protective tariff and non-tariff barriers to protect infant industries. The public sector was given a prominent role in the development process, including direct participation in the production and distribution sectors. Macroeconomic policies emphasized fiscal

SUB-SAHARAN AFRICA

[15] S. Chand and R. van Til. 1988. Ghana: towards successful stabilization and recovery, *Finance and Development*, 25(1).

[16] C. Leechor. 1994. Ghana: frontrunner in adjustment. *In* I. Husain and R. Faruqee, eds. *Adjustment in Africa: lessons from case studies,* Washington, DC, World Bank.

[17] Chand and van Til, ibid. The rate of inflation reflects parallel market prices and not official, controlled prices to which the whole economy was subject.

[18] The 1961-1966 period is considered to have been critical for Ghana's future trade and exchange rate policy. The shunning of the use of exchange rate devaluation as a constructive policy instrument during this period bedevilled Ghana's economic policy for two decades. A large bureaucracy was created to monitor the nexus of import controls and to manage foreign exchange, which "quickly learned the value of the licences it controlled and began to extract some of the rents soon after the system was in place" See S.D. Younger. 1993. *Exchange rate management in Ghana.* Cornell Food and Nutrition Policy Program. Working Paper 38.

expansion to support public investments and current expenditures for an increasing civil service.

The country's fiscal receipts were heavily dependent on the cocoa revenue. Fuelled by the windfall receipts from high cocoa prices between 1953 and 1957, government expenditures increased dramatically during those years and kept increasing throughout most of the period up to 1983. A large part of current expenditures supported an increasingly bloated public sector, including many unproductive and fictitious (ghost) workers. As most public enterprises that constituted the cornerstone of import substitution policies incurred heavy losses, they had to be supported from the government budget.

Declines in international cocoa prices after 1957 and the heavy domestic taxation of cocoa (see The cocoa sector, p. 107), reduced cocoa profitability and eventually production, leading to declines in fiscal revenues that were not matched by reductions in government spending. Thus, the budget surplus of 3 percent of GDP in 1955-57, became a deficit of 4 percent of GDP during the period 1958-71, rising to 10.1 percent for the period 1971-75 and 7.5 percent for the period 1976-82.[15] During the same period, the domestic savings rate was almost halved. Deficits were mostly financed by a highly accommodating monetary policy, with the Bank of Ghana extending large amounts of credit to the government. In certain years (for example 1979 and 1982), the primary source of monetary growth was direct lending by the Bank of Ghana to public enterprises.[16] The money supply grew by an average of 40 percent between 1971 and 1982, giving rise to high inflation which ran at a rate of more than 50 percent per year in the decade before 1982 and reached 123 percent in 1983.[17]

Increases in total imports, both by private importers and by the government to implement its capital-intensive investment programme, could not be met by foreign exchange receipts. Pressures on the country's current account appeared as far back as the beginning of the 1960s.

The *exchange rate policies* of successive governments up to 1983 epitomize the macroeconomic mismanagement in Ghana. A major characteristic of economic policy was the "sanctification" of the fixity of the nominal exchange rate.[18] This was exaggerated to

SUB-SAHARAN AFRICA

the point that attempts to devalue the currency caused governments to be overthrown. In the face of rising inflation, the exchange rate policy resulted in an overvalued real exchange rate and a gap between the parallel market and the official rate, ranging from an average of 17 percent in 1958-66 to 68 percent in 1967-72 and 925 percent in 1973-83.[19]

Policies for the agricultural sector

The cocoa sector. The importance of cocoa for the Ghanaian economy and for its macroeconomic balances (as a source of both foreign exchange earnings and tax revenues) makes the performance of the cocoa sector a determining element in the overall performance of the economy. The macroeconomic policies discussed above provided disincentives for cocoa producers. The overvalued real exchange rate shifted domestic terms of trade against all tradable commodities, but agricultural exports were most affected as industrial tradables were protected through tariff and non-tariff trade barriers. Policies directed at cocoa often added to the negative effects of macroeconomic and exchange rate policies.

The purchasing of cocoa in Ghana was handled by the Cocoa Marketing Board (CMB), established in 1947 to combat cocoa price volatility. The system provided preannounced fixed producer prices and centralized marketing. The CMB levied export duties on cocoa bean exports and local duties on cocoa bean deliveries to local processing factories, and passed those taxes on to the government. The government approved allowances for the CMB's operational expenses.

In 1965, the CMB was required to transfer all operating surpluses to the central government, thus eliminating the distinction between the CMB surpluses and payments to the government. Government revenue from cocoa was the "remainder" from the cedi (¢) equivalent of the f.o.b. price (at the official exchange rate) after payments to farmers and marketing costs had been covered.

Gradually, the cocoa sector became a major and convenient source of general tax revenue. It provided one-quarter to one-third of total government revenues in the 1960-1980 period. Over time, the size of the CMB increased, as did cocoa marketing costs. By 1982, the CMB employed some 105 000 workers. In the face of large fixed costs and increasing inflation, the share of

[19] J.D. Stryker. 1991. Ghana. *In* A. Krueger, M. Schiff and A. Valdés, eds. *The political economy of agricultural price policy, Vol. 3. Africa.* Baltimore, Md., The Johns Hopkins University Press (for the World Bank).

total sales going to marketing costs increased. Thus, according to Stryker (footnote 19, p. 107), in 1981/82, with the parallel exchange rate about 15 times the official rate, the costs of the CMB (excluding payments to farmers) exceeded the value of f.o.b sales at the official exchange rate.

Because the producer price was preannounced, it could turn out to be lower or higher than the price the farmer would have received if the payment was made at the time of the sale (assuming the same marketing cost). In the latter case, the government's revenue was negative. Even when that was true, the *absolute* real price to the farmer was too low relative to its level at the equilibrium exchange rate. The real price to farmers for cocoa decreased from ¢355 per tonne in 1962-72 to ¢165 in 1973-83. In addition to the price-based taxation, the cocoa marketing system was fraught with inefficiencies that resulted in prolonged delays in payments to farmers.

Food crop policies. Imported food commodities that were considered essential (maize, rice, wheat, sugar and vegetable oils) were imported by the Ghana National Trading Corporation (a state monopoly) and were distributed either by the corporation's own shops or by licensed wholesalers. The retail price was determined as the c.i.f price (calculated at the official exchange rate), augmented by a tariff, marketing costs and costs of working capital. The retail price was controlled, the controls being more effective at the corporation's shops and less so at the outlets of the wholesalers.

Because open market food prices were generally higher than controlled prices, especially with the onset of inflation, plenty of opportunities existed for rent seeking and corruption. Part of the imported foodstuffs were finding their way to the open market, and licence holding became a lucrative activity. Open market prices in the late 1970s were up to five times the official price. Many Ghanaians spent an enormous amount of time trying to obtain access to the scarce goods at low prices and profiting from the difference between the official and open market prices (an activity known as the *kalabule* system). There were no policies that directly affected other non-tradable foods. Indirect effects from macroeconomic policies on non-tradable food crops

SUB-SAHARAN AFRICA

were in terms of high transport costs and deteriorating transport infrastructure (see Overall and agriculture-specific effects of pre-1983 policies). Although there is great uncertainty regarding the trend of food prices in Ghana, it is unlikely that real food prices suffered large declines as a result of direct price intervention.[20]

Policies on inputs and agricultural services. Public policy on inputs focused on subsidization of modern inputs and credit. Direct subsidies on imported modern inputs such as fertilizer, sprayers and chemicals were added to the indirect subsidy resulting from exchange rate overvaluation. The effects of such subsidies were uneven across the agricultural sector because not all farmers had access to the subsidized inputs. Government investment in agriculture was biased towards the large-scale mechanized sector, while research and extension for small farmers were neglected.

Overall and agriculture-specific effects of pre-1983 policies

Ghana's economic decline precipitated during the later part of the 1970s and the early 1980s.[21] Until then, various government controls on prices and imports were able to mask the real state of the economy to a degree and keep the deteriorating macroeconomic situation under some control. A turnaround in world cocoa prices after the sharp increase in 1977 and 1978, together with concomitant declines in cocoa production, reduced government tax revenues, aggravated the budget deficit and inflation and reduced foreign exchange receipts and the ability to import. As real producer prices deteriorated, increasing quantities of cocoa were smuggled out of the country and non-productive rent-seeking activities became widespread. The deficit rose to 127 percent of total government receipts in 1978, while inflation reached 116 percent per annum in 1977 and 123 percent in 1983. Ghana's infrastructure was run down, transport capacity was reduced by a lack of spare parts and lubricants and social services were in a state of collapse.

Although GDP grew by an average of 0.2 percent per year between 1970 and 1980, it fell by 6.1 percent between 1979 and 1982 (-3.1 and -9.4 percent, respectively, on a per caput basis). Export volumes fell

[20] See discussion in H. Tabatabai. 1988. Agricultural decline and access to food in Ghana. *International Labour Review,* 127(6): 703-734.

[21] Some authors consider 1975 as the first year of a serious economic decline. See, for instance: N. Chazan. 1983. *An anatomy of Ghanaian politics: managing political recession, 1969-1982.* Boulder, Colo., Westview Press; and J.D. Stryker. 1990. *Trade, exchange rate, and agricultural pricing policies in Ghana.* World Bank Comparative Studies. Washington, DC, World Bank.

by 8.4 percent and agricultural GDP by 1.2 percent annually in the 1970s. The import substitution industrialization development strategy proved to be self-defeating: declining export revenues meant that Ghana could not import intermediate inputs and raw materials essential for other sectors. Industry's decline was equal to that of agriculture – in some industries, utilization of capacity fell to 10 to 15 percent. A lack of investment in the gold industry damaged another source of foreign revenue for the country.

By 1982, Ghana's comparative advantage in cocoa production was severely eroded. In the early 1970s, it had been a leading cocoa exporter with more than 30 percent of the market but, by 1981/82, the share had been almost halved. The government was unable to continue increasing the salaries of the oversized public bureaucracy. This, coupled with high inflation, caused real wages to decline drastically. In 1983 the real minimum wage had fallen to about 13 percent of its 1975 value. The sharp declines in civil service salaries caused severe discontent and a massive exodus of skilled personnel.[22]

In the 1978-1982 period, successive governments attempted to save the formal economy from complete collapse. A number of measures were initiated in 1978, including a devaluation of the cedi to ¢2.75 per US dollar, currency reform, the introduction of an austerity budget and increases in the price of cocoa. They also included an intense anti-corruption campaign and tighter monitoring of compliance with price controls. However, these economic measures were probably "too little too late".

In 1982 and 1983, a number of exogenous shocks caused further hardship for the Ghanaian economy. Nigeria cut oil shipments because of Ghana's inability to pay. Poor rains in 1982 and 1983 caused a severe shortfall in maize production, which tightened food supplies and increased prices. The drought also caused a major shortfall in the hydroelectric power on which Ghana depends heavily. The situation was exacerbated by the influx of one million Ghanaian workers who were forced to return from Nigeria.

Economic decline: the critical role of agriculture
Although there is no one single reason that could by itself explain Ghana's rapid economic decline, it is safe

[22] World Bank. 1983. *Ghana: Policies and programmes for adjustment.* Report No. 4702-GH. Washington, DC; and Chand and van Til, op. cit., footnote 15, p. 106.

to say that at the root of the problem were the severe economic disequilibria caused by the insistence on a fixed exchange rate regime and the lack of proper macroeconomic policies to support it.

Agriculture in general and the cocoa sector in particular played critical roles in the economic crisis. Although the growth of the cocoa sector was essential for foreign exchange receipts and fiscal revenue collection, macroeconomic policies discriminated against cocoa, both directly and indirectly: i) by direct taxation of the cocoa industry in terms of high shares of the cocoa price being used to cover the expenses of an inefficient and highly expensive parastatal bureaucracy; ii) by indirect taxation of real domestic prices as a result of the overvaluation of the currency, high domestic inflation and the relative protection accorded non-agricultural sectors.

In a well-known study,[23] direct and indirect taxation of cocoa in 1975-79 and 1980-84 were calculated and compared. The results show that, for the 1975-79 period, there was a 26 percent direct subsidization (negative taxation) of cocoa producers because of the low world cocoa prices and the system of payments as described above. During the same period, indirect taxation of cocoa was 66 percent. The net result was a total taxation (or negative protection) of cocoa amounting to 40 percent. The situation worsened during the 1980-84 period during which, although direct subsidization increased to 34 percent, indirect taxation increased to 89 percent for a net tax of 55 percent.[24] The situation was very different with imported food products: the data for rice show that, while it was subject to a negative indirect protection of 66 percent in 1975-79, rising to 89 percent in 1980-84, it enjoyed direct protection of 79 and 118 percent, respectively. The combined effect was a positive overall protection for the two periods of 13 and 29 percent, respectively. Those results are in broad agreement with the overall government policy on tradable food commodities, as described previously.

The excessive cocoa taxation policies exacerbated the impact of declines in world prices of this commodity and reduced production by an average of 6.1 percent per year in 1970-83. A comparison with Côte d'Ivoire demonstrates that the loss in cocoa output was not just a result of changes in the world price.

[23] A. Krueger, M. Schiff and A. Valdés. 1988. Agricultural incentives in developing countries: measuring the effects of sectoral and economy-wide policies. *The World Bank Economic Review,* 2(3): 255-271.
[24] The calculations for cocoa take into account the fact that, owing to Ghana's large share in the world cocoa market, a devaluation and the concomitant increase in production and exports would have had negative impacts on the world price of cocoa.

SUB-SAHARAN AFRICA

While Ghana's world market share changed from 26.3 percent in 1970 to 14.5 percent in 1983, Côte d'Ivoire increased its share from 11.6 percent in 1970 to 25.8 percent in 1983.

The disincentive effects of policies on cocoa production created a vicious cycle for the Ghanaian economy. Declines in production and exports meant declining fiscal revenues and foreign exchange receipts, a situation that was dealt with by imposing more controls and increasing inflationary deficit financing, which increased inflation and dampened production incentives. The emphasis on increasing controls to stave off the crisis caused Ghana to become one of the world's most distorted economies during 1970-1980.[25]

Post-1983 policies

Macroeconomic reforms. When the Provisional National Defence Council took over in December 1981, Ghana was on the brink of economic collapse after initial attempts to deal with the crisis through tighter controls on foreign exchange, stricter border surveillance and an anti-corruption campaign. The government first adjusted the exchange rate in April 1983 by establishing a system of export bonuses and import taxes that amounted to a 900 percent devaluation of the exchange rate.[26]

In 1983, in response to the deepening economic crisis, the government launched the economic recovery programme (ERP), covering the period 1983-1986. This was followed by the first phase of the structural adjustment programme (SAP I), covering the period 1987-1988, and by the second phase (SAP II), from 1989 to 1990. In 1983 the ERP was accompanied by nominal devaluations, first to keep the real exchange rate at its April 1983 value and later to create further real devaluations. Two major institutional reforms practically eliminated the overvaluation of the cedi: establishing the exchange rate auction in September 1986 and the launching of the interbank market in April 1992.

Fiscal policies succeeded in broadening the tax base and increasing tax revenue from 4.6 percent of GDP in 1983 to 11.2 percent in 1986 without a major increase in tax rates. Non-tax revenue also increased as a share of total revenue, mainly as a result of the grants which increased from 0.6 percent of total revenue in 1983 to 5.9 percent in 1992. Higher fiscal revenues permitted

[25] World Bank, op. cit., footnote 22, p. 110. Ghana rated top in the World Bank's price distortion index (a qualitative indicator that summarizes the composite distortions in exchange rate, interest rate, wage rate, etc.) with a score of 2.9 out of a maximum of 3.
[26] Stryker, op. cit., footnote 21, p. 109; and Younger, op. cit., footnote 18, p. 106.

SUB-SAHARAN AFRICA

increased spending on civil service salaries, infrastructure rehabilitation and social services and programmes without increasing the deficit. Thus, total fiscal deficit as a percentage of GDP, which stood at 2.7 percent in 1983, became a surplus 1.5 percent in 1992. The structure of spending also changed: the share of capital spending in total central government expenditures increased from 7.9 to 20.1 percent while current expenditures fell from 89.3 to 76.7 percent.[27]

The conduct of monetary policy in Ghana is complicated by large official capital inflows. The need to replenish the foreign exchange reserves of the central bank as well as the need to use foreign aid to finance the domestic expenditure and fiscal revenue gap have been major sources of monetary growth.[28] Thus, growth of the broad money supply increased at an average annual rate of more than 40 percent in 1984-1988. Since 1989, domestic credit policy has been used to offset the growth of foreign assets, so money supply growth decelerated between 1989 and 1991 although it exploded in 1992, an election year. The cause was an 80 percent wage increase for civil service staff, which set the stage for private sector wages to increase by 500 percent. The inflation rate has been decelerating, falling from about 40 percent in 1987 to 10 percent in 1992. On the trade side, most quotas and import restrictions have been removed and tariffs for a wide array of goods have been reduced.

Agricultural sector reforms. Agricultural sector reforms started relatively late in the SAP. Exchange reforms succeeded in raising producer prices despite falling world prices. Thus, real cocoa prices increased continuously between 1983/84 and 1987/88, despite the collapse of world cocoa prices in 1985. As the devaluation effects bottomed out, real producer prices declined sharply in 1989/90 (14.5 percent) and continued declining at a rate of about 5 percent per year between 1989/90 and 1991/92. Farmers benefited from a premium paid to them after harvest (albeit often with a delay). This price compensation ranged from 0.9 percent of the producer price in 1986/87 to 15.2 percent in 1989/90.

There have been gradual reforms in the cocoa marketing system, including the restructuring of the CMB – renamed the Ghana Cocoa Board (COCOBOD)

[27] Excluding capital outlays financed directly by foreign loans.
[28] Leechor, op. cit., footnote 16, p. 106.

– and a reduction of its activities. Thus, the Board has shed some of its plantations, its majority ownership of a pesticide factory and the responsibility of maintaining feeder roads. More than 40 000 workers were laid off in 1985 (some of them ghost workers) and an additional 12 000 were retrenched in 1987. In 1992, competition was introduced in the internal marketing of cocoa. Two new buyers were allowed to buy cocoa from producers alongside the Produce Buying Company, a subsidiary of COCOBOD. Since 1987, the reforms have reduced COCOBOD's operating costs by one-third. Full liberalization has been stalled by, *inter alia*, the fear that the credit market is not capable of handling a large private cocoa trading sector.[29]

The Ghana Cotton Company's monopoly on cotton buying and ginning has been abolished. The government withdrew from fixing producer prices for cotton and lifted the restrictions on cotton exports.

With respect to food crops, the guaranteed minimum price for maize and rice was abolished owing to the ineffectiveness of the scheme and the high costs associated with it. The Ghana Food Distribution Corporation controlled only 10 percent of the market while the rest was controlled by private traders. The government transferred some of its rice mills to the Divestiture Implementation Committee and operates others on a fee basis.

Ghana has also abolished subsidies and price controls on fertilizers and is encouraging private importation, wholesaling and distribution.[30] A phased marketing privatization was launched over a three-year period ending in 1990. In January 1989, the Ghana Seed Company was dissolved to enable the reorganization of the entire seed industry. Imports of agricultural inputs are duty-free.

Policy reforms: assessing the effects and charting the future. The effects of policy reforms in Ghana have been impressive. Overall growth in real GDP increased from an annual average of 1.5 percent in 1970-83 to about 4.7 percent in 1983-91 and 4 percent in 1992.[31] Assuming population growth of 2.6 percent, there has been a real per caput growth rate of more than 1.9 percent per year. The fact that the rate of growth remained continuously positive in per caput terms since 1984 (with the exception of 1990) is also impressive.

[29] H. Alderman. 1991. *Downturn and economic recovery in Ghana: impacts on the poor.* Cornell Food and Nutrition Program. Monograph 10.

[30] Government of Ghana. 1993. *From economic recovery to accelerated growth.* Report prepared for the Seventh Meeting of the Consultative Group on Ghana, Paris, 24-25 June 1993.

[31] AGROSTAT, FAO (Exponential growth rates).

Agricultural GDP, which had declined by about
1 percent annually between 1970 and 1983, increased
by 1.9 percent between 1984 and 1991, and fell again
by 0.6 percent in 1992. Thus, overall per caput growth
in agricultural GDP has been negative throughout the
post-adjustment period, except for short-term recoveries
such as that following the severe drought of 1983.

In response to devaluation and increased domestic
price incentives, cocoa production is slowly recovering
from the record low level of 1983/84. This partly
reflects the diversion of cocoa from the parallel to the
official markets. FAO data show that a 6.1 percent
average annual decline in production between 1970
and 1983 has been turned into an annual increase of
6.75 percent between 1984 and 1992. However, cocoa
production has not reached the high levels registered in
the 1960s to the mid-1970s.

The production of *non-traditional export commodities*
(pineapples, cola nuts, cotton seed, yams, fish and
lobsters) has also picked up as a result of the higher
incentives provided by the devaluation. Export earnings
from non-traditional export crops increased by 66
percent between 1966 and 1990.

The privatization and liberalization of agricultural
inputs has had mixed results. In the case of fertilizers,
consumption has been down from its peak levels of the
late 1970s and early 1980s, when the subsidy
sometimes reached 80 percent of the fertilizer price.
The relative absence of private sector interest in
marketing and distribution is due, *inter alia*, to
inconsistencies in the fertilizer privatization process.
Namely, government control on fertilizer distribution
margins and an indirect subsidy to the Farmer Service
Companies have discouraged the participation of
private dealers. Problems associated with credit
availability are also inhibiting activity by the private
sector in the marketing of inputs. Declining fertilizer
imports cause increases in the per-unit price because
of the consequent loss of cost savings associated with
large bulk orders.

In this context, it is worthwhile mentioning the
activity of Global 2000, a non-governmental
organization (NGO) whose activities have contributed
to significant productivity gains for the participating
farmers. Global 2000 provides extension and payment
in kind (for example, maize in return for fertilizer) to

farmers participating in the scheme. Many of Global 2000's resources (staff, capital and physical flows) are provided by the government. Despite the positive results achieved so far, the scheme may be inhibiting efforts to increase private participation in the distribution process.[32]

From adjustment to growth: constraints, prospects and the role of agriculture

Ghana is one of the few countries in sub-Saharan Africa where issues concerning the transition from stabilization to a sustainable growth path are now being raised. Despite the courageous steps that it has taken towards policy reform and despite its impressive overall growth performance, it is still one of the poorest countries in the world, with a per caput income of $390. It has been estimated that, even if the past decades's high growth rates were to continue, the average Ghanaian would rise above the poverty line 50 years from now. The World Bank estimates that, under the best of circumstances, it will take ten years before Ghana finds itself on the "threshold" of rapid growth.[33]

Future economic role of agriculture. The performance of Ghana's different economic sectors after 1983 leaves some questions to be answered. Given the reversal of the indirect taxation of agriculture, one would expect prima facie the sector to show a strong recovery, given the more favourable domestic environment. This has not happened so far. While industry and services grew on average by about 7.5 percent per year between 1983 and 1990, agriculture only increased by 2.5 percent during the same period.

The explanation for the growth of industry and services rests largely with: i) the availability of substantial unused capacity in factories and mines because of the state of the economy which was near to collapsing before 1983; and ii) heavy government activity in the areas of electrification and road and other infrastructural construction, which accounts for the bulk of non-agricultural investment. The explanation for the lack of a strong response from the agricultural sector lies in: i) the continuous declines in world cocoa prices which eventually reversed the effects of devaluation; ii) the accumulated effects of unfavourable domestic real returns for cocoa producers on tree planting and

[32] For details on Global 2000 (the abbreviated name for Sasakawa Global 2000), see World Bank. 1992. *Ghana: 2000 and beyond: setting the stage for accelerating growth and poverty reduction.* Report No. 11486-GH. Washington, DC.
[33] Ibid.

SUB-SAHARAN AFRICA

replanting; iii) the limited price benefits of liberalization on food crops; and iv) structural constraints that dominate the agricultural sector and inhibit its response to price signals.

In any case, overall growth in Ghana will continue to be largely dependent on agricultural growth for many years to come. This is so in view of the importance of the sector to employment and export revenue as well as its strong input and output links with other sectors (demand for agricultural products, demand for transport services, links with agro-industry). The high proportion of the poor who live in rural areas and depend on agricultural activities make it unlikely that any broad-based poverty-reducing development strategy can be successful without the growth of the agricultural sector.

It is unlikely that the current pattern of sectoral growth led by manufacturing and services is sustainable. Continuous growth of manufacturing and services will require significant increases in capital investments *by the private sector* as well as improvements in human capital resources and infrastructure, which take time to build up. Investment as a percentage of output stood at around 19 percent of GDP in 1993, a rather low percentage since it is estimated that a 13 percent share is required for replacement investment.

Furthermore, the current pattern of agricultural growth is unsustainable: recovery has been based largely on increases in cultivated area rather than yield responses. Despite some improvements in productivity, which have followed policy reforms, Ghanaian Government estimates show that food crop yields are still as low as 40 percent of potential.[34] Likewise, in the cocoa sector yields are low compared with other world competitors. For instance, while Ghana's 300 kg per hectare average yield compares favourably with those of Nigeria and Cameroon (200 and 260 kg per hectare, respectively), they are far from those of Côte d'Ivoire, Malaysia and Indonesia (600, 800 and 1 100 kg per hectare).[35]

The availability of land resources is not a critical constraint in the short term, but their abundance may be exaggerated. Despite Ghana's undulating topography, 70 percent of the territory is subject to sheet and gully erosion.[36] In the longer term, extensive farming may not be possible without jeopardizing the

[34] Government of Ghana, op. cit., footnote 30, p. 114.

[35] V.K. Nyanteng, ed. 1993. *Policies and options for Ghanaian economic development.* Accra, Institute of Statistical, Social and Economic Research, University of Ghana.

[36] Government of Ghana. 1993. *Ghana's achievement of self-sustainability in food production and food security for 10 years: 1983-1993.* Accra. (unpubl.)

sustainability of the resource base (forests and wetlands). Population pressure causes increased settlement of fragile lands, thus exacerbating the serious sheet and gully erosion of the soils. Therefore, the extensive frontier, although not reached yet, may be rapidly declining.[37]

Ghana's accelerated growth strategy aims at maximizing value added in agriculture rather than gross volume increases. Expanding yields rather than the area under cultivation will reduce the volume of investment required for supporting infrastructure, minimize marketing and distribution problems associated with extending the production area and be environmentally friendly.[38]

This discussion leads to two major conclusions: i) the growth of agriculture is necessary if Ghana is to achieve a poverty-reducing development path; ii) agricultural growth should mainly be productivity-based.

Policies for increasing agricultural productivity. Stimulating agricultural productivity in an environment of falling real world and domestic agricultural prices is a major challenge facing policy-makers in Ghana. Given the market-oriented direction that Ghana is following with respect to economic management, trade and prices, policy solutions to low productivity are being sought in largely non-distortive interventions rather than policies directly affecting the prices of outputs and inputs. Such policies try to alleviate the structural problems and bottlenecks facing Ghanaian agriculture.

Increasing the use of modern inputs is the key to increasing soil fertility and productivity in Ghana. Yet there is a decline in the use of fertilizer and agricultural chemicals to which several factors have contributed:

i) An increase in the relative price of fertilizer *vis-à-vis* that of agricultural commodities following devaluation and the abolition of the subsidy. In order to overcome this constraint, policies are concentrated on improving the performance of the marketing system, reducing marketing margins and improving relative prices for the producer.

ii) Reluctance by traditional farmers to expose themselves to the risks of using new technologies with uncertain returns.

iii) A lack of access to credit by small farmers.

[37] World Bank, op. cit., footnote 32, p. 116.
[38] Government of Ghana, op. cit., footnote 30, p. 114.

SUB-SAHARAN AFRICA

iv) A lack of appropriate technologies and inputs (especially seeds).

Constraints ii) and iii) are interrelated. Namely, the lack of a well-functioning rural credit system reduces the risk-taking capacity of farmers who have to rely either on their own savings or on informal credit. The problem is accentuated by the investment uncertainty associated with Ghana's land tenure system which is dominated by traditional tenure arrangements. The legacy of suspicion and harassment of the private sector associated with past policies in Ghana has deprived the country of a class of large traders who could extend credit to small farmers. Constraint iv) is associated with a long-neglected research and extension system which is now undergoing a complete reorganization.

Technology for increasing labour productivity is also necessary. There are already labour shortages in critical periods of the production cycle (land preparation, harvesting) and this is expected to worsen as competition for labour increases from other sectors. At the root of the low level of farm productivity is the very low-level technology, especially tools and implements (even the use of animal traction is rare). Research and extension are critical for developing and disseminating technical packages based on simple technologies and improved cultural practices geared towards small producers who constitute the majority of the rural population and produce the bulk of the nation's food. The Medium-Term Agricultural Development Programme plans a drastic reform of agricultural support services, including unification of the fragmented research and extension services.

If agriculture is to benefit from the demand generated by a growing economy, linkages with other sectors must be strengthened. Thus, the creation of conditions for the smooth functioning of markets is considered essential. From the policy point of view, this means enhancing the physical infrastructure of rural and urban markets including improvements in telecommunications and storage facilities. The public sector will play a key role with a view to leasing or selling the services to the private sector.

Farmers and sellers face an acute lack of adequate *storage facilities*. Estimated storage losses for all food crops (including cereals, roots, tubers and plantain) are between 15 and 30 percent. Proper storage facilities

could reduce losses by 30 to 50 percent. This means that much of the harvest must be sold immediately, weakening the flexibility and bargaining power of sellers and eventually discouraging surplus production. The role of the public sector in planning and constructing storage facilities, with a view to leasing or selling them to the private sector, is essential.[39] To encourage medium-level storage as a part of its Food Security Strategy, Ghana has asked bilateral donors to finance small to medium-sized storage facilities for the private sector.[40] This, along with other measures aimed at a smoother market functioning, will create the conditions for increased arbitrage and the smoothing out of extreme interseasonal and interregional price fluctuations.

In Ghana high transport costs incurred by the poor state of rural roads is considered the single most important factor preventing the integration of small farmers in the market economy. During the crisis years in Ghana, a lack of foreign exchange and fiscal revenues limited the ability of the country to buy spare parts and keep up regular road maintenance. The problem of costly transportation is particularly acute for non-tradable food crops, since such costs represent a large part of their value. The deterioration of roads and the incapacitation of 70 percent of the truck fleet through a lack of spare parts and tires has resulted in 70 percent of the farmers head-loading crops to markets.

The feeder road density in Ghana averages 89 m per km^2 for a total of 21 300 km. Of those, 12 900 km are considered to be in poor or very poor condition while only about 3 200 km are motorable year-round.[41] Head-loading produce to markets causes long delays in delivery, increases wastage and poses serious health risks. It also inhibits the smooth functioning of the rural labour markets. The Ghanaian Government has established the National Feeder Road Development Programme (NFRDP 1992-2000), under which 2 500 km of selected feeder roads will be fully rehabilitated and another 3 500 km will be regravelled. Cocoa roads will also be rehabilitated to facilitate the linking of cocoa production areas to ports.

A major source of vulnerability of the agricultural sector derives from the fact that 87 percent of agricultural production is sent without processing for final sales and consumption. The development of agro-

[39] For details, see: V.K Nyanteng and S.K Dapaah. 1993. *Agricultural development policies and options.* In V.K Nyanteng ed., Chap.4, op. cit., footnote 35, p. 117. See also *Ghana Ministry of Agriculture. 1990. Ghana Medium-Term Agricultural Development Programme (MTADP).* Accra.

[40] See Government of Ghana, op. cit., footnote 36, p. 117.

[41] See World Bank, op. cit., footnote 32, p. 116; and Nyanteng and Dapaah, ibid.

BOX 5
REFORM AND RURAL POVERTY IN GHANA

To understand the impacts of the policy reforms on the poor in Ghana, one has to have a good idea as to i) who and how many the poor are; ii) where they live; iii) their sources of income; and iv) their consumption patterns. If the poor are defined to include those who live in households with a per caput expenditure below two-thirds of the mean (one-third for the extremely poor), according to an analysis of household data in the Ghana Living Standards Survey (GLSS), about 80 percent of the poor live in the rural areas. Thus, poverty is primarily a rural phenomenon. For Ghana as a whole, 35 percent of the population fall below the poverty line while, for the rural areas, 43 percent are considered poor. Further analysis has demonstrated that, amid wide regional variations, the rural poor are "poorer" than their urban counterparts. For instance, the savannah region of the country, with a population share of 12 percent, has 18 percent of the country's poor and 35 percent of the extremely poor. The heads of most poor households are self-employed, poorly educated and own no cocoa land.

Poor and non-poor alike spend a large share of their budgets on food (69 and 66 percent, respectively) but the poor depend on home-produced food for 33 percent of their total food consumption, compared with 22 percent for the non-poor. Thus, the poor depend on the market for a large proportion of their food consumption.

About 88 percent of the total income of the poor comes from self-employment (65 percent from agricultural income and 23 percent from non-farm self-employment). Almost two-thirds of the income derived from agricultural activities constitutes consumption of home-produced commodities, while about one-third constitutes (net) income from sales of commodities. Cocoa and cereals have equal shares in the total crop revenue (about 20 percent each). The data also show that the poor do not dominate the production or consumption of any single commodity vis-à-vis the non-poor. On the other hand, sorghum and millet seem to be the principle elements of diets in regions where malnutrition is the highest and are also the main income sources in those regions (the Upper and Eastern regions and the entire savannah agro-ecological zone).

The data on poverty presented above indicate that macroeconomic policies favouring the agricultural sector in terms of better incentives for cocoa production tend to help the poor and extremely poor who live in the cocoa-producing zones directly (i.e. as producers and as labourers), while their impact on other regions can be positive through labour migration linkages.

As a high proportion of the income of the poor is derived from self-consumption, it is correspondingly isolated from market shocks. On the other hand, the amount of income derived from market sales of commodities is not negligible, implying that market conditions and prices do matter to the rural poor. The smooth functioning of prices and markets also matter for net consumers of purchased food. The data indicate that real prices of food consumed by the poor have probably followed a declining trend since 1984. The decline in real food prices occurred despite the increase in average per caput incomes and increasing demand, thus reflecting increases in food production. The prevalence of parallel markets in Ghana, especially at the peak of the economic crisis, means that the poor had to pay market prices for food. Thus, the removal of price controls may not have caused a deterioration in the ability of the poor to buy food.

As the rural poor derive 88 percent of their income from self-employment, they are unlikely to have been affected by the retrenchment of the state and the reductions in the civil service. Although devaluation tends to increase the cost of living through its effects on import prices, one has to take into account that imports had all but collapsed before the devaluations took place. The role of the parallel markets and the fact that controlled items found their way into those markets means that the biggest effect of devaluation has been on those earning high rents from the previous system. A significant effect of the combined devaluation/liberalization policies on the poor was through increases in the price of kerosene on which the poor largely depend.

Data show that public expenditures on health increased from an average 0.8 percent of GDP in 1981-86 to 1.3 percent of GDP in 1987-90. For the same periods, education expenditures increased from 2.2 to 3.4 percent of GDP. The large external flows into the country following reform have permitted the government to spend more on social services. Although the analysis above suggests no deterioration in the position of the rural poor as a result of policy reforms, the eventual benefits may not have been large enough to permit a drastic change in the overall poverty situation in its several manifestations (malnutrition, poor health, etc.). Overall growth has not been strong enough to make a serious dent in poverty.

Despite the fact that health expenditures have increased in the post-reform period, nutrition and the level and quality of health services provided in Ghana are still extremely low. A 1990 report by the United Nations Children's Fund (UNICEF), showed that 30 percent of all Ghanaian children are malnourished to some degree, 28 percent of the 12- to 23-month-olds were considered wasted and 31 percent of 24- to 59-month-olds were considered stunted.

Even under the most optimistic growth assumptions, it will take several years before Ghana will be able to make a substantial step forwards in poverty alleviation. Thus, although growth is probably the ultimate sustainable answer to the poverty problem, parallel direct interventions are needed to broaden the benefits of such growth to the poorest segments of the population and improve their living and education standards.

The fact that the majority of the poor live in the rural areas emphasizes the need for agricultural growth as a necessary step towards poverty alleviation. Increases in agricultural productivity will greatly improve the position of the poor in the rural areas in terms of higher farm earnings and lower food costs.[1] On the other hand, the fact that the poor do not seem to dominate any one commodity group means that price-based measures (as production or non-targeted consumption subsidies) to help the poor will be associated with high leakages. The building of rural infrastructure, in addition to its beneficial effects on productivity and overall development, can in the short term be an income-generating activity that will contribute to the revival of the rural communities. Income-generation through employment is an important element in the government's new anti-poverty policy. In this context, the government is promoting projects such as the construction of labour-intensive feeder roads, hand-dug wells and low-cost sanitation, priority public works and non-formal education as part of the mainstream development programme.

---

[1] Alderman (1992) has suggested that given the importance of sorghum and millet in the diets and incomes in the regions with high poverty levels, a food security component in an agricultural strategy should consider giving priority to such crops even though this may not be optimal from a strict efficiency standpoint. *Sources:* H. Alderman. 1992. *Incomes and food security in Ghana.* Cornell Food and Nutrition Policy Program. Working Paper 26; Government of Ghana. 1991. *Enhancing the human impact of the adjustment programme.* Accra; E.O. Boateng, K. Ewusi, R. Kanbur and A. McKay. 1990. *A poverty profile for Ghana, 1987-88.* Social Dimensions of Adjustment Paper No. 5. Washington, DC; World Bank. 1994. *Adjustment in Africa: reforms, results and the road ahead.* New York, Oxford University Press; P. Dorosh and D. Sahn. 1993. *A general equilibrium analysis of the effects of macroeconomic adjustment on poverty in Africa.* Cornell Food and Nutrition Policy Program. Working Paper 39; World Bank, op. cit., footnote 32, p. 116.

SUB-SAHARAN AFRICA

industry will permit the carryover of food products between seasons, thus increasing the shelf-life of perishable commodities. Studies have shown that agroprocessing and other value added activities contribute to the revitalization of the rural non-farm sector through a number of input, output and labour market linkages. The government has tried to stimulate investment in agroprocessing by increasing incentives through the waiver of import duties on equipment. Such policies have led to the diversion of equipment to other uses. The use of the corporate tax structure may be more effective for such a purpose.

Poverty alleviation. Box 5 shows the dimensions of the rural poverty problem in Ghana and outlines some of the policies that the Ghanaian Government is implementing with the aim of poverty alleviation. Although the majority of the poor are rural poor, one-third of them live in the urban areas. The government has identified the urban unemployed and those with meagre earnings, especially in the 18- to 25-year-old bracket, as a target group in its poverty alleviation scheme. In contrast to the rural poor, policy reforms have negatively affected the urban poor and have created a new class of poor through the retrenchment of workers from the civil service, state-owned enterprises and inefficient enterprises that closed as a result of market liberalization. In the urban context, and for the unemployed who have not returned to rural areas, the government has introduced a programme of initiatives to help distressed industries. The First Finance Corporation was established to provide venture capital and expertise in restructuring in management, production marketing and finance.

Conclusions

Ghanaians have made a choice as to what the main directions of their economic system should be: a market-based, private sector-driven economy with pragmatic government policies and the concentration of state activity in the areas of education, infrastructure, market development and poverty alleviation. While consolidating the gains from policy reform is a fundamental task for the short term, it is equally important that the benefits of growth be shared widely among population groups. The achievement of these

objectives is critical if economic development is to be sustained. Continued support from donors will go a long way in helping the Ghanaian Government cope with the structural problems that have to be resolved if the economy is to be put on a sustainable growth path.

ASIA AND THE PACIFIC

REGIONAL OVERVIEW

Over the last 25 years, Asian and Pacific developing countries grew at an average annual rate of 6.5 percent compared with the average 4.5 percent for all developing countries. This strong performance continued in 1993, and the Asian Development Bank (AsDB) estimates the average growth for the region to be 7.4 percent for 1993 and 7 percent for 1994. The high-growth economies include China, Malaysia, Thailand and Viet Nam, but almost all countries performed well except Pakistan and the Philippines. In general, countries throughout the region stabilized their economies, reducing fiscal deficits, improving their balance of payments and containing inflation rates.

Major factors contributing to this overall growth performance include market-oriented policies aimed at enlarging private sector participation, enhancing competitiveness in the economic system, attracting foreign investment and participating to a greater extent in world trade. There is a greater convergence of policies followed by Asian countries than ever before.

The overall figures, however, do not tell the full story. There have been significant intracountry and interregional differences in economic growth, daunting poverty problems still persist in many countries and the quest for rapid growth is placing increased pressure on environmental resources while threatening long-term sustainability.

Although the share of agriculture in the region's GDP has declined from around 30 percent in the mid-1980s to 22 percent in recent years, agriculture remains the driving economic force and major employer in many countries. Moreover, the Asian region is the world's fastest-growing import market for agricultural commodities. The region's share of global agricultural imports has increased from 17 percent in the early 1980s to nearly 25 percent today; agricultural imports are increasing by around 6 percent per year, accounting for the bulk of the increase in global imports.

Table 4 provides an overview of recent agricultural GDP performance and the AsDB's estimates for growth rates in 1994. Following are some individual country experiences.

Figure 6

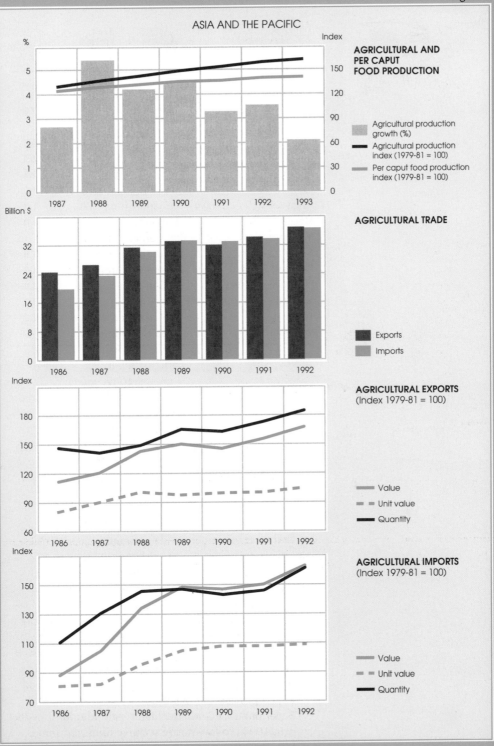

ASIA AND THE PACIFIC

Source: FAO

ASIA AND THE PACIFIC

TABLE 4

Growth rates in agricultural GDP

Country	1991	1992	1993	1994[1]
Bangladesh	1.6	2.2	1.9	2.6
Cambodia	4.7	1.9	3.2	-
China	2.4	4.0	4.0	3.7
India	-1.4	4.6	2.3	2.5
Indonesia	1.4	6.5	1.5	4.5
Laos	-1.7	7.9	0.0	-
Malaysia	0.0	4.3	3.0	1.2
Mongolia	-5.1	-3.9	-7.0	4.0
Myanmar	-2.4	13.6	7.5	-
Nepal	2.8	-1.2	-1.2	5.0
Pakistan	5.0	9.7	-3.9	4.0
Philippines	1.4	-0.1	1.5	2.0
Sri Lanka	1.9	-1.5	5.1	3.5
Thailand	5.0	4.0	2.6	2.5
Viet Nam	2.2	6.0	3.3	6.5

[1] Projections.

Source: AsDB. *Asian Development Outlook 1994*. Manila.

- China's economy remains one of the most dynamic in the world. GDP growth in 1993 was 13.4 percent, the highest among Asian countries. The agricultural sector grew by 4 percent. Cereal production increased by nearly 2 percent, while output in livestock, fisheries, fruit and vegetables achieved double-digit growth rates. The country recently announced the complete removal of administrative controls on cereals by 1996 and further improvement of the grain reserve system.
- India's policy-makers are debating reforms in a number of agricultural input markets, including reducing subsidies for water, fuel and electricity. A reduction in fertilizer subsidies is planned throughout the 1993-1996 period, while reductions in irrigation subsidies are expected to take place more gradually. These reductions are likely to be accompanied by hikes in support prices targeted to smaller farmers. India's agricultural GDP increased by 2.3 percent during 1993.
- Bad weather led to a decline in agricultural production in Pakistan. Excessive rains and floods led to a 3.9 percent drop in output. In addition, a

virus attacked the cotton crop, reducing production by 30 percent. Bad weather also led to livestock losses in Mongolia, contributing to the 7 percent decline in agricultural GDP.

- In Cambodia, agricultural output grew by 3.2 percent in 1993, but the presence of land-mines left over from the war and deteriorating irrigation networks hampered overall performance. Agriculture accounts for 50 percent of the country's GDP and employs 85 percent of the labour force. Rice output increased by 1.7 percent in 1993, other crops increased by 10 percent and the livestock sector increased by 18 percent. Only forestry output fell, as logging restrictions led to a severe production decline of 75 percent in 1993.
- Sri Lanka's agricultural sector grew by 5.1 percent in 1993, as tea production increased by 35 percent after having declined by 26 percent in 1992, in part because of bad weather. Rubber output increased by 19 percent and rice production by 3 percent. Agricultural sector growth was strong in Myanmar in 1993, increasing by 7.5 percent. Rice production expanded as higher procurement prices, improved access to fertilizers and good weather boosted yields.

Public and private sector roles under policy reforms
The positive results of market-oriented policies among the early reformers has encouraged several other countries to follow similar paths of economic and institutional reforms. The basic strategy is to reduce public sector dominance, liberalize markets and emphasize private sector participation. For example, since July 1991, India has made considerable progress in liberalizing the investment, trade and foreign exchange regimes. While agricultural subsidies for water, electricity and fertilizers still exist and trade policy remains biased against the sector, the government's direct involvement in agricultural activities is being reduced gradually.

In recent years, former command economies (Cambodia, Laos, Mongolia, Viet Nam and six central Asian former Soviet republics) either initiated or made substantial progress towards a more market-oriented economic system. The policy reorientation aims to improve overall sectoral efficiency and performance

while preserving the natural resource base and keeping macroeconomic, fiscal and external imbalances within manageable limits. A concurrent concern is to minimize or offset the negative effects on the poor.

Among the command economies, however, the pace of reform, the difficulties encountered and the record of success in surmounting them are quite diverse. For instance, Viet Nam is continuing structural reforms and the economy is performing well; the agriculture sector is responding to improvements in land tenure security, liberalization of input and output prices and an increase in farm credit. In Laos, on the other hand, the privatization plan appears to have slowed down. Only 5 percent of state enterprises have been privatized so far, although the government plans to privatize all such enterprises by 1996.

In Mongolia and the central Asian republics, high rates of inflation and unemployment, falling output levels and constraints to the financing of social safety nets over the last three years have resulted in a gradual erosion of living standards and considerable increases in poverty. These problems are being addressed by reverting to price controls on selected basic goods and services such as food, public transport and housing rent or, where possible, cash compensation to the affected population. Even in China, steps have been taken to control prices of some basic commodities and services in recognition that measures to curb money supply growth and credit restrictions are not enough to curtail the double-digit inflation rate (currently exceeding 20 percent in the cities).

The varied experience with structural adjustment programmes in the market-oriented and transitional economies demonstrates that the design of policy reforms should take into account the country-specific comparative advantage of the private and public sectors for economic functions and support services. In particular, such experience underscores the public sector's role in addressing market failures to enhance private sector efficiency, improve competitiveness and quality of service, and fulfil long-term social welfare objectives, including environmental protection. Moreover, it has also indicated that a conducive institutional framework for a market system must be created prior to, or concurrently with, policy reforms. Without the appropriate institutions, the expected

ASIA AND THE PACIFIC

supply response would not occur and the process would consequently lead to high inflation and impoverishment of the population.

Growing importance of intraregional trade, investment flows and growth triangles

Trade within the Asian region is growing more rapidly than trade with the rest of the world; the share of intraregional trade grew from 30 percent in 1986 to 40 percent in 1992. Trade between China and the rest of the world expanded particularly fast. China's imports surged by more than 25 percent in each of the last two years and a growing share of these imports came from other Pacific economies which are increasingly dependent on China. In fact, China is considered to be the main engine of growth in the Asia and Pacific region.

In part, the growth of intraregional trade has been aided by the lingering recession (since 1990) and growing unemployment, which has given rise to stronger protectionist tendencies in industrial countries. The recent conclusion of the Uruguay Round of GATT negotiations is expected to remove some of these barriers.

Nevertheless, there is concern about the possible internalization of trade in Europe and North America following progress in economic integration within the EC and the North American Free Trade Agreement (NAFTA). Despite recent diversification in trade flows, the Asia and the Pacific region still sells one-third to one-half of its total exports to these two regions.

For the past decade, the region has received an increasing volume of capital inflows, comprising foreign direct investment (FDI) and long- and medium-term credit. Recently, these capital flows have grown rapidly. Two factors contributing to the increase in FDI are the continuing recession in developed countries and the impressive growth record, stability and market-oriented reforms in Asian economies. The AsDB estimates that capital inflows averaged $36 billion annually during 1989-92 compared with $20.5 billion during the preceding four years. Between 1987 and 1992, FDI inflows increased by 27 percent annually. In the past, capital inflows were largely concentrated in Southeast Asia. Today, they are increasingly directed towards China, which attracted $11 billion in 1992, and

India which attracted $5 billion of foreign capital flows in 1993.

The emergence of the so-called growth triangles is the other major development towards greater regional economic integration. Growth triangles link geographically contiguous areas and evolve in response to opportunities for exploiting national complementarities of natural resources, capital and labour. While a number of intergovernmental arrangements for regional cooperation and trade, such as the Association of Southeast Asian Nations (ASEAN), the South Asian Association for Regional Cooperation (SAARC), and South Asian Free Trade Agreement (SAFTA), are still grappling with the design of a workable system, the informal arrangement of growth triangles is rapidly multiplying in the region. This approach is more outward-oriented than trade blocs which focus on enhancing trade within the bloc. Successful examples of growth triangles are the *China Economic Area,* linking southern China, Hong Kong and Taiwan Province of China, and the *Southern Growth Triangle,* linking Singapore, Johore State in Malaysia and the island of Batam in Indonesia.

Implications of the Uruguay Round Agreement for Asian agriculture

Although the Uruguay Round Agreement of GATT does not come into force until mid-1995 and many of its provisions will become operational gradually over the next decade, the signing of the Final Act has generated a great deal of interest among Asian farmers. The net effect of GATT's provisions for agriculture has not been systematically analysed for most countries; in some countries, farmer lobbies and interest groups are expressing strong opinions. For example, some farmers' groups feel that the provision on the Total Aggregate Measurement of Support (Total AMS) would reduce subsidies on fertilizers, water and power and that seed prices may increase if farmers are forbidden to sell seeds covered by intellectual property protection.

In Asian countries, wheat products, meat, fruit and vegetables are being substituted for rice because of rising incomes and growing urbanization. The result is a lower per caput demand for rice throughout the region but an increased demand for higher-quality rice varieties. Demand for feedgrains and oilmeals are

expected to increase, with consequent changes in relative prices. One implication of the Uruguay Round Agreement for Asian countries is to step up investment for improving production technology and marketing as well as processing infrastructure to facilitate crop diversification – induced by changing consumption patterns – in line with the countries' dynamic comparative advantage.

Growth, poverty alleviation and regional development
Sustained economic growth and specific government policy measures have significantly reduced both the proportion and absolute numbers of poor in the region. Yet almost three-quarters of the more than one billion poor people in the world live in Asia; of these, nearly 500 million live in absolute poverty. Therefore, poverty alleviation continues to be a priority and is likely to remain so for many years.

Poverty is generally concentrated in remote rural and resource-poor areas that have poor access to social services and infrastructure. Progress in productivity and, therefore, land-saving technology has mainly accrued to rice and wheat. Thus, regions unsuited for intensive rice or wheat cultivation have tended to lag behind. Large-scale rural poverty is concentrated in regions of poor agricultural performance.

Even in countries with high growth records, uneven regional development has led to severe income disparity and pockets of chronic rural poverty. Inland regions, especially in the northwest of China, the outer islands of Indonesia and the Philippines and the region outside Bangkok in Thailand, are examples of areas identified by the respective governments for special development efforts.

Asian governments continue to implement specific programmes for improving infrastructure, developing the skills of target populations, providing investment incentives, assisting rural enterprise development, creating export processing zones and engaging in integrated development programmes in underdeveloped regions to counter spatial biases induced by macroeconomic and séctoral policies. For example, poverty alleviation measures in India include rural wage employment programmes during the lean agricultural season, integrated rural development programmes and land reform efforts. Bangladesh has

ASIA AND THE PACIFIC

feeding programmes for vulnerable groups, special cooperatives for promoting income-generating activities for the poor, food-aided infrastructural development programmes and special credit and skill training programmes for small farmers. It is increasingly apparent that these programmes must be complemented by adequate attention to technological improvement in crops grown in the targeted regions.

ASIA AND THE PACIFIC

CHINA
Economic overview

The tremendous economic transformations that have taken place in China over the past 15 years have attracted worldwide attention. Economic reform, modernization and opening to the outside world has been accompanied by buoyant economic activity. After having expanded at annual rates of nearly 10 percent during the 1980s, the national economy entered a period of austerity from 1989 to 1991 but accelerated to a growth rate of more than 13 percent in both 1992 and 1993 – among the highest rates in the world. Nevertheless, current levels of per caput income $318 in 1990 at current prices – still place China among the low-income developing countries.[42]

As economic growth has accelerated, major changes in the economic structure have occurred. Output and employment structures have shifted in favour of industry and services. The industrial sector, which only accounted for 36 percent of GDP and 10 percent of employment in 1970, increased these shares to about 55 percent and 22 percent, respectively, in 1990. Conversely, the share of agriculture fell from 47 to 23 percent of GDP and from 81 to 60 percent of employment during the same period. The industrial sector continues to lead economic expansion. Its growth was estimated to be nearly 21 percent in 1993, albeit with wide performance differentials between the dynamic east coast provinces and those in the poorer west and centre. Growth of value added in agriculture has lagged (about 4 percent in both 1992 and 1993) and, consequently, the economic importance of the sector has further declined.

Rapid growth in recent years was fuelled by massive investments, particularly in the industrial sector, facilitated by a relaxed monetary policy and rapid growth in money supply. (Fixed investment grew by more than 60 percent in the first half of 1993.) Concurrent signs indicated that this course was unsustainable and the economy was being stretched to its limits. Transportation bottlenecks, shortages in energy and several key industrial raw materials and accelerating inflation (from 8.6 percent in 1992 to 14.5 in 1993) all pointed to excess demand pressure and the need for tighter monetary policies and financial discipline.

[42] The 13th National Congress of the Communist Party had defined a three-phase development strategy. GDP was expected to double in the first ten-year phase ending in 1990 (this was achieved) and to double again in the second phase ending in 2000 (not unlikely, considering recent trends); by the end of the third phase in 2050, China's per caput income was expected to be that of a medium developed country.

ASIA AND THE PACIFIC

Buoyant domestic demand also caused the trade balance to turn negative in 1993, for the first time since 1989. Import demand sharply increased and export growth slowed as exportable capital and consumer goods were absorbed by the domestic market. Significant liberalization measures related to China's application to rejoin GATT also contributed to strong import growth.

Increasingly restrictive monetary policies and major financial sector reforms are expected in the coming years. Inevitably, these measures will slow growth, although expectations are for still robust rates of 9 to 10 percent in 1994 and 1995. Underlying positive expectations are favourable supply responses to the ongoing reforms, large inflows of FDI, a strong external account position and high levels of foreign exchange reserves.

Despite such optimistic expectations, several fundamental problems remain to be solved. Foremost is the population problem. Demographic growth, with a current annual rate of about 1.3 percent (1.5 during 1980-1990), is still relatively high considering the very large base of more than 1.2 billion. Despite active population control regulations, family planning policies – particularly in rural areas – have encountered major obstacles, in some cases arising from government action itself.[43]

Other issues are the long-term sustainability of high levels of growth as well as the ability to achieve it through a balanced combination of intensive practices – raising factor productivity – and extensive practices – allowing the absorption of the vast and expanding labour supply. An important factor affecting the future pace of growth is the ability to push state-owned enterprises, especially the larger ones, into the market economy so as to increase their vitality and efficiency.

Despite rapid growth, and to a certain extent because of it, income and living standard disparities have widened between rural and urban areas, coastal and inland provinces, favoured economic and development zones and zones with little access to public support and market opportunities. A major challenge facing the government is to prevent a further accentuation of regional and intersectoral disparities. Consolidating a socialist market economy requires converting a liberal economic system that fosters private initiative while

[43] For instance, land for farming and residential housing was leased to peasants on a per caput basis, encouraging them to increase the family size.

preventing social inequities, speculation and corruption.

China's agricultural sector in transition

In the late 1970s, China's policy-makers initiated a series of rural sector reforms aimed at overcoming the country's sluggish agricultural growth. Despite three decades of emphasis on food self-sufficiency and impressive achievements in health and education, policy-makers were dissatisfied with the rural sector's inability to improve the quantity, quality and variety of agricultural production. For more than 30 years, the rural sector required increasing levels of state investment to generate growth, but there was little improvement in productivity. In fact, agricultural productivity stagnated or even fell in some years. Per caput cereal production increased by only 14 percent between 1952 and 1978, while food production barely kept ahead of population growth. Moreover, the country had been a net cereal importer for over one-quarter of a century.

Although the 1978 reform measures were focused on raising agricultural production by providing farmers with improved price and income incentives, they were quickly followed by a complete restructuring of China's agricultural sector. In less than five years, policy changes shifted the control of resources and production from the collective farming system to a household-based farming system. The role of direct state planning in agricultural production was replaced with markets and prices. By the early 1980s, the government had dismantled the commune system, embraced the household responsibility system (HRS) and allowed prices and markets to help determine input use and production decisions.

This shift from central planning to a market-oriented agricultural sector not only profoundly reshaped the role of the state in agriculture, but it also resulted in remarkable improvements in productivity, rural incomes and well-being. For example, since the 1978 reforms, the agricultural sector has grown at an average annual rate of nearly 6 percent, one of the highest in the world and twice the growth rate of the 1953-1978 period. The real value of China's agricultural output has more than doubled since 1978. More important, rural per caput income increased rapidly, reducing by two-thirds the

number of people living in absolute poverty. The most rapid increases in rural per caput income occurred between 1979 and 1984 when it averaged a 15 percent increase per year.

The initial rural reforms. Prior to the 1978 reforms, China's central government planned and directed the country's economic activity. The state established annual economic plans for industry and agriculture and assigned production targets to industrial and agricultural enterprises.

The state was also responsible for providing enterprises with the necessary inputs to meet targets and for procuring and distributing the outputs. For example, the government imposed a compulsory procurement policy, obliging agricultural households to sell their produce at government-set prices. The government then rationed items, including cereals, edible oils, pork, sugar and cotton cloth, to urban residents. At one point, the government rationed more than 100 items to urban residents.

Rural People's Communes carried out the central plan's rural assigned activities. The communes were both government bodies and compulsory cooperatives that implemented state directives and managed small-scale enterprises and shops. A typical commune consisted of ten to 15 production brigades, which were subdivided into about ten production teams of 20 to 30 households each. The average commune included about 5 000 households with 4 000 ha of cultivated land.

Production brigades allocated each team's production and procurement quotas and managed primary schools, health clinics and small non-farm retail shops. Production teams organized agricultural activities and maintained accounting and income distribution systems. Payments to workers were based on a work point formula. The teams also controlled property rights to land and assets.

China's commune system achieved most of the goals for which it was established. The communes constructed and operated rural infrastructure (irrigation facilities, transportation networks, etc.), organized and managed economic and social welfare services (including health care and education) and maintained food self-sufficiency for the rural sector.

Initially, the reforms of 1978 aimed to build on this well-developed physical and human infrastructure by using price incentives to increase overall production. Preliminary measures relaxed central government control over sown area and raised procurement prices by more than 20 percent for cereals, 15 percent for cotton, 25 percent for oilseeds and 25 percent for pigs. In addition, they raised premium prices for above-quota sales by 50 percent and reduced input prices by 10 percent.

Reorganizing the production unit. As a further incentive, the government allowed production teams to experiment with a variety of payment systems, on the condition that the commune's collective ownership and management structure be maintained. Some teams chose to link pay to the type of work; others tied it to the amount of time worked, the type of land or the amount of final output. A group of farmers in Anhui Province adopted what came to be the most successful payment system. Known as "Da Baogan" or "Baogan Dao Hu" (meaning the contracting of all activities to the household), this system divided up the production team's land, assets and quota among individual households. After fulfilling the quota obligations and paying a specified portion of output or revenue to the production team as a tax for community purposes, each household could keep or dispose of surplus production as it wished. This system later became known as the HRS.

At first, the government did not support the HRS, insisting that the production teams remain the basic management unit and that they maintain collective ownership of land and assets. However, it did promote the HRS as an effective measure in the poorer remote and mountainous regions.

In 1982, the government allowed the HRS to become the dominant rural institution for agricultural production in China. Households established fixed-term land-use contracts with production teams. Initial contracts granted land rights for three to five years; by the late 1980s, contracts were extended to 15-year periods; and by 1993 they stretched to 30 years. Households also contracted with production teams to fulfil state procurement quotas and to pay various taxes.

By the end of 1983, 200 million family farms had adopted the HRS and more than 50 000 communes had

been eliminated. During this same period, the government introduced two additional policy changes: first, in 1983 households were permitted to exchange and employ labour for farm work; and, second, the subleasing of land to other households for compensation was sanctioned in 1984. These two reforms aimed at increasing on-farm investment by improving the functioning of land and labour markets.

Product market reforms. Prior to the 1978 reforms, the Chinese Government classified farm products into three categories. The first category, which included cereals, oil-bearing crops and cotton, was subject to "tong gou", or unified procurement: the government was the sole buyer through the compulsory quota system. Production quotas and targets and procurement prices were fixed for three- to five-year periods. Above-quota deliveries were compulsory, but received a 20 to 30 percent price premium. These goods could not be sold on the free market.

The second category included meat, aquatic products, tobacco, tea, silk and sugar and was subject to "pai gou", or imposed purchase: the government set compulsory procurement quotas and prices but permitted free market sales of surpluses. There were no compulsory quotas for goods in the third category, which consisted of vegetables, fruit and some industrial crops. However, government agencies set prices and controlled interregional trade within the country; producers could trade only in local markets.

In the early 1980s, additional market-oriented reforms had legalized wholesale markets and allowed free market trade in cereals (provided the procurement quota was fulfilled). The government gradually reduced the quantity of items covered by procurement quotas and reformed the rural supply and marketing cooperative system. These policy changes fostered farmer-owned marketing enterprises, including both private cooperatives and individual businesses. In the early 1990s, private marketing enterprises reached 3.7 million and employed around 14 million people.

These enterprises purchased farm products from traders in local markets or directly from farmers and then processed, transported or sold them in large wholesale markets. In many cases, they competed with government purchasing agencies (the reformed rural supply cooperatives). By the end of 1993, Chinese

farmers sold about 85 percent of their agricultural products in private sector trades at market prices.

By the mid-1980s, non-agricultural goods also moved progressively out of the mandatory plan and private distribution systems, and market channels gradually expanded. The government introduced "dual track" pricing for industrial goods in 1985 (permitting output above target levels to be sold on the free market) and began phasing out procurement pricing in the late 1980s. In 1980, 90 percent of industrial goods were allocated under the central plan; by 1994, the proportion of industrial goods under state planning declined to less than 10 percent. In addition, the number of consumer goods administered by government agencies, including basic food items, declined from 274 in 1978 to 14 in early 1994.

Rural reforms and agricultural development

The real gross value of agricultural output more than doubled during the 1980s and was accompanied by substantial diversification and increased productivity. For example, between 1979 and 1985, land area planted to cereals declined by 6 percent and crop cultivation's share in agricultural employment declined from 93 percent to 70 percent, as farmers shifted resources and labour to more profitable farm activities such as fruit and vegetables. The total agricultural labour force declined from more than 70 percent of total population in 1979 to 58 percent in 1993, but agriculture's share of national income remained at 33 percent.

Nevertheless, this reallocation of resources did not decrease output. The availability of cereals increased from 305 kg per caput in 1978 to 400 kg in 1984. Total cereal production increased from 304.8 million tonnes in 1978 to 456.4 million tonnes in 1993, a 50 percent increase. Over the past 15 years, yields in cereals, cotton and oilseeds increased by 3.5 percent per year. Increased inputs accounted for most of these productivity gains – chemical fertilizer use tripled and the number of small tractors quadrupled.

Livestock production, fisheries, forestry and other non-crop activities expanded even more rapidly. Over the past 15 years, livestock and fisheries output increased by 10 percent per year, forestry production by 5 percent and other "sideline" activities by 15 percent.

Even though the value of crop output increased by more than 4 percent per year, the share of crops in the total value of agricultural output decreased from 77 to 60 percent. Livestock production's share increased from 14 percent to 26 percent of total output. The relative liberalization of livestock markets and rapid income growth have caused meat production and consumption to expand more rapidly than all other agricultural products. During the 1980s, per caput consumption of pork increased by 200 percent, poultry by 440 percent and eggs by 290 percent.

However, this rapid economic growth and transition to a market-oriented economy has been accompanied by periods of high inflation and macroeconomic imbalances. The government introduced several austerity programmes to curb inflation and cool down the overheating economy during the last half of the 1980s. Consequently, in 1989 and 1990, the rate of growth in real GNP declined to about half the average annual rate experienced during the first years of reform.

In addition, the benefits of growth have not been evenly distributed. For example, strong rural sector growth played an important role in bringing down poverty levels during the first half of the 1980s, but a subsequent slow-down in agricultural growth after 1985 coincided with the stagnation of poverty levels. The number of rural poor declined from 260 million in 1978 to 100 million in 1990 (or from 33 percent of the rural population to around 12 percent). However, during 1985-1990, the incidence of rural poverty remained roughly constant.

In 1978, most of the poor resided in areas where rapid productivity gains were feasible through an increased use of farm inputs and hybrid seeds. By 1985, however, China's remaining poor were concentrated in the less productive rain-fed areas. While some increases in productivity were achieved in these resource-poor areas, available evidence suggests that the gains in agricultural growth were largely offset by population growth.

Ironically, the dramatic increase in cereal availability in the early 1980s led to a second round of policy reforms that adversely affected many farmers. The record-breaking cereal and cotton harvest of 1984 produced a serious fiscal problem for the central government because it was still committed to

purchasing, at relatively high prices compared with consumer prices, all above-quota cereal production from farmers. While the government had raised retail prices on pork, fish and eggs to compensate for increased procurement prices, the retail prices for basic necessities such as cereals and edible oils were not increased. Thus, food subsidies increased from 8 percent of the state budget in 1979 to 25 percent in 1984. This represented an unsupportable financial burden for a country seeking to allocate more investment to the industrial sector.

To reduce this burden, the government converted the 30-year-old procurement system into a "contract purchase" system, eliminating mandatory quotas for cotton in 1984 and for cereals in 1985. The new system established unified prices equal to the weighted average of the quota and above-quota prices at the 1984 level. In addition, it set lower quotas for cotton purchases, raised the cost of input items such as diesel and fertilizers and reduced state investments in agriculture. Lower prices for cereals and cotton reduced both area planted and input use: cereal production decreased by 7 percent in 1985 and cotton by 34 percent.

Rural enterprise development and agriculture

After the commune system had dissolved, the government permitted townships to inherit the administrative functions and property of the communes and villages to assume the functions and property of brigades. These township and village enterprises (TVEs) soon began operating as collective enterprises, producing a variety of goods and services, many of which provided inputs to farmers. Meanwhile, privately owned rural enterprises developed quickly.

In the mid-1980s, when the government began addressing the fiscal problems caused by food subsidies and cereal procurement, a series of policy reforms focused on TVEs and urban industrial enterprises. These included a system of retainable profits, the right to sell above-plan output on the free market and the permission to hire labour (and allowing farmers to work off the farm). The government further encouraged TVEs with tax exemptions and subsidized credit. However, the TVEs expanded beyond all expectations. Between 1978 and 1993, TVE output increased at annual rate of

21 percent, and employment by 12 percent. In 1978, TVE output accounted for only 35 percent of agricultural output but, by the early 1990s, the ratio had increased to approximately 200 percent. Between 1978 and 1993, the number of TVEs increased from 1.5 million to 20.8 million, creating nearly 80 million jobs for peasants who were said to be "leaving the land but not the countryside".

TVEs have had mixed effects on the agricultural sector. For instance, in the first years after the reforms, TVEs contributed to agricultural growth by providing inputs, technical services and improved infrastructure in the community. They also created employment, absorbed surplus labour, increased rural incomes and narrowed the gap between rural and urban sectors. However, the drawback was that TVEs provided higher investment returns than agriculture while competing for the same resources; as a result, farmers and the state gradually began investing more of their new savings in TVEs and less in agriculture. This has had negative effects on agricultural production and created a new income gap between agricultural work and rural industry.

Moreover, throughout the 1980s, while TVE production for urban and export markets increased, the production of agricultural inputs declined: nitrogen fertilizer by 27 percent and farm machinery by 50 percent. Many farmers were forced to travel long distances to purchase these inputs in cities, thereby raising production costs and lowering farm income, which further reduced incentives to invest in agriculture.

As agricultural price incentives were reduced in 1984 and cereal production slackened, the declining profitability of agriculture induced many farmers to invest most of their new savings and labour in these TVEs. By 1993, TVEs' total outstanding loans with the rural credit cooperatives amounted to Y 147.2 billion, while their total deposits amounted to only Y 30.2 billion. At the same time, farmer households' deposits and outstanding loans amounted to Y 286.7 and Y 75.9 billion, respectively. The TVEs had extracted Y 117 billion from the farming sector, an amount roughly equal to 30 percent of the value of total fixed production assets owned by farm households at the end of 1992.

Farmers' investment in agricultural assets as a percentage of their savings decreased from 25 percent in the early 1980s to less than 6 percent in the early 1990s. Likewise, state investment in agriculture fell from 10 percent of the national total during the last half of the 1970s to 3.3 percent during the last half of the 1980s. On average, capital investment in agriculture by the state and farmers together was only 30 percent of the TVE investment between 1985 and 1990. Recent evidence suggests that insufficient farming investment and a weak infrastructure are beginning to limit growth. For instance, irrigated land remains close to the 1979 level and 25 percent of the country's reservoirs are shrinking because of sedimentation and erosion.

TVEs create additional problems for the agricultural sector. For instance, unlike urban enterprises, which attract entire families, TVEs tend to draw the best educated and most able workers from families, leaving less productive household members on the farm. Finally, TVEs are not subject to the same environmental legislation as urban industries and they are degrading agricultural land and irrigation water in many areas.

Future directions in farm organization and agriculture
In 1994, only seven agricultural products were still subject to some type of government control. Price controls on cereals and edible oils were relaxed in mid-1993 and futures markets were introduced for cereals. The central government has announced that administrative controls on cereals and oilseeds will be completely removed by 1996.

As retail price controls are lifted and the rationing system is phased out, urban residents are buying more and more staple foods on the free market. By June 1993, only three provinces (Tibet, Hainan and Gansu) retained the longstanding system of cereal rationing, under which urban residents are entitled to purchase low-priced cereals with coupons. In all the other provinces, cereal coupons have been eliminated and workers given partial compensation in the form of additional wage supplements.

These changes will continue to place numerous pressures on China's agricultural sector throughout the 1990s. High income growth combined with further reductions in basic consumer subsidies will continue to alter food consumption patterns. The higher income

BOX 6
RECENT DEVELOPMENT ISSUES IN THE PACIFIC ISLANDS

The Pacific Island nations include a wide range of economies, landforms, resource endowments and population densities. The countries in the subregion face a number of common constraints, however, including small domestic markets, a narrow resource and production base, relatively high unit costs of infrastructure, a heavy dependence on external trade and vulnerability to external shocks and disasters. In addition, the Pacific Islands lack proximity to a large, high-income market (unlike the Caribbean islands).

Economic growth tends to be erratic, with long-term growth rates just keeping pace with population growth. GNP per caput ranges from $1 830 in Fiji to $560 in the Solomon Islands. Social indicators generally compare favourably with developing countries at the same or higher levels of income. The countries have relatively rich natural endowments, a high ratio of land per person and vast areas of ocean containing significant mineral and fishery potential. The average sea area is more than 24 times that in the Caribbean.

Over the years, the Pacific Island countries have taken advantage of large consessional aid flows, workers' remittances and a natural resource base that is favourable for subsistence living. Absolute poverty is low but relative poverty is still a problem in the Solomon Islands and Vanuatu. Recent food self-sufficiency rate indicators demonstrate high levels for all countries, ranging from 95 percent in Papua New Guinea to 145 percent in Vanuatu.

Per caput income has stagnated since the early 1980s and average population growth rates remain above 2 percent. This low economic growth and stagnation despite high levels of foreign resource inflows and high rates of investment is often referred to as the "Pacific paradox". Owing to limitations of monetary policy in small, open economies with relatively high levels of external grants and workers remittances, fiscal policy is the main macro policy instrument. The most recent common development strategy is to seek export opportunities and efficient import substitutes to promote their domestic economies.

Agriculture, fisheries and forestry are three of the most important activities identified as holding promise for future development (tourism and small-scale manufacturing are two others). Agriculture is the largest employer in the region and is dominated by a combination of semi-subsistence root crops and garden vegetables and by the production of copra, cocoa, sugar and coffee for export. Falling and unstable prices of traditional export crops have stimulated producers to diversify into non-traditional products such as squash, vanilla, melons, coconut cream and range-fed beef for export markets.

Even though sea rights are very large, little domestic investment has gone to the fisheries sector. In the past, leasing fishing rights to foreign ships has been preferred to encouraging indigenous fisheries capacity. More recently, however, many governments have promoted linkages between foreign fisheries and the fledgling domestic industry. The domestic fisheries will need to improve local skills, expand collection and marketing facilities, reserve sections of their economic zones for local fishing communities and provide adequate incentives – fiscal, financial and infrastructural.

The environment in the Pacific Islands is fragile and is coming under stress from various sources and types of degradation. These environmental concerns are emerging as the most important feature in long-term development strategies because of the high degree of economic and cultural dependence on the natural environment. While none of these environmental issues are unique to the Pacific Islands, most are exacerbated by small, low land masses dispersed over part of the world's largest ocean, resulting in vulnerability to rises in sea level, a high degree of ecosystem and species diversity and vulnerability to natural disasters.

Environmental issues that are common across the region include: the impacts of population growth on urban water supply and sewage; degraded watersheds from forestry practices and related deforestation; threats to coastal and atoll aquifers; marine pollution from nutrient contamination (deforestation, sewage and land clearing); land degradation from erosion and soil compaction; loss of biodiversity; and high sea driftnet fishing and overharvesting of marine resources.

elasticities for livestock and feedgrains imply that demand for these commodities will increase faster than for rice. Demand for better-quality wheat, fruit, vegetables and japonica rice also appears to be rising.

Likewise, production supports for cereals will affect incentive structures and farmers' decisions about what to plant. In addition, future agricultural sector growth and improvements in cereal production depend on policy changes regarding investment policy, labour and population migration, property rights and further reforms of cereal production, marketing and storage systems. For example, an important concern facing China's policy-makers is the fragmentation of farmland. When households became independent producers in the early 1980s, a typical farm included four or five parcels scattered in different locations, suitable for different uses and totalling about 0.5 ha. Production incentives increased, but scale economies were lost. Some production teams attempted to consolidate landholdings, but total size was not affected. Moreover, attempts at consolidation often resulted in a conflict of interests among households. Other farmers lack confidence in the long-term land and asset leases.

China's policy-makers are currently discussing measures to further reform farm institutions by allowing the free migration of labour and population, both between regions and from rural to urban areas. The purpose is to encourage some households to leave the land, which would allow others to consolidate holdings and improve efficiency. One barrier is the resident registration system, which assigns a different legal status to rural and urban inhabitants and restricts where individuals can live and work. The government introduced a proposal to reform this system in March 1994.

A second issue is the confusing legal status of landownership and property rights. In the early 1980s, farmers signed contracts with the production team, which represented the formal owner of land and assets. However, the government retained the right to change the time length of land leases. In most rural areas today, the current land tenure concerns are the security, length, transferability and "marketability" of land leases (and the implications for long-term investments). One recent experiment divided all the land in a village into two categories: one for distribution among existing

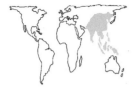

ASIA AND THE PACIFIC

members perpetually and the other for open bidding. Landownership remains a sensitive issue and a practical problem that will persist in the years to come.

LATIN AMERICA AND THE CARIBBEAN

REGIONAL OVERVIEW

In accordance with the widely adopted market-oriented economic principles, most countries in Latin America and the Caribbean have advanced further in the process of deregulation, privatization and external opening of their economies. These policies have continued to make inroads into the longstanding problems of high inflation and external account and fiscal imbalances. Inflationary pressures have slowed, in some cases dramatically. External indebtedness, still a major impediment to full recovery, has nevertheless abated somewhat thanks to debt restructuring and reduction measures as well as the general decline in interest rates since the early 1990s. The new climate of confidence created by improved economic prospects and external openness have given rise to large inflows of private capital. Regional integration has gained significant momentum, a remarkable feature of the current process being a greater openness of regional trading arrangements *vis-à-vis* "outsiders".

These achievements are not exempt from dark areas and uncertainties, however. Economic growth rates did accelerate markedly in most countries during the 1990s, but only a few achieved significant gains in per caput terms. Regional GDP growth in 1993 was still substantial at 3.2 percent (excluding Brazil, 2.6 percent) although well below the annual average of nearly 5 percent for the two previous years. Inflation fell to single-digit levels in Argentina, Bolivia and Mexico and also fell considerably in previously hyperinflationary economies such as Peru and Nicaragua. However, the inflation rate exceeded 2 200 percent in Brazil, which was a destabilizing influence throughout the region. The regional current account deficit increased considerably in 1993 (to 2.5 percent of GDP, compared with about 1 percent in the early 1990s), the trade balance having turned negative for the second consecutive year since the outbreak of the crisis in the early 1980s. The large inflows of capital to economies that are notoriously vulnerable to inflation have created "new generation" problems of economic management. Faced with the necessity to counter an excessive liquidity buildup, governments have operated monetary

Figure 7

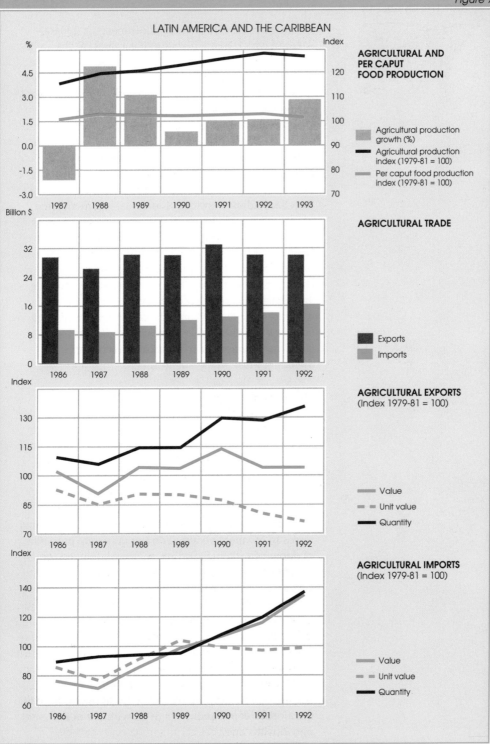

LATIN AMERICA AND THE CARIBBEAN

AGRICULTURAL AND PER CAPUT FOOD PRODUCTION

- Agricultural production growth (%)
- Agricultural production index (1979-81 = 100)
- Per caput food production index (1979-81 = 100)

AGRICULTURAL TRADE

- Exports
- Imports

AGRICULTURAL EXPORTS
(Index 1979-81 = 100)

- Value
- Unit value
- Quantity

AGRICULTURAL IMPORTS
(Index 1979-81 = 100)

- Value
- Unit value
- Quantity

Source: FAO

(and to a lesser extent fiscal) adjustments, a general effect of which being higher interest rates. At the same time, foreign exchange policies have continued to be implemented as instruments for internal stabilization, the result being a progressive overvaluation of national currencies in many countries, which has negatively affected their external competitiveness.

Last but not least, major efforts remain to be made in broadening the base of economic recovery and extending its benefits to the large segments of society who continue to live in situations of extreme poverty. Structural adjustment has at long last begun yielding growth and stabilization dividends and may have set the basis for more stable and sustained patterns of growth in many countries. Nevertheless, market-oriented reform has yet to prove its effectiveness in creating the conditions for a more equitable resource and welfare distribution in the region. The economic recovery provides an opportunity for governments to turn their priorities away from day-to-day problems of crisis management to more structural concerns, including those in the social sphere.

The agricultural sector
Beyond country-specific and climatic factors, agricultural performances in 1993 have been strongly affected by the overall macroeconomic environment. The productive and export capacities of regional agriculture have been negatively affected by the continuation of stabilization measures, which has reduced governments' capacity for supportive intervention; the overvaluation of currencies, involving losses in competitiveness; and the persisting problems of depressed internal and international demand for agricultural products, compounded by unabated protectionism in the main export markets of the region.

As a consequence, in 1993 the index of agricultural production for the region as a whole showed a contraction of almost 1 percent relative to the previous year. This shortfall followed several years of mediocre or poor performances for many countries in the region. Regional agricultural production only rose by an average 1.2 percent yearly during 1990-93, about half the already depressed average growth rate of the previous decade.

The agricultural export sector of the region showed

similarly lacklustre trends, in marked contrast with the relatively dynamic export performances of other sectors since the early 1990s.

Some improvement in the international policy framework surrounding agricultural trade is expected in the coming years, in particular as a follow-up to the conclusions of the Uruguay Round of GATT negotiations. The recent strengthening of agricultural prices for some of the main export products of the region are an encouraging signal in this context.[44] Prices of coffee, sugar, wheat and soybeans have remained well below the averages of the 1970s and most of the 1980s, however. Also, despite a commitment by many countries to reduce levels of support in agriculture and improve market access, the region will continue to face strong competition for its commodity exports as well as the risk of new forms of protectionism such as sanitary and phytosanitary measures.

Sectoral policies. Along with the rest of the economy, regional policies have progressively emphasized the role of market forces in agriculture as the main mechanisms for resource allocation. This process has imposed the difficult task of redefining the role of the public sector, including in agriculture. As shown by the region's recent experience, radical changes in strategy involve the risk of falling from one extreme to another – in this case, from an excessive presence in productive and market mechanisms to an excessive absence of the public sector.

These issues gain relevance in the context of the generally poor performances of regional agriculture in recent years. Among the various factors behind such trends, what has been the role of the new policy strategies? More specifically, do agriculturists overall, or at least large numbers of them, risk being the great losers of free-market reform? Although this much debated question can only be answered in the longer term, the issue has immediate implications for policy-makers. Without adequate government support, large segments of agriculture, a historically neglected sector in the region, risk losing economic viability for the transition period required until market forces place them on a more efficient and self-reliant long-term footing. Support should focus on improving farm productivity and accelerating the process of

[44] Prices of coffee increased by 10.6 percent, sugar 10 percent, beef 6 percent, rice 8 percent, wheat 8.4 percent and soybeans 3 percent.

modernization. This can be achieved by providing farmers with better infrastructure, extension and training, technical and financial assistance.

An increasing awareness of these problems and needs prompted several countries in the region to strengthen the role of sectoral policies in 1993. This was particularly so with regard to institutional policies and instruments of agricultural support.

One important area of institutional reform, with wide implications for agriculture, was the creation of ministries of the environment in Bolivia, Colombia, El Salvador and Nicaragua. This development is particularly significant not only as a sign of growing recognition of the importance of environmental problems in the region but because it also defines a new and important line of policy action for these governments in the context of the redefinition of the public sector's role. It can also be seen as an indication of the improved economic and political environment for policy-making, to the extent that governments are able to channel significant human and financial resources towards longer-term objectives.

Another area of important institutional developments is the process of regional and subregional integration, which is reviewed in the section Trade arrangements in Latin America and the Caribbean, p. 156.

As regards internal policies related to agricultural support, a number of significant developments took place, particularly in Colombia, Mexico and Argentina. In 1993 the Government of Colombia issued a package of measures designed to promote agricultural development in the coming years. These included: the General Law of Agricultural and Fisheries Development, a ten-year plan of land improvement and reclamation, the establishment of a national system of technological transfer; and the creation of a cooperative institution for agricultural research and the establishment of Colombia International, an institution for export promotion. The new General Law defines a number of norms and regulations for agricultural support. These include the elimination of duties at the source for agricultural services, incentives to capital formation in rural areas and the creation of stabilization funds for agricultural prices, crop insurances and peasant family subsidies.

Other measures of agricultural support included

changes in the system of prices to protect agro-industrial enterprises, minimum import prices to counter the effects of subsidized exports and changes in import licences for certain products that have an impact on livestock production. At the same time, the price stabilization fund for cotton was redesigned with a view to improving its operational efficiency and a special agreement was made with Venezuela for regulating bilateral rice trade. Finally, a tax refund certificate was established for productive activities related to agriculture and fisheries.

A significant new development in the process of policy reforms carried out by the Mexican Government since the late 1980s[45] was the PROCAMPO programme. Introduced in 1993, the programme is expected to align domestic prices of programme commodities to world prices by April 1995. PROCAMPO aims at gradually replacing price supports with direct income payments. Direct support is to be provided to producers who have cultivated the main grains and oilseeds in the last three years. Farmers will be free to switch to more profitable crops in the future. Subsistence farmers, rather than commercial producers, are targeted to receive the direct income support. Under the new programme, the government will make direct payments to farmers based on the number of hectares planted to maize, beans, wheat, rice, cotton, soybeans, safflower, barley, sorghum and coffee. Payments per hectare will be kept constant in real terms for ten years and will be phased out from year 11 to year 15. It is expected that maize land will be converted to wheat, cotton, fruit and vegetable cultivation. Subsistence farmers, who generally had not benefited from the guaranteed price support system, will directly benefit from PROCAMPO. Thus, the programme is expected to mitigate the effect of farm labour migration from rural to urban areas. The budget allocated in 1994 for financing PROCAMPO represents an increase of more than 80 percent relative to producer support in 1993.

Within the framework of the programme "*Argentina en crecimiento* (Argentina in expansion) 1993-1995", a large number of agricultural support policies were announced by the Argentine Government in 1993. In order to improve profitability and promote investment in agriculture, taxes on assets and import duties on capital goods were eliminated; a credit programme was

[45] See *The State of Food and Agriculture 1993.*

introduced, with official and private bank participation, for refinancing agricultural debt at interest rates close to those in international markets; enlarged facilities were provided for agricultural export prefinancing; a new agricultural credit facility, amounting to $200 million, was created for the 1993-1995 period; the Argentine National Bank introduced new lines of supervised credit for the reconversion of agricultural production units to sheep, fruit, vegetables, agro-industrial products and agrotourism. This new policy package also included measures to improve agro-industrial competitiveness, improve agricultural extension and reduce climatic risks. A programme of technical assistance was also introduced to help production reconversion and diversification of about 30 000 small and medium-sized agricultural enterprises.

Trade arrangements in Latin America and the Caribbean

The commitment of many countries to a more open trade regime is evidenced by the recent revitalization of old and new trade arrangements in the region. Inspired in particular by the Enterprise for Americas Initiative (EAI)[46] and the North American Free Trade Agreement (NAFTA), many countries negotiated expanding markets through reciprocal privileged access with neighbouring countries, thereby revitalizing old trade arrangements throughout the region.

Regional cooperation schemes are not new in Latin America and the Caribbean. Many of the groups to promote economic integration and freer trade (see Box 7) were formed in the 1960s (the Andean Pact and the Central America Common Market [CACM]), 1970s (the Caribbean Community and Common Market [CARICOM]), and 1980s (the Latin America Integration Association [ALADI]. NAFTA, which took effect in January 1994, is the latest and by far the largest trading bloc in the region (see Selected issues, p. 74). In addition, many other bilateral agreements have been signed. Nevertheless, until recently limited progress had been made in these schemes because of both short-term constraints associated with the economic crisis and factors of a more structural nature (limited complementarity, inadequate transport and marketing facilities, rigid economic structures and high levels of government intervention).

[46] This is a trade and investment initiative announced by the United States in 1990 and aimed at promoting liberalized regional trade, reducing official debt and increasing foreign investment in Latin America and the Caribbean. Its centrepiece was a proposal to move towards a Western Hemisphere Free Trade Area. However, except for some debt reduction commitment, there was no implementing legislation or budget authority for any of the initiative's goals. Nevertheless, the prospect for increased market access to the United States sent a strong economic signal throughout the region and all but three Latin American and Caribbean countries signed the EAI with the United States.

BOX 7
SELECTED TRADING BLOCS IN LATIN AMERICA AND THE CARIBBEAN

Name	**ANDEAN PACT or ANDEAN GROUP (CARTAGENA AGREEMENT)**
	GDP (1992): $151 billion **GNP per caput (1992): $1 408** **Population (1990): 92 million**
Established	**26 May 1969, effective 16 October 1969**
Objectives	**Encourage harmonious development through economic integration**
Members	**Bolivia, Colombia, Ecuador, Peru and Venezuela** **Associate member: Panama**
Current status	**The Andean Pact's external tariffs are 13.6%, down from 41% in 1989. In 1992, Bolivia, Colombia, Ecuador and Venezuela set up duty-free trade. Peru has reached an FTA separately with Bolivia and Venezuela. Venezuela and Colombia eliminated all tariff and non-tariff barriers in January 1992**
Name	**CARIBBEAN COMMUNITY AND COMMON MARKET (CARICOM)**
	Population (1990): 6 million
Established	**4 July 1973, effective 1 August 1973**
Objectives	**To promote economic integration and development, especially among the less developed countries**
Members	**Antigua and Barbuda, the Bahamas, Barbados, Belize, Dominica, Grenada, Guyana, Jamaica, Montserrat, Saint Kitts and Nevis, Saint Lucia, Saint Vincent and the Grenadines and Trinidad and Tobago** **Associate members: British Virgin Islands, Turks and Caicos Islands** **Observer: Mexico**
Current status	**CARICOM is working towards a single market in 1994. External tariffs are expected to be reduced from 45 to 20% by 1998. CARICOM and Venezuela have signed a preferential trade agreement**

Name	**CENTRAL AMERICA COMMON MARKET (CACM)**
	GDP: $33.3 billion **GDP per caput: $1 143** **Population: 30 million**
Established	13 December 1960, effective 3 June 1961
Objectives	Promote establishment of a Central American common market
Members	Costa Rica, El Salvador, Guatemala, Honduras and Nicaragua
Current status	In 1992, Honduras, Guatemala and El Salvador signed an FTA to eliminate all tariffs. Regional tariff rates range from 5 to 20%, with a 15% common external tariff. In February 1993, the region also established the Central American Integration System (SICA) which functions as a Central American parliament, replacing the Organization of Central American States. The CACM signed an FTA with Venezuela and Colombia in 1993. Mexico also signed an FTA with the CACM in 1992, which will be fully effective by 1996
Name	**CHILE-MEXICO FTA**
	GDP (1992): 1987 $86 billion **GNP per caput (1990): $1 880** **Population (1990): 102 million**
Established	February 1992
Objectives	Promote free trade
Members	Chile and Mexico
Current status	The FTA between the two countries will be fully operational by 1 January 1996
Name	**NORTH AMERICAN FREE TRADE AGREEMENT (NAFTA)**
	GDP (1992): $6.2 trillion **GNP per caput (1992): $16 833** **Population: 370 million**
Established	1 January 1994
Objectives	Promote freer regional trade
Members	Canada, Mexico and the United States
Current status	Implementation of NAFTA began 1 January 1994

Name	LATIN AMERICA INTEGRATION ASSOCIATION (ALADI or LAIA)
	GNP per caput (1990): $1 681 Population: 384 million
Established	12 August 1980, effective 18 March 1981
Objectives	Promote freer regional trade
Members	Argentina, Bolivia, Brazil, Chile, Colombia, Ecuador, Mexico, Paraguay, Peru, Uruguay and Venezuela
Current status	ALADI's slow progress towards integration has led some of its members to pursue bilateral and subregional integration
Name	SOUTHERN COMMON MARKET (MERCOSUR)
	GDP (1992): $485 billion GNP per caput (1992): $2 473 Population: 196 million
Established	26 March 1991
Objectives	Promote regional economic cooperation
Members	Argentina, Brazil, Paraguay and Uruguay
Current status	MERCOSUR members plan to eliminate most trade and investment barriers by the end of 1994. Tariffs are being cut by more than half to reach a 20% ceiling. The common external tariff will enter into force on 1 January 1995

Sources: ECLAC/UN; World Bank; and C. Valdés *et al.* 1993. Overview of US agricultural trade with the Western Hemisphere. In *Western Hemisphere Situation and Outlook Report.* RS-93-2. Washington, DC, ERS/USDA.

Since the beginning of the 1990s, the older groups have renewed their arrangements by securing further integration towards a free trade agreement (FTA) or a customs union. For example, the Andean Pact reduced its external tariffs by more than 40 percent, while two of its members, Colombia and Venezuela, also established the Andean region's first binational customs union in January 1992. As a result, Colombia's exports to Venezuela increased by 30 percent in 1993 while Venezuela's exports to Colombia increased by 20 percent. These older groups are now moving faster towards a common market or an FTA with submembers either within or outside the group. New trading arrangements are the Southern Common Market (MERCOSUR), the Chile-Mexico FTA and the Group of Three (G3) – Mexico, Colombia and Venezuela – which are yet to sign the trade accord. Many trading blocs in the region are customs unions or common markets such as the CACM or MERCOSUR (see Box 7).

MERCOSUR, created in 1991, is the largest trading bloc in Latin America and is second only to NAFTA, with a GDP of $485 billion in 1992 and total population of 196 million. Intratrade within MERCOSUR has significantly increased in recent years, especially trade in grains and animal products for which member countries have a comparative advantage. For example, over one-quarter of Argentina's total trade in 1994 is expected to be with the MERCOSUR countries and three-quarters of that figure should be with Brazil. A major obstacle to progress under the scheme and to the achievement of scheduled targets is the discrepancy between Brazil and other member countries with regard to inflation levels and exchange rate policies. As regards agriculture, Brazil has been practising a more active policy support than its partners in the scheme, although Argentina, as seen above, has also strongly activated its policy intervention in favour of agriculture in recent months.

Following are some recent developments in these regional integration schemes.

- In the context of the G3 (Colombia, Mexico and Venezuela), the Mexican market was opened to important agricultural products originating in Colombia and Venezuela. Within agriculture, this agreement covers 80 percent of all tariffs and

**LATIN AMERICA
AND THE CARIBBEAN**

includes such important products as sugar, flowers, green coffee and tropical fruit.

- The Central American Tariff System entered into force on 1 January 1993. The system is based on the norms of the International Harmonized System.

- A Common External Tariff was adopted by the Andean Pact in 1993. Expected to enter into force shortly, this system foresees external tariff levels of 5, 10, 15 and 20 percent, depending on the level of processing, and agricultural products will benefit from special treatment.

- In MERCOSUR, given the difficulties of meeting the 1 January 1995 deadline for achieving a customs union, it was agreed (Decision No. 13) to revise the exceptions and deadlines for the Common External Tariff for tariff levels between 0 and 20 percent. Member countries are allowed to exclude a number of items from the Common External Tariff, provided tariff rates are gradually aligned to the commonly agreed levels within a six-year period.

In addition, a series of bilateral and multilateral cooperation and free trade pacts have been implemented or are being negotiated. For example, Chile has signed a bilateral agreement with Mexico, Bolivia and Venezuela; Mexico has also signed an FTA with Costa Rica which will go into effect on 1 January 1995; and Bolivia has signed a bilateral agreement with Argentina. On July 1994, 25 countries signed an agreement for the establishment of an Association of Caribbean States, with the objective of creating a new economic zone that would include Colombia, Cuba, Mexico, Venezuela and Central American and Caribbean island states.

BRAZIL

The economy

Since the 1980s, the Brazilian economy has undergone a number of stabilization and adjustment programmes. These included the traditional balance-of-payments stabilization package adopted in 1982, the heterodox Cruzado Plan experience in 1986, the heterodox-cum-orthodox Bresser Plan of 1987, the short-lived Summer Plan in 1988 and finally the Collor Plan in 1990. During this period both inflation rates and GDP growth fluctuated widely and, since 1987, hyperinflation has been a persistent threat.

Agriculture was strongly affected by an adverse economic environment, characterized by deep recession during much of the 1980s as well as by institutional and political instability and strenuous efforts to restore equilibrium in domestic and external macroeconomic balances. Thus, agricultural growth slowed from an average annual rate of 3.4 percent during the 1970s to 2.4 percent during 1981-90. Per caput food production barely increased during the latter period but food imports increased sharply. Agricultural exports stagnated, in marked contrast with the buoyant performance of earlier periods. However, in the context of the major economic difficulties faced by Brazil during the past decade, the overall performance of agriculture was considered remarkable by most analysts. The dynamism of the sector is confirmed by the strong recovery that was achieved during 1991-1994.

Stabilization and adjustment programmes since the 1980s

From 1980 to 1994 there were numerous attempts at stabilization and structural reform. The main concern of macroeconomic policy was to address the increasing – and, after 1982, unsustainable – deficit in external accounts through the standard stabilization programmes advocated by the IMF.

As the current accounts were brought to balance, the Brazilian economy entered into its deepest recession ever, accompanied by inflation rates which rose from 100 percent per annum in 1981/82 to 230 percent in 1983/84.

After 1985, having traversed the most critical phase of external balancing, economic policy focused more

on controlling inflation through a series of heterodox stabilization programmes. The main policy experience during this period was the Cruzado Plan, enforced in February 1986 at a time when monthly inflation reached 28 percent. Along with a monetary reform, all prices, wages and the exchange rate were frozen. The formal mechanisms of price indexation were eliminated. In an attempt to foster economic recovery, credit restrictions were eased and abundant and cheap resources channelled to agriculture in particular. However, underscoring the inconsistency of combining price freezes with expansionist monetary and fiscal policies, inflation accelerated to 26 percent in June 1987.

The Bresser Plan followed; it combined heterodox measures (wage and price freezes) with devaluation and restrictive monetary policy. Confidence in the Plan was soon eroded because the government was unable to reach a satisfactory debt-alleviation agreement with foreign creditors, unable to reduce the public deficit and unable to implement fiscal reform.

In 1989, the government introduced yet another stabilization plan – the Summer Plan – based on a wage-price freeze with a fixed nominal exchange rate anchor and tight monetary policy. However, the stabilizing effects of the Summer Plan lasted only one month. The government, having lost control over public spending, relied entirely on highly profitable short-term public bonds to finance its deficit and prevent hyperinflation.

In March 1990, the more radical Collor Plan introduced an unprecedented liquidity squeeze through a general freeze of bank assets, shortly followed by a price freeze. Simultaneously, a structural reform programme was launched which included the privatization of public sector enterprises, administrative reform, trade liberalization and domestic deregulation. Replacing the crawling peg rate of exchange with a floating exchange rate, strongly affected by central bank operations, was particularly important.

In spite of the liquidity squeeze, which virtually paralysed the economy, prices increased and, by the end of 1990, monthly inflation had reached 20 percent. In January 1991, a new phase of the Plan – Collor II – was introduced. It included a new round of price freezing, de-indexation measures and renewed

restrictive monetary policy,[47] but it was soon abandoned in favour of a market-oriented approach. Stronger tax reform and privatization measures were enforced to address the foremost cause of inflation – the public sector deficit. Other anti-inflationary measures included trade liberalization and even more restrictive monetary policies.[48]

The new government that took over in August 1992 accentuated the market-oriented approach. In February 1994, a new adjustment programme – the Real Plan – was announced, with the notable feature that no price freeze was contemplated, unlike previous plans. The Real Plan was implemented in successive phases: balancing the public budget through fiscal reform; creating a unit reference value (URV) for wages, contracts and prices; and, finally, introducing a new currency (the real) which entered into force on 1 July 1994. Although not legally pegged to the US dollar, since its introduction the URV has in fact followed the variations of the dollar.

It is too early to assess the effectiveness and viability of the Plan, but current expectations are on the whole optimistic. The Plan should help consolidate the macroeconomic improvements achieved in recent months. Although the government was unable to gain approval for the entire fiscal reform, the fiscal deficit is expected to be brought down to zero in 1994. At the same time public debt was reduced to an equivalent 10 percent of GDP, foreign exchange reserves rose to a record $40 billion and the external debt was renegotiated on relatively favourable terms and reduced to 15 percent of GDP. Despite high inflation, Brazil once again attracted international capital. In general, the opening of the economy is expected to help overcome supply bottlenecks and contribute to price stability. Finally, the expected record grain harvest in 1993/94 should help normalize the food supply.

National currency appreciation (an estimated 15 to 20 percent since the early 1990s) is undermining recent gains in export competitiveness, achieved through improved productivity and trade liberalization. Despite this, there is still ample margin for improvement through further productivity gains and tax reductions.

The Plan's impact on agriculture is expected to be positive to the extent that sluggish domestic demand – a major limiting factor to sustained growth of the

---

[47] In spite of the "credibility shock" inflicted by the Collor Plan, the liquidity squeeze restored attractiveness to public bond markets and restored some effectiveness to monetary policy. It also helped reduce public debt sharply.

[48] To some extent, the success of the monetary policy backfired on its main target, inflation, as very high rates of interest attracted a massive inflow of capital which became difficult to manage.

sector – would be sustained by the fall in inflation. Moreover, market liberalization and the reduction of inflation are expected to create a better environment for agricultural investment and more efficient resource allocation.

Role and performance of agriculture

Although agriculture accounts for only 10 percent of GDP, it is a key sector of the Brazilian economy. In addition to its traditional role as a source of income, employment and foreign exchange, agriculture also has important upstream and downstream linkages with industry; it has served as a safety valve for social pressures during crisis periods and has played a positive anti-cyclical role since the 1950s. About 27 percent of the labour force is employed in the agricultural sector and nearly 30 percent of the population still lives in rural areas.

The economic crisis of the early 1980s affected agricultural products in different ways. Animal product output rose by 6.3 percent but crop output fell by 5.1 percent during 1981-83. Domestic market production declined or stagnated but production of cotton, cocoa, coffee, orange juice and sugar cane expanded significantly. This shift towards tradables primarily reflected price incentives arising from real currency devaluation during the first half of the 1980s.

The years 1984 to 1989 were a period of stronger agricultural expansion, reflecting government support, some economic recovery and improved international market conditions for certain Brazilian products. The growth of export products continued, albeit at a slower rate, partly because of currency appreciation. By contrast, staple food production accelerated, particularly rice, maize and potatoes. Wheat production expanded most rapidly during this period (12.6 percent per annum).

This overall favourable growth halted abruptly in 1990-1991. Agricultural output fell by 3.7 percent in 1990 (with crops declining as much as 10 percent) and did not recover in 1991. Bad weather played a role but the 1990 shortfall also reflected economic deterioration in the second half of 1989 and the negative impact of the Collor Plan, adopted in March 1990. Rice, bean, maize, cotton and sugar cane production recovered in 1991. However, this was largely offset by a sharp fall in

BOX 8
EMERGENCY AGRARIAN REFORM PROGRAMME

The concentration of landownership continues to be a fundamental problem in Brazilian agriculture. About 50 percent of all farms are small and occupy 2.2 percent of agricultural land; the upper 5 percent of the total are large farms which occupy 69.2 percent of the total land. Such uneven land distribution, together with macroeconomic and sectoral policies that discriminated against family production, resulted in a bipolar modern and traditional agriculture.

Successive governments introduced programmes of agrarian reform. Between 1979 and 1993, about 325 000 families received land from state and federal authorities. Between 1985 and 1991, the federal government alone created 524 settlements in an area covering 4.7 million ha and benefiting 94 000 families.

A recent study, carried out jointly by FAO and the Brazilian Ministry of Agriculture, Supplies and Land Reform,[1] presents a relatively positive assessment of the agrarian reform efforts in Brazil since 1985. In particular, it concludes that 90 percent of those who benefited from reform saw a marked improvement in their welfare and income situation. Their average family income, equivalent to 3.7 times the minimum wage, is close to the national average of 3.82 times the minimum wage.

Despite these achievements, social pressure from the landless poor has mounted in recent years. About 20 000 landless families are camped precariously alongside highways and illegal land occupation has increased considerably.

These problems prompted the government to introduce in March 1993 an Emergency Agrarian Reform Programme with ambitious objectives: through a Special Agrarian Reform Credit Programme, to provide financial support to about 100 000 small producers who had received land since 1986; and to settle 120 000 families on 5 million ha within 1993 and 1994.

Unlike previous plans aimed at reforming large farm agrarian units, this emergency programme reinforces family ownership. Following this approach, policy action is to be implemented in areas facing particular problems of poverty or social tension by utilizing state-owned or unoccupied land. Despite major financial and institutional problems, the objectives defined for 1993 have been achieved and 20 000 families have been settled.

---

[1] Ministry of Agriculture, Supplies and Land Reform and Instituto Nacional de Colonização e Reforma Agraria (INCRA). Programa Emergencial de Reforma Agraria. 1993. Brasilia.

soybean production (from 19.8 million tonnes in 1990 to 14.9 million tonnes in 1991), caused by credit restrictions and pessimistic market expectations.

After the short 1990-1991 crisis, agriculture resumed growth, animal production rose by 5.3 percent and crop output by 6.5 percent in 1992. Maize output increased by 29 percent, to a record 30.5 million tonnes and soybean production recovered somewhat. Improved international market conditions and renewed government support achieved high levels of agricultural production in 1993 despite dramatic reductions in output of cotton and wheat which were negatively affected by the liberalization of trade and a policy shift that accorded less priority to agricultural self-sufficiency. Preliminary official estimates indicate an all-time record for the 1993/94 grain harvest.

Agricultural exports have fluctuated but overall there has been a virtual stagnation, resulting in a marked decline in the sector's share of total exports (from 45 percent in 1980 to 39 percent in 1985 and 28 percent in 1993). Nevertheless, Brazil's agricultural exports ($10.4 billion in 1993) still account for more than 5 percent of the world's total.

Export stagnation was due in part to government policies that discriminated against exports of unprocessed agricultural products. Yet international markets and prices were generally depressed, particularly for tropical products, of which Brazil is traditionally a major producer. Depressed prices defeated efforts to increase export earnings by expanding the volume of agricultural exports. Nevertheless, the sector showed flexibility in adjusting production patterns to market conditions. In particular, the 1980s saw a significant expansion in exports of non-traditional and agroprocessed products, which largely compensated for the decline in traditional exports.

Agricultural products were traditionally a minor import item until 1988, when food imports increased steeply (reaching a peak $3.1 billion in 1991 but falling to $2.1 billion in 1993). This reflected a shift in the domestic production mix, from domestic food staples towards tradables, and the liberalization of trade, particularly of wheat for which natural and climatic constraints impose a large degree of external dependence.

Even favourable agricultural sector performances

have not resulted in commensurate gains at the farm level. Agricultural prices and farmers' incomes have lagged behind general inflation and compared unfavourably with prices and incomes of other sectors. Nominal farm prices deflated by the consumer price index indicate a real price decline, particularly after 1986. Overall, real agricultural prices in the early 1990s had fallen to half their level of ten years earlier.[49] More recently, real prices showed some recovery but their sustainability will depend mainly on the success of the Real Plan. Also, there was a clear inverse relationship between inflation rates and the terms of trade of agriculture and industry after 1986.[50]

A study[51] comparing the evolution of agricultural and industrial prices since 1970 revealed that: i) wholesale agricultural prices were falling and industrial prices were increasing; ii) producer prices had fallen for both domestic and exportable agricultural goods; iii) agricultural prices were more unstable than industrial prices at both wholesale and producer levels; and iv) agricultural price instability had been accentuated at both levels during the second half of the 1980s, indicating increased uncertainty and risk. Another recent study[52] concluded that gross income from Brazil's 20 main crops declined steadily from the second half of the 1980s, except for 1988 and 1991.

All these studies concur that the negative impact of depressed and unstable market conditions, the adverse macroeconomic environment and the effect of stabilization measures more than cancelled out productivity gains and benefits from lower real prices of fertilizers, agrochemicals and fuels.

Sectoral policies in the context of macroeconomic adjustment

Until the debt crisis in the early 1980s, Brazil's macroeconomic policies primarily emphasized industry-led rapid growth. Subsequently, policy-makers were forced to shift priorities in favour of macroeconomic stabilization. Debt-related financial constraints and a deteriorating domestic and international economic environment combined to change overall and sectoral policies' objectives and instruments. Sectoral policies, which during the 1970s had promoted agricultural modernization by using seemingly unlimited financial transfers, became

[49] I. Goldin and G.C. Rezende. 1993. *A Agricultura brasileira na década de 80: crescimento numa economia en crise.* IPEA Serie No. 138. Rio de Janeiro, IPEA.

[50] G.C. Rezende. 1992. Do Cruzado ao Plano Collor: os planos de estabilização e a agricultura. *Revista de Economia Política,* 12(2): 106-125.

[51] C. Contador and L.C.A. Silva Jr. 1992. Inflação, preçosrelativos e risco na agricultura: algumas notas. *Anais do XXX Congresso Brasileiro de Economia e Sociologia Rural.* Brasilia, SOBER.

[52] B.D. Albuquerque. 1993. Brasil: la política de comercio exterior y el sector agropecuario. *In* FAO. *Políticas de desarrollo de las exportaciones en países seleccionados de América Latina.* Documento RLAC/93/09-COEX-48. Santiago.

subordinate to macroeconomic objectives and constraints.

In the new context, agricultural policies also became less development-oriented and more ad hoc in response to short-term stabilization or sectoral concerns. Prior to 1987, there was a high degree of government intervention in agricultural markets, through both sector-specific and trade policy instruments. Despite reduced resources and other constraints linked to the restrictive fiscal and monetary environment, agricultural policies attempted to balance sectoral objectives – such as increasing food production – with macroeconomic objectives, particularly the generation of export earnings and price stabilization. Stabilization objectives and the ad hoc nature of interventions created inefficiencies and distortions. Nevertheless, until the 1987/88 harvest season, support policies did help farmers overcome the effects of unfavourable macroeconomic and market conditions.

During 1988-1991, attempts were made to deregulate and liberalize, first the domestic agricultural markets and, after 1990, foreign trade. Some market intervention mechanisms were deactivated (for coffee, wheat, cocoa and sugar cane) and, although minimum price mechanisms continued to exist, they were ineffective.

The unfavourable macroeconomic environment, together with liberalization measures aimed at short-term stabilization, depressed agricultural output which consequently stagnated during 1990-1991. After 1991, the government continued with the liberalization strategy adopted in 1990 but also partially reactivated sectoral policy instruments to cope with the agricultural crisis and its negative effects on the stabilization effort.

Rural credit. Before the crisis of the early 1980s, the government highly subsidized rural credit, the main instrument used to promote agricultural modernization and strengthen the processing, agricultural input and equipment industries. Since then, rural credit supply fell dramatically, from $26.8 billion in 1979 to $6.1 billion in 1991 and around $8 billion in both 1992 and 1993. Official lending continues to account for the bulk of agricultural loans (more than 82 percent in 1992).

Not only was rural credit supply sharply reduced but also lending conditions and regulations became more restrictive and were adjusted almost yearly throughout

the period 1980-1993. Within the limits allowed by budgetary constraints, credit policies still attempted to compensate farmers for the negative impacts of macroeconomic policies and to direct production decisions in the light of short-term market requirements.

Reducing rural credit subsidies has been a policy goal since the early 1980s. In 1981, rural credit interest rates were only partially indexed to compensate for inflation[53] but, when inflation accelerated, real interest rates became progressively negative. Except for short periods, this has not happened since 1984 when rural credit became fully indexed to general inflation. Although interest rates for rural credit have been progressively raised, they have remained significantly below commercial bank rates.

From 1984 to 1987, preferential real interest rates ranged between 3 and 7 percent, depending on the crop, region and farm size. Small staple producers enjoyed better conditions than large producers and usually had 100 percent of production costs funded under the National Rural Credit System (SNCR). After the Summer Plan in January 1988, real interest rates were raised to 12 percent per year and further to a historical maximum 18 percent per year in 1990/91, at the time of the major liquidity squeeze imposed by the Collor Plan. Two consecutive years of sectoral recession and poor prospects for the 1991/92 season caused the government to announce an emergency "agricultural package" in October 1991. Among measures to stimulate recovery, real interest rates were reduced to 12 and 9 percent for large and small producers, respectively.[54] These rates were still in force for the 1993/94 crop season.

Although the government introduced measures to prevent it, the excessive concentration of credit in large farms continued; they were main beneficiaries of SNCR funding at preferential rates of interest. In 1990, 27 percent of SNCR resources went to small producers, 18.7 percent to medium-sized farmers and 33.6 percent to large farmers.

A study covering the period 1987-1992 suggests that, for seven out of ten crops considered, producer prices lagged behind general inflation rates but increased faster than rural credit costs.[55] This interesting result should be read with caution because monetary correction is automatic and daily but producer prices

---

[53] The nominal value of loans was indexed to a given percentage of changes in the price of government bonds (40 percent for small producers and 60 percent for medium and large producers). Moreover, interest rates remained fixed. After 1984, the outstanding value of loans was adjusted to the general price index or other financial indicators.

[54] Such a difference in interest rate levels was irrelevant in the context of high inflation.

[55] Cotton, rice, beans, orange, cassava, maize and soybeans; prices of cocoa, coffee and wheat increased less than financial costs (CONAB, Anexo 4, CC 93/341).

are linked to market fluctuations. In fact, the financial costs of borrowing can be far greater than the revenues from crop sales because inflation and agricultural prices are not directly linked.

In 1993, 12 percent of farmer borrowers were in arrears compared with an average 2.5 percent in 1981-88. The steep increase seems to indicate an emerging acute financial problem which could severely hamper agricultural growth in the coming years. Between 1986 and 1988, debt forgiveness cost the Banco do Brazil approximately $455 million. Despite this, a recent Banco do Brazil report indicates that 51 000 producers are in arrears amounting to $615 million; 10 percent of 1993 arrears have already been written off by the Bank in 1994. Those in arrears are: large producers, 85 percent; very small producers, 1 percent; and small producers, 8 percent. The report minimizes the role of credit diversion to other uses in the increase of arrears and blames instead the unstable macroeconomic context; competitive losses, particularly in wheat and cotton production; depressed agricultural prices; and a reduction of domestic consumption.

Since 1986, the government has been searching for new non-inflationary sources of funding and encouraging greater private sector participation in agricultural financing. Particularly successful was the savings account "Caderneta Verde" which accounted for nearly half of total rural lending in 1993. However, this was not enough to offset the overall decrease in rural credit. Since 1990, producers have been benefiting from the Constitutional Regional Development Fund (Fundo Constitucional), which provides long-term investment loans at preferential rates, and from the inclusion of agriculture in the FINAME programme, run by the Economic and Social Development Bank (BNDES).

To reduce uncertainty arising from high inflation, Brazilian farmers pressured the government to adopt the "product equivalence" concept which had been established but never implemented in the 1990 farm bill. The concept means that the lending agency bases the loan value on the product value. If, for instance, a bean producer borrows funds equivalent to 100 bags of beans, the repayment will be the current value of 100 bags, plus interest. This system protects farmers but

requires government subsidization for the difference between the product's market value and the loan's real financial cost. This difference can be high in years of abundant crops and falling prices. Nevertheless, for 1993/94 the government has agreed to introduce product equivalence loans for six crops (cotton, cassava, rice, beans, maize and wheat) up to a limit of approximately $200 000. The sector has responded enthusiastically, particularly since the outlook is for a record grain harvest. The follow-up to this interesting experiment deserves monitoring.

Credit, investment and agricultural performance.
Agricultural investment was affected negatively by changes in the volume and terms of rural credit. However, the extent of the decline in agricultural investment and the ultimate effects on agricultural growth are difficult to assess. Available data indicate falling tractor and other equipment purchases, a slow-down in land reclamation on the dynamic central-western frontier, reduced fertilizer consumption and lower investment in soil upgrading and conservation. Nevertheless, contrary to analysts' forecasts, the drop in subsidized credit and investment during the 1980s did not seem to depress agricultural performance. There are several possible explanations for this. Prior to the squeeze, considerable subsidized rural credit had been diverted to non-agricultural purposes; therefore, perhaps the drop in credit affected agriculture less severely than available data suggest. Another possible explanation is that, in view of the reduced access to credit and the risks of contracting indexed loans in periods of high and volatile inflation, many large and medium-sized producers increased self-financing, thus upholding investment and growth.

Minimum price programme. Since the early 1980s, minimum prices have gradually replaced rural credit as the main instrument for stimulating sectoral growth and steering production towards priority crops, particularly basic foodstuffs. Minimum prices have proved to be a powerful influence on crop levels and composition.

Until the early 1980s, the minimum price programme (MPP) was an ineffective influence on producers' decisions because minimum prices were usually considerably lower than market prices.

Minimum prices were normally fixed before the planting season, taking into account the government's expectations of future inflation. However, actual inflation always exceeded expectations and there was great uncertainty about the real value of minimum prices during the harvest season.

In 1981, the government replaced the fixed minimum price with an inflation-indexed base price. For the crop seasons 1983/84 and 1984/85, minimum prices were raised to compensate for reduced official rural credit and for losses incurred from real devaluation. Farmers responded positively by expanding crop output (by 8.5 and 13.1 percent in 1984 and 1985, respectively) and changing the production mix. In fact, the recovery from the 1981-1983 crisis was initially led by crops that had been stimulated by the MPP, such as rice, maize, cotton, beans and soybeans.

To a certain extent, objective technical criteria influenced the determining of minimum prices, as they were generally expected to cover variable costs of production. In practice, price definition was primarily a political exercise because farm needs tended to be subordinated to Treasury concerns. This caused wide fluctuations in minimum prices during the decade, although two broad tendencies did emerge: a general increase from 1981 to 1986 and a sharp decline after 1987. Minimum prices of all products fell to a record low in 1990/91.[56]

Following the 1990-1991 crop shortfall, the government decided to reactivate the MPP on a selective basis by targeting fewer crops (rice, maize and beans) and small and medium-sized producers. In 1993, the MPP was extended to other crops and all producers. Since 1992, the government has fixed more attractive minimum support prices for basic foodstuffs but it has been very slow to purchase products at those support levels. This has created friction between the government and the farmers' association, one of the strongest pressure groups in the country.

The importance of the MPP can be broadly assessed from the extent of producers' utilization of the two MPP instruments: Federal Government Loans (EGF) and Federal Government Acquisition (AGF). During 1980-87, nearly 80 percent of cotton production was either purchased by the government at a guaranteed minimum price or stocked under an EGF. For rice,

[56] Taking as the base period 1981 = 100, real minimum prices for the main crops in 1990 and 1991 were, respectively: 40 and 47 (cotton); 38 and 43 (rice); 51 and 60 (beans); 57 and 59 (maize); 42 and 48 (soybeans).

approximately 50 percent of production in 1985-88 was covered by the MPP. In some years, maize, soybeans and beans were also extensively covered.

During 1981-88, under the MPP, grain production increased rapidly in the central-western (10.8 percent) and northern (7.3 percent) frontiers and a significant proportion of output benefited from the MPP which fixed guaranteed minimum prices without adjusting for the distance from farm to market and related transportation costs.

Overall, the MPP played a significant positive role in agricultural markets until the 1987/88 crop – when the system lost effectiveness and credibility. With all their shortcomings, inflation-indexed guaranteed minimum prices did grant producers some protection against price risks. They also provided basic signals for resource allocation, which the market was unable to provide in the highly unstable economic environment of the 1980s.

Government intervention in marketing
Traditionally, the Brazilian Government has been extensively involved in all activities related to the purchasing, transportation, distribution and external trade of agricultural products but the shortcomings of such intervention became increasingly evident during the critical decade of the 1980s. Particularly after 1986, instead of providing market and price guarantees, government policies became an additional source of uncertainty, which affected not only the more direct targets of policy action – producers and consumers – but also the whole marketing chain.

Private grain stockholding was also constrained by the unfavourable economic and market environment. Depressed markets, high and unpredictable inflation, restrictive monetary policy, marketing credit shortages and the high profitability of public bonds and other short-term financial assets all contributed to shrinking the grain stockholding market. Under these conditions, the government became the main grain purchaser, particularly in the frontier zones.

As a result, the government accumulated large stocks of grain, used mainly to control food prices. However, public sector stock management was inefficient and hardly conducive to market equilibrium. The financial burden of stockholding was increased by transportation

costs from the frontier zones and sales at subsidized prices. In fact, in 1985-88 market intervention accounted for an average 80 percent of total government expenditure in agriculture. There were also important wastes because of storage problems as well as poor public sector handling and controlling capacity.[57] Since 1987, when the government could no longer honour its procurement commitments at the minimum price and sustain the MPP, it began withdrawing from agricultural markets.

In an attempt to discipline and liberalize agricultural markets, foster private sector participation in grain stockholding and reduce expenditures, in 1988 the government defined and introduced the "rules of intervention". Under these, government procurement only took place when agricultural market prices exceeded intervention (ceiling) prices for 15 consecutive days. Moreover, procured commodities could only be sold in the market at break-even prices that covered storage costs. Initially, these liberalization rules were limited to selected products (rice, maize, cotton, soybeans and beans), but they were later extended to beef and wheat.

The 1991 farm bill continued to emphasize the government's role in ensuring food security and price stability but, clearly, its main thrust was freeing agricultural markets from government intervention.

Market deregulation measures included dismantling, in 1991, the government's 30-year monopoly of wheat imports as well as the liberalization of the milling industry which was formerly dominated by a few millers through a government-managed quota system. The Sugar and Alcohol Institute and the Brazilian Coffee Institute were also dismantled. Although the government continued to control sugar trade and alcohol production, the coffee industry was totally deregulated.

Foreign exchange policies and agricultural markets

Foreign exchange and trade policies played a contradictory role in determining real agricultural prices and levels and patterns of agricultural production.

During most of the 1980s, Brazil operated a policy of periodic "mini-devaluations", combined with a number of formal real devaluations of the currency. These policies caused pronounced fluctuations in the real rate

---

[57] In 1988 the government agency responsible for the handling of stocks estimated annual losses of 4 percent.

of exchange but, until the mid-1980s, by and large maintained purchasing power parity *vis-à-vis* the currencies of industrial countries. However, the real exchange rate appreciated markedly after 1985. Although this tendency has subsided in recent years, most estimates still pointed to a 15 to 20 percent overvaluation of the currency in 1993.

The currency depreciation during the first half of the 1980s produced conflicting results. Real devaluations reduced the negative impact of declining agricultural export prices and mini-devaluations reduced monetary instability. But domestic market producers, who were already hurt by stagnating demand, paid more for the imported component of their production requisites. At the same time, import substitution opportunities for domestic producers were to a large extent nullified by ad hoc government food import decisions and price interventions.

The sharp appreciation in the rate of exchange after 1985 had opposing effects. It diminished the competitiveness of tradable crops so that, even though output growth remained generally robust for these crops, the export sector suffered for many years. This problem became particularly acute in 1990 and 1991, when the inflation-indexed exchange rate was replaced by a managed, floating foreign exchange market. During this period, producers of tradables were exposed to the risks of unpredictable exchange rates without much possibility, at least initially, of hedging against them. This contributed to a major extent to the catastrophic agricultural production shortfall in 1990-1991.

Since 1992, central bank interventions in foreign exchange markets have been successfully attempting to set monetary goals compatible with real exchange rate stability.

Trade policies. Traditionally, Brazil's trade policies have emphasized supporting local industry, including agroprocessing; ensuring an adequate supply of food and agricultural products to the domestic market; and increasing and diversifying exports. To this end, the government has operated a wide range of instruments, including trade bans and restrictions, tariff barriers, export and import licensing and export subsidies. Such policies were vigorously implemented until the early

1980s and, although their net effect is difficult to ascertain, most assessments indicate that they were detrimental to agriculture.

During the 1980s, trade policies were redefined in the light of pressing short-term stabilization concerns. For agriculture, this shift meant even more sectoral neglect and it was often a source of confusing market signals and inconsistent policy action. Thus, food imports were allowed at times when the domestic market was unable to absorb even domestic supply; and export incentives or restrictions were sometimes imposed, ignoring the interests or needs of farmers, industries and consumers.[58]

In 1987, the government began gradually liberalizing agricultural exports. Nevertheless, it was not until 1990 that a major trade reform was introduced. The main thrust of the reform was to move away from quantitative restrictions and to establish a tariff system that, while being compatible with GATT and MERCOSUR agreements, could also be used as a means for productive restructuring and controlling inflationary pressures. The reform virtually eliminated administrative and quantitative trade restrictions, simplified administrative trade procedures and eliminated export taxes. Tariffs were significantly reduced, from an average 51 percent in 1988 to 25.3 percent in 1991. The liberalization process has been accelerated in recent years: by early 1994, maximum rates on agricultural imports were 10 percent, except for milk and milk powder (20 percent) and rice (15 percent). Import tariffs on agricultural inputs were also sharply reduced, ranging from 0 (most fertilizer components) to 20 percent (farm equipment and tractors) in 1993. Tariffs on agricultural imports from MERCOSUR partners range from 0 to 5 percent. Overall, nominal rates of protection in 1992 varied from -47 percent (maize) to 8.5 percent (cotton).[59]

It is too early to assess the net effects of liberalization on agriculture. On the one hand, at least in 1990 and 1991 it is likely that food imports accentuated the problems agriculture was facing, particularly since the Collor Plan. On the other hand, farmers benefited from tariff reductions for agricultural inputs and equipment, which allowed the sector to increase its productivity and partly compensated for the negative effects of the overvaluation.

[58] For instance, in 1982/83 a major crop shortfall coincided with a large expansion of exports at the expense of domestic supply; in 1986, exports of beef and poultry meat were restricted with no regard for long-term contracts between the export industry and traditional clients, particularly in the Near East. Poultry exports were severely hampered and never recovered their previous levels.

[59] World Bank (LATAG) Surveillance Project.

Financial markets, inflation and agriculture

In an economic and financial environment dominated by risk and uncertainty, open market operations constituted an effective system to convert assets into liquidity almost instantaneously. Through an increasingly refined use of this mechanism, money holders were able to achieve a large degree of financial safety and profitability.

The development of open market operations had pervasive implications for agriculture through the linkages with inflation, financial markets and agricultural prices and incomes. These interfaces are too complex to be covered here in detail, but some of the main issues are highlighted.

In the short term, producer prices have been strongly affected by changes in demand for stockholding, itself strongly affected by the inflationary environment.[60]

During periods of high inflation and uncertainty the attractiveness of holding indexed, profitable and highly liquid financial assets increases. Thus, many producers opted to sell part of their crop at low prices immediately after harvest, expecting to compensate for the foregone gains by investing the proceeds of their sales in the financial market. Private stockholders and processing industries also reduced demand for stockholding.

Financial markets were even more attractive considering the "imperfect indexation" of agricultural prices. Although industrial prices adjusted almost continuously to both past and expected inflation, agricultural producer prices have tended to be unstable and lag behind other prices, particularly during harvest seasons.

It is only logical that producers with surpluses have opted for a promising financial market rather than to face very unstable and uncertain markets for their crops. To some extent, the farmers' propensity to "sell off" their crops right after harvest and rush to the government bond market was induced by their precarious financial condition which prevented them from holding stocks. While this practice might have protected some farmers, it also depressed agricultural prices during postharvest periods when most farmers sell the bulk of their crops. These opposing effects exemplify the simultaneous crisis and prosperity seen in different segments of Brazilian agriculture during the past decade.

[60] Conventional portfolio theory would indicate that the higher the expected rate of inflation, the faster agents would run away from money and the more they would prefer to hold real assets, including agricultural commodities. On the other hand, the higher the rate of interest on government bonds, the more agents would want to hold them.

BOX 9
SOCIAL PROBLEMS IN BRAZIL

Although per caput GDP levels (around $2 500 in the early 1990s) place Brazil among the upper middle-income economies, the country's distribution of wealth, productive resources and access to social services is extremely unbalanced. About 45 million people, or nearly one-third of the population, are estimated to be below absolute poverty levels (i.e. per caput family income is one-fourth or less of the minimum legal salary).

Absolute poverty, formerly a predominant rural problem, increasingly affected cities during the critical decade of the 1980s; by 1988, approximately half of the destitute were estimated to live in urban areas.

Such a high incidence of poverty has multiple consequences. About 67 percent of the population consumes less than the minimum average 2 400 calories per day recommended by FAO and WHO.[1] Child mortality – 64 per 1 000 births – is the third highest in Latin America and the Caribbean, after those of Honduras and Bolivia.

An estimated 12 percent of urban and 44 percent of rural populations do not have adequate access to drinking-water. About 10 percent of the entire population is estimated to suffer from physical and/or mental forms of permanent or temporary disability.[2]

Only about 59 percent of young people between the ages of ten and 17 are full-time students; 12 percent are employed part-time and 18 percent are full-time workers (working more than 40 hours weekly). Approximately 500 000 girls (under the age of 19) are prostitutes.

Working conditions, especially in the countryside, are harsh for many labourers. In 1980[3] the working time for 35 percent

---

[1] It is estimated that, by the year 2000, about 120 million tonnes of cereals, pulses and soybeans will be needed yearly to cover the nutritional gap, taking into account the expected population increase. This is almost twice the current domestic production levels of these commodities.

[2] According to WHO, 70 percent of such disabilities could be avoided by simple preventive and care measures such as vaccination, ante- and postnatal assistance and health education.

[3] Although complete information is not available for more recent years, indications are that labour conditions may have actually worsened as a consequence of the economic crisis of the 1980s.

of rural workers was at least 49 hours weekly, while the average wage for 60 percent of those working 40 or more hours was below the minimum wage. Furthermore, over 80 percent of rural workers did not have a work contract or social security coverage.

A striking sign of Brazil's socio-geographic distortions is the 11-year difference in average life expectancy between populations in the northeast, historically a depressed region, and those of the more economically dynamic southern region.

Conclusions

For Brazil the 1980s have been a period of extraordinary economic turbulence and a strenuous search for an appropriate policy mix leading to both successes and failures. Overall, the growth rate has been disappointing and the inflation rate catastrophic. The crisis, and measures to cope with it, have affected all sectors and economic activities. Despite this, agriculture has shown a remarkable capacity to resurface in the most adverse circumstances. This has been partly due to the structural and inertial qualities of agriculture, which render it less vulnerable to economic, market and policy shocks than other sectors; but it has also been due to circumstances specific to Brazilian agriculture – its immense territory and rich resource base.

There are also other equally important factors, among which policy. For most of the period – broadly speaking, until 1987 – government sectoral support programmes, despite their shortcomings and inconsistencies, provided an effective shelter for those farmers who had access to them. After 1987, the withdrawal of government support in a context of financial restrictiveness and loss of policy credibility resulted in a deterioration of agricultural conditions which culminated in the short 1990-1991 crisis. However, agriculture subsequently recovered, assisted by the recovery of domestic and export markets; reduced risks, owing to price controls and government market intervention; and more clearly defined and credible "rules of the game". Renewed government support also helped.

Another factor is agricultural self-financing. Despite high inflation and inimical economic conditions during the 1980s, farmers' reduced reliance on loans and their ability to self-finance their investment and maintain reasonably dynamic rates of sectoral growth are striking signs of the strength and potential of Brazilian agriculture. Nevertheless, self-financing would not have been possible in the absence of minimum guarantees offered by sectoral support programmes, particularly minimum prices, and the financial opportunities offered by government bond markets.

While agriculture has responded well to government support and changing market opportunities, its development has also shown limitations. First, not all

farmers have been able to benefit from government support or market and financial opportunities. In the same vein, the benefits of agricultural growth have been uneven across types of crop and regions and categories of producers, and major efforts remain to be made to overcome the structural imbalances that still characterize the rural sector. All evidence indicates that, during the past decade, Brazil's already notoriously inequitable pattern of productive assets and income distribution has become even more pronounced.

The trend towards declining food self-sufficiency can be considered anomalous, in view of Brazil's rich endowments for agriculture and the precarious nutritional status of large segments of its population.

Although it can be argued that emphasis on export agriculture can also help finance food imports, possibly in a more cost-efficient way, it is doubtful whether such reasoning can be applied to a country with Brazil's current and potential comparative advantages for food production, and whether low-income food consumers will benefit from this process in the long term.

The responsiveness of producers to policy and market incentives, even during the particularly difficult decade of the 1980s, and the recovery in agricultural production after 1990-1991 augur well. The gradual resurfacing from the economic crisis and the emerging liberal policy environment should create unprecedented opportunities for future growth in agriculture. In the new market-oriented framework, sectoral support policies are expected to emphasize the provision, particularly to small farmers, of basic conditions for overall sectoral development, such as infrastructure, technology, rural extension and education, rather than short-term direct support.

NEAR EAST AND NORTH AFRICA

REGIONAL OVERVIEW
Economic and agricultural performance in 1993

The Near East and North Africa region is entering a demanding period of economic adjustment, in the face of lower oil prices, widening budget deficits, balance-of-payments difficulties and unsettled political issues. The economies of many of the region's countries have been buffeted by a sharp and prolonged decline in petroleum prices, their principal source of foreign exchange. Reduced petroleum earnings forced many of the region's petroleum exporters to cut back spending and study new ways of raising revenues. Some countries have also had to tackle increasingly daunting debt-service obligations. Different remedies are being applied, including debt rescheduling and export diversification. In the case of Saudi Arabia, some pressure has been lifted by stretching out payments schedules. The Islamic Republic of Iran has persuaded its creditors to reschedule debts and Algeria is moving towards a multilateral rescheduling.

Some countries made substantial economic progress but faced increasingly unmanageable inflation rates and growing deficits in their balance of trade and often in their current accounts. Among these were Turkey, Iran and Algeria.

Hopes were raised by the signing of the long-awaited peace agreement between Israel and its Palestinian neighbours. The Syrian Arab Republic, Jordan and Lebanon moved ahead in attempting to reconcile their historical differences with Israel.

The region was marked by civil unrest which bit into foreign exchange earnings and the tourist industry, particularly in Egypt. In Algeria, violence caused the exodus of many foreigners and slowed investment in an already dismal economic climate.

Agriculture fared well in most countries in 1993, with the exception of Morocco and Algeria, which suffered damaging droughts. The region's index of agricultural production rose to 155 in 1992 (1979-81 = 100), with per caput production rising to 113. Growth in output has generally enabled regional food production to keep pace with population growth, except for weather-induced fluctuations. Most countries

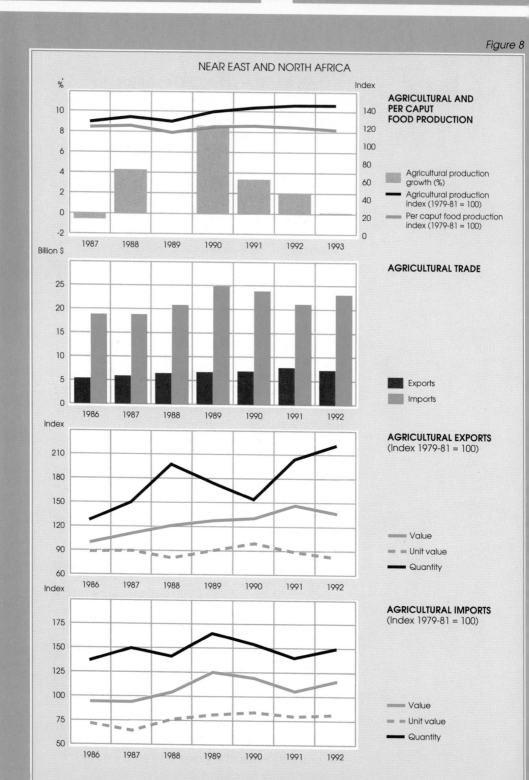

Figure 8

NEAR EAST AND NORTH AFRICA

AGRICULTURAL AND PER CAPUT FOOD PRODUCTION

Agricultural production growth (%)
Agricultural production index (1979-81 = 100)
Per caput food production index (1979-81 = 100)

AGRICULTURAL TRADE

Exports
Imports

AGRICULTURAL EXPORTS
(Index 1979-81 = 100)

Value
Unit value
Quantity

AGRICULTURAL IMPORTS
(Index 1979-81 = 100)

Value
Unit value
Quantity

Source: FAO

**NEAR EAST
AND NORTH AFRICA**

achieved substantial gains in food production; the index
stood at 153, with per caput food production at 112
(1979-81 = 100). Per caput caloric intake in the region
rose by 3.8 percent between 1981 and 1990 to an
estimated 2 928 calories.

Morocco, one of the region's largest agricultural
producers, suffered its second consecutive major
drought in 1993, necessitating substantial and higher
than normal grain imports. Algeria's cereal output was
1.9 million tonnes which reflected the severity of a
drought in the western region and necessitated imports
of 5.2 million tonnes, a 24 percent increase over 1992.
In Egypt, changing price signals and the lifting of
planting controls resulted in a substantial shift in crop
mix since 1986. As a result of the adoption of high-
yielding varieties (HYV) over the past decade, wheat
yields have risen by nearly 50 percent, wheat area by
nearly 80 percent and output by 172 percent.

Iraq's food situation continues to deteriorate from
levels prevailing before the Persian Gulf conflict.
Revenue losses resulting from the UN embargo on Iraqi
oil exports have caused a steep reduction in agricultural
imports, leading to a precipitous decline in the output
of livestock products and little gain for overall crop
production. This caused a sharp increase in food costs,
reducing the average daily per caput caloric intake from
3 250 in 1990 to about one-third less in 1993.

In Iran, the agricultural sector's performance over the
last five years (ending in 1993) was more stable than the
rest of the economy. Following a decline of 2.5 percent
in 1988/89 because of drought, the sector's output rose
by an average of 5.3 percent in the four-year period
ending in 1992/93. In Saudi Arabia, the spectacular
growth in the agricultural sector has been a result of a
vigorous price support policy and other incentives as
well as the adoption of modern cultivation techniques.
However, a shift is occurring in the grains sector
because the government is reducing the extraordinarily
high price supports and subsidies which nevertheless
remain far above global wheat and barley prices.

In Afghanistan, shortages of agricultural inputs,
damage to irrigation networks and insecurity – the
results of a lingering civil war – continue to limit
agricultural production throughout the country. Total
cereals output in 1993 was estimated to be 2.5 million
tonnes, somewhat higher than in 1992 but still below

normal. The indices of both agricultural and food production have continued their downward spiral, falling to below 80 (1979-81 = 100) in 1993. Staple food prices remain high relative to earnings. The miserable food situation, resulting from successive below normal cereal harvests and the return of hundreds of thousands of refugees, was further exacerbated in 1993/94 by poor winter conditions.

In the Sudan, the civil war and the weather dictate the performance of the agricultural sector which accounts for one-third of the GDP. In the late 1980s, the Sudanese economy was characterized by very low growth, high government expenditures, triple-digit inflation and a widening trade deficit. In 1991, the government implemented a three-year recovery programme, which aimed at deregulating price and profit controls, privatizing government parastatals, lifting fuel and food subsidies, liberalizing the trade environment and stabilizing the exchange rate. Although the economy has shown signs of recovery since the implementation of these reforms, many problems remain, including large trade imbalances and budget deficits.

In Lebanon, past conflicts have taken a heavy toll on the country's infrastructure, financial markets, labour and capital. Like other sectors, agriculture has suffered heavily, including from neglect of tree crops, livestock losses and the destruction of storage facilities. However, recent years have seen a remarkable recovery and growth of the sector. Little information is available on Lebanon's irrigation facilities which used to cover one-quarter of the country's cultivated area.

Although not verified, it is believed that much farmland was abandoned in southern Lebanon by people fleeing the continuous fighting in that region.

Agricultural value added constitutes an estimated 8 to 10 percent of the country's GDP, while food and agricultural exports, which include forestry products, provide about 10 percent of merchandise export earnings. In recent years, the sharply depreciating Lebanese pound enabled the agricultural export subsector to withstand rising domestic transport costs and external competition (from Turkey). Although sales to the Persian Gulf state markets were severely curtailed by the Persian Gulf crisis, more recently they have recovered somewhat.

The region remains a huge importer of agricultural products – with agricultural imports estimated to have been worth $25.2 billion in 1992, 9 percent above the previous year and comparable to the levels recorded before the Persian Gulf conflict. The region's leading suppliers continue to be the EC, with a share of approximately one-third, and the United States, with approximately 12 percent. Other important suppliers include Australia, Canada, Argentina, Thailand and Turkey. The leading importers in the region are Saudi Arabia, Egypt, Algeria, Iran, the United Arab Emirates and Turkey. Turkey, Egypt, Saudi Arabia, Morocco and Israel are important exporters of agricultural products such as cotton, horticultural products and tobacco.

Wheat self-sufficiency has increased slightly as a result of strong production gains relative to consumption. In 1992, Near East wheat production was 91 percent of consumption, compared with 80 percent in 1980. For North Africa, production was 39 percent of consumption in 1992 compared with 36 percent in 1980. Regional self-sufficiency levels are a composite of varying performances of individual countries. For example, Saudi Arabia has become a major exporter in recent years, exporting about one-half of its crop. Turkey became a substantial wheat trader in the late 1980s and Iran has made strong headway in increasing wheat output. However, for most of the region's countries, imports account for an increasing share of wheat consumption.

Policy reforms and issues

Despite the disruptions caused by the Persian Gulf crisis, economic reform remains high on the agenda of most countries. The region as a whole continued its march towards policy reforms and liberalization, with reduced government intervention and increased private sector investment. However, structural adjustment programmes were slowed by domestic political problems. Iran and Lebanon continued their rehabilitation of economic infrastructure. Egypt continues its structural adjustment programme, public enterprise reform and privatization.

The reform process has been more difficult in Yemen and Algeria, largely because of changes in government leadership and continuing social tensions in Algeria and

the confrontation between northern and southern Yemen.

Most countries within the region introduced some privatization of marketing and trade as part of a broad policy shift towards market liberalization and reform. Yet, wheat-producer support policies are being maintained in most countries. All countries have subsidized consumer purchases of wheat flour and bread, which has helped transform the region into a mature wheat market where per caput consumption is among the highest in the world. Since 1980, per caput consumption has stabilized, and growth in total use correlates with population growth.

In some countries, including Morocco, Egypt and Tunisia, recent policy reforms included reducing or eliminating consumer subsidies for staple foods, including some breads. Algeria continues to subsidize bread and wheat flour but controlled prices are being increased for other food items, implying reduced subsidies.

The region shares a number of social problems, including unemployment. It has a large pool of skilled, relatively cheap labour and a dynamic and entrepreneurial trading sector with great expansion potential. However, unemployment remains a chronic issue, averaging around 15 percent in Egypt, Iran, Morocco and Tunisia; 20 percent in Algeria and Jordan; and 25 percent in Lebanon and Yemen. In many countries, this situation is exacerbated by the imbalances between population and economic growth. In agriculture, unemployment and underemployment are somewhat more difficult to measure. The capital-intensive nature of a large share of investment and increased mechanization on the land continues to free up already underutilized labour at a time when domestic employment generation has slowed (petroleum earnings are declining). Also, Western countries, which in the past absorbed some of the excess labour, are undergoing economic slow-downs and have sharply reduced expatriate employment.

Water issues
Control over water resources has long been regarded by nations as a vital security interest. This is especially true in the Near East and North Africa because periodic droughts and rapidly growing populations have

compounded the problems of water scarcity. In the past, the major emphasis was on assuring an adequate and reliable supply of water. It has only been in recent years, as problems of salinity and pollution have increasingly threatened the quality of water supplies, that governments have begun to focus on the potentially harmful environmental effects of development projects and unregulated private water use.

Two water-related issues are of an immediate threat to the sustainability of agriculture in the region. The first is environmental – the deterioration of irrigation water quality – and the second is the diversion of irrigation water for urban use. Solutions will require both political and scientific cooperation among the region's nations. These issues affect each country and will be critical determinants of viable agriculture and urban life in the near future. While water issues have been most often couched in terms of regional conflicts, the necessity of developing a regional water strategy may, in fact, drive nations towards regional peace.

Most governments in the region have called for greater attention to water issues, including sewage disposal, salinity, water source pollution and inefficient, wasteful water delivery systems. In many cases, municipal water supply has priority over other uses. Water that had been used for agriculture is now being diverted to urban use. This is the case in Damascus and Aleppo in the Syrian Arab Republic and Amman in Jordan. Other urban areas are relying on desalinated sea water transported over long distances.

In 1993/94, high temperatures and a critical shortage of rain reduced the Near Eastern grain harvest. In Turkey, for example, unusually dry autumn conditions prevented wheat and barley germination in many areas. Grain output forecasts are significantly lower than in 1992/93; similar circumstances apply in neighbouring countries such as the Syrian Arab Republic, Iran and Iraq. This dry spell underscores the vulnerability of the region's economies to weather. In North Africa, growing conditions have been favourable for winter grain crops in Morocco and Algeria, forecasting good grain crops for the 1994/95 season. Increased crops will mean reduced grain imports, following record levels in Morocco in both 1992 and 1993 and near record levels in Algeria.

TURKEY
Agriculture's role in the economy

Historically, the agricultural sector has been Turkey's largest employer and a major contributor to the country's GDP, exports and industrial growth. However, as the country has developed, agriculture has declined in importance relative to the rapidly growing industry and services sectors. Agriculture's share of GDP declined from 35 percent in 1970 to 22 percent in 1980 and to 15 percent in 1992. Agricultural employment declined from 75 percent of the population in 1950 to an estimated 40 percent in 1992. This reflects rural-urban migration and an increase in foreign employment. Crops represent 55 percent of the agricultural sector, livestock represents 34 percent and the rest comprises forestry and aquaculture.

Turkey is the largest producer and exporter of agricultural products in the Near East and North Africa region. Exports of agricultural commodities, including tobacco, pulses, vegetable oils, dried fruit, hazelnuts and other nuts, forest products, wheat and cotton, were valued at $3.4 billion in 1992 and accounted for 23 percent of Turkey's total export earnings. The country has a vast agricultural resource base with significant potential to expand output, particularly through increased crop yields. However, agricultural production is constrained by factors such as weather variations exacerbated by low irrigation rates; ineffective technical support services; inadequate access to agricultural credit; inefficient agricultural marketing systems; inadequate input use; and fragmented landholdings.

Government intervention

In the past, the Turkish Government has intervened heavily in its agricultural sector through price supports, input subsidies, import protection, marketing monopolies and export subsidies or taxes. Some government objectives have been to increase food self-sufficiency and rural development, stabilize farmers' incomes, provide adequate nutrition and affordable food and promote exports. Since implementing its first SAP in 1980, Turkey has developed an ongoing series of agricultural policy reforms designed to privatize markets, reduce agricultural subsidies, remove trade barriers and integrate Turkey into the global economy. Policy measures adopted under the SAP included

currency devaluation, price and trade liberalization and the opening of financial markets.

Crop production was supported primarily through domestic price supports and input subsidies and was bolstered by restraints on imports. These policies raised yields and improved cultivation practices, thereby increasing production and farmers' incomes. Levies were also introduced to protect domestic production of agricultural inputs. In the livestock sector, the government sought to raise productivity, particularly milk yields, by improving genetic characteristics and nutrition of the herd as well as veterinary services and the marketing of livestock products.

Since 1980, the government has departed from its traditional agricultural trade policies which included quantitative restrictions, a heavy reliance on public production and administered prices. Instead, trade barriers have been substantially reduced in accordance with the government's overall move towards a market-oriented agricultural policy. Both the IMF and the World Bank supported this strategy; the World Bank provided five structural adjustment loans (SALs).

During this period currency overvaluation ceased, duties were reduced, many prices were liberalized, nearly all quantitative border restrictions were removed and financial markets opened. As a result, trade increased and imports as a share of GDP rose from 17 percent in 1980 to 30 percent in 1990. Exports as a share of GDP rose from 6 percent to 17 percent, with both value and volume rising. Rapid growth occurred throughout the 1980s, led by manufacturing but also by agro-industry and a resurgence of both domestic and foreign investment in Turkey. Reform of the foreign exchange system left exporters largely free of restrictions in international transactions. Trade policies, which included tax rebates, export credits and credit subsidies, also enhanced export performance. Furthermore, the war between Iran and Iraq greatly increased demand for Turkish agricultural products by both countries.

At times, especially during the early 1980s, the government sought to protect consumers by moderating food price increases through price control and, until the mid-1980s, by restraining taxes on exports, thereby moderating rises in domestic producer prices. This has frequently been the case for ex-factory prices of sugar,

and occasionally for cereals. Although there was a value added tax (VAT) on food, it was kept below that of most other goods: in late 1993 the VAT for food was 8 percent while the general VAT was 15 percent.[61]

In 1980, as part of a package of economic reforms, crop support subsidies were reduced and the number of supported commodities dropped from 30 to 17. During the next several years, the share of support purchases in total agricultural GNP declined and the number of supported crops fell to 11 by 1990. However, the number rose again in the early 1990s owing to a government programme to improve farming conditions and the social welfare of farmers and villagers. The programme sought to reduce rural unemployment and improve extension and research capacities by organizing rural industries. By 1992, input subsidies were increased so that producer prices for wheat and other crops were above border prices, even though the price support scheme had not been enlarged.

Government policies have been implemented through government-owned state economic enterprises, agricultural sales cooperative unions, agricultural credit cooperatives, state-owned banks and other agencies. Despite the move towards liberalization and reduced government intervention, a large number of ministries, agencies, state economic enterprises and banks continue to administer price supports, credit measures, extension and research activities and irrigation projects. Overlapping responsibilities and a lack of coordination have often diluted the effectiveness of government activities, while political considerations have caused yearly variations in the number of supported commodities.[62]

[61] OECD. 1994. *Review of agricultural policies in Turkey.* Directorate for Food, Agriculture and Fisheries. Paris.
[62] H. Ogut. *The restructuring and financing of agricultural support.* Turkish Union of Engineers and Architects' Association of Agricultural Engineers, Symposium on Agricultural Support Policies, January 1993.

The effects of intervention on output. Turkey's SAP created a steady real depreciation of the lira which improved agricultural export competitiveness and increased output and trade. From 1980 through 1992, the overall volume of agricultural production rose by an average of 3 percent per year. Output and yields of the major grains (wheat, barley and maize), sugar beet, oilseeds, potatoes and cotton increased steadily. The index of agricultural production reached an average of 130 in 1991-93 (1979-81 = 100), while the index of per caput agricultural production dropped slightly below 100.

NEAR EAST AND NORTH AFRICA

During this period a number of changes occurred. Cultivated land area rose by an estimated 2.4 million ha, approximately 14.5 percent. The most dramatic change occurred from 1981 to 1982, when fallow area dropped by 1.6 million ha, as a result of large input imports, particularly seed and fertilizer. In the last 12 years, rice area fell by almost half because of water shortages and attractive import prices, supported by exporter credit in other countries. The area sown to barley rose by 23 percent because of high support prices, HYVs and, more recently, wheat disease problems. A strong push in the production and export of pulses tripled the area devoted to those crops. While overall yields have risen, there are often wide regional differences. Field crop yields are usually two to three times higher in the milder coastal areas (Aegean and Mediterranean regions) than in the colder and generally drier areas of central and eastern Turkey – on the Anatolian plateau.

Wheat is the major grain produced in Turkey. Although its output stagnated in the early 1980s, it has recently expanded because of increased fertilizer and irrigation use, a result of price and input subsidies, particularly for fertilizer. Per caput consumption of wheat has been one of the highest in the world but continues to decline as incomes rise and urbanization increases consumption of fruit, vegetables and meats – particularly poultry. In the past, Turkey imported wheat during shortfalls and exported during surpluses. More recently, lower-quality wheat has been exported while higher-quality wheat has been imported for blending.

Over the past decade, the government has initiated measures to raise the productivity of its livestock sector. Among these are genetic improvement of meat and dairy herds through dairy cattle and bull semen imports and improved nutrition and veterinary services. During the 1980s, milk production per cow more than doubled to 1 350 kg per year. This is still low by European standards because approximately two-thirds of the national herd comprises local breeds (only 7 percent are pure-bred animals) and much of the expansion is taking place without selective breeding. Similarly, most of the sheep are domestic breeds. Insufficient attention to the special nutrient and micronutrient needs of imported cattle may also be a contributing factor to low yields.[63] Special emphasis has been placed on

[63] Animal numbers and livestock production data are debatable in Turkey. In 1984 the government ceased publication of official data, as census data differed significantly from previously published series. While the publication of livestock inventories resumed in 1992 (1990 data), two sets from the same organization still differ significantly.

developing animal husbandry in the eastern and southern Anatolia regions and on expanding fodder crop production.

Domestic animal output is below domestic demand, thus animal slaughter has tended to exceed animal birth rates; animal and meat imports are on the rise and exports of live animals and meat have declined. Without serious policy changes, Turkey will become increasingly dependent on imports of livestock products.[64]

In 1993, with FAO's assistance, the government undertook a comprehensive study of the livestock sector, which brought to light some policy shortcomings. For example, in the 1980s livestock sector subsidies were 7 percent compared with 32 percent for crop subsidies. Credit is not properly utilized by livestock producers owing to a lack of programme support. Also, since the producers are smallholders, the servicing and marketing of produce is difficult and marketing systems, when they exist, are poorly organized and inefficient.

As the livestock sector began to expand and demand for feed rose, the government strongly supported maize production by introducing hybrid seeds, new irrigation facilities, fertilizers and improved cultivation practices. In the 1980s, area declined by 6 percent but maize yields rose sharply.

A desire to shift consumption from red to white meat and to raise feed efficiency spurred a major effort to increase the output of poultry meat, particularly chicken meat. The government provided poultry producers with limited incentives such as a rebate on capital investments and an export subsidy. Although support has been far below that provided by other major producing countries, output has grown steadily since 1980 to a record 436 000 tonnes in 1992.

Among industrial crops, cotton has been strongly supported by the government, with PSEs rising to a high of 71 percent in 1987 and declining to about half that level by 1992. Raw cotton was a major export prior to the 1980s but, owing to the dramatic expansion of textile manufacturing and high internal prices, most cotton is now processed. In the three-year period 1990-1992, Turkey became a net importer of cotton.

More recently, a new cotton production support system has been introduced which is somewhat similar to that of the United States and the EC. It provides a

[64] United States Foreign Agricultural Service. *Livestock and Products Annual,* July 1993. TU3023. Ankara, United States Embassy.

larger role for the private sector and allows for market-determined prices while guaranteeing a premium to all cotton producers. The deficiency between the selling price and the government-set target price is covered by the government. This system requires the documentation of all cotton transactions and sales must be registered at commodity exchanges. This will eventually help to create future markets and stronger commodity exchanges and to assist the government in tax revenue collection.

Despite a large and widening overall trade deficit, the agricultural trade balance is significantly positive, providing some relief to external accounts. Trade liberalization and rising regional demand resulted in agricultural exports rising from $1.8 billion in 1980 to $3.4 billion in 1992. In recent years, food and animal exports constituted 17 percent of total export earnings, a figure that would be substantially higher if other agriculture-based products, such as textiles and cigarettes, were included. Livestock exports rose dramatically from $123 million in 1980 to a record $528 million by 1982. However, production could not keep pace with demand and, for some commodities, domestic prices rose and consumption declined. As livestock prices rose, exports declined and, by 1983, had fallen to $312 million. Restrictions resulting from animal health problems exacerbated the decline of live animal exports and, by 1992, they had fallen to $173 million.

Reduced import restrictions under the SAP also led to a dramatic rise in agricultural imports – from an average $326 million in 1980-82 to an average $1.7 billion in 1990-92. In the past, imports were constrained by strong domestic production, import substitution policies and restrictive government regulations on expenditure of foreign exchange. As economic growth increased domestic demand, it became necessary to import chemical fertilizers, machinery, seeds, dairy animals and raw commodities to supply an expanding processing sector. Major agricultural imports included vegetable oils, hides and skins, wool, tobacco, cotton, rice, wheat and feedgrains.

Changes in rural and urban consumer demand
A longstanding goal of the Turkish Government and a central component of the five-year development plan is

to provide an adequate and balanced diet for a growing population and, in particular, to increase per caput consumption of animal proteins. As economic development increases dietary diversity, the country's caloric intake is approaching European levels. However, Turkey remains one of the world's largest per caput grain consumers and the average diet, particularly in rural areas, continues to be derived largely from grains, fruit and vegetables.

Over the last three decades, Turkey's population has been migrating not only to urban areas but also to other countries. In 1950 the rural population represented 75 percent of the total; four decades later, it has dropped to 40 percent. In the 1980s, urbanization grew at an annual rate of 6 percent.

As Turkey has urbanized, food consumption and dietary patterns have changed. From 1980 to 1990, the caloric intake of vegetable-based products rose by 10 percent, while those of animal origin dropped by 19 percent. There was a marginal change in the consumption of cereal products but pulse consumption doubled to 15 kg per caput per year. The steady supply of fruit and vegetables increased consumption by 15 percent over the same period.

Despite a steady increase, consumption of livestock products remains significantly below the regional average. Livestock products account for only 7 percent of the 3 200 calories consumed on average by Turks, although demand has grown in recent years. Poultry meat and dairy product consumption have grown most quickly, largely displacing traditional meats such as lamb, mutton and goat. Poultry consumption – which was about 6 kg per caput per year in 1992 – remains more than 50 percent below regional consumption levels. Turkey is the largest milk producer in the region.

However, per caput milk consumption, although approaching the regional average, remains well below European standards and, in fact, declined by one-third during the 1980s. Overall milk production has stagnated – output of cow's milk has increased but milk from other sources has decreased.

Production outlook
Within the Near East and North Africa region, Turkey probably has the greatest potential to expand

agricultural output. However, to meet its agricultural sector objectives, many ongoing programmes will have to be accelerated. Trade liberalization and reduced market intervention should continue, including the removal of export levies, the phasing out of input subsidies and a reduction in costly purchase and storage price support operations.

Policy reform continues within the framework of Turkey's Five-Year Development Plans. Some of the goals are to raise farmers' incomes and improve dietary diversification through increased crop and livestock production and to expand agricultural export markets, particularly in Central Asia, Eastern Europe and the Baltic states. Targets include production growth rates of 3.7 percent per annum for crops and 5 percent for livestock; an increased use of hybrid seeds, pesticides, fertilizers and irrigation; the expansion of double cropping programmes; and the continued reduction of fallow land.

The government has conducted a comprehensive study of the horticultural industry, seeking to improve internal marketing, quality, standards and yields. The study also examined export potential and opportunities and noted that the global market for Turkey's products is becoming increasingly competitive.

Although Turkey has a comparative advantage in producing wheat, barley, cotton, oriental tobacco, sunflower seeds, olive oil and melons, crop yields are below the rates of many of its competitors. For example, wheat yields stagnated in the 1980s at 1.9 tonnes per hectare and were only slightly higher in 1992. By comparison, United States wheat yields were 2.3 tonnes per hectare in 1991 and those of the EC countries were 5.4 tonnes per hectare.

There are large economic disparities between rural and urban areas and between the more developed western part of the country and the underdeveloped and relatively isolated eastern and southeastern portions of the country.

Consequently, developing these areas is a high priority. The government will strengthen infrastructure, communications, and the agricultural resource base and expand employment opportunities by upgrading local enterprises and attracting new industry. The focus of this policy is the development of the Southeastern Anatolia Project.

Resource and environmental issues

Turkey's agriculture still suffers from chronic structural and institutional weaknesses. Farm size and land fragmentation are major obstacles to agricultural progress and efficiency. In 1980, less than 10 percent of the total number of farm holdings were single-plot units whereas 64 percent were highly fragmented. The recent agricultural census indicates an increase in the total number of farms from approximately 3.6 million in the early 1980s to an estimated 4.2 million a decade later. This is an alarming development because the average farm size declined from 6.4 ha to an estimated 5.3 ha. In the mid-1980s, the government set up a programme to encourage neighbouring farmers to exchange landholdings and initiate land consolidation but the programme has been ineffective.

Turkey is subject to sharp weather changes which have a profound effect on agriculture because of the relatively low percentage of irrigated land – currently about 13 percent of the cultivated area, or 3.5 million ha.[65] This figure represents about 40 percent of the country's potential irrigated land and results from delayed project completions, particularly of secondary and tertiary canals and drainage works. Irrigation is a means of reducing weather-induced production variations. Therefore, the government is giving high priority to improving land and water resources and expanding irrigation. It has designated about two-thirds of total public agricultural investment for land and water improvement.

Low education levels remain a major problem in rural populations. In 1985, it was estimated that one-third of persons over 12 years of age and employed in agriculture (about four million people) were illiterate, compared with an estimated 5 percent of workers employed in manufacturing. Most of the remaining one-third of agricultural workers had only completed primary school. As a result, productivity and incomes among agricultural workers are considerably below those of workers in the non-agricultural sector despite the fact that, since 1988, both sectors have had the same minimum wage (except for workers younger than 16).[66]

Environmental degradation and resource conservation are of increasing concern to the agricultural sector. Intensifying production, especially by using subsidized

[65] Approximately 2.4 million ha are under large-scale irrigation works of the State Hydraulic Works. Another 1.1 million ha are under the General Directorate of Rural Services.
[66] OECD, p. 40. Op. cit., footnote 61, p. 192.

chemical fertilizers, pesticides and irrigation, puts further pressure on the environment. Moreover, the practice of using polluted water for irrigation is still common, posing an immediate threat to human and livestock health and contaminating the soil. The need for adequate drainage for irrigation systems is now widely recognized in Turkey and investments to improve drainage are under way.

Soil erosion has been one of the most serious aspects of soil deterioration in Turkey. It is exacerbated by inappropriate agricultural practices, such as downhill ploughing on steep-gradient land (about 6 million ha of steep-gradient land are currently being farmed) and overgrazing. Some 72 percent of the cultivated area is affected by water-borne erosion and some areas, mainly in central Anatolia and certain coastal regions, are affected by wind erosion.

Environmental problems caused by agriculture are compounded by burgeoning volumes of urban solid waste – a result of rapid population increases, urbanization, industrialization, tourism and rising living standards. Waste materials necessitate numerous rubbish dumps on the outskirts of urban areas, rendering the affected soil unfit for agricultural use. Rapid urbanization is also leading to the uncontrolled construction of housing and factories on fertile arable land. Effluent and sewage are discharged into water from which irrigation water is often drawn.

Government responses to these problems have been stepped up in recent years. Regulations on the use of arable land for purposes other than agriculture were brought into force in 1989 to reduce urban encroachment on agricultural land. In 1991, new regulations were introduced to control solid waste disposal and the use and disposal of hazardous chemical substances and products. It will be some time before the effect of such programmes is evident.

Projects are being carried out to gather information about agriculture's contribution to water pollution and the results will help policy-makers in formulating their decisions. These include establishing the extent of water pollution and its effect on fisheries. Measures are being taken to combat agricultural pests such as grasshoppers, sunn pest and plant lice, some of which come from neighbouring countries.[67]

After a decade of experimenting with liberalization

[67] OECD, op. cit., footnote 61, p. 192.

and structural adjustment, Turkey's economic performance has been mixed. Externally, the SAP policies achieved an impressive growth in exports and contributed to restoring international creditworthiness. GDP growth has also been impressive, increasing by 4 percent annually during the 1980s and by 6 percent in 1993. Prior to the SAP, economic growth in the 1970s stagnated and declined sharply in 1979 and 1980 while, in the 1960s, very fast growth prevailed.

Reforms moved Turkey further into the international arena because growth was primarily driven by an increase in domestic demand. However, they also resurrected problems which originally forced the 1980 policy reforms, primarily high fiscal deficits and inflation. Thus, while the external sector continued to benefit from growing tourism, foreign investments and worker remittances, this surge was accompanied by a sharp rise in budget and current account deficits.

Continuing economic liberalization resulted in a sharp divergence between external and domestic sector performance. Imports continue to outpace exports because excess demand is absorbed by higher imports. In 1993, Turkey's trade deficit reached an alarming record of $12 billion while its current account deficit, which was $937 million in 1992, rose to an estimated $5 billion. Part of this trend is due to the trade embargo on Iraq which has closed the substantial trade between Turkey and Iraq. The embargo has also curtailed remuneration from Iraq's petroleum pipelines running through Turkish territory to the Mediterranean Sea as well as transit fees from vehicles traversing Turkish territory to Iraq.

Economic policies of the current and past governments have openly and widely criticized support and subsidy programmes of the state economic enterprises. These enterprises are under review as the agricultural sector and government initiate privatization. Privatization has featured prominently in government economic programmes since 1986 but it has progressed slowly. Many state economic enterprises have a large workforce and operations that are inefficient and costly. In 1992, the government decided to privatize the Turkish Feed Industries (YEM SAN), Meat and Fish Organization (EBK), Turkish Dairy Industries (SEK) and Wood Products Industry (ORUS). Since these constitute only a small component of the

NEAR EAST AND NORTH AFRICA

state economic enterprise system, eliminating the resource waste indicated by the huge government assistance for the public sector will require more drastic measures.

Turkey has already taken steps to improve its agricultural support for cotton and this support is being expanded to include other commodities such as tobacco, tea and hazelnuts. The government's grain purchasing agent (TMO) has begun offering storage services, charging farmers or other market agents a daily fee until the grain is sold. Plans to introduce grain commodity exchanges are under way. The government has signalled the important change in its approach to supporting producers by beginning to replace intervention purchases with deficiency payments. This change is expected to benefit consumers, improve the efficiency of assistance to producers and, perhaps, foster a market environment that will develop the institutions and expertise required by a market-driven agricultural sector.

Despite agriculture's diminished role, Turkey's economic well-being still depends on the viability of its agricultural sector. Nearly 40 percent (just over 23 million) of people still live in villages where job opportunities are scarce and incomes are considerably below those of urban dwellers. The government has pursued policies to raise rural incomes and levels of living by generating employment through cottage industries, handicrafts and non-agricultural jobs. Several projects supported by international institutions are aimed at providing employment opportunities and, therefore, higher incomes. The Southeastern Anatolia Project is one such project that is being developed to redress regional disparities in income and technology. A second project aims at reducing fallow land and increasing irrigation. The ongoing double cropping programme has made substantial gains, particularly in maize output. The government has been very active in pricing and marketing agricultural products and now seeks to establish regional commodity markets.

Despite great progress, problems remain. Inputs are available for many commodities but are not optimized. Seed generation is insufficient for the country's needs and the situation is exacerbated by a poor distribution system. Problems also arise with seed certification and origination rights. Artificial insemination of dairy

animals has expanded but falls far short of the livestock industry's requirements. The programme still rests primarily in the public sector, with the private sector relegated to a small role. The use of pastoral land and rangeland remains a problem. Since these lands are considered community property, they tend to be overgrazed and overstocked, thereby losing substantial productive resources. Land fragmentation is a major obstacle to crop optimization. Where irrigation has been established, land consolidation has occurred; where rain-fed agriculture remains, fragmentation has increased.

Recently, government involvement has been limited but intervention is viewed as a social contract. In the context of the sector's lower income, government supports have been a measure used to reduce the income gap. However, this has not often resulted in optimal production and economies of size.

Agricultural potential has not been fully realized nationwide. The government is looking to agriculture to meet the increasing demands of a growing higher-income population. To fulfil that challenge, agriculture must become more efficient, more competitive and economically viable, with minimal intervention.

REGIONAL REVIEW
II. Developed country regions

CENTRAL AND EASTERN EUROPE

This section reviews the status of economic and agricultural reform in Central and Eastern Europe and focuses more closely on four selected countries that have had quite different experiences in their attempts at economic and agricultural reform: the three Baltic republics, which have moved decisively towards reform since regaining independence; and Ukraine, one of the countries in the region that has been most hesitant in embarking on thorough reform.

REGIONAL OVERVIEW
Economic performances in the countries in transition in Central and Eastern Europe and the former USSR are showing increasingly differentiated patterns. Past years had seen an almost universal contraction in production, as countries struggled with the initial shocks following the beginning of the reform process and the severe contraction in intraregional trade. A much clearer relationship is now emerging between economic performance and the scope and intensity of economic reform as well as the continuity and consistency of stabilization policies. In 1993, Poland recorded positive real growth for the second consecutive year, with real GDP increasing by 4 percent.[67] Also in the Czech Republic, economic reforms and macroeconomic stabilization are beginning to translate into positive economic growth; the rate of change of real GDP turned positive in 1993 (0.5 percent) for the first time since the beginning of market-oriented economic reforms. The positive growth performance in both countries is expected to be consolidated in 1994.

The most spectacular economic upturn in 1993, however, was staged by Albania which recorded an expansion in global output of no less than 11 percent, following a severe contraction from 1989 to 1992.

[67] Estimates and forecasts of economic growth in this section are from IMF. *World Economic Outlook*, May 1994.

CENTRAL
AND EASTERN EUROPE

Albania is thus beginning to see the first highly visible results of its successful macroeconomic stabilization and decisive steps to reform the economy, although unemployment reportedly remains extremely high.

In the other economies of Central Europe, a recovery in economic activity has not yet occurred, although GDP is estimated to have stabilized in Slovenia in the course of 1993 and the slide in real output may be approaching the end in Hungary, Slovakia, Bulgaria and Romania, thanks to progress in macroeconomic stabilization, particularly in the former two countries.

In the former USSR the short- to medium-term economic outlook is significantly bleaker. The three Baltic republics have moved decisively towards economic reform and economic stabilization, and their economic growth is expected to resume in 1994. However, output in the other former Soviet republics is continuing to decline, with limited prospects for a turnaround in the short to medium term in the face of ineffective macroeconomic policies and hesitant economic reforms.

Regional agriculture is still struggling with the impact of the economic reform process and the need for adjustment. Agricultural production in the region (excluding the former USSR) increased in 1993 for the first time since 1989, although by a modest 2.1 percent. The pattern of agricultural production in 1993 differed, however, between crop and livestock production. Crop production increased by an overall 13 percent, as production picked up significantly from the severely drought-affected level of 1992 in the two major producing countries, Poland and Romania. However, in spite of the recovery in 1993, crop production in the area is still 16 percent below the level of 1989, the sharpest declines being in Hungary, Bulgaria and Albania.

Livestock production in Central and Eastern Europe in 1993 continued the slide that has been ongoing since the peak production level of 1990, declining by a further 9.8 percent following contractions of 7 to 8 percent in each of the previous two years. The cumulative contraction in livestock production since 1990 amounts to 23 percent, somewhat more pronounced than that of crop production. The pattern of continuously declining livestock production, common to all countries in the area, probably represents a

permanent structural response to the shift in relative prices resulting from price liberalization and the sharp reduction in subsidies. Indeed, livestock products in most countries tended to be heavily subsidized prior to reform, and consumption levels were thus artificially inflated relative to those prevailing in countries at similar income levels. The contraction in demand for livestock products has been further accentuated by the decline in income levels, as such demand tends to be relatively income-elastic.

Although reliable indices for aggregate agricultural production in the former USSR have so far not been compiled, agricultural production in 1993 appears to have declined in most of the former Soviet republics. Agricultural production declined sharply in the Russian Federation (-7 percent) and Kazakhstan (-14 percent) while, in Ukraine, the estimated decline was in the order of 2 to 3 percent.

As regards economic reforms affecting agriculture, the countries in Central and Eastern Europe are still proceeding with differing speeds and to some extent in different ways, although the basic areas of reform are fundamentally the same across the region. After the initial thrust of price and trade liberalization, the various countries are now proceeding with the more complex issues of land reform, privatization and demonopolization (see *The State of Food and Agriculture 1993* and *1992*).

In addition to the policy developments and reforms in the above-mentioned areas, new agricultural policies of a more protectionist nature are emerging in some of the more advanced transitional countries. Immediately following the initiation of economic reforms, agricultural policies in the transitional countries became highly liberal, as prices and international trade were deregulated and subsidies eliminated or reduced. Subsequently, in many countries pressures for support and protection have been mounting. Some of the countries that are more advanced in the economic reform process have already introduced agricultural market regulation systems, to some extent inspired by the Common Agricultural Policy (CAP) of the EC or other Western models.

Much will depend on how such market regulation regimes are operated but there is a risk that they will become permanent market price support mechanisms,

as has been the case in most OECD countries. The transitional countries have the opportunity of avoiding this policy mistake, which has proved costly for the Western economies and would likewise impose heavy costs on the newly emerging market economies. Market price support policies, by raising prices above levels that would prevail in free market conditions or above world market levels, distort production and consumption decisions. Not only may they induce significant budgetary costs, they also represent an implicit taxation of consumers and impede the promotion of efficiency in agricultural production.

The background to the introduction of market price support and protection mechanisms is the weakness, inefficiencies and lack of competitiveness of the agricultural sector, including its current adjustment difficulties, in the transitional countries. Beyond this general justification, two specific rationales for such measures would appear to be: first, the need to protect domestic agriculture from the competition of heavily subsidized Western agricultural exports and to penetrate protected Western markets through export subsidies; and, second, to adapt agricultural policies to the EC's CAP in view of possible future European Union (EU) membership. As regards the former, even though OECD agricultural support and trade policies are undoubtedly damaging to the transitional countries, attempting to counter these policies by similar mechanisms may represent a misuse of scarce funds which could possibly be put to better use in improving domestic farm efficiency and competitiveness as well as physical and institutional infrastructure.

As for the latter, it may be noted that the CAP is a moving target. At the future date of accession of any of the transitional countries to the EU, the policy is likely to have been reformed further in the direction of greater market orientation. More important, however, the food sectors of the new market economies will be better equipped to benefit from free access to the vast EU market if, in the meantime, efficiency and competitiveness of the sector has not been hindered by market support, protective barriers and export subsidies.

Another protective policy in some of the transitional countries has been the introduction of export restrictions with a view to increasing supplies to the domestic market. This type of policy may provide a

**CENTRAL
AND EASTERN EUROPE**

relief to short-term domestic supply problems and help protect low-income consumers. Nevertheless it tends to be self-defeating in the medium to long term, as it depresses domestic prices and thus reduces incentives for expanding agricultural supply.

ESTONIA, LATVIA AND LITHUANIA

The three Baltic republics, Estonia, Latvia and Lithuania, have made significant progress in their transition to a democratic, market-oriented system. Despite sharp drops in national income and trade flows during the period following their 1991 independence, prospects appear favourable for economic recovery over the next two to three years, given continued adherence to sound monetary and fiscal policies and progress in privatization. However, economic stabilization in the other former Soviet republics would also be positive for the Baltic republics' prospects for recovery.

The agricultural sector

Although agriculture has traditionally played a sizeable role in the Baltic economies, the sector's share in aggregate output has been declining over the last few years. Indeed, while the share of agriculture in GDP in 1989 amounted to 18 percent in Estonia, 20 percent in Latvia and 27 percent in Lithuania, according to preliminary OECD estimates, the share in 1993 had declined to 8 percent for Estonia, 14 percent for Latvia and 20 percent for Lithuania. The share of labour employed in the agricultural, fisheries and forestry sectors has declined slightly from previous levels, ranging from 15 percent in Estonia (1992 data) to 19 percent in Lithuania in 1993.

The agricultural economies of the Baltic states are oriented towards livestock production, particularly for dairy products, reflecting climatic and geographic conditions that limit crop cultivation. The share of livestock in total Baltic agricultural production ranges from 60 to 70 percent in value terms. While the share of livestock production relative to crop output in Lithuania and Latvia has remained relatively stable, the livestock sector's share of total agricultural output in Estonia has declined over the last three to four years. Prior to 1990, livestock production in Estonia represented nearly 70 percent of total output whereas, in 1992, the share was 60 percent.

The primary livestock products produced in the Baltic states are beef and veal, pork and dairy products. While Baltic livestock output accounted for only 3 to 6 percent of the former USSR's total, on a per caput basis the Baltic republics produced twice as much as the

Soviet average. Moreover, livestock productivity was higher than in the other Soviet republics.

Traditionally, the Baltic republics were net exporters of most livestock commodities. However, after being incorporated into the USSR, their livestock sectors were further specialized to provide meat and dairy products for the other Soviet republics. In return they received feedgrains, either imported or produced within the USSR.

Limited by a short growing season and cultivable land area, Baltic crop production consists primarily of cereals (winter wheat and rye, spring barley), feed crops, potatoes, vegetables and sugar beet (Latvia and Lithuania only). A small amount of flaxseed and rapeseed is also grown. While wheat is primarily used for human consumption, most of the Baltic states' coarse grain and oilseed production is utilized to feed livestock. The Baltic states are net cereal importers, mostly of coarse grains.

Agricultural production has declined in all three countries since 1990. A particularly sharp contraction took place in 1992 when the cereal harvest was affected by drought. A partial recovery occurred in 1993 in Estonia, where agricultural production increased by 9 percent, and in Lithuania, where agricultural production increased by 8 percent, while agricultural production declined by a further 19 percent in Latvia.

While cereal production recovered somewhat in 1993 (particularly in Lithuania), the drop in 1992 severely affected the Baltic states' struggling livestock sector. There were significant drops in all animal inventories, largely owing to increased costs for mixed feed (in part the result of decreased grain supplies from domestic output and interrepublic deliveries) and lower consumer demand for livestock products, particularly in the former Soviet republics to which the Baltic states previously exported.

Economic reforms
The economic transition of the Baltic agricultural sector has been characterized by the following main reforms: price liberalization, land privatization and trade liberalization. The Baltic states have to some extent followed similar paths in introducing and implementing these measures.

Price liberalization. Under the Soviet system, farmgate and retail prices were set by the state. Massive subsidies were provided to both consumers and producers to keep state-set prices low relative to actual costs. Price reform began in the Baltic states in 1990-1991 and, to date, most producer and consumer prices have been fully liberalized or decontrolled to a large extent.

Estonia was the first Baltic republic to liberalize retail prices, beginning the process in 1990 when the prices of paper products, furniture, vegetables and potatoes were fully decontrolled. During 1990-1991, the government liberalized most retail prices and, at the end of 1991, the retail prices of only 10 percent of the consumer basket remained under the state pricing system, while 30 percent was subject to some level of state regulation. In 1992 retail prices were further liberalized and, in October of that year, retail prices of flour, cereals, bread and sugar were fully decontrolled.

Producer prices in Estonia also increased significantly during 1990-1992, but generally by less than the input prices facing farmers. Producer prices are set through negotiations between regional producers and processors, with minimal, if any, intervention by the state.

Lithuania and Latvia have moved more slowly in liberalizing prices. In 1991 producer and consumer prices in both countries were allowed to increase within state-set margins. During 1991-1992, price liberalization proceeded in both Lithuania and Latvia.

By the end of 1992, Lithuanian retail prices for most products had been fully liberalized, with the exception of energy, public services, communications, alcoholic beverages and tobacco. In addition, the Lithuanian state procurement system was replaced in 1992 by a price support mechanism, which was supposed to cover farmers' production costs. However, by mid-1992 these support prices had to be indexed to take rising costs and retail price inflation into account, and additional subsidies were provided for farmers when output prices fell below the support price. These subsidies were a significant burden to the budget and were phased out by the end of 1992 as part of overall price deregulation. In mid-1993, support prices were announced for major crops and were set to reflect world prices. Cereals received the highest support prices; however, it appears that insufficient funds to buy cereals at the set price led

to state purchases that were lower than planned. Most farm output prices are currently negotiated between producers and buyers.

At the end of 1991, Latvian farmgate and retail prices were almost fully liberalized, although minimum support prices for certain agricultural products and profit margins for processors and retailers were established. By the end of 1992, most retail price controls were abolished, except for cereal products, and less than 8 percent of retail goods and services remained subject to state control. Farmgate prices in Latvia are now largely determined by producers and processors. One exception is for cereals, of which a certain amount is purchased by a state grain bureau at minimum guaranteed prices, which for 1994 are near world prices. The Latvian Government allocated 2.9 million lati ($5.1 million) from the 1994 state budget for these purchases.

Price liberalization has greatly affected agricultural production and consumption. Many producers, particularly of livestock products, found themselves in a severe price-cost squeeze situation, as input prices increased more quickly than the prices producers received for their output. Prices for agricultural inputs such as fertilizers, diesel fuel and lubricants sharply increased as the higher cost of producing these products with petroleum purchased almost at world prices was passed on to end users. While farmers faced higher input prices, farmgate prices were constrained by weak consumer demand and the monopsonist behaviour of processors. However, the higher prices forced farmers to economize on inputs by using them more efficiently.

For consumers, the primary effect of price liberalization was reduced purchasing power, since retail price increases outpaced wage increases. This contributed to a shift in consumption away from income-elastic commodities such as meat and dairy products, to more inelastic goods such as bread, potatoes and vegetables. For example, in 1992 per caput consumption of meat, milk, eggs, fish, sugar and vegetable oil in Latvia declined by 20 to 50 percent from 1988 levels, while consumption of grain products and potatoes remained stable or increased slightly. However, these declines were also partly the result of reductions in the substantial consumer subsidies which, during the Soviet period, had resulted in a higher per

caput consumption of some products, particularly meat, than in other countries with a comparable per caput income.

Land privatization. At the turn of the century, agricultural production in the Baltic republics was organized in the form of small, private family farms which averaged around 10 to 25 ha. However, when the Baltic republics were incorporated into the USSR after the Second World War, land was expropriated and private farms were transformed into large state and collective enterprises. In 1990 a typical state or collective farm in the Baltic republics consisted of 3 000 to 4 000 ha, smaller (significantly so in the case of state farms) than the Soviet average of 15 000 and 6 000 ha, respectively. Total employment on state and collective farms in the Baltic republics averaged around 350 workers per farm in 1990, approximately 100 workers less than the Soviet average but with a significantly higher ratio of workers per hectare owing to the different characteristics of the Baltic enterprises which were more oriented towards livestock production.

By the late 1980s, a notable share of the Baltic republics' total agricultural production (crops and livestock) had shifted from the state sector to the private sector, which at that time primarily consisted of small, subsidiary plots and gardens. Indeed, before the breakup of the USSR, Soviet agricultural production in this private sector averaged 25 percent of total agricultural output on all farms, while in the Baltic republics it ranged from 21 percent (Estonia) to 31 percent (Lithuania). Private sector production of vegetables, potatoes and some livestock products in particular was significant.

The Baltic states were among the first to expand the legal basis of the newly emerging private sector. Beginning in 1989, prior to independence, land privatization was initiated in all three Baltic republics, with the enactment of the Law on Peasant Farms. This law was designed to circumvent ownership constraints under Soviet law and to provide the basis for developing private farming operations. However, a true land market could not be created by this law, as Soviet legislation permitted only usufruct land rights, meaning that land could be inherited but not sold or traded.

Subsequent legislation in each of the Baltic states during 1990-1992 expanded and solidified property rights.

The second step in the process of decollectivization was land restitution, whereby previous owners and their descendants were awarded first priority in receiving land. This component, intended to address certain political issues and to stimulate private ownership, led to bureaucratic delays and a lack of confidence in landownership rights, given that there were competing claims and unclear procedures for awarding ownership. The process of restitution was also complicated by the fact that land privatized under the 1989 Law on Peasant Farms could not be restituted to former owners. Another issue that has not been fully resolved is the form of compensation for previous owners who choose not to reclaim their land. Difficulties in setting land values in the absence of a functioning land market, along with concerns over substantial budgetary outlays, have further complicated land restitution in the Baltic states.

The third element of Baltic land privatization is the reorganization or liquidation of state and collective farms. The decollectivization of these farms generally occurred through the issuance of privatization vouchers or through auctions, with present workers given ownership shares in relation to the number of years they had worked on the farm. This process has led to the formation of new enterprises of various categories, including joint-stock companies, limited liability companies and cooperatives. Despite the restructuring of these farms, there has been little improvement in overall productivity and economic management. In part, this stems from the continued uncertainty of land rights during the process of restitution. There has also been little coordination among the processes of restitution and decollectivization, such that conflicts over land and assets have occurred between private landowners and shareholders of reregistered state and collective farms.

The fourth step to take place in land privatization will be the de facto privatization of subsidiary and garden plots. Generally located on state and collective farms, these plots were allowed during the Soviet period for agricultural workers to supplement their personal consumption. During the Gorbachev period, output from these plots could be sold in farmers' markets,

---

BOX 10
BALTIC FISHERIES

The fisheries sector is an important component of Baltic agriculture. The combined coastal area of the three states totals nearly 4 400 km, ranging from 3 800 km in Estonia to 99 km in Lithuania. Latvian and Estonian statistics indicate that the fishing industry accounted for 1 to 2 percent of total GDP in 1992. The number of employees in the three Baltic fisheries sectors in 1991 totalled 30 000 in Estonia, 29 000 in Latvia and 15 000 in Lithuania. At the end of 1993, there were 40 000 people employed in the distant-water fishing sector (including the associated industry) but this number is probably declining.

From 1970 to 1976, Baltic fish catches grew dramatically from 1.1 million to 1.7 million tonnes, an increase of more than 50 percent. After 1976, annual fish production declined to around 1.5 million, remaining steady until 1989. During the period 1970-1990, Latvia held the largest share of the Baltic fish catch, generally 35 to 45 percent of the total.

After 1990, the catch began to decline, recording particularly sharp drops in 1992/93. Preliminary data for 1993 put the total Baltic fish catch at around 0.42 million tonnes, with the Latvian and Estonian catches at 0.15 million tonnes each and Lithuanian output at 0.12 million tonnes.

The breakup of the USSR and the restructuring of the Baltic economies are the primary reasons for the significant decline in Baltic fish catches. During the Soviet period, the Baltic deep sea fishing fleet was significantly expanded, ending the predominance of coastal fishing which is traditionally practised in the Baltic area. Around 70 percent (Estonia and Latvia) to 90 percent (Lithuania) of Baltic fish catches came from areas outside the Baltic Sea, primarily from areas in the Atlantic Ocean. However, since the USSR's dissolution in 1991, the deep sea fishing fleet has been facing major difficulties, partly through loss of access to Soviet deep sea fishing rights which require new fishing licences, but primarily because of the new profitability requirements as well as the discontinuation of subsidies and logistic and financial support in general, leading to substantially decreased catches. For example, 1992 Baltic fish catches in the Atlantic and Pacific Oceans were down by 50 to 100 percent from 1991 levels. Left with an oversized fishing fleet, reduced access to deep sea fishing grounds, decreases in both subsidized energy supplies and export demand from the former USSR, the Baltic states were forced to reduce or idle much of their fleet, resulting in lower catches. Privatization of the fisheries sector has also disrupted fishing activities to some degree.

Given the economic conditions in the Baltic republics, it is unlikely that the volume of catches will increase substantially from the lower levels of the 1990s, as reduced fishing area, ongoing privatization and strong competition in the world market will probably continue to constrain any significant growth in the short to medium term. In 1992, for instance, 75 percent of the catch was composed of low-value small pelagics.

With this type of catch, it is difficult to operate with a profit and catches will thus tend to decrease further.

Coastal fishing may be expanded during this period, while growth in freshwater aquaculture could also occur, particularly in Latvia where extensive freshwater areas have not yet been fully developed. However, the increase in coastal fishing without regulations and regular monitoring could, and probably has already, lead to environmental degradation and lower fish yields. The Lithuanian region of the Courland Lagoon, one of the richest fishing areas of cod, sprat and herring, has already been affected by industrial pollution, and fish yields in that area have been halved from historical levels. However, the Baltic states have begun to adopt international fishing regulations and accounting standards to reduce the risk of environmental damage.

generally at higher prices than those charged in state stores. In all three Baltic republics, the size of these plots was allowed to increase from 0.5 ha, and the average size of private plots currently ranges from 2 to 4 ha. In Lithuania, it is planned that these plots will be fully privatized by mid-1994.

A problem that all the Baltic states are facing in the creation of private farms is farm size. On 1 January 1993, nearly 170 000 private farms had been formed in the three Baltic states, comprising more than 2 million ha, slightly less than 30 percent of total agricultural area. The average size of these farms ranged from 9 ha in Lithuania to 25 ha in Estonia, which is significantly smaller than the former state and collective farms but very close to that of the farms that existed during the Baltic states' previous independence earlier this century. Nonetheless, there is recognition by the Baltic governments that the creation of such small landholdings is not entirely healthy, as certain economies of size that were developed in the state and collective farm system are lost with the creation of small family farms. Moreover, machinery and other inputs designed for larger farms are often less effective in these smaller landholdings. Structural policies to encourage larger farms are being implemented in all three Baltic states, such as offering landowners land for housing construction in urban areas in compensation for farmland.

Trade liberalization. The Baltic trade regime that has evolved since independence in 1991 can generally be characterized as liberal, with relatively transparent trade barriers and controls. Unlike in the other former Soviet republics, most Baltic foreign trade activity takes place in the private sector, with limited state involvement. In addition, there are few if any constraints on foreign exchange earnings, such as surrender requirements on export proceeds.

The Baltic export policies are for the most part characterized by moderate taxes, with no subsidies and very few quantitative restrictions. The Baltic import regimes are also relatively free from quantitative restrictions and consist of uniformly imposed tariffs and taxes. There are very few import controls, most of which are for health and security reasons. Baltic import tariffs generally range from 5 to 20 percent. By the end

of 1992, several Estonian import taxes were converted to excise taxes. Generally speaking, Lithuania and Latvia have instituted more import tariffs on agricultural goods than Estonia. In March 1994, efforts to liberalize agricultural trade between the Baltics were hindered by Lithuania's and Latvia's rejection of an Estonian proposal to eliminate import tariffs on agricultural goods.

The three Baltic states have also established independent currencies which have full (Latvian lat) or current account (Estonian kroon and Lithuanian lita) convertibility. Lithuania and Latvia established central banking systems and a floating exchange rate when they established their currencies, although Lithuania recently pegged the lita to the US dollar to improve its stability. Estonia established a currency board when it introduced the kroon, pegged to the German mark. The introduction of these new currencies has helped to facilitate trade with developed countries, but Baltic export competitiveness has diminished somewhat as these currencies have appreciated in real terms. Further, while the early exit from the rouble zone allowed the Baltic states to take control of monetary policy and insulate their economies from the inflationary environment of that zone, it also contributed to the sharp reduction in Baltic trade with the other former Soviet republics.

Main policy issues and outlook
The general outlook for the Baltic agricultural economies is one of continued restructuring, as these countries move towards becoming full-fledged market economies. Continued progress in privatization and growth in private sector economic activity are expected in all three Baltic states. In addition, the IMF expects economic growth to resume in 1994, following four years of contraction. Estonia is generally considered to have the best prospects for economic growth in 1994, given its strong economic performance at the end of 1993. Nevertheless, Baltic economic recovery will be dependent on the continuation of sound fiscal and monetary policies and, to some extent, on the rate of progress made by the other former Soviet republics in their transition to market economies.

Given this setting, the following outlook for agriculture can be offered:

- Steps to reduce the level of state support to agriculture have been taken and are likely to continue. Quantifying the level of agricultural subsidies is difficult, but all countries appear to have sharply curtailed direct and indirect subsidies to agriculture. In 1994 agricultural support in all three Baltic republics is primarily directed at cattle production, crop programmes (primarily to support seed production), credits, the development of extension services and the creation of family farms.
- Wholesale and retail markets for agricultural goods will continue to develop in the short to medium term. Privatization of downstream enterprises, which has proceeded more slowly than in primary agriculture, and increased competition among these enterprises will play an important role in agricultural market development.
- The Soviet economic system established in the Baltic republics after the Second World War resulted in high levels of regional concentration in the processing industry, such that one mill, meat kombinat, etc., processed all the agricultural output produced in that area. With this system still in place during the Baltic republics' transition to a market economy, these processors have been able to act as monopsonists and little progress has been made in developing more efficient wholesale markets.
- The current financial and technological condition of the Baltic agro-industrial sector is generally not good, and only through increased privatization, foreign investment and competition, both domestically and from imported goods, will this sector be able to produce in a cost-efficient manner and therefore be competitive in external markets. There has been pressure for increased protection of domestic producers and processors, which to some extent has been granted in the form of import tariffs on certain agricultural imports. However, by protecting domestic producers, the process of market development is arrested and the creation of cost-efficient competitive enterprises delayed. Moreover, consumers – particularly the poor – are hurt by protectionism which, in the absence of subsidies, leads to higher retail prices.
- Nevertheless, even with significant advancements in competitiveness, Baltic agricultural producers and

processors will continue to face substantial trade
barriers for their output in the short to medium term.
However, as the Baltic republics move closer to
GATT membership and the former USSR begins its
economic recovery, the Baltic republics could
regain or develop new export markets for their
agricultural production. It is not expected, however,
that exports of livestock and dairy products will
return to the artificially high levels of the Soviet era.

CENTRAL
AND EASTERN EUROPE

UKRAINE

Ukraine has been one of the region's most conservative countries in implementing economic reforms. Aggregate output continued to decline steeply in 1993, while inflation has been running high (at around 2 500 percent in both 1992 and 1993, according to the OECD). To counter the declines in output, the government has been subsidizing enterprises and farms. Prospects for economic recovery appear poor in the absence of more decisive economic reforms and stringent macroeconomic policies.

The agricultural sector

Agriculture plays a very large role in the Ukrainian economy, accounting for 33 percent of Ukraine's net material product (NMP) in 1993 and employing about 20 percent of the workforce. Agriculture and food account for about 9 percent of Ukraine's total exports and 6 percent of total imports.

Ukraine has some of the richest soils for agricultural production in the former USSR and in the world. About 54 percent of the country is in part of the chernozem soil zone, which Ukraine shares with the Russian Federation. These deep black soils have a humus layer of 40 to 50 cm or more in depth and abundant mineral and organic nutrients. Ukraine is divided into three agroclimatic bands running from southwest to northeast: the forest zone has acidic soils and an annual precipitation of 600 to 700 mm; the forest-steppe zone has plentiful chernozem soils and an annual rainfall of 450 to 600 mm; and the steppe zone, mostly chernozem, has 350 to 450 mm of annual precipitation.

Ukrainian agriculture is practised predominately in the southwest and south. The southwestern region (including Kiev and western Ukraine) forms the heart of Ukrainian cereal, sugar beet and cattle production and related food processing industries. The southern economic region includes the dry steppes near the Black Sea and the Crimean Peninsula. This area is also dominated by agriculture and agriculture-related industry, including viticulture and such crops as wheat, sunflowers, vegetables, fruit and rice.

As a result of the country's rich soils, crop yields in Ukraine are quite high compared with other former Soviet republics and rival or exceed United States yields, except for maize. Moreover, Ukrainian crop

yields regularly exceed those of the Russian Federation by 50 to 100 percent.

Livestock products currently make up 53 percent of the value of total agricultural production in Ukraine (in 1983 rouble prices). The main meats produced are beef and veal and pork, which account for 49 and 35 percent, respectively, of total meat production by weight. Crops make up the remaining 47 percent of total agricultural production value in Ukraine (in 1983 rouble prices). The main crops are cereals, sugar beet, sunflowers, potatoes, flax and vegetables. The main cereals cultivated are winter wheat and spring barley.

Agricultural production in Ukraine, along with the GDP, has been falling since 1990; agricultural production declined by about 2 percent in 1993 after larger declines in 1991 and 1992.

The structure of agricultural production has also changed since 1990, as the demand for and the production of livestock products has fallen relative to crops. This is a consequence of the drop in real incomes and rise in the relative consumer prices of livestock products following price deregulation and the reduction of consumer subsidies for livestock production in 1992. Indeed, under the Soviet regime, consumer subsidies stimulated consumption of meat and other livestock products, leading to a per caput meat consumption in Ukraine and the USSR in 1990 that was considerably higher than that of other countries with a similar per caput GDP. Thus, livestock production as a portion of total agricultural production in Ukraine decreased from 57 to 53 percent between 1991 and 1992 (in constant 1983 prices).

Ukraine has regularly produced an exportable surplus of agricultural products, except for cereals. Net cereal exports have depended on the harvest, normally ranging from about +0.5 million to +2 million tonnes in good years to -0.5 million to -1.5 million tonnes in bad years (with average production in the period 1990-93 lying in the range of 40 million to 45 million tonnes).

Trade statistics are relatively poor and frequently contradictory. However, trade both with former Soviet republics and other countries appears to have fallen off sharply in 1991, 1992 and 1993. Ukraine has been a net importer of about 0.5 million to 1.8 million tonnes of cereals for the past three calendar years (1.8 million tonnes in 1993). Ukraine is normally a net exporter of

sugar, almost exclusively to former Soviet republics. Whereas as recently as 1990 these exports totalled about 3.5 million tonnes, in 1993 Ukraine exported less than 1 million tonnes of sugar. It was also traditionally a net exporter of livestock products, exporting nearly 2 million tonnes of milk and 650 000 tonnes of meat in 1990, mostly to other former Soviet republics. By 1993, however, net milk exports had shrunk to 300 000 and meat to less than 100 000 tonnes. In addition, in 1993 Ukraine had net exports of fruit, vegetables and eggs.

Economic reforms

There has so far been little effective reform in the Ukrainian economy, with the exception of price reform starting in 1992. Otherwise, Ukrainian agriculture continues to operate in much the same way as it did before 1992. State organizations continue to supply farms with inputs, albeit at deregulated prices. Those operating at a loss continue to be supported by the state through budget subsidies and liberal credits. Agricultural producers are free to market commodities outside the state channels, but receive subsidies and inputs and are granted export licences only if they sell part of their output to state processors at state-set prices. According to a government decree of November 1993, they are obliged to sell an average of 40 percent of their output to the state. Finally, there has been almost no privatization of Ukrainian agricultural producers or processors, and private farmers are few and have limited resources.

However, an increasing portion of agricultural commodities are now (primarily) bartered or sold directly to the public. As a result, the percentage of production procured by the state has fallen since 1990. For instance, whereas the state procured nearly 40 percent of grain production in 1988, in 1992 less than 30 percent went directly to state mills. Sunflower procurement dropped from 82 to 60 percent of production over the same period, while vegetable procurement dropped from nearly 70 percent of production in 1988 to 33 percent in 1992.

Nevertheless, high inflation in Ukraine has forced changes on agricultural producers, just as it has on consumers. Ukrainian farms and processors are chronically short of working capital to purchase inputs and pay workers, not only as a result of an unfavourable

CENTRAL AND EASTERN EUROPE

movement in the terms of trade for agriculture, but because of high inflation, which has been running at around 2 500 percent in 1992 and 1993. High inflation has prompted agricultural producers to sell more of their output through barter and to lobby constantly for additional credits from the central bank.

Price reforms. Ukraine followed the Russian Federation in beginning deregulation of most retail and producer prices on 2 January 1992. Deregulation meant that most retail prices were freed from direct state control. This, however, did not imply the complete liberalization of retail prices, as maximum profit margins were imposed on many downstream processors, wholesalers and retailers and most factor prices were still controlled centrally. Only about 20 percent of retail prices were fully liberalized in January 1992 in the sense that downstream processors of the goods were not subject to margin regulation.

About 12 percent of retail prices and 17 percent of producer prices remained under direct central control. Centrally controlled retail prices included many basic foods such as bread, dairy products, some cereal products, sugar, salt, vegetable oil and margarine. Producer prices that remained controlled included those for coal, crude petroleum, refined petroleum products, natural gas, electricity, freight transportation and communications.

In the course of 1992 further price liberalization took place. At the end of March, retail meat and milk prices were decontrolled and, in July, prices for most other foods were deregulated, with the exception of low-quality bread. Retail and producer prices were deregulated further in December 1992, as the scope of centrally fixed retail and producer prices was further reduced. Notably, retail prices for refined petroleum products were freed, although wholesale controls remained. Retail prices for a number of basic foods were also deregulated, and some goods were moved from the fixed price to the regulated price category. Moreover, price levels were raised for a number of commodities for which prices continued to be fixed.

In 1993 there was no significant further deregulation of prices in Ukraine and fixed prices were raised periodically. The Ukrainian Parliament legislated a moratorium on retail price increases in May, which it

subsequently lifted in June. In November, wholesale and retail controls were reimposed on certain prices that had previously been freed.

Despite controls, both retail and producer prices have risen at an increasing rate. Price controls meant that food shortages persisted in Ukraine throughout 1992, although prices in state stores were periodically raised to follow those in free markets, albeit with a lag.

As for farm prices, on 2 January 1992 agricultural input prices were deregulated and farms were no longer formally required to deliver agricultural production to state enterprises at fixed prices. However, the state maintained a variety of ways of influencing both commodity prices and marketing which effectively means that, to a large extent, farms continue to deliver agricultural commodities to the state at fixed prices.

Price deregulation led to a price-cost squeeze for farms, since farm costs of production rose faster than agricultural commodity farmgate prices. The price-cost squeeze is a result of three factors. First, whereas input prices have been deregulated, output prices are still heavily controlled. Second, many inputs are purchased by the Ukrainian Government from other former Soviet republics and the prices of these purchases have tended to rise towards world levels. Third, subsidies for input suppliers have fallen in the past two years, and they have correspondingly raised their prices to compensate.

The farm price-cost squeeze threatened to cause farms to reduce production and prompted the Ukrainian Government to reintroduce agricultural producer subsidies in June 1992. Moreover, consumer subsidies through payments to agricultural processors (such as flour mills) were maintained. In 1992 the share of subsidies for agriculture and food amounted to about 6 to 10 percent of GDP. The reintroduction of government fiscal support for agriculture is an attempt to counter the effects of price liberalization on production and tends to inhibit the restructuring of production according to price signals.

Both budgetary subsidies and liberal credits to agricultural producers continued in 1993. For instance, in June 1993 farms received 5 trillion karbovanets ($1.1 billion) worth of credit at an annual interest rate of 30 percent. Such loans, made at highly negative real interest rates, are part of the Ukrainian Government's policy of budgetary and credit support for the economy

with scarce attention to the macroeconomic consequences. Thus, in early 1994 the official interest rate of the central bank was 240 percent in spite of a recorded inflation rate in 1993 of 2 600 percent. The result has been hyperinflation and an accelerating downturn in economic performance in the first quarter of 1994.

Land reform. Ukraine has enacted legislation allowing the establishment of limited private landownership. However, this legislation does not provide for clearly delineated and transferable property rights. Moreover, private farms in Ukrainian agriculture are intended as a supplement to collective agriculture, which is still the dominant form of farm organization.

The Supreme Soviet took the first steps towards the establishment of private landownership in the USSR between November 1989 and March 1990 in the Law on Leasing, the Law on Property and the Law on Land. These laws permitted the long-term lease of land and granted individuals the right to individual proprietorship. Proprietorship was quite limited in that it allowed for lifetime inheritable rights to work the land, without the right to buy, sell or mortgage it.

Subsequent Ukrainian legislation further expanded the right of landownership. The Ukrainian Law on Peasant Farms of 20 December 1991 allowed for lifetime, inheritable rights to land as well as private ownership of land after it has been farmed for six years. The farmer then has the right to transfer the land to another person, but only with the permission of the local council and at a regulated price. The Land Code of 13 March 1992 expanded the provisions of the Law on Peasant Farms. Private owners are allowed to lease their land for agricultural use for a term of up to three years, although more recent legislation has imposed limits on lease payments (Law on Payment for Land of 3 July 1992).

Legislation on landownership permits the formation of private farms in Ukraine, although the law is highly restrictive. A private farm may be established by an individual, whether currently engaged in farming or not. Nevertheless, a successful application for land requires some training or experience in farming. Land is provided without payment, with a six-year moratorium on sale, and the hiring of labour is not allowed. The

maximum landholding is 100 ha, 50 ha of which may be arable land. However, farmers may lease additional arable land.

The number of private farms in Ukraine grew from 82 on 1 January 1991 to 27 700 at the beginning of 1994. The increase in the number of farms in Ukraine has been much less rapid than in Armenia and the Russian Federation, which are the two leaders in the number of private farms in the Commonwealth of Independent States (CIS). Moreover, private farms in Ukraine are small compared with those in the Russian Federation: the average size of a private farm in Ukraine is 20 ha, compared with an average of 42 ha in the latter.

Private farming is a minor part of total private production of agricultural products in Ukraine. Private farms produce less than 1 percent of Ukraine's individual crop and livestock production. Private plot production is much more important as a portion of total production.

Private plots on state and collective farms are quite important for Ukraine's agriculture and have become even more so in the past two years. Production on private plots accounted for 37 percent of total agricultural, 35 percent of crop and 39 percent of livestock output in 1992, up from 27, 22 and 31 percent, respectively, in 1990. In 1992, 85 percent of potatoes, 52 percent of vegetables and 69 percent of fruit and berries were grown on private plots. The proportions for livestock products are also significant: private plot production accounted for 35 percent of total meat production, 32 percent of milk production and 45 percent of egg production in 1992.

State and collective farms in Ukraine are currently reregistering, as in the Russian Federation. State and collective farms have the option of reregistering as joint-stock companies, maintaining their current organization or dividing into a number of private farms, etc. Just as in the Russian Federation, however, on the whole, the behaviour of formerly state and collective farms has yet to change appreciably.

Prospects for food and agriculture
The prospects for agriculture in Ukraine in the coming few years depend on a number of economic constraints and policy changes. One primary problem for agricultural production is hyperinflation which, in

1994, has caused a fall in real incomes and the elimination of producer working capital. It also imposes an exorbitant tax on holders of nominal balances and forces all economic agents to expend a great deal of resources in order to avoid the tax. Demand for agricultural and other goods, as well as GDP, will continue to fall as long as hyperinflation continues. Stabilization would not only have the beneficial effects of reducing the tax burden and transaction costs for farms, but would force the government to impose stricter limits on state support for agriculture. Less opportunities for state support would force farms to pay greater attention to reducing costs of production.

Agricultural producers would be likely to benefit from substantial liberalization of the foreign trade regime although such changes are probably not possible without macroeconomic stabilization. Ukrainian crop procurement prices are well below world market prices, while poor-quality agricultural machinery is likely to be overpriced. Thus, agricultural terms of trade could probably be improved by foreign trade liberalization. A major obstacle to receiving the full benefits from foreign trade liberalization is the reluctance of many Western markets to allow access to imports of former Soviet republics' agricultural commodities and the current oversupply of livestock production potential in both the former Soviet republics and Eastern Europe. While consumers would benefit from foreign trade liberalization and the ensuing increased supply of higher-quality imported food, the Ukrainian food industry would be under considerable competitive pressure to improve quality and reduce costs.

Regardless of the above, the livestock sector will probably continue to contract, simply because livestock in Ukraine (and the former USSR in general) is a particularly high-cost industry (compared with world standards). As producer and consumer subsidies continue to shrink as a result of falling government revenues, increasing inflation or macroeconomic stabilization, levels of livestock consumption near those attained in the Soviet period will be found to be unsustainable.

Ukraine possesses a very rich agricultural resource base and has the potential for being a major net exporter of agricultural products. However, the country's full realization of its agricultural potential

**CENTRAL
AND EASTERN EUROPE**

requires significantly more decisive economic reforms and the implementation of effective macroeconomic stabilization policies.

OECD COUNTRIES

Within the OECD review, *The State of Food and Agriculture* has traditionally included a report on changes in agricultural policies in both the European Community (EC) and the United States, since their policies have significant effects on other member countries, mainly through the global trading system. In the case of the EC, again this year some important changes have occurred and are reported below. In the case of the United States, however, the present farm legislation is scheduled to expire at the end of 1995. *The State of Food and Agriculture 1993* reported on the likely issues that would drive the 1995 farm bill debate. Since then, little has changed in the implementation of the 1990 farm legislation or in the issues that are likely to come under debate, beginning in the autumn of 1994 and lasting until a 1995 farm bill is passed by the United States Congress, perhaps in late 1995. A section on the United States is therefore not included this year.

Instead, the recent changes in the agricultural situation and policy in Canada have been highlighted. In recent years, Canada has experimented with some innovative policies and programmes, particularly related to social safety nets for farmers, while at the same time finding other aspects of its agricultural policy difficult to reform.

AGRICULTURAL POLICY DEVELOPMENTS IN CANADA
Slow-growth high-deficit economy
Three policy issues currently dominate Canadian agriculture – supply management, grain transportation and farm safety nets. The resolution of these issues is likely to be affected considerably by factors external to the country's agricultural sector, including the recent weakness in the Canadian macro economy, falling real prices in world commodity markets and changes in international trading rules.

Canada has emerged from the prolonged recession of 1990 and 1991 into a period of slow growth, especially in the domestic market. Modest GDP growth is expected for the next two years, with the February 1994 federal budget assuming a 3 percent growth in 1994 and 3.8 percent in 1995. In early 1994, the prime

lending rate declined to a 30-year low (it has subsequently increased). With slow growth in the economy, very high unemployment levels (more than 11 percent) and low energy prices, the inflation rate is expected to remain well under 2 percent for the next two years. The low inflation rate has occurred despite a 16 percent depreciation in the value of the Canadian dollar against the US dollar, falling from US$0.89 in 1989 to under US$0.72 in the spring of 1994. Domestic demand has remained very weak but cost pressures have also been dampened.

Both federal and provincial governments have continued to run very large annual deficits during the past two decades. The deficit, aggravated by the recession, reached about 7 percent of GDP in 1993. Pressure is mounting on both levels of government to take stronger action to reduce the deficit and to do this via spending cuts rather than continuing the recent practice of raising taxes. The deficit continues to influence government programmes and has, for example, resulted in reductions in subsidies to industrial milk producers and for grain transportation.

The Canadian economy is heavily dependent on trade. As a result of recent trade agreements, the Canada-US Free Trade Agreement (CUSTA) and NAFTA and now the Uruguay Round of GATT negotiations, the economy is becoming even more open to trade. Increased competition following the implementation of these trade agreements has forced restructuring in the food processing sector in particular to compete in North American and global markets. The Canadian economy in total, and increasingly its agricultural and food sector, is heavily tied to trade with the United States market.

Structural adjustment in the primary sector

Structural change in the Canadian agricultural sector continues in response to pressure from declining real prices and reduced government support. The average farm size has continued to increase in the past 20 years, growing by 29 percent to 242 ha, and the number of farms has declined by more than 24 percent. Structural adjustment in the dairy sector has been even faster than the average for the sector as a whole; the number of dairy farms has declined by 42 percent in the past decade. However, despite marked decreases in the

number of farms, employment in the agricultural sector declined slowly from about 500 000 in 1970 to about 450 000 in 1991.

Another important aspect of structural adjustment has been the diversification of farm labour to off-farm employment. Off-farm income now accounts for about 60 percent of total farm family income, particularly for the smallest farms. This trend has enabled average farm family incomes to remain very close to the average income for all families in Canada.

Total farm debt rose quickly during the first half of the 1980s, as farm prices were strong from relatively high world cereal prices and a weak Canadian dollar. When these two factors reversed in the mid-1980s, bankruptcies rose by more than 400 percent from the 1979 level to reach their peak in 1985. Since 1986, total farm debt has remained relatively stable and farms in payment arrears have declined from about 12.5 percent of all farms to 6.5 percent in 1993. Bankruptcies have stabilized at an annual level of 0.2 percent of all farms. The improvement in the farm debt situation should continue as the prime interest rate has dropped from 14 percent in 1990 to 5.5 percent in early 1994. More recent increases could slow the recovery.

Agriculture is highly dependent on world trade
Agricultural and food exports are a very important source of income, generating about C$21 000 per full-time farmer. However, there are significant regional differences; exports are much more important in western Canada. In July 1993, recognizing the importance of trade to growth in the sector, the federal and provincial agriculture ministers set an objective to increase agricultural exports to C$20 billion, a 65 percent increase, within the period 1992-2000.

In the past few years, growth in Canadian agricultural exports to the United States has been the most rapid among all export destinations, especially for processed food products: the United States accounted for about 45 percent of agricultural exports in 1992.

On the other hand, the value of Canadian agricultural exports to Japan, other Asian countries and the EC fell during the 1988-1992 period. Also, the former USSR sharply reduced its imports of Canadian agricultural products in 1992 and again in 1993. As a result, Canadian agricultural and food trade destinations now

parallel more closely those for non-agricultural trade, that is they are heavily tied to the United States.

High levels of government assistance for the sector
Expenditures by both federal and provincial governments for support of the agricultural sector in 1992/93 were estimated to be C$7.04 billion, about 60 percent from federal and 40 percent from provincial governments. This represents about 31.5 percent of the agrifood GDP and about 2.9 percent of total federal and 1.9 percent of provincial government expenditures.

In the mid-1980s, government expenditures increased sharply in response to the abrupt decline in world grain and oilseed prices and were highly concentrated in the prairie provinces. For example, in Saskatchewan, federal and provincial government agricultural support expenditures exceeded the total agrifood GDP output in two of the past eight years. In Manitoba and Alberta, federal and provincial government expenditures exceeded 50 percent of the agricultural GDP in four of the past eight years.

Because of low grain prices, most government expenditures are for income support – commodity programmes, transportation and storage subsidies, tax rebates and programme operation. The majority (about two-thirds) of all government payments go to farms with sales of more than C$100 000. Relatively little assistance has been directed to new government priorities such as expanding international trade, enhancing market development programmes or protecting the environment. Equally limited are expenditures currently devoted to traditional public sector activities such as research and food safety.

A second important means of support to the agricultural sector is provided through regulations such as import restrictions, production controls and price supports. These instruments are used mainly for the supply-managed commodities (largely dairy products, poultry and eggs). In this case, the agricultural sector receives support through transfers from domestic consumers. An estimate of the importance of this support can be obtained from the value of PSEs. The OECD estimates that, in 1993, the net PSE for dairy, poultry and eggs totalled C$3.1 billion, or 76 percent of the value of production for dairy products and 37 percent for poultry.

Government expenditures, while remaining a large percentage of the agricultural GDP, declined from C$8.93 billion in 1991/92 to C$7.04 billion in 1992/93 and are forecast to drop to C$5.98 billion in 1993/94. Further declines are likely. As part of a general deficit reduction programme, the federal government reduced the subsidy for industrial milk producers and western grain transportation for 1993/94 and 1994/95 by 10 percent. Expectations of generally strengthening world prices, devaluation of the Canadian dollar and support prices based on moving averages will also contribute to reductions in safety net payments.

Policy process

Because agriculture is a shared responsibility between the federal and provincial governments, programmes must often be developed jointly. Under the Canadian constitution, interprovincial and international trade are the responsibility of the federal government, while marketing and education are provincial responsibilities. This division increases the need for consultation to develop national commodity marketing programmes and may result in some duplication of programmes between the two levels of government.

The Agriculture Policy Review (see *The State of Food and Agriculture 1991*, p. 73-74) initiated a comprehensive reassessment of all facets of Canadian agrifood policy in December 1989, involving extensive consultation with federal and provincial governments and industry. The review introduced two new safety net programmes – the Gross Revenue Insurance Plan (GRIP) and the Net Income Stabilization Account (NISA). Other task forces that reviewed supply management for dairy and poultry production and grain transportation provided a number of recommendations, but there was no broad consensus for their introduction. Furthermore, the delay and uncertainty surrounding the GATT agreement dampened the potential for change in both supply management and grain transportation.

Current policy issues

Dairy and poultry supply management. The marketing of milk and poultry in Canada is regulated through compulsory producer marketing boards. The basic elements of this supply management system are the control of domestic production, border controls and an

administered pricing system. Its policy objectives are to maintain a minimum level of domestic self-sufficiency,[68] the regional sharing of production and processing and prices based on the cost of production.

The current form of supply management in Canada was largely introduced in the 1970s. Supply management programmes operate through a complex series of regulations. For example, imports of industrial milk and processed dairy products (with at least 50 percent dairy content) have quantitative restrictions under the Import Control List. There are tariffs on products with fixed import quotas (e.g. 20 400 tonnes of annual cheese imports). Industrial milk producers require production quotas to be eligible to produce milk and receive direct subsidy payments. Prices to producers for industrial milk are set by a cost-of-production formula and these are maintained through dairy product prices which are supported by a government offer-to-purchase programme for butter and skim milk powder. Industrial milk production is based on a national-level quota which is allocated on a historical basis to each province which, in turn, allocates quotas to individual producers. Producer levies are assessed to pay for surplus product disposal, largely for export. Processors pay variable prices for industrial milk depending on its end use. Processed dairy product producers may also face plant allocation quotas.

In the Uruguay Round of GATT negotiations, Canada had sought to maintain the current supply management system through a strengthened Article XI, paragraph 2(c). The level of tariff equivalents replacing quantitative restrictions on imports, however, is not likely to require fundamental changes to the supply management programme. CUSTA includes no specific measures relating to the liberalization of trade in supply-managed products, but discussions with the United States were held regarding the introduction of the new tariffs permitted under GATT and the implementation of the GATT panel (October 1989) which ruled that the Canadian import restrictions on ice-cream and yoghurt were inconsistent with GATT.

A task force on orderly marketing, headed by the Parliamentary Secretary to the national Minister of Agriculture, is currently studying options that are compatible with GATT and address the industry's ability

---

[68] The target levels of self-sufficiency vary by product: for industrial milk, the target level is 100 percent self-sufficiency of domestic butterfat consumption; for fluid milk, it is 100 percent of domestic consumption; for chicken broilers, it is 92 percent of domestic consumption; and for eggs, 97 percent.

to respond and compete. Recently, ministers reaffirmed their commitment to the maintenance of orderly marketing systems for dairy products and poultry. They established ad hoc review committees for each commodity to address the operation of tariff rate quotas under the Uruguay Round Agreement, future federal-provincial agreements, institutional structure and other operational and programme issues. The task force plans to submit recommendations to ministers in the autumn of 1994.

Grain transportation. The majority of Canadian cereals and oilseeds are produced in the prairies and exported as primary commodities. Regulated transportation of grains and oilseeds from western Canada has a long history and now forms an integral part of agricultural policy in Canada.[69] In 1983, the Western Grain Transportation Act (WGTA) institutionalized several ad hoc compensation programmes of the Crow Benefit with payments made directly to the railroads. The WGTA also required the producers' share of the freight cost, 42.8 percent of the total in 1993/94, to increase gradually through time.

The federal government commitment under the WGTA will be decreased by 10 percent in crop years 1993/94 and 1994/95. The February 1994 budget further reduced its commitment by 5 percent to C$615 million.

A number of studies have shown that the WGTA subsidy has resulted in higher on-farm prices for cereals in western Canada. As a result, livestock production in western Canada has been reduced. To offset the negative impact of this cereal transportation subsidy on livestock producers, provincial governments introduced subsidies for livestock producers.[70] The last of these programmes, however, was terminated in 1994 as a result of provincial budget pressures and the expectation of a change in the method of payment for the WGTA programme.

In June 1993, the federal government proposed (but did not pass) legislation to change the current method of payment from that of paying the subsidy to the railroads (in compensation for reduced producer rates) to that of paying the subsidy directly to the producer through the farm safety net system. This would result in transportation rates to producers increasing to the full

[69] In 1897, the Crow's Nest Pass Agreement fixed the statutory rates for the transportation of grains from the prairies to the great lakes "in perpetuity" in exchange for the railroad's commitment to build a rail line through the Rocky Mountains.
[70] In 1985 the province of Alberta introduced a programme on grain used for livestock feeding. Payments were initially C$21 per tonne but were reduced to C$10 per tonne by 1989. More limited programmes were introduced in Saskatchewan and Manitoba in 1989.

OECD COUNTRIES

compensatory level. The Producer Payment Panel was established to make recommendations on how the WGTA benefit should be delivered to producers. It proposed that payments to producers be made initially on an acreage basis and eventually (after seven years) be part of a national farm safety net programme for all producers in Canada.[71] The conclusion of the Uruguay Round of GATT negotiations has given an additional incentive to change the WGTA. This is because the transportation subsidy for cereals that go through the west coast and Churchill ports is classified as an export subsidy under GATT.

Safety net programmes. The Farm Income Protection Act (1991) established the basis for current safety net programmes in Canada. The programmes are: i) voluntary (producers agree to participate); ii) cost-shared through producer premiums and cofunded by the two levels of government; iii) market-oriented, using triggers based on moving averages of market variables; iv) based on performance triggers for payments such as prices, costs, gross revenue or net income; and v) actuarially sound, with premiums set to maintain the integrity of the fund for the programmes.

There are three main types of programme which support grains, oilseeds, red meats and horticultural products. The first type of programme, the National Tripartite Stabilization Programme (NTSP), makes payments to cattle, hog and lamb producers and a number of horticultural and speciality crop producers when market prices adjusted for costs drop below 80 percent of a five-year moving average.

The second type of programme is the Gross Revenue Insurance Plan (GRIP) which consists of a yield protection (crop insurance) and price/revenue protection. GRIP makes payments to cereal, oilseed and speciality crop[72] producers when the producer gross revenue from the market falls below a certain percentage (which varies by region from 70 to 90 percent) of the target revenue. This target revenue is based on the previous 15-year moving farmgate average price (with a three-year lag), adjusted for inflation, and on individual long-term average yields. Premium rates are set by an independent actuary and fluctuate from year to year depending on historical payouts and future price trends. Net payouts from the programme (i.e. total

---

[71] *Delivering the Western Grain Transportation Act Benefit to Producers.* **Final Report of the Producer Payment Panel, June 1994. This Report also recommended that, during the first seven years, C$70 million be allocated to Canadian whole farm safety nets.**

[72] **These crops include buckwheat, canary seed, broad beans, lentils, mustard, peas, beans, safflower, sunflower, triticale, white pea beans, coloured beans and kidney and cranberry beans.**

payouts less premium) were C$1.586 billion in 1991/92, C$972 million in 1992/93 and are estimated to be C$350 million in 1993/94. However, payouts are likely to increase slightly in 1994/95.

The third type of programme, the Net Income Stabilization Account (NISA), enables producers to make cash withdrawals from their individual accounts when their net income from eligible products (currently cereals, oilseeds, speciality crops and horticultural products) falls below the previous five-year average or when their taxable income falls below C$10 000. Producer contributions to their individual accounts of 2 percent of eligible sales are matched by federal and provincial governments. In addition, producers can contribute up to another 20 percent of their eligible sales (to a maximum of C$250 000), which is not matched by the government.

Budget pressures, loss of international competitive performance, substantial inequities among products and regional coverage and trade actions by the United States have led governments and producers to seek better solutions for safety net programmes. The Uruguay Round Agreement also emphasized the need to move from commodity-specific, coupled price support programmes to a support that is broadly based and decoupled. In response to these concerns, federal and provincial agriculture ministers proposed that all safety net programmes be converted to a whole farm approach similar to a NISA programme. Several programmes have already ended – the NTSPs for beef, lamb and pork producers were terminated in 1994. Red meats are to be added as eligible commodities for NISA. The province of Saskatchewan has indicated that it will opt out of GRIP in 1995.

At a major industry policy conference on safety nets in February 1993, it was agreed that the industry would move from the current GRIP and NTSP to include all commodities (except those under supply management) in a whole farm income protection programme. Companion programmes, such as disaster assistance and price supports, would also be part of the safety programme. A National Safety Nets Consultation Committee was established with a secretariat, steering committee and technical working groups. In July 1994, the Minister of Agriculture agreed as an interim measure that, for the 1994 year, NISA would be extended to all

commodities except those under supply management, in provinces wishing to extend this coverage. A further refinement of options will be proposed to ministers in November 1994.

The red meat NTSPs are being terminated at the request of producers. A key factor has been the trade actions or threat of trade actions by the United States. A significant share of Canadian production of live cattle and hogs and red meats is exported to the United States. A countervailing duty on Canadian live hogs entering the United States since 1988 has meant that little of the government subsidy is retained by Canadian hog producers. Programmes for Canadian beef producers have also been the subject of a Section 22 investigation by the United States International Trade Commission but no further action has occurred.

Canadian beef producers have proposed replacing the NTSP by a whole-farm approach programme (similar to NISA). A companion programme will be the Risk Management Agency which will operate commodity futures market programmes. A pilot project is expected in the autumn of 1994. Pork producers are considering this option and other cost-of-production or enhanced NTSP approaches.

Impact of policies

The Canadian economy is adjusting to the trade liberalization which has resulted from CUSTA, NAFTA and the Uruguay Round as well as previous rounds of GATT. Also, the globalization of markets for investments, services and information as well as the trend towards more deregulation all increase the pressure on the economy to adjust and compete. To meet the agricultural export target of C$20 billion in 2000, the agrifood processing sector must also become more competitive. Essential actions are to improve integration of the primary sector within the total food system and to provide an adequate supply of competitively priced products. Income support programmes have not always furthered this objective.

Supply management. Supply management for poultry and dairy products in Canada was instituted to improve producer prices, production stability, producer bargaining power and regional equity. Programmes have been effective in promoting these goals but, at the

OECD COUNTRIES

same time, they may have increased production costs, reduced efficiency and restricted growth in demand and consumption.

Under supply management programmes, the quotas for the right to produce have generated high values, requiring considerable capital investment. These values are bid up, as the most efficient farmers purchase quotas from the less efficient. An industrial milk producer would require an investment of about C$13 000 per cow or C$600 000 for an average farm. With the higher risk and restrictions on credit available to the enterprise, this is probably one of the main reasons for the smaller average herd size in Canada (34 cows) compared with many of its competitors such as New Zealand (164 cows), Australia (104 cows), the United Kingdom (63 cows), the United States (50 cows) or the Netherlands (41 cows). Data on production costs show that important economies of size exist. Thus, quotas reduce competitiveness because of the smaller herd size.

Productivity estimates using yield per cow show that Canada remains significantly below the United States. Comparisons of the cost of production in adjoining areas of Canada and the United States indicate that the average total cost of production is about 25 percent higher in Canada. However, the cost of production among producers is quite variable. For example, the lowest-cost 20 percent of Canadian producers have costs below the average United States producer.

Future reductions in the tariff equivalents established under GATT could result in lower domestic producer prices for supply-managed commodities. An initial adjustment would be a decline in the value of production quotas. As a result, the adjustments to obtain economies of size would be made easier by the reduced investment requirements under the production quota regime.

Production quotas for supply-managed products cannot be traded among provinces, which prevents production shifting to the most efficient producers and regions. Proposals by a national committee[73] to have a national milk pool for both producers and processors were not accepted by industry stakeholders. Neither have the national supply management supervisory agencies been able to devise acceptable principles for reallocating quotas among regions. Some minor

---

[73] **Report of the Consultative Committee on the Future of the Dairy Industry.**

regional adjustments have been made to accommodate markets where population has expanded the fastest, such as the province of British Columbia, and where quota cuts would have affected the viability of the processing sector (e.g. the Maritime Provinces). The Ontario Chicken Marketing Board substantially increased its production quota (by 24 percent) in 1994. British Columbia has already opted out of the national quota programme and has increased its market share. These extreme measures appear to be required to make regional production reallocations.

The poultry boards have been very conservative in the allocation of production quotas, despite a rapidly growing demand for poultry meat. Per caput poultry consumption in Canada has remained at about 75 percent of the United States level during the past few years. The conservative setting of quotas has limited promotions by supermarkets and new product development by the processing sector because there is no guarantee of adequate supplies. The highly processed products have had the highest growth but the supply management programme has reduced opportunities for participation.

The high support prices for milk have been an important factor in reducing dairy product consumption and hence milk production quotas (industrial milk quotas were reduced by 17 percent prior to the 1993/94 dairy year). Retail dairy product prices were 15 to 40 percent higher in Canada than in the United States (1991 estimates), resulting in significant cross-border shopping by Canadian consumers. Retailers in some provinces have also been prevented from using special prices for milk.

The pricing system for dairy products has limited the extent of the market orientation in the sector. For example, it has tended to encourage the production of butterfat, despite a clear preference by consumers for low-fat products. In all other OECD countries, the price of butter relative to skim milk powder has declined much more rapidly, reflecting this shift in consumer preference. This results in distorted consumer signals being sent throughout the whole inputs, production and processing sector. Producers have resisted a shift to multiple component pricing, which would allow a much more market-oriented pricing of milk.

The regulatory environment at the primary level has

also had an impact on the downstream industries which have been protected against imports of processed dairy products and faced considerable regulation of pricing practices, sources of supply and ability to export. The liberalization of the manufacturing sector of North American markets will enable increased imports of processed food products containing dairy and poultry ingredients and Canadian food processing firms will find themselves at a cost disadvantage when purchasing these agricultural inputs. The competitiveness of the sector will be most affected in the further processing of dairy and poultry products where there has been little incentive or ability to expand.

Grain transportation subsidies. The WGTA was introduced to maintain low transportation costs for cereals and oilseeds and to improve the bargaining power of producers. It has been an important means of income transfer to cereal and oilseed producers, but it has undoubtedly been capitalized into land prices. At the same time, however, it has created a number of production distortions and increased costs. It is central to a series of changes required to lower costs and improve the efficiency, viability and competitiveness of the entire grain transportation and handling system in Canada.

The WGTA increases domestic cereal and oilseed prices, shifts production in western Canada towards unprocessed bulk commodity exports – the slow-growth component of international trade – and reduces opportunities for value added processing and employment in the prairies. It has also limited adjustment to commodities which are not eligible for the transportation subsidy but which would be of higher value to the economy. As a result, structural adjustment in the prairies has been delayed, diversification has been limited, economic returns have been reduced and rural outmigration has been accelerated.

If the WGTA compensation was paid as a decoupled, direct payment to producers instead of to the railroads, the result would be a decline in farmgate prices for cereals and oilseeds. This decline in prices, coupled with the projected reduction in government safety net assistance, could substantially reduce the area currently devoted to cereals and oilseed production. It has been estimated that, under those conditions, up to 2 million

ha currently in cereal and oilseed production could no longer even cover the cash costs of production.[74] This land is likely to shift either to forage production for cow and calf operations or to new, lower-cost management for cereals and oilseed production which would increase total economic benefits. This change in the WGTA benefit payment would also improve the grain producers' competitive position in the eastern prairies compared with the adjoining areas in the United States, which would increase the potential for exports from Canada to this region.

Safety nets. Because of the differences in support levels among commodities and the fact that the NTSP and GRIP are commodity-based programmes, the safety net programmes in Canada have caused some production and marketing distortions. Producers have shifted production to crops with relatively higher support levels, regardless of current or expected market prices.

For example, the introduction of GRIP increased wheat area at the expense of feedgrains because of the relatively higher support level (based on 15-year moving average prices) compared with expected market prices. For certain speciality crops with thin markets, the potential oversupply has required changes in support levels to prevent major market disruptions. The province of Saskatchewan moved to a "basket of commodities" approach to avoid such problems.

The current safety net programme has affected the competitiveness of Canadian agriculture. High levels of support for certain commodities have maintained those commodities at the expense of both the search for more profitable alternatives and structural adjustments in the sector.

The movement of safety nets from commodity-based support programmes such as GRIP and the NTSP to income-based programmes would improve equity among products and regions and remove many of the production and marketing distortions. The NISA programme, which is the first attempt to design an income programme in Canada, permits the targeting of a more desirable performance measure than prices. Moreover, because of its sector-wide availability and non-distortive impact, NISA is likely to be considered a "green" programme in terms of future trade actions.

[74] **Technical Report of the Producer Payment Panel, March 1994, p. 48, Table 5.1.**

OECD COUNTRIES

Conclusion

In summary, much of the emphasis in Canadian agricultural policy during recent years has been to ensure equity and stability for producers. While achieving these objectives, the programmes have affected structural adjustment for the industry and reduced its competitive position in domestic and international markets. This lack of competitiveness has been most noticeable in the rapidly growing international trade in processed food products. Moreover, the large income-support expenditures are difficult to maintain in a period of sizeable fiscal deficits and there is a recognized need to provide programmes that improve competitiveness and environmental sustainability.

THE EUROPEAN UNION

The most important institutional event in the European Union (EU) over the last year with wider implications for the European Community (EC) and its agricultural sector was the progress made towards further enlargement of its membership. Indeed, in early 1994 the EU reached agreement on conditions of accession with four applicant countries: Austria, Finland, Norway and Sweden. Subject to approval by referendums, the four countries will become new members of the EU on 1 January 1995. Austria, the first country to hold such a referendum (12 June 1994) has already pronounced itself in favour of accession.

The demographic impact of the EU's enlargement will be relatively modest. The four new member countries will add only 26 million people to the current EU population of close to 350 million. The impact on the EC's Common Agricultural Policy (CAP) and market balances is also expected to be relatively moderate. The contribution of agriculture (including forestry and fisheries) to the GDP in the four countries ranges from 2.1 percent in Sweden to 3.8 percent in Finland (1991). The addition of the four new countries would increase the EC's total area of arable and permanent cropland by about 9 percent. Its agricultural labour force of 8.6 million would increase by some 0.7 million.

All four new member countries are major agricultural net importers. However, in aggregate they are net exporters of cereals, dairy products and meat. Their average yearly cereal production over the period 1989-93 amounted to approximately 15 million tonnes. Their net exports of cereals in the 1989-1992 period have ranged from a minimum of only 1 million tonnes to 3.2 million tonnes. For meat, total production in the four new member countries represents about 6 percent of production in the EC-12. Their net exports of meat in recent years have represented significantly less than 1 percent of EC-12 total production. Milk production in the four new member countries is fairly significant, representing 9 to 10 percent of EC-12 production. The value of their net exports of dairy products has dropped from 1990 to 1992, falling from more than 10 percent of EC-12 exports to only about 4 percent.

The main problems of the accession, as far as the agricultural sector is concerned, stem from the higher levels of support and the often particular regional

OECD COUNTRIES

TABLE 5

Aggregate production of main agricultural commodities in the four new member countries as a percentage of production in EC-12					
Commodity	1989	1990	1991	1992	1993
	(................................ % ....)				
Cereals	8.8	10.2	8.2	6.9	8.5
Meat	6.2	6.1	6.0	6.1	6.2
Milk	9.6	9.6	9.4	9.5	9.6
Sugar	5.7	5.7	5.1	5.2	5.7

Source: FAO.

TABLE 6

Net exports of major agricultural commodities from the four new EC member countries				
Commodity	1989	1990	1991	1992
CEREALS				
Million tonnes	1.04	2.29	3.16	2.34
Million $	121	202	244	210
MEAT				
'000 tonnes	69	75	45	39
Million $	102	118	31	24
DAIRY PRODUCTS				
Million $	286	346	222	149

Source: FAO.

circumstances (difficult climatic and mountainous conditions) characterizing agriculture in the new member countries. According to OECD estimates, in the new member countries levels of agricultural support in relation to the value of agricultural production expressed in percentage PSEs are substantially higher than in the EC, with the exception of Sweden, where agricultural support has dropped significantly since 1991 (in large part owing to a significant depreciation of the Swedish currency reducing the gap between domestic and international prices). When measured in

OECD COUNTRIES

terms of total transfers to agriculture per full-time farmer equivalent, agricultural support levels, according to the OECD, exceed those of the EC in all four applicant countries.

All four countries provide support to their agricultural sector, to varying degrees, both through market price support and direct payments to producers. Market price support is high in all four countries, as their average domestic producer prices are well above world market levels. With the exception of Sweden, all the new member countries also have rates of market price support that are significantly above those of the EC, which are also expected to decline in the medium term as a result of the implementation of the 1992 CAP reform.

The obverse of market price support to agricultural producers is the implicit taxation of consumers by keeping domestic consumer prices above world market levels, although consumer subsidies may in some cases reduce, if not altogether eliminate, the price wedge. According to OECD estimates, the price wedge between domestic and world market prices on the consumption side is substantial in the EC-12, but even more so in the applicant countries (with the exception of Sweden, which approaches EC-12 levels). Membership in the EU should thus be followed by lower prices for consumers in the new member countries.

As regards the modalities of the accession, the fourth enlargement of the EU occurs within a significantly different framework from the three previous ones. The creation of a single market no longer admits border controls on the movement of goods and services between the member countries. As a consequence, unlike the case of previous enlargements, the new member countries will be adopting the basic mechanisms of the CAP – including its institutional prices – from the day of accession. In order to facilitate the adjustment of agricultural producers in Austria, Finland and Norway to the lower support levels prevailing in the EC and to avoid undue strain on producer incomes, degressive national aids paid from national budgets will be authorized for a transitional period of up to five years. In addition, adjustment assistance is also authorized for facilitating adjustments in the food industry.

On accession, the new member countries will be

able to benefit from a wide range of EC programmes, i.e. for disadvantaged areas, structural adjustment and regional development. They will become eligible for structural support for mountainous and less-favoured areas within the framework of existing EC programmes as well as for support in favour of agro-environmental measures. They will also be eligible for the direct payments introduced within the context of the 1992 CAP reform to compensate farmers for the reduction in support prices. In addition, the accession agreement allows the payment of long-term national aid in certain areas – in principle, north of the 62nd parallel – in the Nordic countries, in order to ensure continued agricultural activity without leading to an increase or intensification of production. Specific conditions for such assistance are that the eligible areas have a low population density (less than ten inhabitants per km^2) an agricultural area representing less than 10 percent of total area and arable cropland representing less than 20 percent of agricultural land. The national aid should not be distortive and should not be linked to current agricultural production, but rather to physical factors of production (e.g. hectares of land) or historical levels of production. Likewise, Austria will be allowed a ten-year transition period to continue national aid to small-sized farms, in case EC rules do not offer equivalent compensation for natural handicaps.

For the period 1995-1998, the four new member countries will be granted compensation from the EC budget for a total of about ECU 3 billion to take account of problems deriving from adjustment to the CAP. A part of this compensation, to be provided in 1995, is to take account of the impossibility of applying certain CAP aids in the new member countries already in 1995, as well as the necessary lags involved in implementing structural policies introduced with the 1992 CAP reform. The other part of the compensation will be provided to the new member countries in order to take account of the costs of assisting the adjustment to lower EC agricultural support levels.

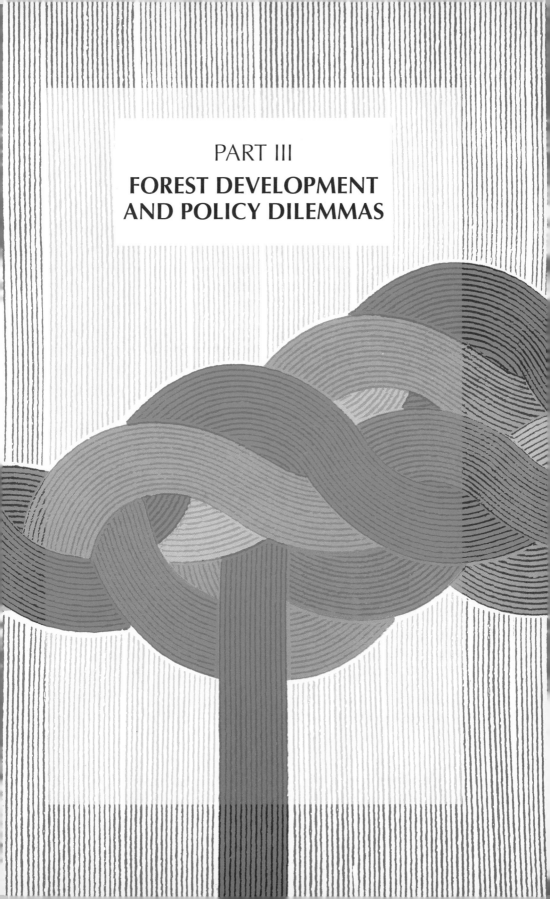

PART III

**FOREST DEVELOPMENT
AND POLICY DILEMMAS**

FOREST DEVELOPMENT AND POLICY DILEMMAS
I. Forests in transition

INTRODUCTION

The world's foresters must have welcomed the 1987 report by the Brundtland Commission, which urged sustainable development, as a long-awaited recognition of their core principle. It is in the context of forestry, after all, that the basic elements of sustained resource management originated many centuries ago. The Chinese grappled with questions of long-term sustainable timber supplies in the fourth century BC. In India and Sri Lanka, rulers began establishing forest reserves, controlling cutting and regulating hunting more than 2 000 years ago.

Western cultures later developed similar protective measures. The Canton of Schwyz in Switzerland passed legislation in 1343 to maintain forests for a constant supply of fuelwood and timber and for protection against avalanches.[1] In the sixteenth century, German states tried to prevent deforestation by imposing ordinances to regulate wood supplies; laws required households to plant hedges and dig ditches instead of building wooden fences, forced builders to substitute bricks for wood

---

[1] A.H. Gron. 1947. The economic foundations of forest politics. *Unasylva*, 1(3).

shingles in roofs and regulated charcoal making. Saxony called for all new houses to be built entirely of stone and permitted only designated foresters to decide which trees were to be cut, even in private forests.[2]

Over time, forestry policies and management practices evolved and adapted to changing economic demands, social needs and political circumstances. For centuries, European governments set aside forest reserves to maintain a reliable source of wood for warships. Later, forest management looked on trees as the primary fuel source for the industrial revolution. By the middle of the nineteenth century, European foresters had developed sustained yield practices to balance timber utilization with forest growth. North American foresters then broadened the sustained yield concept to include the conservation of non-timber values and ecological services.

While the term "sustained yield" may mean different things to different foresters, this tradition of managing forests for the indefinite future has remained a guiding principle of forestry thinking. Foresters developed biological models to maximize long-term timber production, pioneered economic techniques for evaluating optimal harvest rotations and introduced an ecosystem approach to sustainable forest management.[3] This experience should provide a model for balancing economic and social demands with nature's productivity. Instead, the competency of foresters to manage and control forest practices is being increasingly questioned and criticized by the public.

A widely held public opinion is that we are "cashing in" our forests; an initial reading of many vital signs does not reassure us that we are doing otherwise. A frequently cited study by the International Tropical Timber Organization (ITTO) asserts that fewer than 1 million ha of tropical forests out of the 828 million ha within ITTO member countries were under sustained yield management in the mid-1980s.[4] FAO estimates that 15.4 million ha of tropical forests were lost each year during the 1980s and that the area of severe forest degradation is perhaps even larger than the area of forest depletion.[5]

The general perception is that commercial logging is the major cause of accelerating tropical deforestation and temperate forest degradation. Critics point to the lack of attention paid to forest values other than timber,[6] including the value of wilderness, wildlife, non-wood products, environmental services,

[2] J.G. Laarman and R.A. Sedjo. 1992. *Global forests: issues for six billion people.* New York, McGraw-Hill.

[3] P.H. Pearse. 1993. Forest tenure, management incentives and the search for sustainable development policies. *In* W.L. Adamowicz, W. White and W.E. Phillips, eds. *Forestry and the environment.* Wallingford, UK, CABI.
[4] D. Poore. 1988. *Natural forest management for sustainable timber development.* London, IIED.
[5] FAO. 1993. *The challenge of sustainable forest management. What future for the world's forests?* Rome.
[6] A.V. Korotkov and T.J. Peck. 1993. Forest resources of the industrialized countries: an ECE/FAO assessment. *Unasylva,* 44(174).

ecological linkages and biodiversity. When logging operations conflict with these values, people believe forestry policies favour the timber industry. This discontent about how forests are managed as well as concern for the natural environment are increasing the pressure on governments to develop policies that address the multiple and competing demands on forest resources.

Forests are complex ecosystems capable of providing a wide range of economic, social and environmental benefits. Forests and woodlands are essential for human life, but their benefits and services are valued differently by different people and different groups. Local, national and international interests in forest resources also differ greatly across landscapes. Moreover, the numerous roles that forests are expected to play in local, national and global development change dramatically over time.

These multiple benefits and changing roles in the development process are challenging concepts and institutions that evolved during simpler times when forests were regarded as distant reserves to be managed as sources of public revenue and foreign exchange, treated as reservoirs of new land for cultivation or protected as nature reserves. Today, forests are no longer viewed as being separate in space, narrow in political interest or sectoral in their economic function. They directly affect and are affected by local, national and international concerns.

The roles of forestry (i.e. the knowledge, concepts, institutions and practices through which diverse and competing demands on forest resources are sought) are changing as well. The changes began in the 1970s, when growing awareness of how local communities control and depend on forests prompted efforts to strengthen local stakes in forest management, programmes and activities. New types of cooperative activities emerged between local communities and national governments, including community forestry, farm forestry, joint forest management and small-scale forestry enterprises. These activities highlighted the role of forests in broader rural development and, at the same time, eroded confidence in exclusive state control. Forests became symbols in a larger debate over centralized and decentralized governance.

The importance of forests to local communities led governments, NGOs and donors to consider a variety of rights, obligations, incentives and supports that would motivate people to invest in growing and managing forests. Countries throughout the world paid greater attention to local interests in forests and the capacity of communities to manage them alongside national interests. They explored new organizations, structures, rules and tenurial forms to enhance the productivity of forests, protect environmental qualities and empower rural communities to use forest resources for economic and social needs. As these various interests and objectives were not necessarily compatible, they gradually expanded rather than resolved contentious forest issues.

By the 1980s, countries began to recognize that forests have a global role in the stability of the biosphere, in the maintenance of biodiversity and in the protection of threatened indigenous and traditional cultures. This expanded role placed additional pressures on national governments. While in the 1970s they were compelled to develop better means to work with local communities, governments of the 1980s were expected to act as intermediaries between international interests in forests and local actions and demands for forest resources. Forestry policy-makers searched for ways to balance growing international expectations with the dispersed, diverse activities and needs of households and local communities.

Forests again became symbols in a larger debate; this time the subject was the sovereignty of nations and their right and capacity to govern land, and therefore people, in the national interest. While forests had played an international role as sources of tradable commodities for decades, their role in the provision of non-tradable global services now required a much more diverse range of international relationships.

In the 1990s, forests are a primary focus of policy discourse about sustainable development. Despite its message of harmony, the concept of sustainability raises tensions between market-driven economic growth, social pressures for a more equitable distribution of economic opportunities and the need to maintain environmental productivity, ecological services and biodiversity to fulfil future economic and social aspirations. The forces behind these pressures are unlikely to meet their goals without some compromise.

THE POLICY CHALLENGE

Society's shifting and sometimes conflicting expectations create difficult policy challenges related to both the forest sector and national development. Earlier centralized and sectoral policies were often motivated by the need to generate revenue and foreign exchange for national economic development. New national development strategies require policies that integrate forests in rural development efforts and that balance economic and environmental needs among national, local and international interests. Moreover, these strategies must acknowledge that forest conditions are a consequence of development, displaying the imprint of competitive uses.

Forest resources are now in the forefront of national policy debate about how to restructure entire economic and political systems as well as how such structural changes can be made consistent with national interests in local action, social and sectoral distribution, international obligations and sovereignty. Today's governments are searching for pragmatic policy frameworks that deal coherently with both the contributions of forests to development and the institutional and organizational structures required to make better use of these contributions.

International organizations, non-governmental organizations (NGOs) and research centres are producing important studies aimed at helping policy-makers address these complex issues. FAO, the World Bank, the regional development banks, the ITTO, the World Wide Fund for Nature (WWF), the World Conservation Union (IUCN), and the World

Resources Institute (WRI), among others, are gathering, analysing and distributing information to raise the public's awareness and improve its capacity to respond to forestry problems.[7]

Concern about forestry's evolving roles moved on to a crowded stage at the United Nations Conference on Environment and Development (UNCED) in June 1992. UNCED highlighted forestry development and environmental issues by developing a set of "forest principles", devoting a chapter of its document Agenda 21 to combating deforestation (Chapter 11) and focusing on the importance of non-wood functions of forests in the biodiversity and climate change conventions.[8] A number of countries have launched specific international programmes to follow up on UNCED forestry recommendations. This broad consensus on principles of sustainable forest management represents the first-ever commitment of responsibilities beyond national boundaries. Turning these principles into practice, however, presents a more formidable task.

Developing effective forestry strategies and policies involves an array of difficult choices. For example, while we know that forest clearing for crops and pasture, overcutting for fuelwood, uncontrolled commercial logging and expanding infrastructure all contribute to deforestation and degradation, the fundamental problem facing policy-makers is how to address the underlying causes, which include poverty, hunger, access to land, a lack of jobs and income-generating opportunities and growing economic demands for forest goods and services.

Ironically, some government policies frequently exacerbate these underlying causes, producing intense and lasting impacts on forest resources.[9] A growing body of literature now demonstrates convincingly that taxes, terms of forest concessions, administered prices, controlled transportation of forest goods, land and tree tenure insecurity, tariff and non-tariff barriers to international trade, investment incentives, agricultural sector strategies and macroeconomic policies all affect economic motivations as well as the management and conservation of temperate and tropical forests. In many cases, these policies directly encourage or unintentionally subsidize deforestation and degradation.

Today, countries are seeking more appropriate economic policies, regulatory mechanisms, financial incentives, organizational structures and tenurial arrangements to promote sustainable forestry practices. In many countries, the search for policies takes place alongside a wider examination

---

[7] Among the many recent studies are: FAO, op. cit., footnote 5, p. 252; N.P Sharma, ed. 1992. *Managing the world's forests: looking for balance between conservation and development*. Dubuque, Iowa, Kendall/Hunt; and Laarman and Sedjo, op. cit., footnote 2, p. 252.

[8] J.P. Lanly. 1992. Forestry issues at the United Nations Conference of Environment and Development. *Unasylva*, 43(171).

[9] A. Contreras-Hermosilla. 1993. *Forestry policies in India*. Paper prepared for the South Asia Region Seminar on Forestry Management and Sustainable Development, Kandy, Sri Lanka, 4-9 October 1993.

of the role of government as regulator of the market place, as landowner and as forest manager. This examination is prompted partly by governments' own need to optimize resource efficiency, and partly by public dissatisfaction with government performance and, in particular, with the performance of forest services and their policies.

The current public pressure on governments for rapid innovation and institutional change is tremendous. The contributions of forests to national development depend on how well this challenge is met.

PURPOSE AND SCOPE

The purpose of this special chapter is to enhance our understanding of how economic and social policies affect forest resources. While it does not attempt to lay out an agenda for action or establish a set of correct policy choices, the chapter aims to raise awareness and inform a full range of professional and public interests so that forest issues can be better understood and appreciated.

Choosing policies to influence and manage forest ecosystems are among the most controversial challenges facing the world community. The political mainstreaming of forestry issues has forced the forestry profession to reassess its knowledge, roles, attitudes, limits, responsibilities and practices. This process has involved productive debates leading to innovative responses to public concerns. Here an attempt is made to encourage further debate, stimulate thinking about the way we manage and use forest resources, promote change and help interest groups recognize that some goals are incompatible, that not all groups can achieve every one of their goals and that, without cooperation and compromise, none may achieve their objectives.

The perspectives and demands of politically diverse groups are proliferating, placing a significant strain on current institutions and policies. The analysis presented here illustrates that macro and sectoral policies are blunt instruments that attempt to encourage behaviour across broad sweeps of land with diverse social and ecological settings. Economic, social and environmental impacts depend not so much on the effect of policies on one forest, but their net effects across these diverse settings. This special chapter stresses the need to view forests from this macro perspective and to map out the ecological potential, social motivations and organizational capacities which provide the basis for judging the net impacts of national policy.

The chapter is organized in five sections. This first section reviews the current state of forest resources and their importance to economies, societies and the environment.

Section II provides an overview of the changing role of forestry in development strategies and national economies. It describes how forests have evolved out of a narrow sectoral prerogative to enter mainstream political interests involving highly diverse groups.

Section III discusses key issues facing policy-makers and examines how economic policies affect forest resources. It reviews the literature examining macro, intersectoral and forestry sector policy implications. This section also introduces the concept of landscape formation models as an example of how to recognize, explain and direct policy interactions that influence how people use forests.

Section IV explores the relationship between forest trade policies, forest management practices and their environmental impacts. The costs and administrative implications of certification schemes for forest products are reviewed and compared.

The final section examines future directions for forestry policies in contributing to sustainable development. It suggests that a major task for governments is to develop national frameworks to deal explicitly with the consequences of their overall policy choices on forests and to establish priorities between forests and other national interests.

THE STATE OF FOREST RESOURCES

Forests are classified, assessed, described, mapped, evaluated and studied in a variety of ways. Despite several decades of attempts, no single, widely accepted forest classification system exists. Even common definitions are difficult, in part because nature is not easily compartmentalized, and in part because different cultures, languages, professional disciplines and interest groups view forests from their own perspectives.

Forest assessments estimate the extent and evaluate the condition of various forest zones. Forest vegetation is classified and then divided into these zones based on geographic-climatic features or physiognomic-structural characteristics. Physiognomic-structural classifications combine forest appearance (e.g. open woodland or closed forest) with vegetative structure (e.g. evergreen or moist deciduous). Each classification has a number of variations which reflect different economic, geographic and biological information. Each approach has its advantages, depending on who is collecting, using and evaluating the information.

Extensive knowledge about forest regions and ecosystems is indispensable to today's foresters, policy-makers and scientists. For instance, forest geneticists have shown that the geographic source of tree seed used to regenerate forests is crucial to their survival. Building this knowledge base, however, is a daunting task. Foresters are asked to provide information about entire forest ecosystems and their internal processes, which can involve thousands of species interacting in a constantly changing environment. Forest ecologists must characterize and classify regions and geographers must delineate them in a way that describes meaningful ecological zones. A recent attempt in Canada resulted in the identification of 5 428 forest ecodistricts.[10]

FAO's first forest assessment, the 1947 World Forest Inventory, focused on wood production capacity. Over time, new concerns emerged and the need to evaluate forests for their many other values became more apparent. Subsequent FAO global forest assessments continued to cover wood production capacity but also attempted to capture information about fuelwood resources (1970s), tropical deforestation (1980s) and forest fragmentation, logging intensity, biomass conditions and plantations (1990s). The 1990 temperate forest resources assessment included a review of forest functions by area.

In its most recent resource assessment, FAO estimates world forest area to be 3.4 billion ha, or 26 percent of the earth's land area. FAO's definition of forests includes ecological systems with a minimum of 10 percent crown coverage of trees. In addition to areas classified as forests, 1.6 billion ha contain woody vegetation and other woodlands consisting of shrubs and scrub. Woodlands often have forest characteristics but do not meet the minimum tree cover definition of open or closed forests.

The regional distribution of world forest cover is presented in Figure 9.

---

[10] **Forestry Canada. 1993. *The state of Canada's forests*. Ottawa.**

Figure 9

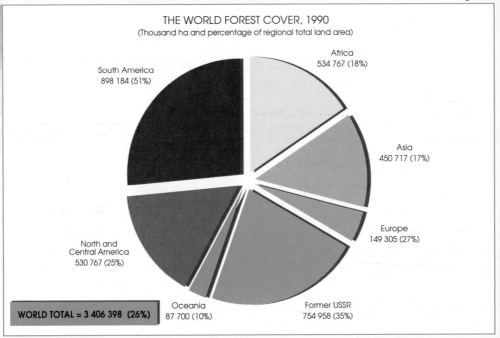

THE WORLD FOREST COVER, 1990
(Thousand ha and percentage of regional total land area)

South America
898 184 (51%)

Africa
534 767 (18%)

Asia
450 717 (17%)

Europe
149 305 (27%)

North and
Central America
530 767 (25%)

WORLD TOTAL = 3 406 398 (26%)

Oceania
87 700 (10%)

Former USSR
754 958 (35%)

Source: FAO

Four countries account for more than 50 percent of the world's forests: the Russian Federation (22 percent), Brazil (16 percent), Canada (7 percent) and the United States (6 percent). Table 7 lists the most forested countries in the world according to total land area, proportion of land area and forests per inhabitant.

Some of the least-forested countries have extremely arid climates, for example Algeria, Egypt and Saudi Arabia. Others include countries which were once heavily forested but which cleared most of their original forests for agriculture, human settlement and infrastructure. Examples include Bangladesh, Haiti and the United Kingdom.

Temperate and boreal forests: resources and issues

Temperate and boreal forests occupy 1.64 billion ha, just less than half of the world's forest cover. More than 70

percent of these are located in the Russian Federation (45 percent), Canada (15 percent) and the United States (13 percent). In general, the aggregate size of temperate forests in industrial countries is stable or even increasing slightly through afforestation efforts. In Europe, the forested and wooded land area increased by 2 million ha between 1980 and 1990.

The temperate zone includes two basic ecological formations: mixed temperate forest and boreal forest. The mixed temperate forests comprise coniferous, broadleaf, deciduous, evergreen and other forest types found in the non-tropical zone and on mountain ranges in subtropical and tropical countries. The boreal forests extend between the arctic tundra and the temperate zones in a circumpolar belt of mainly coniferous trees. The boreal forests are vast; they cover 920 million ha, make up 27 percent of the

TABLE 7

The top ten most forested countries, 1990

7A

Total forest area

Country	Total forest cover	Percentage of land area	Hectares per caput
	('000 ha)		
Former USSR	754 958	35	2.6
Brazil	561 107	66	3.7
Canada	247 164	27	9.3
United States	209 573	23	0.8
China	127 780	14	0.1
Zaire	113 275	50	3.1
Indonesia	109 549	61	0.6
Peru	67 906	53	3.0
Colombia	54 064	52	1.7
India	51 729	17	0.1

7C

Forest area per caput

Country	Hectares per caput	Total forest cover	Percentage of land area
		('000 ha)	
French Guyana	86.9	7 997	91
Suriname	36.6	14 768	95
Guyana	17.7	18 416	94
Gabon	15.6	18 235	71
Botswana	11.1	14 261	25
Belize	11.0	1 996	88
Central African Rep.	10.5	30 562	49
Congo	10.0	19 865	58
Namibia	9.4	12 569	15
Canada	9.3	274 164	27

7B

Proportion of total land area

Country	Percentage of land area	Total forest cover	Hectares per caput
		('000 ha)	
Suriname	95	14 768	36.6
Guyana	94	18 416	17.7
French Guyana	91	7 997	86.9
Belize	88	1 996	11.0
Brunei Darussalam	87	458	1.7
Papua New Guinea	80	36 000	9.0
Guinea-Bissau	72	2 021	2.1
Gabon	71	18 235	15.6
Cambodia	69	12 163	1.5
Brazil	66	561 107	3.7
Finland	66	20 112	4.0

earth's forest area and contain more than 70 percent of its coniferous forests.

Temperate zone forests are widely recognized for their enormous contribution of global industrial timber supplies as well as for their non-wood products, recreation and environmental services. However, they are often less appreciated for their plant and animal life than the tropical rain forests, even though they contain some of the tallest and oldest trees in the world. North America's redwoods and Douglas firs and Australia's eucalyptuses can grow to almost 100 m, and some bristlecone pines in the southwestern United States are estimated to be more than 4 800 years old. The pharmaceutical value of biodiversity in the temperate zone is also substantial. For example, the Pacific yew contains the chemical taxol, which is an effective medicine against several forms of cancer. A recent study found that 28 percent of Canadian trees have medicinal properties.[11] Box 11 presents an overview of the carbon storage and biodiversity values of temperate and boreal forests.

Forest quality and management issues in the temperate zone. Public concern about how temperate forest resources are managed and used is widespread and growing.[12] Forest quality, health and vitality are the major concerns: interest groups are questioning the ability of current forest policies, management practices and ownership structures to balance forest quality with competing demands for timber, jobs, wildlife conservation, water resources, landscape and recreational benefits.

Attempts to measure and define "forest quality" show how differently it is viewed from different standpoints.[13] To forest industries, the old-growth forest in the Pacific Northwest of the United States may be overmature. To conservationists, this forest is the perfect age for a biodiversity reserve. To most vacationers, old-growth forests are aesthetically more pleasing than the cropped rows of even-aged plantations.

The strongest pressure for changing timber management practices comes from groups interested in non-timber forest functions. In Europe, these groups are calling attention to the expansion of intensively managed single species plantations, the afforestation of rare ecosystems and water acidification related to afforestation. North American groups are especially concerned about logging practices, stumpage fees and the rate, level and intensity of timber extraction in old-growth forests.[14] In Canada, land-use planning conflicts over clear-felling and timber concession policy led to a new consultative management approach and the "model forest" programme. Ten model forests cover an area of 7 million ha, in which the most ecologically sound forestry practices are to be used. Each model forest is managed for a sustainable supply of timber, but most also integrate a range of other important functions, including water quality, biodiversity, wildlife habitat, community stability and recreation and cultural and spiritual values.[15]

Logging in the Pacific Northwest of the United States and afforestation of the Scottish flow country in the United Kingdom have led to conflicts over bird conservation. In both countries, the disputes focused on the value of birds as an indicator of the health of forest ecosystems. In both cases, the problem was perceived as a conflict between jobs and birds and between the needs of local communities

[11] D.E. McAllister. 1991. **Estimating the pharmaceutical values of forests, Canadian and tropical.** *Canadian Biodiversity,* 1(3).

[12] A.V. Korotkov and Peck, op. cit., footnote 6, p. 252.

[13] N. Dudley, J.-P. Jeanrenaud and S. Stolton. 1993. *Towards a definition of forest quality.* WWF-UK.

[14] WWF. 1993. *What is happening to the global forestry policy?* **Background paper for the Forests of the World Conference. Copenhagen.**

[15] Forestry Canada, op. cit., footnote 10, p. 258.

BOX 11
TEMPERATE FORESTS' VALUES: CARBON STORAGE AND BIODIVERSITY

In addition to their economic importance, temperate and boreal forests play an important role in biodiversity and the earth's carbon budget – the balance between carbon release and accumulation. Carbon dioxide (CO_2) is one of the main gases associated with the greenhouse effect. Because a considerable amount of carbon is temporarily stored in forests, they influence the build-up of carbon in the atmosphere, both through emission from fire, decay, harvesting and processing and through their absorption and storage capacity as they grow. FAO's Forest Resources Assessment 1990 documents the continuing expansion of temperate and boreal forest resources, which is leading to increased carbon absorption and storage.

The potential effects of global warming on temperate and boreal forests include changes in tree growth rates, in species composition, in the extent of the effects of fire, pests and disease, and shifts in forest boundaries. Some changes, such as the apparent fertilizing effect of CO_2 emissions on tree growth, may be beneficial. Others, including the shrinkage of the boreal forest zone from its southern boundary, could be damaging to economies dependent on forests.[1]

Some boreal forest countries are attempting to minimize the extent of global warming. In Canada, for example, forest managers are being asked to pay more attention to the types of forests logged, the amount of timber harvested and the effects of harvesting on forest soils, as these factors influence the amount of stored carbon. Canada's forests are a net carbon sink, accumulating 45 percent more carbon than they release. To improve the carbon budget further, Canada's policy-makers are examining ways to encourage processing and consumption that maximize the temporal extent of the carbon stored in forests.

With generally fewer tree species per hectare than tropical forests, boreal forests are considered to contain a relatively low level of biodiversity. New information, however, particularly about the soil biota and invertebrates, is encouraging a reassessment

_____

[1] B. Street, B.J. Stocks, D.C. MacIver and R.B. Stewart. 1993. *Impacts of climate change on Canadian forests.* Paper presented to the 14th Commonwealth Forestry Conference, Kuala Lumpur, Malaysia.

of boreal zone diversity. For instance, recent studies reveal that two-thirds of all micro-organisms and plant and animal species found in Canada reside in forests.

The forests that regenerate in Canada's boreal zone following harvesting have higher proportions of poplar and birch and lower quantities of spruce and pine. In Sweden, the conversion of old-growth forests to uniform spruce and pine plantations threatens 200 forest-dwelling species of plants and animals with extinction and a further 800 with decline. These include lichens, fungi and invertebrates that depend on dead wood, a rare component in plantations. Some 880 species of beetles depend on dead trees and help to recycle nutrients in the forests. In Finland, more than 50 percent of 1 692 threatened species of flora and fauna are located in the remaining areas of old-growth forests.[2]

Wider recognition of these boreal forest values has led to expanding research and protection efforts. Examples include:
• The Boreal Ecosystem Atmospheric Study (BOREAS), an international research and monitoring effort established to improve our understanding of the interactions between boreal forests and the atmosphere.
• The International Working Group on Boreal Forests and Taiga Rescue Network, two international scientific and NGO forums for information exchange, awareness raising and joint scientific and environmental activities;
• Increases in the protected area of old-growth forests in the principal boreal forest countries; for example, protected areas in Canada have tripled over the past 30 years, and Canadian forestry and environment ministers are committed to protecting 12 percent of the most significant habitats.

The overriding requirement is to increase our knowledge of the ecological systems inherent in unaccessed boreal forests, ascribe values to the non-timber benefits and forest qualities and determine appropriate silvicultural practices from an objective understanding of sustainable forestry.

---

[2] Taiga Rescue Network. 1992. Forests and forestry in Scandinavia: a status report. *Taiga News* (July).

dependent on forests for employment and the interests of "outsiders" who value the forests' environmental services. Moreover, both disputes showed the high level of importance that forestry issues receive in industrial countries; the President of the United States intervened to resolve the situation in the Pacific Northwest while the Minister of Agriculture, Fisheries and Food acted on the problem in the United Kingdom.

These two cases illustrate the kinds of problem that temperate forest policy-makers face in balancing competing values and interests, including those values that can be quantified in financial terms and those values that, while providing wider public benefits, as yet have no market.

The tropical forest zone
The tropical forest zone contains 1.76 billion ha, divided into six ecofloristic zones: the tropical rain forests, the moist deciduous forests, the dry zone, the very dry zone, the desert zone and the hill and mountain forests. Table 8 presents the regional distribution of these six categories. Ninety-six percent of tropical forests occur in the following four formation types.

Tropical rain forests are found in areas with more than 2 500 mm of annual rainfall. They are evergreen, luxuriant and rich in animal and plant species. More than half the world's 718.3 million ha of rain forests are located in two countries: Brazil (41 percent) and Indonesia (13 percent). Rain forest composition and structure vary with distance from the ocean, distance from rivers, altitude and geographic position.

Moist deciduous forests occur in areas with an annual rainfall of 1 000

to 2 000 mm. Forest structure varies depending on the amount and distribution of rain, the type of soil and the length of the dry season. Some dominant tree species may lose their leaves towards the end of the dry season. This forest type is generally less diverse than rain forest.

Dry zone forests are found in tropical areas receiving between 500 and 1 000 mm of rainfall per year. They are relatively open and include thornland, shrubland, savannah and other short and sparse woody vegetation. Dry zone forests tend to be fragile and are easily degraded. More than half are in Africa. Dry forest types include oak, mesquite, piñon-juniper, maquis and acacia.

Tropical upland forests are forests above 800 m and include cloud forests (montane rain forests), which are shorter, floristically simpler and more heavily laden with mosses and lichens than lowland rain forests. Tropical upland species are similar to temperate forest species. The upland zone covers the Himalayas, parts of Myanmar, Thailand and Viet Nam, the highlands of Mexico, the Andes and the highlands of Ethiopia and mountains around Lake Victoria.

More than 200 million people live in clearings in tropical forests. They include groups who have lived in the same forest for generations, often referred to as indigenous or tribal peoples; people who have recently moved into the area, often described as settlers or squatters; and people who live part-time in the forest working as small-scale harvesters of forest products.[16] These forests

---

[16] FAO, op. cit., footnote 5, p. 252.

TABLE 8

Area of tropical forest formation, 1990

Region	Total forest area	Rain forest	Moist deciduous	Dry deciduous	Hill and mountain	Very dry	Desert
	(.... '000 ha ....)						
Africa	527 586	86 616	251 143	92 527	35 256	58 660	3 385
Asia	310 597	177 371	41 832	41 108	47 163	37	3 085
Latin America and Caribbean	918 116	454 309	294 306	44 944	121 895	1 045	1 616
TOTAL	1 756 299	718 297	587 281	178 579	204 314	59 742	8 086

Source: FAO.

contribute to food security by providing sources of food, income, jobs, fuelwood, medicine and construction materials. Hunting for forest wildlife provides a significant proportion of the protein requirements of forest dwellers and the rural poor in many countries.

Forests also provide important indirect services. For example, forests surrounding towns, villages and communities offer critical soil erosion protection on hillsides and near streams. Deforestation in nearby watersheds may lead to flooding of lowland areas, displacement of populations and reductions in food production, as happened recently in Thailand and Madagascar.[17]

Tropical deforestation. The rates, causes and effects of deforestation differ greatly from one country or region to another. These differences are due to population density and growth rates, the extent and quality of forest resources, levels and rates of development, the structure of property rights and cultural systems. Recent estimates suggest that nearly two-thirds of tropical deforestation worldwide is due to farmers clearing land for agriculture.[18] Table 9 provides data on deforestation rates by region for the four major forest zones. As FAO points out in its recent book on sustainable forest management (footnote 5, p. 252), tropical forests are not being destroyed for trivial reasons. They are being cleared to provide expanding populations with land for food and cash crops. Many growing economies depend on wood products as a source of jobs, income, tax revenue and export earnings. Logging concessions and industrial roundwood production, from which sawnwood, panels and pulp and paper originate, provide these opportunities.

The largest losses of forest area are

---

[17] N.P. Sharma, R. Rowe, K. Openshaw and M. Jacobson. 1993. World forests in perspective. *In* Sharma, ed., op. cit., footnote 7, p. 255.

[18] R. Rowe, N.P. Sharma and J. Browder. 1993. Deforestation: problems, causes, and concerns. *In* Sharma, ed., op. cit., footnote 7, p. 255.

TABLE 9A

Forest cover and deforestation in the tropical zone

Region	Total land area	Forest area 1980	Forest area 1990	Annual change in area 1981-90	Annual rate of change
	(.. million ha ....)				(%)
Africa	2 236	568	527	-4.1	-0.7
Asia	892	350	311	-3.9	-1.2
Latin America	1 650	992	918	-7.4	-0.8
WORLD TOTAL	4 778	1 910	1 756	-15.4	-0.8

TABLE 9B

Deforestation in the tropical rain forest zone

Region	Total land area of zone	Total forested area 1990		Annual deforestation 1981-90	
	(million ha)	(million ha)	(% of zone)	(million ha)	(% of zone)
Africa	118.5	86.6	73	0.5	0.5
Asia	306.0	177.4	58	2.2	1.1
Latin America	522.6	454.3	87	1.9	0.4
WORLD TOTAL	947.1	718.3	76	4.6	0.6

TABLE 9C

Deforestation in the moist deciduous forest zone

Region	Total land area of zone	Total forested area 1990		Annual deforestation 1981-90	
	(million ha)	(million ha)	(% of zone)	(million ha)	(% of zone)
Africa	653.6	251.1	38	2.2	0.9
Asia	144.6	41.8	29	0.7	1.5
Latin America	491.0	294.3	60	3.2	1.0
WORLD TOTAL	1 289.2	587.2	46	6.1	1.0

TABLE 9D

Deforestation in the dry and very dry zones

Region	Total land area of zone	Total forested area 1990		Annual deforestation 1981-90	
	(million ha)	(million ha)	(% of zone)	(million ha)	(% of zone)
Africa	823.1	151.2	18	1.1	0.7
Asia	280.6	41.1	15	0.5	1.1
Latin America	145.4	46.0	32	0.6	1.3
WORLD TOTAL	1 249.1	238.3	19	2.2	0.9

TABLE 9E

Deforestation in the tropical upland formations

Region	Total land area of zone	Total forested area 1990		Annual deforestation 1981-90	
	(million ha)	(million ha)	(% of zone)	(million ha)	(% of zone)
Africa	169.2	35.3	21	0.3	0.8
Asia	102.6	47.2	46	0.6	1.2
Latin America	429.1	121.9	28	1.6	1.2
WORLD TOTAL	700.9	204.4	29	2.5	1.1

Note: Table 9A gives figures on forest cover in the tropical zone as a whole, including forests growing in zones not regarded as zones of natural forest growth, such as deserts or alpine areas. The data for Tables 9B to 9E are restricted to the zones of natural forest growth. The sums of the figures in these tables do not necessarily agree with Table 9A. Source: FAO, op. cit., footnote 5, p. 252.

taking place in the tropical moist deciduous forests, the zone best suited for human settlement. In the decade 1981 to 1990, an estimated 61 million ha were deforested, which is more than 10 percent of the remaining moist deciduous area. The proportion of moist deciduous area still forested is 46 percent (only 29 percent in Asia). In contrast, 76 percent of the world's rain forest zone is still covered in forest. During the past decade, the total area of rain forest cut was 46 million ha.

Plantations

The available data on tree plantation areas suggest that the 100 million ha of plantations in the world provide for 7 to 10 percent of the world's present commercial wood consumption.[19] An additional 14 million ha of rubber and coconut oil palm plantations are not included in the area of forest

[19] J.J. Gauthier. 1991. *Plantation wood in international trade.* Paper presented at the seminar, Issues Dialogue on Tree Plantations – Benefits and Drawbacks, Geneva, CASIN.

plantations. These are mainly in Asia and the wood obtained from them is increasingly important.

Statistics on plantations must be treated with caution because some reports use figures based on the accumulated area planted without any deductions for the areas felled. In other cases, figures are based simply on the numbers of seedlings distributed to farmers or communities and not on the numbers planted or surviving. On the other hand, the figures may omit the numbers of trees planted by farmers from their own seedlings.

Plantations cannot provide the full range of goods and services supplied by a natural forest. They are tree crops, analogous to agricultural crops, with a simplified ecology of one or, at most, a few species usually chosen for their yield and ease of management. The primary purpose of most plantations is to produce wood or other products quickly and cheaply. Their role, which is a highly valuable one, complements national or global forestry management strategies.

Plantations can be highly

BOX 12
MALAYSIA'S COMPENSATORY PLANTATION PROGRAMME

Malaysia has a long history of experience with tree plantations. To meet projected timber requirements, the country established teak plantations in its northern peninsula in the late 1950s. A decade later, fast-growing tropical pine plantations were planted to provide long-fibre pulp for an expanding pulp and paper industry. Prime lowland natural forest was cleared to plant *Pinus caribaea, P. merkusii* and *Araucaria* spp.

In the 1980s, a number of factors prompted policy-makers to expand plantations. First, revised projections made it clear that natural forests alone could not entirely meet the growing demand for logs. The initial growth rates and production estimates of the country's selective management system proved to be overoptimistic. Second, three-decades of agricultural development had reduced much of Malaysia's natural production forests to less productive and harder to manage hilly areas. Third, overharvesting in many areas resulted in a significant backlog of secondary forest in need of silvicultural treatment and rehabilitation.

The government responded by establishing the Compensatory Forest Plantation Programme. As the name suggests, this large-scale programme was intended to compensate for the declining timber production from Malaysia's natural forests by establishing 188 000 ha of fast-growing, utility-grade tree plantations. As development programmes converted natural forests to agricultural and other uses, the timber would be used by an expanding wood processing industry. An important objective of the compensatory plantation programme was to maintain timber production at levels that could support the country's wood processing capacity.

In the early 1980s, international donors promoted fast-growing species such as *Acacia mangium, Gmelina arborea* and *Paraserianthes flacataria* as a means of relieving pressure on natural forests. The Malaysian Government accepted funding to plant these species even though the performance of the principal species to be planted, *Acacia mangium*, was largely unproven in Malaysia. Nor was this

species well established in domestic or international markets.

Over time, problems with the performance of *A. mangium* became evident. Although the tree grows rapidly, it has poor form, is vulnerable to heartrot and is not a reliable source of utility-grade timber. To date, its wood appears to be more suitable for wood chips, a much lower-value end use. As a result, the government has halted the Compensatory Forest Plantation Programme.

productive. The increment of timber from a tropical plantation may be 30 m³ per hectare compared with 2 to 8 m³ per hectare from a managed natural forest. Annual yields of up to 70 m³ per hectare have been attained in Brazil from clones of hybrids of eucalyptus species. Such figures must be treated with caution, however (see Box 12). Experience shows that the yields assumed at the planning stage of many plantations are overestimated, often by a factor of two or more.[20] Tree plantations that are well planned and managed can be highly productive and are ideal for supporting large-scale wood industries.

In tropical countries, the net area of plantations (taking into account the estimated survival rates) is estimated to be about 30 million ha, counting industrial and community plantations but not including trees planted by farmers themselves on their own lands.[21] The area dedicated to plantations is growing at an average rate of around 2.6 million ha per year; about half of this area is in communally owned plantations.

A recent review of tropical plantations concluded that planning is generally poor, particularly for vital issues such as matching species and site. The study also noted that plantation projects are often designed in haste, with scant attention paid to important issues because of time and financial constraints.[22]

Temperate countries also have numerous examples of plantations that have failed or sites that have been degraded because large blocks of single-species plantations have been established, unsuitable species have been introduced and even-aged plantations have been planted. Case-studies describe improperly managed temperate plantations as degrading key natural habitats, increasing soil erosion, modifying local hydrological cycles, intensifying pest and disease attacks and elevating levels of agrochemical pollution.[23]

In the developing countries, further development of plantation forestry is constrained by the shortage of land. With expanding farming populations using all the unforested land for food production, the areas available for plantations are becoming increasingly restricted. The experience of the past two decades demonstrates that degraded or "waste" land may be the only resource available to the landless poor. There are, however, large areas where the natural forest has been badly degraded or where soil fertility has been lost through overcultivation, which could be used for plantations.

---

[20] FAO, op. cit., footnote 5, p. 252.
[21] D. Pandey. 1992. *Assessment of tropical forest plantation resources.* Umeå, Uppsala, Swedish University of Agricultural Sciences.
[22] Ibid.

---

[23] N. Dudley. 1992. *Forests in trouble: a review of the status of temperate forests worldwide.* Gland, Switzerland, WWF.

FOREST DEVELOPMENT AND POLICY DILEMMAS
II. Forests and national development

When international attention turned to the developing countries in the early 1950s, economists were caught unprepared. They had no readily available conceptual model with which to analyse the economic growth process in these mostly agrarian societies.[24] Many economists reasoned that developing countries would need to follow the same path taken by the world's richer nations in their transformation from agrarian to industrial economies. Development models described this growth process as a series of linear stages through which all countries must pass.

Natural resources such as forests received little or no attention in these initial models. Instead, development strategies highlighted capital formation and technical progress as the major factors responsible for rising incomes and economic growth. In general, forests were viewed as a source of land to be converted to more productive uses. While they could also be a source of revenue and foreign exchange, forests were seen as relatively unimportant in the struggle to promote sustained economic development.[25] Forest industries other

[24] M.P. Todaro. 1985. *Economic development in the Third World.* New York, Longman.
[25] G. Robinson. 1965. Forests and economic development in Latin America. *Journal of Forestry,* 63(2).

than pulp and paper were considered too small to be significant for industrialization efforts.

FORESTS IN EARLY DEVELOPMENT STRATEGIES

International donors also ignored the forestry sector relative to other activities. The World Bank did not establish a policy paper on forestry development until 1978. Between 1949 and 1968, it funded only two forestry projects in developing countries – a chemical pulp and newsprint mill in Chile and a paper mill in Bangladesh.[26]

During the same period, lending for land colonization projects, dam construction, road building and related development projects resulted in the removal of forests. The World Bank's first forestry loan, focusing on soil conservation and watershed management, was made in 1980.

FAO incorporated forestry in its mandate in 1945. For the next 15 years, the Organization produced forest inventories, statistical and outlook reports and market analyses, but paid relatively little attention to the sector compared with its other activities. During the 1950s, FAO concentrated on four basic aims: increasing the yield from forests; reducing waste from logging operations and wood industries; accessing virgin forests in tropical countries; and planting new forests.[27] Even after the 1960 Conference of FAO had approved a reorganization, establishing large departments for Administration, General Affairs and Information and Development, forestry

[26] World Bank. 1991. *Forestry development: a review of bank experience.* Washington, DC.
[27] M. Leloup. 1985. The first ten years. *Unasylva*, 37(148).

remained the responsibility of a division in the Technical Department. FAO finally established a Forestry Department in 1970.

Perhaps the most negligent among the early development specialists were the economists. The development economics literature of the time contributed very little to our awareness of the role of forests in development. Development economics tended to neglect the forestry sector because it ignored the role of natural capital as a basis for economic growth. As a result, economists did not develop the conceptual and practical capacities to value natural capital.

On the other hand, forest economics did what development economics did not do by developing optimization models that dealt explicitly with the relationship between natural capital, growth and income. However, these optimization models and techniques examined specific forest properties rather than the macro problems important to development economics.

Foresters began addressing questions of long-term optimization and the trade-offs between present and future choices in the middle of the last century. For example, the German forester Faustman developed a long-term optimization model for optimal harvest time (or rotation age) in 1849. The early models focused on the relative merits of biological and economic efficiency to determine the optimal harvest time. In general, biological models maximize the volume of timber production from a stand, depending on the forest's growth rates. Economic models maximize the present value of the net benefits from the wood; criteria include the timber's value, the time value of money and other costs associated with planting and harvesting.

The optimization question is by far the most fully analysed issue in forest economics, but its focus has remained at the micro level (examining specific timber stands).[28] In the recent past, development economics began addressing questions of present-future choices at the macroeconomic level for non-renewable resources such as oil and minerals. Only more recently has it begun the process of applying the lessons learned from the optimization debate about renewable forest resources to a national scale.

---

[28] Sharma, ed., op. cit., footnote 7, p. 255.

FORESTS IN NATIONAL ECONOMIES

While most early development strategies generally ignored the forestry sector, there are two noteworthy exceptions. First, in 1958 Hirshman[29] emphasized the importance of spacial attributes and forward and backward linkages. Hirshman's analysis highlighted important economic growth linkages of lumber, wood and paper manufacturing.

Second, Westoby[30] led a team at FAO to challenge the conventional approach to forestry in the special chapter of *The State of Food and Agriculture 1962*. The FAO study reasoned that those responsible for setting development priorities were unaware of the potential contribution of forests to industrial-based development. The report drew on Hirshman's concept of growing points, lagging regions and backward and forward linkages to demonstrate how the forests (as natural capital) could play a more vital role in promoting economic growth. Among the many arguments presented are the following:

- Forest industries are based on a renewable resource that all developing countries possess or could create.
- These industries have considerable flexibility regarding both their scale of operations and

technology; they also have pronounced backward and forward linkages, implying important multiplier effects on the whole economy.

- Because of their remote location, forest industries can create development poles and provide a wide range of products, including basic necessities, for poor populations.
- Forest products can substitute for expensive imports and can earn valuable foreign exchange when exported. Most developing countries are net importers of forest products (exporting logs and importing higher-valued products). Internal demand is expanding as populations grow and incomes increase.
- Forests offer a multitude of raw materials for domestic industries and for export.
- Forest industries have acquired great importance in advanced countries, providing a renewable raw material for a whole range of industries.
- Capital requirements are relatively low and labour needs are high compared with many other industries. In addition, the investment range is wide, allowing smaller investors to start up businesses.
- Harvesting time is flexible within considerable limits, permitting adaptation to short-term fluctuations in demand, without danger of spoilage or excessive storage problems.
- Fuelwood can contribute to growth in South Asia, where dung is burnt instead of being returned to the soil. Village fuelwood plantations

[29] A.O. Hirshman. 1958. *The strategy of economic development.* New Haven, Connecticut, Yale University Press.

[30] J. Westoby. 1962. The role of forest industries in the attack on economic underdevelopment. In *The State of Food and Agriculture 1962*. Rome, FAO.

may be a key to increasing agricultural productivity.

Westoby's study helped attract international attention to the forestry sector. Over the next decade, the frequency and funding for forestry projects increased substantially and projects were more carefully prepared, documented and justified than in the past.

Two additional factors motivated donors to increase funding. First, market analyses predicted large increases in industrial countries' demand for timber and wood products from the developing world. Second, forestry projects demonstrated higher success rates than other types of development projects.[31]

More than a decade later, however, when Westoby looked back on how the forestry sector had developed, he rejected his initial vision. In a paper presented to the Commonwealth Forestry Association in 1975,[32] he concluded that the exploitation of massive tracts of virgin tropical forest had been, for the most part, reckless, wasteful and even devastating. Westoby argued that nearly all operations lacked a profound or durable impact on the economic and social life of the countries in which they had taken place. Too many forestry projects failed to contribute to vital local needs.

Several other studies arrived at similar conclusions, reporting that forestry projects contributed little to the industrialization process, created few jobs and had a minimal impact on the overall growth process. In 1980 the Director of FAO's former Forestry Industries Division argued that:

"Forests, on the whole, are simply being mined, taking out the easiest to get and the most highly priced trees without any real concern for what happens afterwards. For the forests and the people who are dependent on them, the only obvious lasting effect is retrogression."[33]

By the late 1970s, changes in the overall concept of economic development had created a new role for forestry. Experience revealed that development assistance strategies focused solely on promoting industrialization were not working satisfactorily. Poverty increased steadily in many countries, even though their economies expanded at a strong pace. To address this dilemma, development experts turned their attention to poverty reduction, employment generation and improved equity. Furthermore, policy-makers began to recognize that natural resource degradation seriously impedes economic development and poverty alleviation. Sustainability gradually emerged as the major development principle. At the same time, natural resource and environmental economics flourished, strengthening analytical techniques and enhancing macroeconomic development models.

---

[31] J. Westoby. 1987. *The purpose of forests.* New York, Blackwell.
[32] Ibid.

[33] A.J. Leslie. 1980. **Logging concessions: how to stop losing money.** *Unasylva,* 32(129).

Today, forests are recognized as an integral part of national economies. Forests contribute to development in many ways, for instance in the form of natural capital, production inputs and environmental goods. But forests also constrain and limit development. In some countries, forests are viewed as obstacles that must be removed before productive activities are possible. For example, in the past, land tenure legislation in many countries required settlers to remove all trees on a parcel before ownership rights were granted. In other circumstances, forests are treated as a scarce natural resource that must be protected from all types of exploitation. Several factors help explain how forests both contribute to and limit policy choices for national development strategies.

First, roads, commerce and agrarian populations have penetrated and settled much of the world's forest land; few forest areas remain unused or disconnected from national interests. Forest areas have undergone "agrification", involving the use of forests and trees in farming systems and the formation of agricultural mosaics within forest systems. Forests are increasingly managed for their range of resource flows, their ability to support rural well-being and their capacity to promote industrial opportunities. Forests provide large, albeit different, ranges of goods and services for virtually all patterns of human settlement and livelihood. They are not contiguous blocks of timber beyond the frontier, but are active parts of life everywhere.

Second, economic development strategies are beginning to include the capital values of forests in national policies and programmes that modify forest stocks, qualities and distributions. Forests are now widely acknowledged as both *productive capital stocks* and as components of *public infrastructural systems*. As ecological analogues of industrial capacity and physical infrastructure, forests are entering the central equations of macroeconomic growth, often with new definitions of what the forest is and does.

Advances in national accounting make it possible to incorporate explicitly the capital value of forest resources as *productive stocks*, and to assess the effects of changes in them on national productive capacity. Conventional national accounting systems overstate sustainable income in two ways. First, the accounts disregard depreciation of forest and other natural capital. Second, the costs of mitigating or offsetting the side-effects of resource depletion (e.g. anti-sedimentation measures in a deforested watershed) are not subtracted from national income.[34] This conveys the wrong message: that income gained from depleting forest resources can continue forever.[35]

Some countries are establishing new accounting systems that measure the depreciation of forest resources in

_____

[34] S. El Serafy and E. Lutz. 1989. **Environmental and resource accounting: an overview.** *In* Y.J. Ahmad, S. El Serafy and E. Lutz, eds. *Environmental accounting for sustainable development.* Washington, DC, World Bank.
[35] C.A. Meyer. 1993. **Environmental and natural resource accounting: where to begin?** *Issues in development* (November). Washington, DC, Center for International Development and Environment.

excess of their reproductive capacity (both quantitative and qualitative). For instance, the French system shows trade-offs between the economic, ecological and social functions of natural resources. This system, known as the "natural patrimony accounts", records separate accounts for forests, wildlife, water and soil.

As *infrastructure*, forest systems provide services that would otherwise require capital expenditures or reductions in human well-being. For example, by storing water, regulating flows, protecting channels and cleansing impurities, forests form a structure of hydrological services akin to structures for transportation and communication. Recent economic methods make it possible to account for these infrastructural services on a national rather than project scale.

Third, forests represent productive assets that are increasingly used as a means for attaining national development objectives, including equity, stability, investment and growth. Programmes in community forestry have become central to agrarian reforms that seek to build more productive relations between rural communities and public lands. Community forestry programmes are widely implemented to strengthen investment incentives and encourage civic participation in the growth and use of forests and trees.

Fourth, forests have emerged as significant factors in economic and political relations among nations. For example, forests have taken on foreign policy dimensions through their roles in both economic and environmental trade. (Box 13 presents an example of environmental trade.) Forest conditions increasingly affect national

dependence on processing capacity, wood products and international trade. Trading patterns grow more complex as nations shift emphasis from primary to secondary and tertiary forms of production, increase their purchasing power and diversify their consumption requirements.

Furthermore, changes in the extent and quality of forests have become the subject of global environmental concerns. Changing forest conditions represent factors in biodiversity, relations between industrial and non-industrial nations which occupy and use the same global atmosphere as a carbon source and sink and expressions of interdependence between nations. Such developments create pressure on national governments to consider forests in the realm of international relations. Some nations are already moving towards international agreements that tie matters of economic and environmental trade together in the service of larger, global interests.

For all of these reasons, national forest politics and policies have evolved out of a narrow sectoral prerogative to enter pluralized mainstream political interests involving highly diverse groups. Throughout the world, forests are the topic of discussion among articulate groups of populists, industrialists, statists, internationalists, consumers, environmentalists, farmers, indigenous forest communities, city dwellers, scientists, educators and humanists.

The perspectives and demands of these politically diverse groups have proliferated, placing a significant strain on the institutions of forest policy that evolved when forests meant only timber belonging to the state and were

BOX 13
ENVIRONMENTAL TRADE: DEBT-FOR-NATURE SWAPS

Many developing countries are heavily burdened with foreign currency debts to commercial banks, to the governments of industrial countries and to international lending agencies. For the poorest countries the possibility of paying off these debts within decades, if ever, is extremely low.

Debt-for-nature swaps represent an attempt to benefit the environment by capitalizing on lenders' willingness to discount (or sell at less than face value) some of their longstanding debts and to accept an immediate reduced payment rather than a deferred full payment that may never come. The swap is organized by a third party, such as an environmental NGO or the government of an industrial country, which buys the debt at a reduced rate from the lender and agrees to cancel it provided the debtor country makes a specified investment in an environmental project, such as a tropical forest reserve of particular ecological significance.

In this way, the developing country rids itself of the debt without having to repay any foreign currency but assumes responsibility for certain environmental activities.

By the end of 1992, a total of 24 debt-for-nature swaps with a face value of more than $122 million had been arranged, generating conservation funds of more than $75 million but costing just over $23 million. The overall impact is small in relation to the total debt of the developing world and the rate at which deforestation is taking place. In addition, it is difficult to ensure that the conservation programmes are realistic and capable of being implemented and maintained on a sustainable basis. An initiative in Bolivia, for example, ran into trouble because both local indigenous people and loggers who had been awarded concessions laid claim to the land to be managed.

Debt-for-nature swaps have also been criticized as a form of "eco-colonialism", in which industrial countries set the priorities of developing countries. Swaps may work in countries that are badly mismanaging their economies, but not in those that display economic discipline. The economic and ecological benefits of debt-for-nature swaps may overshadow the needs of the people living in the area. It is nevertheless generally accepted that prudently chosen and well-planned debt-for-nature swaps are a viable, if rather complicated, measure that can make a contribution to forest conservation.

Source: FAO. 1993. _The challenge of sustainable forest management. What future for the world's forests?_ Rome.

controlled by a small professional cadre. These competing pressures, combined with a wider understanding of the importance and complexity of forests' non-wood services and values, are strongly influencing forestry policy today.

Forests as a source of national development

Individual forest ecosystems provide many protective, scientific and commercial services, ranging from living space and food to climate regulation and genetic resources (see Box 14). At the national level, however, countries are interested in their entire forest system (in the macro sense, the forest is any area where there are trees) and how they contribute collectively to national development as sources of goods and services, as forms of insurance against excessive risk and as economic and social assets.

Sources of revenue, foreign exchange and financial equity. Forests supply materials for export and for import substitution in the form of wood, fibre, processed products, energy and a growing variety of medicinal, ornamental and speciality forest products.

Timber typically has been a primary source of capital for forested nations, through the trade of wood for currency, the use of forests as equity for loans and debt relief and the exchange of concessionary rights for physical infrastructure. Canada, India, Indonesia, Italy, Malaysia, Norway, Sweden, the Russian Federation, Thailand and the United States, among many other countries, have relied on the transformation of forest capital to help build their industrial and agricultural capacities; Laos, Myanmar and Viet Nam appear to be pursuing a similar strategy today.

Beyond this initial stage of forest transformation, some nations attempt to create employment and increase incomes by building industrial capacities to process wood into finished goods. Germany, Indonesia, Italy, Malaysia, Singapore, Thailand and the United States have followed this path, using wood from both domestic and foreign sources. Thailand derives substantial foreign exchange from trade in furniture, orchids, speciality foods, medicinals and wildlife. This stage requires more complex market and tenure systems than those that prevailed when timber was the forest's main contribution. Japan's forest industries rely heavily on imports of tropical and temperate hardwood logs; the country accounts for 30 percent of global industrial roundwood imports and about 45 percent of all tropical hardwood imports. Although Japan's own forests are capable of providing for industrial production, environmental considerations and high extraction costs mean that imports are preferred.[36]

Forests also attract recreational users. Since tourism and recreation may require infrastructural investment beyond the requirements of a processing industry, this economic activity usually awaits later stages of industrial and commercial growth.

[36] F. Nectoux and Y. Kurada. 1989. *Timber from the south seas: an analysis of Japan's timber trade and environmental impact.* Gland, Switzerland, WWF.

BOX 14
**THE ROLE OF FORESTS
IN FIVE DOMAINS OF
HUMAN WELFARE**

Protective services and influences
• Climate regulation
• Regulation of atmospheric composition
• Stabilization of slopes, stream banks, water catchments and sand dunes
• Shelterbelts, soil moisture retention
• Streamflow regulation, flood reduction
• Land reclamation
• Buffers against the spread of pests and diseases
• Nutrient storage, distribution and cycling
• Wildlife habitat
• Conservation of biodiversity

Consumption of plants, animals and derivatives
• Timber: logs, pulpwood, posts, poles
• Fuelwood: firewood and charcoal
• Food products: fish, game, fruit, nuts, berries, seeds, mushrooms, spices, eggs, larvae, honey, syrups, teas, other beverages
• Herbs, flowers, medicinal plants
• Gums, resins, lacs, oils, tannin, waxes, distillates
• Livestock fodder (grass, leaves)
• Thatch, ropes and string, weaving materials, silk
• Non-wood structural materials (e.g. bamboo, rattan)
• Skins, feathers, teeth, bones, horns
• House plants and pets

Psychophysiological influences
• Recreation, tourism, sports
• Sense of stewardship, peace, harmony with nature
• Inspiration for art, literature, music, myths, religion and philosophy
• Historic sites and values

Source of land and living space
• New lands for cropping and grazing
• Habitat of indigenous (aboriginal) people

Education and scientific services
• Research on ecosystems and organisms
• Zones for monitoring ecological changes
• Specimens for museums, zoos, botanical gardens
• Wild stocks of foods, chemicals, biological control agents
• Environmental education

_____

Source: J.G. Laarman and R.A. Sedjo. 1992. *Global forests: issues for six billion people.* New York, McGraw-Hill.

Thus, nations must make strategic trade-offs between converting forest capital for industrial and commercial activities, providing access to non-timber products, using forests as energy sources and increasing future income streams from tourists attracted to pristine forests.

Sources of rural income. Rural populations depend on forest products as well as on their environmental services. Forests contribute to food security. In some areas, forests are the primary source of protein, energy, oils, medicines and even staple foods. In general, they are most important during seasonal or periodic famines or shortages of crop-based foods.

As sources of income, forests are important in a distributive sense, creating opportunities that cannot be generated on a national scale or through incipient market systems. National accounts typically do not record such in-kind forest incomes, although these are essential to the well-being of hundreds of millions of people (especially those groups who depend on the forest as their only source of cash income).

Rural populations also use, protect and create forests as sources of agricultural inputs; they depend on tree products to sustain soil fertility and structure, to feed livestock and to maintain desired moisture regimes and water flows.

Such non-monetized production inputs are not recorded in national accounts, although their decline would reduce monetized production, require compensation through augmented monetized inputs of capital and labour or increase pressure to clear forest for cultivation.

At early stages of market participation, rural populations use commercial forest products to generate cash income. For instance, India has extensive commerce in "minor" forest products which resident communities harvest, process and sell. Examples include silk, cigarette wrappers, food and feed, charcoal, oils, lac and resins, spices and medicines. Box 15 highlights the significance of minor forest products in the West African humid forest zone.

Shares of national assets. Forest tenures have become part of broader strategies designed to distribute national assets to achieve a desired mix of economic growth, equity and stability and to conserve environmental opportunities for future generations.

Tenurial patterns have diversified over the past several decades, reflecting the variety of forest functions, growing populations and political expectations, and expanding technical, financial and organizational capacities. To pure *de jure* state or de facto local control have been added a wide variety of quasi-public structures of land and market control, systems of state-local cooperative management, local management structures and private tenures for forest activities on corporate, farm and household scales. Forest distribution therefore involves choices within and among fiscal, educational, industrial, agrarian and stabilization policies.

Land reserves. Forests provide habitats and livelihood opportunities for landless people who otherwise would be absorbed or subsidized in more expensive ways. Forests also provide

BOX 15
**MINOR FOREST
PRODUCTS
IN WEST AFRICA**

Forests have traditionally been valued as a source of timber, pulp and fuel. All other products, regardless of their value to local people, have been classified by foresters as "minor" forest products. Yet this term often refers only to those products, such as gums, resins and tannins, for which there is an industrial market. For rural West Africans, the forests are valued for a much broader array of products.

Like many forests around the world, the West African humid forest zone is extremely diverse, incorporating many different political and economic systems, cultures, histories and land-use practices. The forests provide food, medicines, household equipment, building material and raw materials for processing. They support agriculture by providing materials for farm implements, harvesting and transportation equipment, crop storage containers and dryers as well as fuel for crop processing. Forests and trees are also socially and culturally important, serving as temples, symbols, gathering places and locations for rites such as initiation ceremonies.

The multitude of "minor" ways in which a single forest species may be used is well illustrated in the example of the *Ceiba pentandra* of Ho in Ghana. This fibrous fruit is used in making medicines, pillows and a commercial product to plug up holes in canoes; its seed oil is prescribed for rheumatism, sold commercially for soap making and used as a fire-lighter; its leaves are consumed in soups and used as fodder for goats; its ash provides a good mulch; its bark and stems are used as a medicinal mouthwash; and its roots are used in the treatment of leprosy. It is also valued as bee fodder for honey production. In addition, a favoured mushroom grows at the tree's base. Finally, it is a sacred tree; its leaves and bark are believed to expel spirits.

_____

Source: FAO. 1990. *The major significance of "minor" forest products.* Rome.

opportunities to grow commercial crops that would be more expensive to grow elsewhere. Although some of these activities may deplete environmental capital, many nations choose to tolerate them because forests provide a flexible alternative to more costly national responses.

Ecological systems providing biodiversity. The world's forests are both laboratories for the natural selection of genetic resources of plants and animals and dynamic storage banks for these genes. Tropical forests contain an estimated 50 percent of all the living species on the planet, including a great proportion of higher plants and mammals. For example, there are 50 indigenous tree species in Europe north of the Alps. In Malaysia, an area of forest covering just 50 ha was found to contain 830 tree species and, in Peru, nearly 300 species of trees have been recorded on a single hectare.

Infrastructure. Forests provide infrastructural services without which development opportunities decline. They stabilize streamflow and microclimates; protect land and earth structures, such as roads and canals; and drain, shade and purify. Urban trees cool towns, conserve energy and absorb pollutants, substituting for more conventional infrastructure which would otherwise be needed. Strategically placed trees can reduce home air-conditioning needs by 10 to 15 percent by providing shade and can reduce heating requirements by shielding wind.

Forests are ecological systems that provide insurance against reductions in national well-being. The economic and social consequences of changes in ecosystems are difficult to predict. Changes in the dynamics of river basins, ecological regions or wildlife systems, for example, may reduce or increase different aspects of human well-being; without sufficient knowledge, the unpredictability of the consequences tends to rise with the extent of change. The inundation of logs through Thai villages, boulders falling on to Nepalese villages and habitat-deprived elephants rampaging through Indian villages are recent examples of catastrophes that forests can prevent.

Although the concept of "forest as infrastructure" is not yet widely supported, the absence of forests clearly requires constructed infrastructure at the expense of other potential uses of scarce capital.

Sources of energy. Forests supply energy that would otherwise be unavailable or would cost more to obtain. Wood continues to be the primary fuel in most tropical nations and a significant fuel in many others. Wood may substitute for fossil fuels and agricultural biomass, alleviating cost pressures on competing needs for these resources.

Nutritional problems arise where people lack sufficient fuelwood to cook their food adequately and where its substitution with dung reduces the fertility and productivity of their fields. Fossil fuel replacements, whether for energy or fertilizer, can be expensive in foreign exchange or in lost future opportunities for domestic use. Energy policies in nations of South Asia and Africa have placed significant emphasis on fuelwood plantations.

CHANGING FOREST CONDITIONS: INDIA, THAILAND AND THE UNITED STATES

Forested regions offer incentives for both clearance and preservation. The national balance depends on how combinations of economic, social, ecological and political circumstances change over time. Factors include site quality, the distribution of landholdings, non-farm employment opportunities and the strength of communities.

In *India*, for example, there has been a simultaneous depletion of state forests and rapid growth of farm forests outwards from urban centres. Natural forest depletion has been driven by the growth of population relative to non-farm employment opportunities and the resulting quest for additional land. The most extreme depletion has occurred just outside protected public forests, displaying a backwash effect against the protective boundaries.

Forest growth and investment in tree crops occurring outwards from cities are driven by market incentives, including rising prices for wood products relative to agricultural crops, input prices and wage differentials. Forest growth also occurs within irrigated areas, where tree crops fit in with other production activities through complementary uses of the same inputs, household management systems and market networks. Although India continues to experience high official rates of deforestation, these tend to reflect the jurisdictional definitions of hinterland forests and do not take into account the impressive growth of forest cover on private agricultural land. This shift in the aggregate forest cover from hinterlands towards settled areas is accompanied by significant changes in the species composition and social organization of forests.

Thailand displays a direct relationship between deforestation and agricultural expansion. Over the last three decades, this expansion has been driven by the growth of urban markets and road networks, new production technologies and export opportunities for agricultural crops. Liberal trade and commodity market policies, the aggressive development of the nation's road network and a strong urban demand for rural land have all shaped forest distribution.

At first, the landless population not absorbed in non-farm employment converted forested land to farmland, thus increasing agricultural production. Over time, beginning first near cities and then extending outwards, non-farm opportunities increased dramatically, consequently raising wage rates, reducing agricultural labour supply and increasing agriculture's capital dependence. Meanwhile, agricultural land was converted to residential and industrial uses, leading to further clearance of forests in more remote areas.

In 1989, the Government of Thailand banned logging of public forests. The ban increased incentives to grow wood on private land, while the underutilization of mill capacity created incentives to expand forest extraction into neighbouring countries. As a result, the nation's forest cover shifted towards private land and market centres; debates over local relative to national control of national forests intensified; and the bulk of wood extraction shifted beyond national boundaries.

The State of California in the United States provides an extreme example of the same changes occurring in India and Thailand. The state's population has quadrupled in four decades; its economic structure has shifted from primary to secondary and now to tertiary activities. The cities, supported by huge imports of water, have radiated outwards in sprawling suburban settlements, extending urban park forests, tree-lined streets and residential gardens and reserves across former farm and forest lands.

California's industrial forest, the economic base of many rural localities, has been depleted and fragmented. Imported wood is less expensive, forest land is more valuable when sold for housing development and timber investment opportunities look unattractive compared with the alternatives. National forests, increasingly pressed to favour non-wood services, no longer fill the slack in mill capacity and labour utilization.

The state's aggregate forest is increasing in size but shifting away from traditional forest sites, regions and communities towards urban, agricultural and "non-forest" wooded lands. Despite the compelling force of these changes, forest policy continues to focus on timber production in conventional private and federal forest holdings.

These examples illustrate how national development and policy choices affect the quality and location of forests, while changing forest conditions shape and constrain available options.

A number of African countries illustrate similar relationships between development, energy and forest dynamics. In many countries, wood continues to be the dominant household energy source because alternative energy prices are relatively high. In some cases, economic policies keep energy prices high with import restrictions, market controls and taxes. In other cases, countries lack alternative domestic supplies or capital to develop them. Both the scarcity of alternative energy sources and the means that would relieve such scarcity have an impact on the distribution and quality of forests.

Sources of potentially tradable global services. Forests supply many global benefits: they store carbon; maintain diverse, unique and rare forms of life; store biotic potential; and encompass natural phenomena that have yet to be understood. These global attributes are gaining value rapidly as institutions evolve to protect them and develop means to translate them into tradable forms. The Global Environmental Facility (GEF) was established to finance national provision of such services.

Debt-for-nature swaps, long-term purchases of forest carbon storage for industrial atmospheric emissions, environmental conditions in trade agreements and international contracts for biological prospecting rights are early examples from the gradual development of international trade in global environmental services.

Heritage. Forests contribute to social cohesion that may enhance the success of productive enterprises or, with the help of government subsidies, that may ensure that weak enterprises are made productive. Throughout the world, forest groves provide a focus for community life and form part of a social and cultural regime for managing an economic and ecological system; in some countries, for example, sacred forest groves are located in the hills above irrigation systems. More generally, the groves are natural temples, ancestral places and spiritual retreats that contribute to the strength of the community. As cooperative movements have demonstrated consistently, such strength is difficult to create. Natural parks appear to have analogous functions in urban societies.

In recent years, forests have become more widely recognized as homes of cultures. International concern and appreciation for the value of traditional cultures and their knowledge of nature have contributed to the preservation of forest regimes as a matter of national interest.

Forests as a consequence of national development

While forest conditions affect opportunities for national development, the development process shapes what these forest conditions are, what they do and what they will become. For example, as development proceeds, population pressure on land increases and then declines; urban demand and prices for wood products and energy increase; urban incomes and savings rise; non-farm employment opportunities grow; road systems and water resource developments expand; governmental capacities to protect forests, subsidize forest growth in agricultural areas and cooperate with local populations in forest management increase; and the strength of environmental interests relative to extractive interests and the extent of their international integration increase.

These dynamics determine the motives for cutting and growing trees in different places and at different times. Box 16 presents examples of the relationship between forest conditions and national development in India, Thailand and the United States.

Forest conditions reflect the consequences of policies that create and modify the opportunities for people to grow and cut trees. For example:

- Relative market prices between agricultural and wood products and between fossil and forest fuels influence the growth of farm forestry and rates of natural forest depletion.
- The development of market infrastructure influences price structures and relationships.
- Changes in the labour force, non-farm employment opportunities and the expansion and intensification of agriculture are all fundamental forces affecting how forests change.
- Income and its distribution between and within urban and rural populations affect the availability of resources for, and spatial distribution of, investment in trees.
- The capital value of trees as growing stock and as protection against avoidable costs in soil and aquatic productivity is of growing importance to macroeconomic considerations of the national roles of forests.
- Trade policies and international environmental agreements alter property rights and tenure systems.

Thus, the use, development and conditions of forests are fundamental consequences of the wider configuration of national policy and economic development. National development is constantly creating incentives and capacities both to exploit and to enhance forest resources. Economic growth and social conditions tend to shift the location and composition of forest resources. On a national scale, the nature of this relationship depends on a country's particular economic, demographic and political circumstances. Where forest cover shifts away from traditional jurisdictions and commercial species, national accounts are likely to understate not only the amount of forests, but also the economic, social and environmental importance of forest resources. Two cases illustrate this point:

i) In Bangladesh, 14 percent of the land area is classified as forest under forest department jurisdiction, but more than 50 percent of the nation's wood and energy supplies come from homestead gardens (comprising less than 1 percent of the nation's land), which are not considered forest and receive relatively little governmental attention. From the air, the actual forest of Bangladesh, i.e. the aggregation of its trees, appears as tens of thousands of small islands in an alluvial plain as well as forest-lined ridges and streams between agricultural clearings and governmental and commercial logging sites. Forest department jurisdictions provide weak indications of actual forest conditions. Analogous patterns are apparent in densely populated regions of Indonesia (Java), Sri Lanka and Viet Nam.

ii) Vast areas classified as national forest in the western United States are treeless. Private irrigated orchards, riparian woodlands, hardwood savannahs and town tree cover in the same region have no legal definition as forests. However, private forest is included under the legal definition, whatever the vegetation or character of contiguous cover, if ownership is above a certain minimum size. Timber industry ownerships are classified as forest even when cleared in a pattern

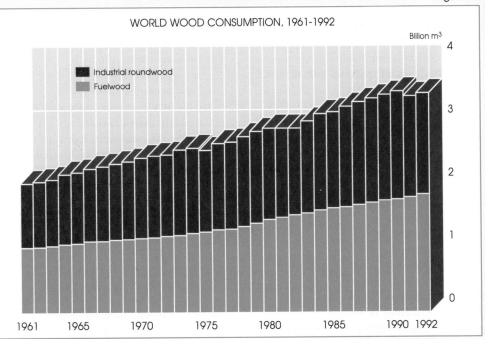

Figure 10

WORLD WOOD CONSUMPTION, 1961-1992

Source: FAO

that resembles shifting cultivation in Asia, but 14 million ha of United States farmland planted to trees in agricultural conservation reserves are not called forest. Many metropolitan areas look like forest from the air and function ecologically as such but are not considered forest because of their forms of ownership.

Examples of such jurisdictional distortions are ubiquitous. They raise an interesting point with regard to global attributes of forests. Since trees, not hectares or jurisdictions, conserve and store carbon, their location and arrangement, form of ownership and potential for other uses are irrelevant. Trees in the city store as much carbon as the same species in similar sites in the forest, and their shade reduces emissions from energy required to cool offices and houses. If forests were defined according to what aggregations of trees do, rather than according to certain customs of

placement, form and control, the accounts of their national contributions would differ significantly from those cited for jurisdictional purposes.

In the future, the trade-offs between international obligations and national interests and government readiness to negotiate international dimensions of forests (in terms of both commodity trade and environmental services) will further influence policy choices, national development and forest conditions.

The economic contributions of forests
Many direct economic contributions of forests are well documented, particularly the value of wood energy and solid wood and fibre products. An estimated three billion people depend on fuelwood as their main source of household energy, consuming more than one-half of the world's wood production. In many urban areas of developing countries, families may

BOX 17
ECONOMIC SERVICES PROVIDED BY FOREST ECOSYSTEMS

SERVICE   **ECONOMIC IMPORTANCE**

Gene pool   Forests contain a diversity of species and habitats. They provide the gene pool that can protect commercial plant strains against pests and changing conditions of climate and soil and provide the raw material for breeding higher-yielding strains. The wild relatives of avocado, banana, cashew, cacao, cinnamon, coconut, coffee, grapefruit, lemon, paprika, oil palm, rubber and vanilla – the exports of which were worth more than $20 billion in 1991 – are found in tropical forests.

Water   Some 40 percent of developing country farmers depend on forested watersheds for water to irrigate crops and to water livestock. In India, forests provide water regulation and flood control valued at $72 billion per year. In most countries of Europe and in the United States, Japan and Australia, more than 20 percent of the forest area is regarded as important for the protection and conservation of water supply.

Watershed   Forests keep soil from eroding into rivers. Siltation of reservoirs costs the world economy about $6 billion per year in lost hydroelectricity and irrigation water.

Fisheries   Forests protect fisheries in rivers, lakes, estuaries and coastal waters. Three-fourths of fish sold in the markets of Manaus, Brazil, are nurtured in seasonally flooded *varzea* forests, where they feed on fruits and plants. The viability of 112 stocks of salmon and other fish in the Pacific Northwest (North America) depends on natural, old-growth forests; the region's salmon fishery is a $1 billion industry.

Climate   Forests stabilize climate. Tropical deforestation releases the greenhouse gases, carbondioxide (CO_2), methane (CH_4) and nitrous oxide (NO_x). Replacing the carbon storage function of all tropical forests would cost an estimated $3.7 trillion – equal to the gross national product of Japan.

Recreation   Forests serve people directly for recreation. The United States Forest Service calculates that, in eight of its nine administrative regions, the recreation, fish, wildlife and other non-extractive benefits of national forests are more valuable than timber, grazing, mining and other benefits. In most countries of Europe and in Australia more than half the area of public forests is regarded as important in providing recreational services.

Sources: Table 2 in A.T. Durning. 1994. *Saving the forests: what will it take?* Worldwatch Paper 117. Washington, DC, Worldwatch Institute; and ECE/FAO. 1993. *Forest resources and the temperate zones. The UN-EC/FAO 1990 forest resource assessment.* Vol. II. *Benefits and functions of the forest.* New York, UN.

TABLE 10

Economic value of Swedish forests

	SKr billion	Percentage of GDP
FORESTRY AND WOOD PROCESSING		
Stumpage value of wood	8.0	0.9
Value of manufactured products	90.0	10.0
NON-WOOD GOODS AND SERVICES		
Forests and habitat	0.3	...
Forests as virgin environment	0.1	...
Recreation and services	0.7	...
Hunting	1.6	...
Non-wood crops: berries	0.8	...
mushrooms	0.5	...
Total	4.0	0.4
Imputed value of CO_2 sequestration	8.0	0.9

Source: T. Jones and S. Wibe. 1992. *Forests: market and intervention failures – five case studies.* London, Earthscan.

TABLE 11

Production of forest products, 1992

Product	World	Developed countries	Developing countries
	(............... million m³ ....)		
Roundwood	3 477	1 433	2 044
- Fuelwood	1 873	244	1 629
- Industrial roundwood	1 603	1 188	415
Sawnwood	450	343	107
Wood-based panels	122	92	30
	(................. tonnes ....)		
Paper	245	200	45

spend 20 to 30 percent of their income on fuelwood and charcoal.[37] In 1992, global wood consumption included 1.87 billion m³ of fuelwood and 1.6 billion m³ of industrial roundwood (see Figure 10).

The total value of fuelwood and wood-based forest products is estimated to be more than $400 billion. Wood for industrial uses accounts for 75 percent. No comparable global estimate is available for non-wood services and benefits of forests, but some country estimates do exist. An FAO study of non-wood forest product use in Greece, Italy, Morocco, Spain, Tunisia and the coastal zones of France and Algeria indicate that Mediterranean trade in cork, resin, mastic gum, honey, mushrooms, wild fruit and wild game, added to the value of trees used in livestock production, had an estimated value of more than $1 billion in 1992, with a development potential of up to $5 billion per year.[38]

Table 10 shows that the estimated value of non-wood goods and services from Sweden's forests is 50 percent of the wood value but only 5 percent of the value of the products manufactured with wood. Box 17 assembles a variety of non-wood forest values (estimated by different methods for different purposes).

Global per caput consumption of forest products has increased by nearly

---

[37] Rowe, Sharma and Browder, op. cit., footnote 7, p. 255.

[38] FAO. 1993. *More than wood.* FAO Forestry Topics Report No. 4. Rome.

1 percent per year over the past three decades. Between 1961 and 1991, the value of global wood consumption more than doubled in real terms, growing by an average of 2.7 percent per year.

During the same period, global roundwood production increased by 75 percent, fuelwood nearly doubled and industrial roundwood increased by 50 percent. Among processed products, sawnwood increased by 20 percent, wood panels by 600 percent and paper by 350 percent. The 1992 production volume is presented in Table 11. Three countries, Canada, the Russian Federation and the United States, account for more than one-half of all the world's industrial roundwood production.

These substantial increases in the volume of wood-based products have been achieved with a relatively small increase in industrial roundwood production. This is explained by improved efficiency in sawnwood and plywood production, the recovery of

TABLE 12

Fuelwood in world energy consumption

Region	Share of fuelwood in energy consumption		
	1970	1980	1990
	(.............. % ....)		
World	5.1	5.2	5.0
Developed countries	1.0	1.1	0.9
Developing countries	24.0	19.0	15.0
Africa	67.0	56.0	58.0
Latin America	20.0	15.0	15.0
Asia	19.0	16.0	11.0

Source: FAO.

Figure 11

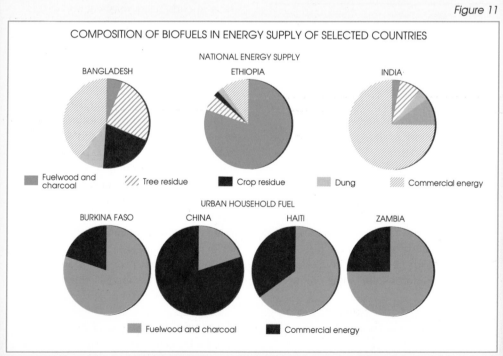

COMPOSITION OF BIOFUELS IN ENERGY SUPPLY OF SELECTED COUNTRIES

NATIONAL ENERGY SUPPLY

BANGLADESH   ETHIOPIA   INDIA

Fuelwood and charcoal   Tree residue   Crop residue   Dung   Commercial energy

URBAN HOUSEHOLD FUEL

BURKINA FASO   CHINA   HAITI   ZAMBIA

Fuelwood and charcoal   Commercial energy

Source: FAO

wood residues for the manufacture of other wood-based panels and in paper manufacture, and increased recycling of used paper in paper manufacture. In addition, wood residues make important contributions as a fuel source, improving energy efficiency in many wood industries.

The developed countries consume most of the world's sawnwood and wood-based panels (300 m^3 per 1 000 people per year for housing and furniture) and paper (150 tonnes per 1 000 people per year for communications, packaging and hygiene). Average annual developing country consumption of sawnwood and wood-based panels is 30 m^3 per 1 000 people and consumption of paper is 12 tonnes per 1 000 people.

In developing countries, 80 percent of wood is consumed as fuel. Fuelwood accounts for 58 percent of energy use in Africa, 15 percent in Latin America and 11 percent in Asia (see Table 12). In more than 40 countries and in many of the least-developed countries, wood is the source of more than 70 percent of national energy consumption. Wood supplies the basic energy needs in communities where people lack access to or cannot afford alternative fuels; where wood supply is scarce, twigs and leaves may be used. Figure 11 compares the role of fuelwood in national energy supply for Bangladesh, Ethiopia and India; and fuelwood use in urban households in Burkina Faso, China, Haiti and Zambia.

FOREST DEVELOPMENT AND POLICY DILEMMAS
III. Forests in national policy

POLICY CHOICES AND FORESTS

Governments tend to deal with forests through programmes and projects rather than as elements of a national system. Forests are nonetheless analogous to other systems of national interest such as infrastructure, education, finance, transportation and energy. Policies chosen to express and serve these interests influence the aggregate quality, composition, distribution and use of a country's forests.

Governments are concerned with several types of national policy interest, including: i) maintaining national sovereignty and a balance in international relations that preserves the discretion of a nation to set its own course; ii) stabilizing socio-economic forces to permit the security, growth and effective use of national discretion; iii) sustaining economic growth; and iv) distributing wealth and power in ways that serve security, equity, stability and growth. Any national policy engages all of these concerns in varying degrees.

In terms of forests, *sovereignty* is most obviously related to the right to: i) use forest products for export or for import substitution (e.g. for energy, as industrial raw materials, to enhance foreign exchange balances and to reduce dependence on external sources of capital); ii) accept or reject international provisions (e.g. for biodiversity, carbon storage, watershed protection and forest or wildlife management), depending on the relative gains and losses in financial, economic and political terms; and iii) develop a natural reserve system (e.g. to encourage, discourage or channel tourism and its economic and social effects).

Stabilization interests of forests tend to focus on specific needs. For example, rates of forest exploitation are increased or reduced to help avoid excessive fluctuations in economic performance: the forest is used as a treasury to dampen cycles through both subsidies and forced savings, perhaps simultaneously among different groups. Pressure by landless groups for agricultural land or demands for more reliable electricity supplies (which require reservoirs) encourage policies that accelerate forest clearance.

Rapid industrialization may require the preservation of forests for their infrastructural, material supply and environmental stabilization values, or to satisfy the recreational and amenity demands of a growing middle class.

Growth interests include the conversion of forests to other forms of capital, to agricultural land uses, or for immediate income and consumption. On the other hand, governments may expand forests to provide a source of productive capital, infrastructure or renewable fuel to conserve fossil fuels. They may preserve forests to earn future income or obtain capital for global environmental services or they may enhance educational opportunities and human skills through study, practical involvement or by using forests to finance educational facilities.

Distributional interests of forests relate to policies that: modify access to public forests; redistribute public holdings to private owners or communities; develop cooperative systems of forest management between national and local governments; shift relative subsidies or taxation of farm forestry and other farm products; and change market and industrial structures that determine the amount and distribution of forest benefits.

Forests are closely tied to the overall policy configurations chosen to affect nationwide political, social and economic relations. These policy configurations create different incentives and opportunities for forest use throughout a country. How forests are used in any one location depends on the degree of competition for non-tree uses of land, the degree of access to markets and resources for tree growth, the rights provided to local forest-dependent communities, the cost of alternative sources of forest values and the social basis for the negotiation and enforcement of rules. Such factors reflect the nation's economy and society as a whole as well as the policies a nation chooses to affect them.

The urban, hydrological and jurisdictional preserve models of landscape formation presented in Box 18 suggest means of recognizing, explaining and directing the policy interactions that influence how people use forests. These landscape formation models have close counterparts in national policy models that differentiate the urban or industrial and the rural or agricultural sectors. They provide a basis for examining,

BOX 18

LANDSCAPE FORMATION MODELS AND FORESTS

Three broad paradigms of forest transformation are suggested from historical evidence. They are dynamic models driven primarily by urban or industrial development, water development, and enforced public protection of forest boundaries.

THE URBAN SYSTEM

The complex urban or urban and industrial mix of demographic density and concentrated economic and political activity i) penetrates a receding hinterland with its roads, markets, administration and technologies; and ii) pulls people and primary products towards it. Land-use and associated forest patterns change because of the opportunities and the controls to which the urban system allows access. The following is one example of a model of the urban system's effects on forest distribution.

The classic hinterland forest – extensive, sparsely populated areas of trees – disappears as roads and authorities penetrate it for commerce, settlement and control. Trees rise instead near population centres and along roads, where authorities are strong enough to protect them, where the urban economy creates a slack in land use by attracting farm labour to non-farm jobs and where urban land markets increase their value for non-agricultural ownership.

As the wealth, power and urban base of a nation increases, trees radiate outwards from its population centres and roads to form growing, star-like aggregations, between which the gaps are filled in over time. The hinterland forest still recedes, but at a slowing rate. This retreat eventually stops when the growth of non-farm jobs surpasses the growth of the labour force at which point the radial forest approaches and then protects hinterland boundaries by satisfying the needs that would otherwise encourage people to breach them.

During this process, the forest grows first where boundaries are enforceable – within homesteads or on lands of wealthier, secure owners and public agencies – and on sites where, for ecological or institutional reasons, trees are the sole, the best, or a complementary potential use; the forest grows last where social cohesion and compensatory external powers for protection are absent.

The configurations of policies specific to this system are generally contained within national strategies for industrial and commercial development and for strengthened central and market institutions.

THE HYDROLOGICAL SYSTEM

The distribution of water shapes the distribution of trees. The human dynamics that change the distribution of water over space and time also create characteristic forest formations. Water control intensifies production in irrigated areas, "extensifies" or intensifies it in the uplands and stabilizes environmental conditions in the cities. By drastically modifying the relative productive potentials, agricultural opportunities and social organization of land, such changes provoke new distributions of land-use and forest patterns. The following shows the effects of the hydrological system on forest patterns.

Initially, natural riparian forests form patterns that widen on alluvial fans, at river bends and in estuaries and that narrow in steep or straight stretches. The construction of dams and irrigation systems segments these riparian forests and increases the biological, technical and financial opportunities in irrigated areas and for cities that depend on water and electricity imports as well as flood control.

In irrigation systems, people intensify production

and, over time, gain a sufficient slack in land, surplus income and social stability to plant and protect trees on their holdings. The forest becomes a net of trees on bunds and paths, with scattered clumps on rises, in seeps and along residual segments of the riparian system.

People in the unirrigated upland areas suffer if irrigated production depresses crop prices. They clear forest for agricultural expansion if land is available, leaving patchy and sprinkled distributions of residual trees; they create high-rise homestead forests if land is scarce, using leaf surface to expand productive area; they migrate to towns and irrigated areas if neither option is possible.

In urban areas, water control permits the expansion of settlement and economic activity. Scattered remnants of natural forest are replaced over time by exotic species in structure-determined patterns of open space, for example yards, parks and streets. The extent of replacement depends on the strength of rural migration, thus partly on the effect of water redistribution on irrigated and upland agricultural opportunities and on relative food prices.

Over time, population densities climb and holding sizes fall in irrigated areas. People form high-rise homestead forests and shift towards horticultural production. Tree lines along bunds and paths break and decline. The forest becomes a pattern of household groves. The original riparian forest is replaced by a forest patterned by households and villages, with weak fringes or clumps of residual trees at the margins of cultivation. The upland forest has become a pattern of scattered remnants and planted groves distributed by household or village.

The configurations of policies specific to this system are generally contained within national strategies for agricultural and water resource development and for strengthened systems of specialized administration in agricultural areas and around hydroelectric facilities.

JURISDICTIONAL PRESERVE SYSTEM

Exclusive boundaries form land-use and forest patterns around them. This last model shows the complex of forces that seal off areas from incursion in order to maintain sovereign control. Its effects on forests arise from social differentiation of opportunities among groups of people in the region of the preserve. For example:

By closing access to land and its resources, a preserve transfers human needs for land to adjacent areas and possibly into illicit activities. It generally favours those with larger holdings and political power because they are in a better position to capture opportunities that the preserve creates. It forces others towards forest clearance elsewhere and poaching in the preserve.

The resulting forest pattern has the preserve at its centre; it is a large forest island surrounded by a mix of relatively tree-covered larger ownerships amid general deforestation that leaves feathery patches in less accessible or rocky spots.

Over time, the forest island contracts to the extent that population pressures increase relative to governmental capacities for defence; it is maintained to the extent that cooperative arrangements with the surrounding populace are developed; and it grows if public investment programmes or land reforms are undertaken to enhance the stable economic base for the region.

The configurations of policies specific to this system are generally contained within national strategies for public finance, internal and external boundary control, public regulations and international relations.

comparing and coordinating the effectiveness of policies that otherwise appear to lack a common denominator.

Forests are living systems which evolve over time with or without human intervention. These changing forest formations create a kaleidoscopic movement of trees and land uses over space. Understanding the reasons behind these changes provides the basis for predicting the direction and consequences of future changes. Understanding how national policies affect forests provides the basis for achieving desired types of forest formations, including the aggregate contributions they provide, and the required trade-offs with other national objectives. But while the overall economic implications of national policy models are reasonably well understood, aggregate forest landscape formations have been ignored.

Forests and the resources devoted to growing, maintaining and protecting them depend on combinations of many different policies: environmental, energy, land, commodity, trade, industrial and agricultural policies; price, wage, income and investment policies; and the terms of international agreements. The analytical task is to relate policy combinations to forest consequences in diverse conditions and to identify those that are likely to serve local, national and international interests in the best way.

This task is complicated by growing global interests in forest conditions. In environmental matters, national governments increasingly function as mediators between international interests, domestic needs and local actions (as they do in international trade matters) rather than as national authorities over local resources. International cooperation requires reasonable congruence between a nation's choices and the trade-offs involved in cooperation. The task facing policy-makers is to develop national-level frameworks that deal explicitly with the consequences of their overall policy choices on forests and to establish priorities between forests and other national and international interests.

Domestic policies and forest management

An important step towards understanding how overall policy choices affect forest resources was taken in the 1980s, as development strategies shifted from project-based assistance to policy-oriented programmes. During this period, policy analysts turned their attention to the impacts of intersectoral policy linkages on the forestry sector. They recognized the inability of traditional forestry strategies to slow the accelerating pace of deforestation and forest degradation and realized that the roots of forest degradation and depletion often lay outside the forestry sector.[39] In the industrial countries, the effects of pollution (acid rain) on temperate forests highlighted this problem. In the developing countries, population growth, land tenure

---

[39] M.R. de Montalembert. 1992. Intersectoral policy linkages affecting the forestry sector. In H. Gregerson, P. Oram and J. Spears, eds. *Priorities for forestry and agroforestry policy research.* Washington, DC, IFPRI.

systems and agricultural sector policies were seen as underlying causes of deforestation.

Repetto[40] suggested that one useful way of conceptualizing how these intersectoral policy linkages affect forests is to visualize a set of concentric circles moving outwards from the forest.

- At the hub are *policies that directly affect forest management:* forest revenue structures; tenurial institutions governing the privatization of forest land and enforcement of traditional use rights; reforestation incentives; and administration of timber harvesting concessions.
- In the next circle are *policies directly influencing the demand for forest products:* trade and investment incentives to promote wood-using industries and energy pricing to encourage fuelwood substitutes.
- In the third circle are *policies directly affecting extensions of the agricultural frontier and the rate of conversion of forest land:* agricultural credit, tax and pricing incentives for frontier agriculture, including polices affecting the relative price of new forest land; incentives for cultivation at the intensive as opposed to the extensive margin; and the concentration of landholdings as well as public investments that indirectly spur frontier expansion in the form of road building and public services, such as agricultural research and extension.
- In the outer circle are *macroeconomic policies that indirectly affect deforestation:* exchange rate policies affecting tropical forest product exports; policies affecting capital markets which influence investors' time horizons; demographic policies; trade and investment policies affecting labour absorption; and rural-urban migration.

It is important to note that the macro scale could just as easily be placed at the hub or in one of the intermediate circles, depending on a country's particular circumstances and where the primary interest resides. Repetto's example reflects primary interest in the forest unit. On the other hand, the evidence suggests it often belongs in circles above those in which Repetto placed it: specialized direct policies have proved to be remarkably ineffective without a macro or sectoral policy context allowing them to work properly. How these policy linkages are defined and interpreted depends on whether forest issues are: viewed from a national (macro) or a forest unit (micro) perspective; evaluated using development-oriented or resource-oriented concepts of capital, space and location; and analysed with macroeconomic or microeconomic methods (therefore establishing macro or micro sets of policy priorities).

The ongoing research on the efficiency and sustainability implications of these linkages may be consolidated in four key areas: i) market failures and incentive structures; ii) policy failures; iii) forest sector policies; and iv) impacts of

[40] R. Repetto. 1990. Deforestation in the tropics. *Scientific American,* 262(4).

timber trade policies on forest use and the environment. Following is an examination of the first three groups for the forestry sector; the fourth group is covered in Section IV, which deals specifically with trade issues.

Market failures and incentive structures. Market failure occurs when incentives offered to individuals, households and firms encourage behaviour that does not meet efficiency criteria, i.e. private and social prices (costs and returns) diverge. When public goods, including public environmental goods and externalities are present, incentive structures may lead to market failure. The market does not confront users with the full social costs of their actions. For example, markets that fail to reflect environmental values fully can lead to excessive environmental degradation. Some form of public or collective action involving regulation (command and control), market-based incentives or institutional measures is required if market failures are to be corrected.

Forests may be affected in several ways. For example, the market prices of widely traded timber products typically do not reflect the environmental costs of their production. Market prices fail to account for indirect use values (e.g. watershed protection or nutrient cycling) as well as future use and non-use values (e.g. option value or existence value), which may be lost or degraded by the production or consumption of forest products. Many environmental benefits are public goods and thus have no market price.

If all goods and services, including environmental services, provided by forests could be bought and sold in efficient markets, the trade-offs among forest functions and between forest and non-forest uses of land would be determined by the public's willingness to buy different services. If the public preferred the services of an intact forest over timber, the private landowner would be paid more to preserve the forest than to harvest it. Since it is not possible to restrict environmental benefits to those who pay for them, no market for these services exists and most landowners undervalue and thus underinvest in environmental forest functions.

In these cases, private and social costs and benefits diverge. Logging companies, for example, may disregard the impact of their activities on wildlife and landscape. The resulting loss of value for hunting or tourism falls outside the private cost and benefit calculations of the timber firm. When external costs are consistently ignored throughout an industry, prevailing market prices will tend to fall below the socially optimal level. Ideal policies would induce landowners to weigh the social costs and benefits of their land-use decisions equally with the private costs and benefits. Policies that attempt to induce this behaviour include taxing landowners to cover the social costs they impose on society or subsidizing landowners to prevent them from imposing the damages.

Property rights also shape the system of incentives and disincentives for forest use. The structure of property rights defines the rules, rights and duties within which users of the forest operate. Economic policy-makers place great importance on property rights systems because they govern the efficiency of resource use throughout the economy as well as the distribution of income.

Forest tenure systems range from exclusive rights to open access. Public forests in many developing countries are often open access resources from which no one can be excluded. In countries with extensive tropical forests, the public sector's claims on tree-covered land far outstrip its ability to manage or control forest resources.[41] In an open access situation, one individual may want to conserve the forest or set it aside for future use, while another may decide to extract timber for personal gain. The risk and uncertainty associated with abstaining from current use creates an incentive to maximize short-term returns by harvesting forest products immediately. Thus, the opportunity costs of resource use (at long-term social prices) are not taken into account.

This type of economic behaviour is not limited to open access situations. If the owner of a forest parcel is so poor that the revenue from selling trees is needed immediately, the discount rate applied to tomorrow's benefit is infinite and the parcel would therefore be logged today.

Institutional and legal arrangements governing land tenure and transactions can also have significant effects on forest land use. In the past, property laws and land reform legislation in many countries required settlers to

_____

[41] D. Southgate and C. Ford Runge. 1990. *The institutional origins of deforestation in Latin America.* Staff Paper P90-5. St Paul, Department of Agricultural and Applied Economics, University of Minnesota.

clear land in order to secure title to forested areas. Large areas that could have been exploited for commercial timber and non-wood products on a sustainable basis were lost in this way.

With the exception of remote frontier areas of tropical forests, very little forested land exploited for timber is subject to pure open access conditions. However (as discussed below), the failure to design appropriate concession arrangements for public forest lands and insecure tenure rights to plantations can create conditions similar to an open access situation. That is, private individuals and businesses make harvesting decisions based on short-term profit-maximizing objectives and have little regard for the potential for greater returns from timber stands in the future.

Government policies and forest use. Macroeconomic policies and public investment decisions may distort market prices of traded forest products and services. It is often difficult to discern how the linkages between macroeconomic, trade and sectoral policies affect forestry. Economic policy interventions at various levels can alter the profitability of forest-based activities *vis-à-vis* other domestic sectors and their competitiveness relative to foreign producers.

Macroeconomic policies, such as exchange rate devaluations and the level of debt-service ratios, influence forest resource use in a variety of ways (see Box 19). For instance, an overvalued exchange rate lowers the price of tradable goods relative to non-tradable goods. In this case, a real devaluation would remove economic distortions and provide enhanced incentives to domestic production of tradable goods (including forest products) relative to non-tradable goods. This may encourage forest harvesting and increase deforestation rates through the expansion of wood production for international markets.

More generally, macroeconomic policies can affect underlying demand and supply conditions, having an inevitable impact on the forest industry and forest resources. Habito[42] describes how the Philippines encouraged capital displacement of labour through macroeconomic policies that subsidized exports of manufactured goods and that taxed labour relative to capital at a rate five times higher than in developed countries. Many of the displaced labourers and their families migrated to upland public forests where they cleared parcels to grow crops. Without secure tenure, the squatters lacked incentives to invest their labour or capital in conservation practices or to plant tree crops. In many of these upland areas, the resulting soil erosion caused downstream sedimentation of reservoirs, harmed offshore coral reefs and fisheries and depleted soil fertility, thereby forcing further forest conversion.[43]

The impacts of macroeconomic performance and policies on the forest sector are difficult to assess; few studies have attempted to examine the macroeconomic linkages to temperate deforestation, and studies of tropical deforestation often produce conflicting conclusions. One study found a significant negative correlation between debt-service ratios and deforestation.[44] In contrast, another study found a positive relationship between tropical deforestation, public external debt and the levels and changes in debt.[45]

One study concludes that the high availability of external funds in the early 1970s may have reduced the pressure to use domestic forest resources in tropical forest countries. However, the results also indicate a negative correlation between exchange rate devaluation and tropical deforestation. Thus, some policy responses to correct or service the debt problem may indirectly lead to forest use and deforestation.

Public investment often has direct effects on forest-based activities, particularly where transport infrastructure and public services are

[42] C. Habito. 1983. *A general equilibrium model of the Philippine economy and an inquiry into tax policy.* Cambridge, Massachusetts, Harvard University (Ph.D. dissertation).
[43] W.D. Cruz, H.A. Francisco and Z.T. Conroy. 1988. The onsite and downstream costs of soil erosion in the Magat and Pantagangan watersheds. *Journal of Philippine Development*, 15 (first semester).

[44] A.D. Capistrano. 1990. *Macroeconomic influences on tropical forest depletion: a cross country analysis.* University of Florida (Ph.D. dissertation); and A.D. Capistrano and C.F. Kiker. 1990. *Global economic influences on tropical closed broadleaved forest depletion, 1967-1985.* Food Resources Economics Department, University of Florida.
[45] J. Kahn and J. McDonald. 1990. *Third World debt and tropical deforestation.* Department of Economics, New York, SUNY-Binghampton.

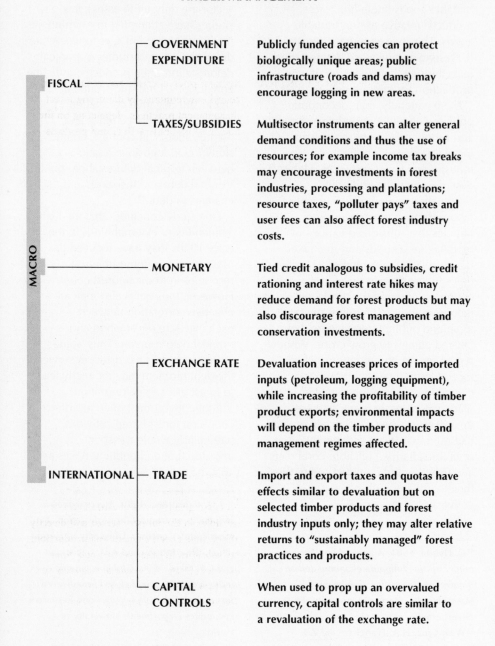

BOX 19

ECONOMIC POLICY AND POTENTIAL IMPACTS ON
TIMBER MANAGEMENT

FISCAL

GOVERNMENT EXPENDITURE — Publicly funded agencies can protect biologically unique areas; public infrastructure (roads and dams) may encourage logging in new areas.

TAXES/SUBSIDIES — Multisector instruments can alter general demand conditions and thus the use of resources; for example income tax breaks may encourage investments in forest industries, processing and plantations; resource taxes, "polluter pays" taxes and user fees can also affect forest industry costs.

MONETARY — Tied credit analogous to subsidies, credit rationing and interest rate hikes may reduce demand for forest products but may also discourage forest management and conservation investments.

INTERNATIONAL

EXCHANGE RATE — Devaluation increases prices of imported inputs (petroleum, logging equipment), while increasing the profitability of timber product exports; environmental impacts will depend on the timber products and management regimes affected.

TRADE — Import and export taxes and quotas have effects similar to devaluation but on selected timber products and forest industry inputs only; they may alter relative returns to "sustainably managed" forest practices and products.

CAPITAL CONTROLS — When used to prop up an overvalued currency, capital controls are similar to a revaluation of the exchange rate.

MACRO

SECTORAL

PRICE CONTROLS   Sectoral price controls may stimulate or retard environmentally damaging forest management practices, depending on the nature of timber practices and products affected.

TAXES/SUBSIDIES   Reforestation taxes, stumpage fees, concession fees, plantation subsidies, processing subsidies and other taxes or subsidies in the forestry sector will directly affect timber management and production; tax subsidies in other sectors may have indirect effects, for example subsidies on livestock production may promote deforestation in timber areas.

extended to previously inaccessible forested areas. This type of investment may be an important subsidy for the logging and wood processing industry, because it reduces the costs of gaining access to forest resources. Likewise, it represents a subsidy for consumers, as it brings forest products to market less expensively. Public investment in remote forested areas also acts as an impetus to human migration and agricultural expansion, which is the major cause of forest clearing in many countries.

Forest sector policies. Examples of policies that aim directly at forest management include tax credits or subsidies for forest conversion, afforestation and wood production. Forestry is also affected by policies that alter incentives and impede competition in downstream industries or related sectors, such as wood processing and construction.

In the past several years, a great deal of applied research has focused on the economic linkages between forest policies and deforestation.[46] Many

studies conclude that forest pricing and management policies often distort costs in two ways. First, the prices for tropical timber products or the products derived from converted forest land do not incorporate the lost economic values, such as foregone timber rentals, foregone non-wood forest products, forest protection and ecological functions or the loss of biodiversity. Second, the direct costs of harvesting and converting tropical forests are often subsidized (or distorted in other ways), thus encouraging overuse and waste.

An important role of policy analysis is to determine whether the benefits of incorporating these foregone values into decisions affecting forest use balance the costs of reduced timber production, trade, jobs and income (as well as the costs of implementing such policies). The next step is to correct the distortional domestic government policies and market failures that drive a wedge between private and social rates of forest use. Economically efficient policies internalize the ecological costs of forest use in production decisions.

Policies that permit imperfect competition in the forest industry can have important effects. Barriers to entry can prevent the most efficient firms from operating, thus leading the industry as a whole to extract more timber than necessary to provide a given supply of products. Inefficiencies in the processing sector are particularly damaging in this respect, as they tend to increase the raw material requirements and, consequently, timber exploitation through poor log conversion rates and overexpanded capacity. Imperfect competition may also lead to the

[46] For recent comparative reviews of how public policies affect deforestation, see: E.B. Barbier, J. Burgess, J. Bishop, B. Aylward and C. Bann. 1993. *The economic linkages between the international trade in tropical timber and the sustainable management of tropical forests.* Final Report for the ITTO; W.F. Hyde, D.H. Newman and R.A. Sedjo. 1991. *Forest economics and policy analysis: an overview.* World Bank Discussion Paper 134, Washington, DC, World Bank; and R. Repetto and M. Gillis, eds. 1988. *Public policies and the misuse of forest resources.* Cambridge, Massachusetts, Cambridge University Press.

failure to adopt technologies and management practices designed to improve forest harvesting activities that minimize environmental degradation.

Finally, public management is often a source of inefficiency. A study of United States national forests, for example, estimates that charging recreational visitors as little as $3 per day would generate more revenue than selling timber does now.[47] The study suggests that if the United States Forest Service's budget depended solely on user fees from all activities ranging from camping to logging, the agency would allow fewer high-impact activities such as clear-felling and grazing.

Forestry policies and management practices

Forestry policies may lead to management inefficiencies in a number of ways. Hyde, Newman and Sedjo[48] characterize forestry policies according to how they affect: i) the level of *privately efficient* harvests; ii) the level of *socially efficient* harvests when accounting for environmental externalities; iii) alternative *royalty, contract* and *concession* arrangements and their implications for trespass, high-grading and other environmental losses;[49] and iv) the level of *rent distribution*. Box 20 illustrates the example of a concessionaire who

contracts with a forestry ministry to extract timber from public forest land. The example could easily be extended to describe a forest operation on private land.

Designing forestry policies to reduce the inefficiencies of existing management practices and to control excessive degradation through logging activities is a complex process requiring careful attention to harvesting incentives. More often than not, policies actually create the conditions for short-term harvesting by concessionaires and, in some instances, even subsidize commercial harvesting at inefficient levels.[50]

Unless specifically regulated, short concession periods for logging operations on public lands reduce incentives for sustainable management, while low stumpage fees and licences fail to reflect the scarcity value of standing timber. Moreover, many governments are unable to control harvesting and management on public forests effectively, which results in illegal encroachment or logging. All of these factors reduce incentives for the sustainable

---

[47] R. O'Toole. 1988. *Reforming the Forest Service.* Washington, DC, Island. Cited in A.T. Durning. 1994. *Saving the forests: what will it take?* Worldwatch Paper 117. Washington, DC, Worldwatch Institute.
[48] Hyde, Newman and Sedjo, op. cit., footnote 46, p. 304.

---

[49] *Trespass* refers to losses through logging theft, which could also be extended to include losses through bribery. *High-grading* refers to the removal of high-value timber, leaving a degraded timber stand.
[50] For further examples and discussion, see: M. Gillis. 1990. *Forest incentive policies.* Paper prepared for the World Bank Forest Policy Paper; D.W. Pearce, E.B. Barbier and A. Markandya. 1990. *Sustainable development: economics and environment in the Third World.* London, Edward Elgar-Earthscan; and Repetto and Gillis, eds, op. cit., footnote 46, p. 304.

BOX 20
**CONCESSION PRICING
AND LICENSING**

Hyde, Newman and Sedjo (1991) suggest that *concession pricing* and *licensing* arrangements are key incentive mechanisms which determine whether timber harvesting levels are both privately and socially efficient. If a timber concessionaire is committed to a forest management plan that maximizes the future value of timber production from the concession, the concessionaire is attaining a *privately efficient* harvest level. If, in addition, the concessionaire is paying for any external environmental costs arising from timber harvesting, such as the loss of any potential non-timber forest values and ecological services (e.g. watershed protection), then the concessionaire is also

extracting timber at a *socially efficient* harvest level.

The Figure illustrates these conditions. If p is the competitive price for delivered logs, V is the harvest volume and MC_1 is the short-term private marginal cost curve of the concessionaire for delivered logs, then V_1 is the optimal short-term and private harvest level. That is, the private concessionaire is concerned only with short-term financial returns from harvesting and not with the potential long-term returns from the stand or with any of the external environmental effects of logging. However, this level of extraction, V_1, is not privately efficient over the long term because it excludes the user costs of

management of forest resources by private firms.

Throughout Southeast Asia, the allocation of timber concession rights and leasing agreements for short periods, coupled with the lack of incentives for reforestation, has contributed to excessive depletion of forests managed for timber production. In the Philippines, the net gain from logging old-growth forest was found to be negative (around -$130 to -$1 175

per hectare), once the costs of timber stand replanting, depletion and off-site damages were included.[51]

Short-term concessions encourage rent seeking; that is, concessionaires

_____

[51] R. Paris and I. Ruzicka. 1991. *Barking up the wrong tree: the role of rent appropriation in sustainable forest management.* Environment Office Occasional Paper No. 1. Manila, AsDB.

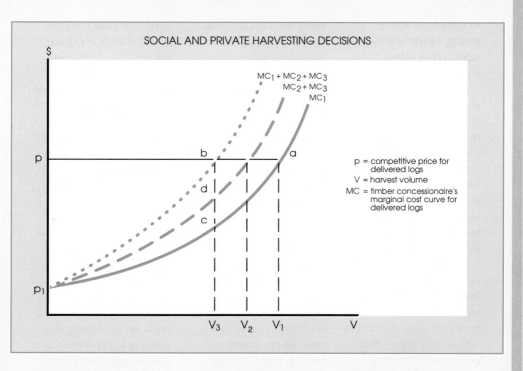

SOCIAL AND PRIVATE HARVESTING DECISIONS

p = competitive price for delivered logs
V = harvest volume
MC = timber concessionaire's marginal cost curve for delivered logs

| short-term harvesting, i.e. the discounted future returns from leaving the residual stand undamaged and growing or from | avoiding high-grading and other practices that degrade the stand. This level of harvesting is not socially efficient either because it | ignores external environmental costs of timber extraction (e.g. watershed degradation, downstream sedimentation, |

open up additional stands for harvesting in order to mine timber for high short-term profits. In addition, inappropriate pricing and revenue policies allow timber operators to obtain excessive rents.[52] By charging insufficient stumpage fees and taxes or

by selling harvesting rights too cheaply, governments have allowed the resource rents to flow as excess profits to timber concessionaires and speculators.

Table 13, p. 310, indicates government rent capture from tropical timber in five countries. Rent is the value in excess of the total costs of bringing trees to market as logs or wood products. Timber rent includes the actual rents that accrue to

disruptions to nutrient cycling, loss of natural habitats, loss of non-timber products).

Improved contractual arrangements between the forestry ministry and the concessionaire could ensure that the latter "internalizes" any additional user costs and thus attains a privately efficient level of harvest. Long-term contracts that coincide with optimal harvesting/regrowth rotations could ensure that the concessionaire has an incentive to take account of these user costs, denoted by MC_2 in the Figure. Other arrangements, such as imposing provisions for the continuation of short-term contracts conditional to the use of "sustainable" practices or even to the

outright sale of the land, could also be applied. If successful, such contractual arrangements would ensure that the concessionaire would attain the optimal long-term harvest level, V_2, and deplete less timber. Finally, if MC_3 represents the additional off-site environmental costs of timber harvesting, then these costs can also be "internalized" by imposing a tax equal to bd on the concessionaire.

It is possible that the national forestry ministry might want to impose a single tax to cover both user and environmental costs, in which case the optimal tax would be bc in the Figure. Hyde, Newman and Sedjo argue that such a tax does nothing to extend the horizon of an operator

after short-term gains and would actually encourage high-grading, trespassing and tax avoidance, especially for inframarginal stems and stands. The result is that the concessionaire now harvests at the socially optimal level, V_3, which is lower than the private short- or long-term level.

As indicated in the Figure, the concessionaire is making an economic rent equal to pap_1, or pbp if all social costs are accounted for. The forestry ministry can capture all or part of this rent through harvest taxes. An *ad valorem* (flat rate) tax or royalty that is a percentage charge on net revenues will not affect the harvest level (i.e. it will not move the concessionaire from V_1 to V_3) but will increase the incentive to

governments and timber businesses (timber concessionaires, mill owners and traders) as well as potential rents, i.e. rents destroyed by logging damage, inefficient processing and high grading.[53] The potential rent column in Table 13 accounts for rent

that would have accrued if all harvested logs were allocated to uses (direct export, sawmills, plywood) that yield the largest net economic rent.[54]

---

[53] J.R. Vincent. 1990. Rent capture and the feasibility of tropical forest management. *Land Economics*, 66 (May).

---

[54] Rent capture *per se* may not be as fundamental to an efficient outcome as ensuring a proper "internalization" of the user costs of timber exploitation through appropriate contractual and concession terms. That is, even if government rent capture is

high-grade, trespass and ignore off-site environmental costs.

A uniform fixed royalty, which is a flat fee per unit of harvest, does alter the marginal harvest decision, but it also increases the incentive to high-grade, trespass and ignore off-site environmental costs on the inframarginal land.

Moreover, increasing this royalty may actually *decrease* tax revenues if the elasticity of the marginal cost curve is greater than 1, and could reduce harvests below the socially optimal level, V_3.

Internalizing user and environmental costs while also capturing a greater share of rents requires a more sophisticated combination of policies: first, sorting out long-term contractual arrangements and an environmental tax equal to bd as outlined above; second, charging a competitively bid lump sum fee for the right to harvest the stand, equal to pbp_1, so as to capture the economic rent generated at V_3.

Source: W.F. Hyde, D.H. Newman and R.A. Sedjo. 1991. *Forest economics and policy analysis: an overview.* World Bank Discussion Paper 134. Washington, DC, World Bank.

Boado estimates potential rents from the Philippines' forest sector to have been more than $1.5 billion during 1979-1982, while actual rents were

slightly more than $1 billion.[55] The difference represents inefficient processing at plywood mills. A log exported as saw timber or in raw form brought higher net returns than the same log used for plywood. During this period, the government's total

low, it can still ensure that the stand is harvested at the private long-term efficient level. However, in many countries poor rent capture and poor concession policies combine to produce short-term management and rent-seeking behaviour in concessionaires.

[55] E.L. Boado. 1988. Incentive policies and forest use in the Philippines. *In* Repetto and Gillis, eds, op. cit., footnote 46, p. 304.

TABLE 13

Tropical timber rent capture

Country	Potential rent from log harvest	Actual rent from log harvest	Official government rent capture	Official government share in:	
				Potential rent capture	Actual rent capture
	(............................ $ million ....)			(................. % ....)	
Indonesia (1979-82)	4 954	4 409	1 644	37.3	33.2
Sabah, Malaysia (1979-82)	2 198	2 094	1 703	81.3	77.5
Philippines (1979-82)	1 505	1 033	171	16.5	11.4
Côte d'Ivoire	204	188	59	31.5	28.9
Ghana	...	80	30	38.0	...

Source: Repetto and Gillis, eds, op. cit., footnote 46, p. 304.

revenue from forest charges and export taxes represented around 11 percent of potential rents. Boado concludes that the government's inability to capture a larger share of the available rent promoted rapid deforestation by encouraging timber booms throughout the country.

Although the total area of production forest in the Philippines is 4.4 million ha, the total area under timber concessions is actually nearly 5.7 million ha – almost 90 percent of the entire country's forest area. Concessions are awarded for a period of five to 25 years, even though the minimum realistic felling cycle is 30 years, and the rotation cycle 60 years. In general, decision-makers other than forestry officials ultimately determine concession policy and allocation.[56]

Forestry departments, particularly in developing countries, often find it difficult to administer and collect timber fees and taxes. For example, in Malawi, the Forestry Ministry collects less than 50 percent of the receipts due from timber harvests. Much of the problem may stem from the complexity of fee structures and concession arrangements, which make the enforcement and supervision of revenue collection difficult.

In a review of forest pricing in West and Central Africa, Grut, Gray and Egli conclude that appropriate concession policies can encourage and support sustainable management and conservation, reflect the values of the forest resources and finance forest

---

[56] D. Poore, P. Burgess, J. Palmer, S. Rietbergen and T. Synnott. 1989. *No timber without trees: sustainability in the tropical forest.* London, Earthscan.

management.[57] They found that: forest revenues are generally low compared with what they could be, owing to low fees and low collection rates; "valueless" forests are the first to go; and a lack of concession fees encourages acquisition rather than management of concessions. The authors suggest establishing an annual concession rent, set by competitive bidding, and replacing logging concessions with forest management concessions that would be regularly inspected.

Timber fees and taxes also have an important influence on the pattern of forest-based industrialization and its implications for long-term economic development and deforestation. For instance, stumpage prices (the prices of harvested logs at the stand) play a crucial role in timber reserve depletion and processing expansion, particularly in facilitating the transition of the forest sector from dependence on old-growth to second-growth forests, and in coordinating processing capacity with timber stocks.[58] In most developing countries, however, stumpage prices tend to be determined administratively and not by the market, in which case stumpage values are understated and fail to reflect increasing scarcity in old-growth forests. As a result:

- old-growth forests are depleted too rapidly;
- forest land is inappropriately cleared for agriculture or other uses;
- inadequate and inappropriate investments are made in second-growth forests;
- inefficient processing facilities are installed;
- decisions on log and lumber trade policies are inefficient and encourage unsustainable management practices;
- elaborate and counterproductive capital export controls are needed to ensure that resource rents are not repatriated.

Industrial countries face similar revenue policy questions related to logging fees and royalties for timber harvested from public lands. The standard calculation for determining royalties is to take the lumber price at the mill minus harvest, extraction and (log to lumber) conversion costs.[59] Such pricing methods are not related to long-term user costs or environmental values and, in many instances, do not even approximate market and economic scarcity values for timber.

For example, Australian state forest agencies generally use administrative means to set timber harvesting royalties, which are then negotiated with individual buyers as part of a package that includes processing commitments. The royalties are usually adjusted in the short term in line with changes in inflation, and in

---

[57] M. Grut, J.A. Gray and N. Egli. 1991. *Forest pricing and concession policies: managing the high forests of West and Central Africa.* World Bank Technical Paper No. 143. Washington, DC, World Bank.
[58] J.R. Vincent and C.S. Binkley. 1991. *Forest-based industrialization: a dynamic perspective.* Development Discussion Paper No. 389. Cambridge, Massachusetts, Harvard Institute for International Development.

---

[59] Hyde, Newman and Sedjo, op. cit., footnote 46, p. 304.

the long term in line with changing market conditions. A recent study compared the resulting administrative royalty pricing in the 1980s with market-derived prices. This study indicated that processors were prepared to pay 49 to 74 percent above royalty levels for low-grade logs, 34 to 48 percent extra for medium-grade logs and 27 to 40 percent extra for higher-quality logs.[60] Old-growth hardwood sawlogs and softwood sawlogs were generally priced below market value; pulp log royalties were found to be both above and below market price.

In another study, Wibe highlighted problems associated with ensuring that private investors and concessionaires in industrial countries produce timber at a long-term privately efficient level.[61] First, market imperfections prevent any investment in forestry from being fully capitalized by selling the standing timber or planted stand. For example, restrictive market regulations apply to forest lands in France, Germany and the Nordic countries. In addition, regulations on the purchase and sale of forest land usually imply large transaction costs, especially when holdings are small, which is normally the case. The result is that private forest owners tend to invest too little in regeneration and/or reforestation.

Second, the major problem concerning publicly owned forest lands in industrial countries is securing efficient contracts with private forestry activities. For example, in Canada, where 11 percent of forest land is owned by the federal government and 80 percent by the provinces, provincial governments sell licences to private concessionaires for 20- to 50-year periods. The concessionaires usually have the right to harvest the area once, with some restrictions on maximum annual cuts. They can also obtain volume licences which allow them to harvest a certain volume of timber in an area. However, such contracts often do not regulate long-term damage and degradation of the stand or any environmental impacts (see Box 21, Clear-felling practices). Nor is the loss of these values reflected in the licence fee, which is usually set very low and, in some areas, close to zero.

Several recent case-studies demonstrate that subsidies in OECD countries, particularly for plantation establishment, have direct environmental impacts.[62] In Sweden, the subsidization of land drainage to increase timber production has led to the loss of more than 30 000 ha of wetlands annually. In the 1980s, the United Kingdom increased tax concessions for afforestation but not for land purchases. This encouraged investors to minimize land purchases and increase their tax shelters by locating plantations on land of poor or negligible agricultural value, such as

[60] **Resource Assessment Commission. 1991.** *Forest and timber enquiry,* **Vols 1 and 2. Draft report. Canberra, Australian Government Publishing Service.**
[61] **S. Wibe. 1991.** *Market and intervention failures in the management of forests.* **Report to the Environment Committee. Paris, OECD.**

[62] **T. Jones and S. Wibe. 1992.** *Forests: market and intervention failures – five case studies.* **London, Earthscan.**

BOX 21
CLEAR-FELLING PRACTICES

Clear-felling is a widely practised harvesting system in temperate forests. Its advantages are its simplicity, adaptability and efficiency. However, it is blamed for soil loss, for upsetting the hydrological balance and for the rapid alteration of ecological conditions to the detriment of forest-dwelling taxa. It is perceived to be aesthetically unpleasant. Moreover, it creates physically and ecologically unstable conditions around forest edges and affects and fragments the habitats of species that require extensive undisturbed habitats, such as the Northern spotted owl.

The environmental effects of clear-felling in the boreal zone are compounded because: i) the forests affected are often undisturbed primary forests; ii) soils are fragile and felling disrupts the water cycle; iii) the scale of the felling coupes is large; and iv) regrowth contains less diversity of tree species and tree ages.

Boreal forests are renewed through extensive fires; some argue that clear-cuts replace the role of this natural force. However, a forest inventory undertaken by Forestry Canada in 1991 shows a higher proportion of poplar and birch in harvested forests than in undisturbed boreal forest, and a fall in the area of spruce and pine. In pine forests swept by fire, pine regrows. On the other hand, the inventory shows little difference in the age composition between regenerated and undisturbed forests.

Research in Canada and Finland shows marked differences between the bird communities of mature forests following logging and those of unlogged forests. Some of the ninefold increase recorded in bird densities in virgin forests as opposed to the young spruce plantations may be explained by the stage of growth of the respective forests.

Research demonstrates that many of the detrimental effects of clear-felling can be reduced by: retaining seed trees and old trees to provide seed sources and nesting sites for birds; providing wildlife corridors to allow movement of mammals; keeping rivers free of logging brash; building logging roads and trails as far apart as possible to minimize fragmentation; and reducing the size of felling areas.

wetlands, heath, moorland and other areas with a high environmental and amenity value. The tax concessions were repealed in 1990, although they have been replaced by direct afforestation grants to farmers.

The long-term economic effects of subsidizing forest plantations may also have indirect environmental impacts. When subsidies lead to more afforestation on agricultural land or wetlands, the expansion in supply could reduce prices and profitability. In Italy, this has caused skilled managers of established plantations to be replaced by new (subsidized) and less skilled owners, with negative implications for productive efficiency and timber stand management over the long term.

In Germany and the United States, state intervention has facilitated below-cost sales of public forest timber, reducing profitability for the whole sector and discouraging private investment. The result has been inefficient forest management and suboptimal levels of exploitation. In Spain, the fact that the environmental benefits of holm and cork oak woodlands in the Dehesa regions are not priced has led to underinvestment in private holdings; government intervention led to the planting of conifers, poplars and eucalyptus, which have altered the characteristics of plantations in these regions and actually increased local environmental degradation.

All these domestic market and policy failures have important implications for sustainable forest management. If public policies are to be redirected to achieve efficient and sustainable management of forest resources, then changes are required.

The economic valuation of current policies plays an important role in determining the appropriate policy responses. Often, however, insufficient economic data and information exist to allow a precise estimation of the economic costs arising from domestic market and policy failures. Although in most cases cost estimates as orders of magnitude and indicators of the direction of change are sufficient for policy analysis, in many cases we are not even at this stage of "optimal ignorance".

Domestic market and policy failures also have a major influence on the conversion of forest land to agriculture and other uses. As this is the single largest cause of deforestation in the world, addressing only market and policy failures that directly affect the forestry sector will by no means be sufficient to halt deforestation and forest degradation in most countries.

FOREST DEVELOPMENT AND POLICY DILEMMAS

IV. Forests, trade and the environment

The environmental impacts of international trade are among the most divisive issues facing national policy-makers. Some environmental and advocacy groups interested in the trade environment debate argue that further trade liberalization will increase the demand for tropical timber. Not surprisingly, these groups tend to distrust regional and global trade agreements aimed at removing trade barriers. A number of interest groups advocate more restrictive trade measures in multilateral negotiations to control excessive forest depletion, encourage sustainable timber management and raise compensatory financing for timber-producing countries that lose revenues and incur costs by changing their forest policy.

Important concerns in the trade and environmental debate include: i) logging of old-growth forests in some regions of the world to service the trade; ii) the impacts of market, policy and trade distortions on the incentives for timber trade; and iii) the inability of many countries to make a sustainable transition from dependence on old-growth to second-growth forests and to match domestic processing capacity with the availability of timber stocks.

After a brief overview of the structure of world trade in forest products, this section examines the debate about forest product trade

TABLE 14

World trade in forest products

Region	1961		1992	
	Total	Roundwood	Total	Roundwood
	(.... $ million ....)			
World	6 039	708	103 331	9 876
Developed countries	5 493	408	86 455	6 402
Developing countries	546	300	16 876	3 474

barriers, timber export and import restrictions, trade bans and environmental restrictions related to trade, including environmental labelling and timber certification.

While the purpose of this section is to examine the nature of the forestry-related aspects of the environment-trade debate, a number of additional issues are important to keep in mind. For instance, trade liberalization raises important questions regarding social distribution of wealth, resources and income. More open markets tend to concentrate wealth and redistribute it to economically efficient groups at the expense of less advantaged and less efficient segments of society. These shifts require public interventions to adjust for imperfect competition and market failures. How to sustain productive distribution and regulate conflicts over forest resources is a fundamental question in the new world of liberalized trade, and nations are only beginning to confront the complexity of these problems.

WORLD TRADE PATTERNS IN FOREST PRODUCTS

About one-quarter of global timber production enters into international trade; it reached more than $102 billion in 1992, representing about 3 percent of world merchandise trade (see Table 14). Trade in wood-based products is growing more rapidly than production. The developed countries dominate trade flows, accounting for more than 80 percent of total trade. Moreover, trade is concentrated in a handful of countries; the top five importers, shown in Figure 12, account for 50 percent of world imports while the top five exporters account for more than 50 percent of world exports. Brazil, Indonesia and Malaysia account for 10 percent of world exports and 50 percent of developing country exports.

For several major exporters, forest products are an important component of their external trade; in the case of Cambodia, the Central African Republic, Equatorial Guinea, Finland, Laos, Liberia, Myanmar and the Solomon Islands, timber products exceed 20 percent of total exports; in the case of Canada, Cameroon, Congo, Côte d'Ivoire, Gabon, Fiji, Finland, Indonesia, Malaysia, New Zealand, Swaziland and Sweden, they

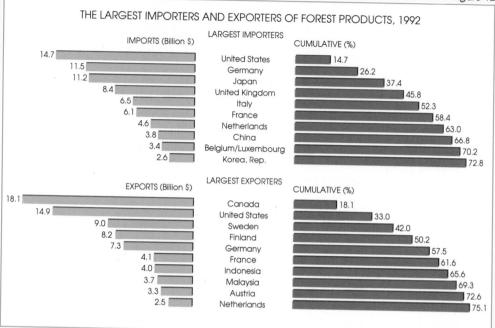

Figure 12

THE LARGEST IMPORTERS AND EXPORTERS OF FOREST PRODUCTS, 1992

LARGEST IMPORTERS

IMPORTS (Billion $)   CUMULATIVE (%)

14.7	United States	14.7
11.5	Germany	26.2
11.2	Japan	37.4
8.4	United Kingdom	45.8
6.5	Italy	52.3
6.1	France	58.4
4.6	Netherlands	63.0
3.8	China	66.8
3.4	Belgium/Luxembourg	70.2
2.6	Korea, Rep.	72.8

LARGEST EXPORTERS

EXPORTS (Billion $)   CUMULATIVE (%)

18.1	Canada	18.1
14.9	United States	33.0
9.0	Sweden	42.0
8.2	Finland	50.2
7.3	Germany	57.5
4.1	France	61.6
4.0	Indonesia	65.6
3.7	Malaysia	69.3
3.3	Austria	72.6
2.5	Netherlands	75.1

Source: FAO

exceed 10 percent. Canada exports almost 50 percent of its production. Other countries are heavily dependent on imports. This is particularly the case with paper; some 80 developing countries depend on paper imports for more than half their supply. Even the United States, which is the world's largest producer and second largest exporter of forest products, is also the largest importer of forest products.

An important trade feature among the developing countries has been the increase in manufactured products as a share of their total exports. In 1961, 54 percent of export value was unprocessed roundwood while, by 1991, this proportion had dropped to 20 percent of a much larger total.

While tropical timber accounts for only a small portion of world trade and of total timber production, it is significant in a number of countries. In Malaysia, the export of sawnwood and wood-based panels accounted for

more than 60 percent of production in 1991 and 1992. Indonesia exports more than 80 percent of its wood-based panels and plywood. Other countries with high export shares include the Congo, Côte d'Ivoire, Gabon, Ghana, Liberia and Papua New Guinea.

Around 80 percent of industrial roundwood from tropical countries is imported by four Asian countries – China, Japan, Thailand and the Republic of Korea. Japan is the single largest importer, accounting for 45 percent of imports in 1992.

TRADE POLICIES AND FOREST MANAGEMENT

In addition to using restrictions for revenue purposes or to reduce import dependence, countries with forest industries may use restrictive trade policies to protect their own forest-based industries, to stimulate value-added processing or to reduce the log content of timber product exports. Trade barriers include tariffs, quotas and other controls that limit the type and volume of forest products traded relative to what would be traded in a free market. Tariffs and quotas on imported forest products provide protection for domestic forest industries. Subsidies and product standard rules are used to discriminate against imported forest products. Taxes and bans on log exports are intended to promote value added processing and restrict harvesting.

Over the past four decades, international trade negotiations have attempted to reduce trade restrictions on a wide range of goods and services including forest products. Fora such as GATT provide a means for reaching agreements on trade rules, settling disputes and reducing trade barriers.

Export restrictions

Log export bans and related export restrictions are often used in producer countries to allow domestic processors access to lower-cost logs and to increase value added activities as well as employment. Proponents argue that export bans are also good for the environment because: falling external demand reduces log harvests; once the processing industries expand and become dependent on a regular wood supply, incentives to invest in and manage forest resources increase; and log export bans are needed to counter high tariffs imposed by many industrial countries on finished wood products.

Although this is a complex issue, current evidence does not support these arguments; log export bans have led neither to better forest conservation nor to the development of efficient processing industries. The bans do not reduce the overall demand for logs; instead they shift the location of processing. While restrictions on log exports may stimulate short-term growth and employment in domestic processing, over time they tend to result in the undervaluing of logs, losses in value added and resource rents, processing overcapacity and inefficient production practices.[63]

Moreover, with elastic internal demand for logs as inputs, deforestation rates will probably increase.[64] For example, when export

[63] See J.R. Vincent. 1992. A simple, non-spatial modelling approach for analyzing a country's forest-products trade policies. *In* R. Haynes, P. Harou and J. Mikowski, eds. *Forestry sector analysis for developing countries*. Proceedings of Working Groups, Integrated Land Use and Forest Policy and Forest Sector Analysis Meetings, 10th World Forestry Congress, Paris; J.R. Vincent. 1992. The tropical timber trade and sustainable development. *Science*, 256: 1651-1655; and L.F. Constantino and D. Ingram. 1990. *Supply-demand projections for the Indonesian forest sector*. Jakarta, Ministry of Forestry, Government of Indonesia and FAO.
[64] P.N. Varangis. C.A. Primo Braga and K. Takeuchi. 1993. *Tropical timber trade policies: what impact will eco-labelling have?* Policy Research Working Paper WPS 1156. Washington, DC, World Bank.

bans cause log prices to fall, tropical forests are treated as an inferior land use and timber as an abundant good. If export restrictions lead to overcapacity, the pressure for logging increases over the medium and long term. In the case of Indonesia, government policies aimed at promoting processed timber product exports relative to logs led to economic losses, inefficient processing operations and accelerated deforestation.[65] Nevertheless, Indonesia doubled the value of its exports in a decade and increased its share of world plywood trade from 0 to 30 percent. Industrial roundwood production increased by 50 percent, but roundwood exports dropped from 20 million m^3 to virtually nil.

Import restrictions

Although import tariffs on tropical forest products are generally low and declining in major developed consumer markets, non-tariff barriers (NTBs) may be significant and increasing.[66] In some cases, major importers have increased NTBs (in spite of commitments to reduce tariffs) to maintain some protection for domestic industries – particularly plywood industries. In many

developed countries, increases in NTBs may reflect growing pressure from advocacy groups to reduce consumption of tropical timber which they perceive, rightly or wrongly, to be produced in environmentally harmful ways.

Import restrictions affect forest resource use by depressing global demand for tropical timber products, reducing stumpage values in producer countries, discouraging investments in more efficient processing and, in some cases, eliminating incentives for better forest management. Moreover, import restrictions on processed wood products prompt producer countries to argue for subsidies and log export restrictions to compensate their domestic processors.

Tropical timber import bans

In some industrial countries, bans on tropical timber product imports or selective bans on those products that are not sustainably produced have been introduced. Some 450 city councils in Germany and more than 90 percent of the Netherlands' local councils have banned the use of tropical timber in their own activities. In the United States, the States of Arizona and New York prohibit the use of tropical timber in public construction projects.[67] However, despite their popular appeal, such bans are unlikely to encourage sustainable management in tropical timber-exporting countries for several reasons.

Producer countries argue that a

[65] See Repetto and Gillis, eds, op. cit., footnote 46; and Barbier, Burgess, Bishop, Aylward and Bann, op. cit., footnote 46, p. 304.

[66] I.J. Bourke. 1988. *In FAO. Trade in forest products: a study of the barriers faced by the developing countries. FAO Forestry Paper No. 83. Rome; and I.J. Bourke. 1992. Restrictions on trade in tropical timber.* Paper for African Forestry and Wildlife Commission, Rwanda.

[67] Cutter Information Corp. 1991. *Global Environmental Change Report*, 3(16) (Arlington).

trade ban on tropical timber products is discriminatory because similar rules for sustainable practices are not imposed on temperate and boreal timber producers. Furthermore, in order for existing multilateral trade agreements to sanction a ban, both tropical and temperate producers need to agree. To extend the ban to include temperate product trade is even less feasible. Given that the global market for temperate wood products is much larger than that for tropical wood products, governments would resist hurting their own forest industries by extending the ban to cover all timber product trade. Box 22 examines this issue in the context of how temperate forest policy-makers attempt to influence forest policies in tropical countries.

More important, the evidence demonstrates that a ban on tropical timber products would be ineffective in reducing either tropical deforestation or trade in unsustainable timber production. The share of tropical timber produced for export is small and declining, while the share of tropical timber exports absorbed in South-South trade is increasing. In response to a tropical timber ban imposed by current importers, the major tropical timber exporters could divert some timber supplies to domestic consumption or to newly emerging export markets. For tropical zone countries where timber exports are neither significant nor a major factor in deforestation (e.g. in Latin America), a ban may have little impact on timber management or overall deforestation. In addition, a tropical timber import ban would have little impact on the economic incentives for sustainable management at the concession level and may actually encourage poor management practices. It is domestic policies that determine whether environmental costs are internalized and most of these affect user decisions.

Proponents of free trade assert that, by eliminating the gains from trade, a ban on tropical timber imports would decrease the value derived from timber production and thus actually reduce the incentives for tropical countries to maintain permanent production forests. Faced by declining export prospects and earnings from tropical timber products, these countries may decide to convert more forests to alternative uses. Thus, while the purpose of the ban may be to reduce log production and exports, it may increase overall deforestation in the medium and long term.

Many of the problems associated with a complete import ban on tropical timber products also apply to a selective import ban on unsustainably produced timber (tropical or temperate). A selective import ban may be counterproductive for similar reasons, namely:

- *Diversion of trade to other markets* (domestic markets and export markets without bans). If these markets are for lower-value products, producer countries may need to supply higher volumes of timber to generate comparable earnings, thus putting more pressure on timber resources.
- *Lower political leverage of importing countries* to influence forestry policies in producer countries.
- *Little positive reinforcement of the incentives for sustainable*

BOX 22
NORTHERN INFLUENCES ON TROPICAL FOREST POLICIES

Tropical forests are the focus of a great deal of international research, debate and controversy centred in the temperate countries. Much of the controversy concerns the regional and global benefits that are lost when tropical forests are cleared, logged or fragmented. Many environmental advocacy groups and scientists argue that the economic, environmental and social costs of converting 154 million ha of tropical forests during the 1980s are well above the benefits.

Proposals to halt tropical forest destruction and secure its sustainable management are a prominent feature of current development assistance programmes and policy advice. The GEF, the ITTO, the World Bank, WRI, WWF, regional development banks, the follow-up activities to UNCED, and the Tropical Forests Action Programme, together with numerous other NGOs and bilateral donors, are pressuring tropical forest countries to adopt sustainable forestry practices.

To many tropical countries, it appears as though the donors' goals of ecological protection are in conflict with their own goals of economic development. In recent international meetings, representatives of tropical timber countries have pointed out the greater scale of annual felling of primary forests in North America than in most tropical countries; they argue that the extent of protection forests and reserves is often greater in underdeveloped countries than in boreal and temperate areas and that countries with a very small forest area because of past extensive deforestation are acting unsustainably by relying on other countries' timber. In short, the South is accusing the North of hypocrisy.

Proposals to introduce production standards and trade barriers, including ecolabelling (see Environmental labelling, certification and sustainable management, p. 326), are perceived to discriminate against only tropical timber producers. Some consider that temperate exporters are using these measures to maintain their share of global timber markets while masquerading as environmentally correct advocates of trade in sustainable timber. Some countries use these countercriticisms to deflect attention from their own environmentally damaging practices. When criticized for the deforestation of the Amazon, Brazil shifts attention to destruction in the Tongass National Forest of Alaska and in Canadian forests.[1]

At the 1991 International Workshop on Global Forestry Management in Bangkok, Malaysia's representative expressed dismay at the overemphasis on tropical forests and called for a careful assessment of the problems besetting the world's forests.[2] She supported the call for quantification of the respective values of forests from different zones, in terms of both environmental services and internationally traded products. This type of assessment is a prerequisite for establishing national targets to deliver global benefits such as carbon sink plantations. (It may also help to determine appropriate levels of funding for the GEF.) If Malaysia's demands for minimum levels of forest cover are to be set, particularly in developed countries, sustainable development criteria must be developed.

The potential difficulties inherent in this global approach quickly became apparent. In January 1994, developing and developed countries signed a revised International Tropical Timber Agreement (ITTA) to promote sustainable forestry practices throughout the world. During the negotiations, developing countries attempted to decrease the tropical emphasis of the agreement, insisting that industrial countries should be held to similar standards of sustainability, as proposed in the original 1983 ITTA for tropical producers. The industrial countries were willing to pledge only to adopt appropriate guidelines and criteria for sustainable management of their forests.[3]

[1] N. Dudley, J.-P. Jeanrenaud and S. Stolton. 1993. *Towards a definition of forest quality.* WWF-UK.

[2] W.L. He Ting. 1991. Intervention notes by Malaysian Ambassador to Italy. In *Proceedings of Technical Workshop to Explore Options for Global Forestry Management.* London, IIED.

[3] Cutter Information Corp. 1994. *Global Environmental Change Report,* 6(2) (Arlington).

management. Selective bans would have an immediate impact on a country's ability to derive value from timber production and would act as a disincentive in the medium and long term to maintaining forests as opposed to converting the land to agriculture and other uses.

- *Incentives to circumvent the ban.* There is generally a high elasticity of substitution for tropical timber products from different sources of origin, particularly for higher-valued products such as plywood.[68] Thus, producer countries would gain significantly if they could "pass off" their "unsustainably" produced timber as being sustainably produced.
- *Reduced incentives* to salvage and use timber from land cleared for agriculture and infrastructure.

FOREST TRADE AND ENVIRONMENTAL POLICIES

The timber industry is directly affected by concession terms that require the reforestation or rehabilitation of logged areas. The forestry sector may be constrained by: limits to the intensity and type of logging; the creation or expansion of public parks and reserves; the legal protection afforded certain endangered species of forest plants or animals; or the reservation of forested areas for the exclusive use of indigenous populations. All of these public initiatives can effectively reduce both the scale and the profitability of forestry activities.

From a general economic welfare perspective, the changes are justified if the net gain from these other demands and requirements exceed the costs of reduced timber earnings. (Distribution issues add another dimension to the debate.) Different uses of forest land, whether for timber production, conversion to an alternative use or reservation as a protected area, must be analysed to determine the relative benefits and costs of each option.[69] In practice, such benefit-cost analyses (whether *ex ante* or *ex post*) to determine the appropriateness of a particular environmental regulation or land-use option are rarely conducted. One report in northeastern Australia

---

[68] Evidence on these elasticities is presented in section 4 of Barbier, Burgess, Bishop, Aylward and Bann, op. cit., footnote 46, p. 304.

[69] For further discussion of the methodology employed in such approaches, see: LEEC. 1993. *The economics of tropical forest land use options: methodology and valuation techniques.* Report prepared for the Natural Resources and Environment Division, United Kingdom Overseas Development Administration. London.

324

confirmed that reduced-impact logging procedures introduced in the early 1980s increased marginal costs by less than 3 percent.[70] A study in Malaysia indicated that natural forest management with reduced impact logging produced higher economic returns than both the current practices and range of alternative land uses, confirming an earlier study carried out by FAO in Sarawak.[71]

Failing to carry out benefit-cost analysis may lead to underestimation of the full production and trade impacts of environmental policies and can even undermine the intended objectives. This has become particularly evident in developing countries, where environmental restrictions have been increasingly imposed on forest management and logging operations in recent years.

In the United States, recent studies suggest that the combination of environmental and trade restrictions on logging in the Pacific Northwest have significant impacts on timber output as well as on prices both domestically and abroad. Three harvesting restrictions (mainly affecting Douglas fir) are implemented in the region:

- Export ban on state-logs. The 1990 Forest Resources Conservation and Shortage Relief Act passed by the United States Congress banned the exports of most state-sold logs, with the exception of Alaska's logs and 25 percent of state-owned timber in the State of Washington.
- Replanning. Coinciding with a revised outlook for harvests on private lands, the replanning of timber harvests on national forest lands will cause a substantial reduction in regional harvests.
- Spotted owl reserves. Specific geographic zones, mostly on public old-growth forest lands, have been proposed as reserved habitat for the spotted owl. In addition, revised harvest scheduling has been proposed for all private and public forest lands that are considered essential for restoring owl populations.

The spotted owl reserves represent an environmental restriction on timber operations, and replanning has elements of both a timber and an environmental restriction, whereas the log export ban is unambiguously a trade restriction. Flora and McGinnis[72] have analysed the incremental and cumulative impacts of these restrictions on domestic and export timber flows and prices for both logs and milled lumber from the Pacific Northwest. Their results indicate substantial decreases in both domestic prices and export trade. Another study

[70] D.S. Cassells. 1994. *Considerations for effective international cooperation in tropical forest conservation and management.* Paper presented at the University of Oslo Conference on Rain Forest Management in Asia, March 1994.
[71] Ibid.

[72] D.F Flora and W.J. McGinnis. 1991. *Effects of spotted-owl reservations, the state log embargo, forest replanning, and recession on timber flows and prices in the Pacific Northwest and abroad.* Review draft. Seattle, Washington, Trade Research, Pacific Northwest Research Station, United States Forest Service, USDA.

estimates that environmental legislation may reduce the total volume of timber sold on public and private land by 44 percent.[73]

Trade liberalization and the environment

Little evidence exists to show how the removal of either import and/or export restrictions affects the environment. One study in the Philippines investigated some of the possible connections between broad export trade liberalization (i.e. the removal of export restrictions) and tropical deforestation.[74] The study concludes that trade liberalization would expand timber harvesting by 6.5 percent, wood-based exports by 28.5, wood industry investment by 2.8 and forest industry employment by 13. The study identifies the wood-based manufacturing sector, which is highly export-oriented and receives no nominal tariff protection, as the major potential beneficiary of trade liberalization.

A recent ITTO study examines the implications of a 10 percent across-the-board reduction in transfer costs (i.e. the difference between export prices and import prices) as a proxy

for the removal of both tariff and non-tariff barriers to tropical timber products. The report also simulates the complete removal of log export bans in Malaysia, Indonesia, Papua New Guinea, the Philippines and West Africa.[75]

The results indicate that trade liberalization is likely to produce significant gains for importing countries, particularly those with log processing capacity. The impacts on tropical timber-exporting countries are mixed. In the simulation's policy scenario, the rise in producer log prices could provide an important incentive for sustainable timber management – but the scenario assumes that policies promoting sustainable harvesting levels will be in place by the year 2005. Without such policies, higher prices could conceivably lead to increased felling of the remaining commercial timber reserves in those countries.

The various studies to date imply that, to take advantage of trade-expanding strategies, countries need to address existing policy failures and the incentive structure underlying deforestation by, for example, internalizing externalities, improving access to farmland, expanding employment opportunities and providing increased tenure security for common and private property.

General trade liberalization for tropical timber products may not be

---

[73] J.M. Perez-Garcia. 1991. *An assessment of the impacts of recent environmental and trade restrictions on timber harvests and exports.* CINTRAFOR Working Paper 33. Seattle, Center for International Trade in Forest Products, University of Washington.

[74] R. Boyd, W.F. Hyde and K. Krutilla. 1991. *Trade policy and environmental accounting: a case study of structural adjustment and deforestation in the Philippines.* Columbus, Department of Economics, Ohio State University.

[75] The policy simulation was conducted using the CINTRAFOR Global Trade Model (CGTM) for forest products, which is included in Annex K of Barbier, Burgess, Bishop, Aylward and Bann, op. cit., footnote 46, p. 304.

politically realistic in the current global trade climate. Agreements between exporting and importing countries on wide-sweeping reductions in existing trade restrictions are often difficult to reach. For example, GATT negotiations over removing just one import restriction – the EC plywood quota system – failed to obtain agreement. Exporting countries are reluctant to remove export restrictions on logs, particularly if it means giving up processing capacity to importing countries.

Eliminating even the most visible quantitative restrictions and tariffs across all countries is probably equally unrealistic. Both importing and exporting countries are likely to continue employing trade restrictions as part of their national strategies to promote forest-based industrialization and to protect domestic industries. Thus, the political will for a general liberalization of the tropical timber trade may simply not exist.

A more feasible approach involves selective trade liberalization steps, such as:

- Encouraging importing countries to revise policies that clearly discriminate against tropical timber exporters, such as the tariff quota or ceiling system of the EC and Japan for non-coniferous plywood exports.
- Encouraging exporting countries to review the impacts of their trade restriction policies on sustainable timber management, in particular the extent to which trade restrictions exacerbate problems caused by poor domestic forestry regulations and policies. Such trade restrictions should only be continued if: i) they do not contribute to greater timber-related deforestation; and ii) the exporting country demonstrates progress made towards achieving sustainable timber management, most notably by implementing well-enforced sustainable forest management policies and regulations.

Environmental labelling, certification and sustainable management

Environmental labelling is both an environmental and a trade policy instrument. Timber certification is one form of environmental labelling designed to evaluate the performance of forestry operations. Four certification schemes are currently operational, covering an estimated 1.5 million m³ of timber and timber products in 1993.[76] This volume represents less than 1 percent of world timber trade.

Many additional certification schemes are being planned: the EC has a programme to establish uniform criteria for a number of products (not just timber products) and a single label that can be applied throughout Europe; WWF began a "1995 Club" in the United Kingdom under which 24 retailers have agreed to sell wood from sustainable sources; and the African Timber Organization (ATO) has proposed a regional ecolabelling programme for West and Central Africa.[77]

---

[76] **B.H. Ghazali and M. Simula. 1994.** *Certification schemes for all timber and timber products.* **Yokohama, Japan, ITTO.**
[77] **Varangis, Primo Braga and Takeuchi, op. cit., footnote 64, p. 318.**

The Forest Stewardship Council (FSC), an environmental NGO established in late 1993 to promote good forest management worldwide, accredits the various private certification systems and certifying organizations to establish the authenticity of their claims. In June 1994, the FSC established a set of principles and criteria to be applied to all tropical, temperate and boreal forests. The scale and intensity of forest management operations, the uniqueness of the affected resources and the relative ecological fragility of the forest are considered in all certification assessments.[78]

Environmental labelling programmes are intended to complement trade policy options encouraging sustainable forest management; the main objective is to facilitate rather than restrict the flow of timber products while providing an incentive for increased sustainable management.

The term certification is used in various ways to mean:

- *Product labelling.* Labelling products that contain wood to indicate whether or not it is sustainably produced.
- *Concession certification.* Certifying that the timber produced by a specific concession is sustainably produced. A close alternative is *company certification.*
- *Country certification.* Certifying timber products from a country that can prove that it has begun complying with internationally

agreed sustainable management guidelines, for example those of the ITTO.

Product labelling is difficult to implement and verify because of the vast array of timber products traded and the stages of processing involved in producing final products. For instance, the end uses of timber are often not discrete products but components of products and composites or parts of basic structures, fixtures and fittings. Free trade advocates argue that product labelling would be used as a powerful NTB to discriminate against the imports of tropical timber in general.

Concession certification involves: i) assessing a forest concession for compliance with sustainable management guidelines; ii) monitoring forestry practices in the concession, including volumes sold and destination, up to the retail level; and iii) ensuring that each product produced with timber from that concession has appropriate certification to verify its origin.

The concession certification approach appears to be a good means of guaranteeing that timber comes from sustainably managed sources. Certification allows traders and timber companies to gain brand name recognition. This represents an important selling point in consumer markets where premium prices are paid for organically grown and environmentally friendly products.

These positive features of concession (or company) certification provide incentives for companies to promote their products through voluntary labelling schemes. Groups of consumer and producer countries

---

[78] FSC. 1994. *Principles and criteria for natural forest management.* Oaxaca, Mexico.

could also develop common voluntary labelling schemes. Such efforts are elements of good marketing and export promotion strategies.

This type of scheme has to address a number of obstacles. First are the potentially high costs of monitoring, enforcement and verification. Moreover, the questions of who pays these additional costs, how the money ought to be raised and how such a mechanism is to be implemented are not easy to resolve, especially if not all concessionaires in producer countries are willing to accept a mandatory scheme.

Second, producer countries and companies may object to intensive monitoring of all aspects of their forest industry production. It is unlikely that a team of visiting international inspectors would be allowed to monitor all levels of the wood chain in all producer countries.

Third, concession or company certification in itself does not provide support for forest management administration and services of producer countries. If anything, a comprehensive mandatory scheme may impose additional costs on forest departments.

Fourth, concession-level monitoring requires the scrutiny of products at the retail end of the trade. Verification is fairly straightforward for consumer products composed solely of one type of wood derived from a single source. However, for composite products containing two or more different timber components, or for timber used as part of basic structures, fixtures and fittings, the process is more difficult.

The purpose of *country certification* is to ensure that participating countries are implementing policies, regulations and management plans that lead towards a sustainable management target. In return, the tropical timber products of that country would be certified as originating from a well-managed forest, giving them easier access to import markets in developed economies.

Proponents of country certification suggest it is more effective than other schemes because it is less costly, easier to administer, more acceptable to producer countries and simpler for consumer countries to implement (see Box 23, p. 330). Problems include the following: if a country has been certified and later criticized for a particular forest concession, the credibility of the whole system is in question; no international organization is in a position to issue certificates to temperate and tropical forest countries; and, under the existing international framework for certification established by the International Organization for Standardization, only individual companies or operations are certified, i.e. there is no precedent for country certification.

Balancing trade and the environment
A recent study of the many issues related to the ongoing trade-environment debate proposes four principles of balanced environmental and trade policies in an ideal world.[79] In real world situations, however, the issues become more complex if trade

---

[79] C. Ford Runge, F. Ortalo-Magne and P. Vande Kamp. 1994. *Freer trade, protected environment.* New York, Council on Foreign Relations.

policies lead to environmental damage or environmental regulations impose trade burdens. Thus, these principles serve as a focus for discussion and a basis for reform. The first principle states the logic of matching targets and instruments; the next two consider trade and environmental policies and how the domain of each might be reasonably determined; the fourth principle extends this logic to the international setting.

Principle 1. In general, trade targets should be matched with trade instruments and environmental targets with environmental instruments.

Principle 2. In general, trade policies should aim to reduce trade barriers while remaining environmentally neutral.

Principle 3. In general, environmental policies should aim to conserve natural resources and improve the quality of the ecosystem while remaining trade-neutral.

Principle 4. National governments should be encouraged to pursue similar trade and environmental objectives, i.e. both trade and environmental policies should be coordinated across national borders.

Another study on forestry suggests how trade policies can match these principles and provide incentives for sustainable management.[80] Trade policies are most effective when:

- they improve rather than restrict access to import markets of forest products so as to ensure maximum value added for sustainably produced tropical timber exports;

- they are employed in conjunction with and complement improved domestic policies and regulations for sustainable forest management within producer countries;

- they assist producer countries in obtaining the additional financial resources required to implement comprehensive, national plans for sustainable forest management.[81]

The first condition requires producer countries to review forest sector policies to determine how existing domestic and trade policies influence forest use. Addressing any policy distortions that undermine sustainable development of the forest sector is a necessary step.

The second condition aims at removing barriers to forest imports into consumer markets, particularly among those producer countries that demonstrate a commitment to sustainable forest management and policy reform. The removal of specific tariff and non-tariff barriers on imports could take place on a case-by-case basis, according to verifiable progress within each exporting country. This could occur through normal bilateral trade negotiations or through multilateral agreements and organizations.

The final condition raises contentious issues concerning sovereignty, the need for international compensation, the scale of resource transfers required and the possible mechanisms for implementation.

---

[80] Barbier, Burgess, Bishop, Aylward and Bann, op. cit., footnote 46, p. 304.

[81] The scope for using direct trade interventions for raising this money, such as import or export surcharges, is probably limited.

BOX 23
COUNTRY CERTIFICATION

Recent studies examining country-level certification suggest the following advantages:

i) Certification at the country level is less costly and easier to implement. Periodic inspection tours by internationally certified teams, monitoring at customs ports and reviews of forest policy and management plans would probably be sufficient to ensure the effectiveness of such a scheme.

ii) Producer countries would find country certification more politically acceptable, provided that:
• producer countries could

help determine the certification scheme as well as any verification process under international auspices;
• certificates of origin could be issued by the exporting country or companies authorized by that country;
• the producer country would be responsible for developing a national sustainable management plan to address any problems posed by production (from conversion forests, plantations, afforestation, etc.) – once this plan was internationally verified, all timber products from all types of forests in the country would be certified;
• development of a national sustainable management

forest policy and land-use plan would in turn support efforts by companies and concessionaires to develop more sustainable forest management practices, which they could then promote voluntarily through product labelling;
• it would be up to the producer country to ensure compliance with the sustainable management plan, and the relevant forest authorities would have primary responsibility for monitoring operations at the concession and industry level in cooperation with independent inspections;
• in exchange for adopting the scheme, exporting countries could receive improved access to international markets for

SUMMARY
Trade measures are often not the most appropriate means for addressing concerns about deforestation and degradation, for several reasons. First, substantial distortions may already exist in the timber trade, the environmental effects of which are not well known. Further interventions to achieve environmental objectives may

add to these uncertainties and prove to have unintended and even counterproductive effects.

Second, market and policy failures have a significant impact on forest management. Domestic environmental policies can have substantial effects on timber production, trade and prices. Trade interventions, on the other hand, address these problems

their sustainably managed products and, hopefully, international financial assistance to implement their sustainable management plans.

iii) Consumer countries may also find country certification more feasible to implement because:
• they could help determine the certification scheme as well as any verification process under international auspices;

• all trade products from a certified country could be safely imported and any inspection could be conducted as routine port of entry (customs) procedures;
• country certification would require a policy commitment by producer country governments to manage their production forests sustainably under the ITTO guidelines and Target 2000, to set up viable national plans for

implementing this policy as well as a mandate to correct domestic market and policy failures that encourage timber-related deforestation;
• it is easier to target bilateral and multilateral financial assistance for sustainable forest management. That is, such flows could now be conditional on producer countries complying with the certification scheme.

Source: E.B. Barbier. 1993. Policy issues and options concerning linkages between the tropical timber trade and sustainable forest management. Paper presented at the 14th Session of the International Tropical Timber Council, Kuala Lumpur.

only indirectly at best. Trade measures imposed unilaterally by importing countries would have little influence on domestic policies within producer countries.

Third, empirical studies contradict the view that logging for the international timber trade is a major cause of deforestation and environmental degradation.[82] The

evidence suggests that, in many countries, a large portion of logging is for domestic consumption. Because the majority of tropical forests are cleared for agriculture and the majority of wood is consumed for energy, only about 6 percent of the

[82] See footnote 46, p. 304.

total amount of wood cut in the tropics enters the international timber trade.[83] Moreover, country case-studies indicate that, however well-intentioned they may be, regulations such as logging bans aimed at protecting forest resources may be counterproductive, resulting in even higher economic and environmental costs.

Finally, trade measures have their most direct impact on cross-border product flows and prices. As noted above, changes in these international flows may have very little influence on the main causes of deforestation and forest degradation in producer countries. Even for forestry operations, there may be little effective control on how these trickle-down effects influence economic incentives at the level of the timber stand.

However, trade policies can play a role in encouraging trade-related incentives for sustainable forest management. Such policies should be used in conjunction with and to complement forest sector policies and regulations that improve forest management. Certainly, other sectoral and macroeconomic policies that influence the pattern of deforestation and forest land use must also be addressed.

---

[83] FAO, op. cit., footnote 5, p. 252.

FOREST DEVELOPMENT AND POLICY DILEMMAS
V. Forests and future directions

In the past, national governments treated forests as bounded stocks of wood that could be enhanced, maintained or converted to improve national welfare. These earlier approaches made use of centralized ministries and sectoral policies to generate revenue and foreign exchange. Today, governments are recognizing that sources of wood are found beyond conventional forest jurisdictions and that forest benefits and services go beyond wood.

This broader view of what forests are and what they contribute requires national strategies and policies to integrate forests in rural development efforts and balance economic and environmental needs among local, national and international interests. Governments are searching for pragmatic policy frameworks that deal coherently with both the contributions of forests to development and the organizational structures required to make better use of these contributions. In this context, forests are now in the forefront of national policy debates about how to restructure economic and political systems and how such structural changes can be made consistent with national interests in local action, social and sectoral distribution and international obligations.

However, governments are also

increasingly making commitments to policy norms that may not be compatible with one another: market liberalization, poverty alleviation, deficit reductions, decentralization, free trade, food security, global relations, privatization and sustainability. In this context, local, national and global policy interests in forests differ widely and, at all these levels, policies provide opportunities and incentives to increase or decrease forest goods and services. These sometimes conflicting expectations create difficult policy challenges in dealing with both the forest sector and national development.

Evolving concepts and shifting priorities are also placing additional strains on national capacity to manage individual forest units. For instance, sustainability in forestry has evolved from focusing on sustained yield of timber to a much broader concept of managing ecological processes, environmental services and economic and social goods. Like the concept of sustainable development, incorporating this broad range of values into sustainable forestry management is appealing, but difficult in practice. The approach to sustainability depends on the perspective adopted.

In addressing the wide spectrum of priorities between local and global perspectives and responding to interest groups which may have competing objectives, trade-offs are inevitable. Critically important issues of equity and morality arise when the interests and welfare of local communities, with limited options and capacity to find alternatives for their subsistence, differ with national or international priorities. Consulting and

compensating those who are poorly served by the priorities selected is essential; the public must be involved in setting priorities.

For all these reasons, national governments are challenged to mesh people's needs with national and global interests; to use policies that determine forest conditions in ways that help improve opportunities for people and communities; and to understand better how interactions among sectoral policies and macro-policies influence people's use of forests and the consequences of such use on national development.

This final section examines the practical ways in which nations are attempting to resolve these complex issues. For instance, by: introducing new types of community forestry programmes; strengthening organizational and analytical capacity to carry out sustainable forestry management; and making use of international strategies to move forestry forwards.

COMMUNITY FORESTRY

Recent experiences at the local level, in community forestry programmes, provide lessons in new forms of local governance aimed at addressing the interests of people who depend on the forest. There is now a need and an opportunity to invest these lessons in arrangements that also capture the intersectoral and macro policy relations that determine what people do with forest resources.

Until the early 1970s, central governments tended to blame rural communities for forest destruction; local communities overharvested fuelwood, allowed livestock to overgraze and illegally converted land to crop agriculture. Local needs increasingly conflicted with national needs and, during much of this period, governments responded by nationalizing forests, restricting local access, curtailing community rights and introducing police authority. Over time, this authoritarian approach displaced community-centred cultures, broke up well-established common property resource traditions and resulted in increased forest destruction.[84]

State control meant keeping people away from forests. Agriculture and forestry were considered separate and, to some extent, mutually exclusive land-use activities. However, it became evident that the expansion of state control and curtailing of community rights ignored fundamental linkages between the forests, agriculture and people as integral components of the rural ecosystem. Food security, income, nutrition, employment, energy sources and overall well-being of rural families were linked to the forests.

During the 1970s, as the importance of these linkages became more apparent (and as attention focused increasingly on rural development issues) new types of national-local cooperative forestry activities emerged. Governments and donors realized that deforestation would not be solved through technical interventions and state control. A broader approach, involving local communities, was needed to address the social, economic, and demographic issues related to rural societies. This reassessment prompted policy-makers to ask several basic questions, such as: What should be the prime concern, communities or forests? Are communities to be used for forestry development or should forests be used to facilitate community development?

The answers to these questions resulted in a new approach that attempted to integrate forestry and communities into a single framework of policy and action, especially in areas with endemic poverty and severe forest depletion. The re-oriented policies and programmes aimed at supporting forestry for people and encouraging rural populations to participate in forestry and conservation efforts. Community forestry is the well-known umbrella term for these participatory activities, which include farm forestry, social forestry, joint forest management and extractive reserves. There are subtle

[84] M. Sarin. 1993. *From conflict to collaboration: local institutions in joint forest management.* Joint Forest Management Working Paper No. 14. New Delhi, Ford Foundation.

distinctions among programmes, but all involve a form of forestry that is based on local interests and depends on community participation – not industrial timber production.

Community forestry attempts to account for diverse situations by strengthening local stakes in management. Nonetheless, community programmes and activities must operate in the context of national-level approaches that involve uniform policy structures. For instance, macro and sectoral policies affect local-level forest use by influencing such factors as: i) the level of competition for non-forest land uses (agricultural, grazing and industrial uses and the relative prices for their products); ii) ease of access to forest products (unguarded public forests, low-cost agricultural wood, commercial fuels and other fodder sources); and iii) access to markets and availability of services. Community forestry activities attempt to work within this policy context by directly influencing the use of individual forests through formal and informal agreements between the government and local groups.

Community forestry arrangements are often in the form of contracts which establish the terms of the programme (e.g. who invests what and how the products are distributed) and the participants' relative capacities to provide and control resources and technical expertise.

The overall policy environment creates opportunities for using forests – opportunities that vary from site to site – while the contracts determine the means and extent to which these opportunities are fulfilled.

Community forestry experiences from around the world illustrate diversity in: the products harvested; the organization of local users; the politics surrounding access; the initial conditions; and contractual arrangements. The variety of products, services and interested parties makes it difficult to classify cases and policies into successes and failures. However, it is evident that different types of users can cooperate and manage programmes, plant trees and restore forests.

On the other hand, as a result of top-down planning, many projects more accurately reflect planners' perceptions of people's needs rather than local people's ideas of their own needs. A recent FAO review of community forestry notes several patterns that differ from what had been assumed or intended by the planners:[85]

- individual participation was more successful than communal participation;
- neither individuals nor groups perceived planting trees to provide fuelwood as a priority;
- by contrast, individual farmers in many places vigorously pursued tree planting for sale and for fodder and fruit;
- trees as cash crops attracted considerable criticism in some countries because it had negative impacts on food supplies, rural employment and the environment.

Other studies question community forestry achievements and some of its

---

[85] J.E.M. Arnold. *In* FAO. 1992. *Community forestry: ten years in review.* FAO Community Forestry Note No. 7. Rome.

BOX 24
JOINT FOREST MANAGEMENT IN INDIA

India's current forest policy emphasizes the subsistence needs of forest dwellers and encourages people's participation in programmes and projects to manage and utilize forest resources. State governments involve village communities and voluntary agencies in the regeneration of forest land through a programme called Joint Forest Management.

The programme's components include: i) identifying target groups and areas of degraded forest as well as the linkages between the two; ii) organizing and consulting local people for planning purposes; iii) using policies to empower local people; iv) defining authority and responsibility among the participants for forestry initiatives; v) supporting institutional development; and vi) monitoring, evaluating and adjusting the programme. More than 1.5 million degraded forests in ten states are now under Joint Forest Management.

This approach became necessary as policy-makers recognized that a forest can only remain stable if it produces enough to meet the demands placed on it by humans and animals. By the end of the 1980s, research suggested that the demand for forest products was outstripping supply by a factor of almost four to one. For example, 235 million m^3 of firewood were consumed, while the sustainable level of consumption was 58 million m^3; and some 90 million cattle grazed in forests with a maximum carrying capacity of 31 million cattle.

Past attempts to correct this unsustainable situation were hampered by contradictions between national forestry policy and forestry legislation. Examples include, property laws that provide disincentives to undertake tree farming; the absence of legal means to ensure that property rights and concessions, including grazing, are limited to carrying capacity; policy statements that customary rights of tribal communities and other people living within and near forests should be fully protected, but no support provided by the government; and policy statements that grazing fees should be levied as a disincentive to maintaining large herds of non-essential livestock, but no actual enforcement.

ISSUES PERCEIVED BY THE LOCAL STAKEHOLDERS
Although Joint Forest Management is a significant departure from earlier approaches, evaluations suggest that much work is

needed before a genuine shift to participatory planning from top-down planning and decision-making happens. So far, few states have actually consulted local people about sharing benefits from and authority over forest areas.

In the states of West Bengal and Gujarat, forest protection groups are demanding at least 50 percent of the returns from timber pole harvesting instead of the 25 percent provided by the state. Forest regeneration through community protection requires little monetary outlay by the government because most of the costs are borne by the local people. Some of these costs include: the considerable labour inputs of local people; the forest produce for subsistence needs which cannot be collected while the forest regenerates; the risk of being assaulted by timber smugglers or others with vested interests; and damage to crops and homes and injuries to people caused by increased wildlife in the regenerating forests.

Despite the risks and costs to stakeholders, virtually none of the state Joint Forest Management resolutions have empowered local people to maximize sustained benefit flows to themselves or to punish forest regulation offenders.

To date, commitment to gender equity is the weakest aspect of India's Joint Forest Management programme. Most of the programme's state resolutions treat the household as an economic unit and assume that benefits accruing to it are shared equally among family members (despite widespread evidence that this approach does not work). Consequently, there is a danger that the contributions of women to conserving and using trees and forests will be lost if only men are consulted and considered as the main actors in community organizations.

Some states have specifically asked for "a man and a woman" per household, or joint husband/wife membership in local organizations. During recent discussions with female and male programme members at three project sites, women requested that 50 percent of the shares be given to them directly, since they do 50 percent of the work. For instance, the de facto exclusion of women from decision-making meant that firewood did not emerge as a major issue in Joint Forest Management. Consequently, women are forced to reduce the amount of time they spend on other productive activities

because they must walk longer distances searching for cooking fuel. Their alternative is to switch to poorer fuels. When women help decide on priorities, such problems are avoided or more quickly resolved, hence gender equity is essential to better tree and forestry management.

Sources: U. Bannerjee. In FAO. 1994. Community forestry in India; J.B. Lal. In FAO. 1984. Forestry planning: new challenges in Indian forestry; and M. Sarin. 1993. From conflict to collaboration: local institutions in Joint Forest Management. Working Paper No. 14. New Delhi, Ford Foundation.

aims.[86] Criticisms include the following: people did not participate to the expected level; the extensive practice of monoculture has been ecologically destructive in some cases; many fuelwood plantations produced industrial and commercial timber rather than relieving fuelwood shortages; and a weak commitment to gender equity (many programmes treated the household as a unit) has worsened rather than strengthened women's economic position and productivity (see Box 24, Joint forest management in India).

The experience with community forestry offers some important lessons. First, just as different branches of the government often support conflicting uses for forests (such as agricultural expansion, timber production, watershed production, government revenue or local economic development), community interests differ and conflict among activities, users, user groups and communities (see Box 25). Because access to political power and economic opportunities are not uniform within a community, it is not surprising that some groups fare poorly under arrangements intended to benefit local users as a whole. This is especially true for women who are often responsible for collecting fodder, fuelwood and food items from the forest. In these cases, women are penalized by forest management policies designed to promote forest

growth by reducing access to forest products.[87] Addressing these concerns through national policies is feasible but may inhibit local initiatives.[88] It is more effective for women to decide on their own priorities and negotiate these with competing interest groups.

Second, the more successful examples from around the world point to the need to lay out explicit contracts where the returns to the parties are roughly proportional to the respective levels of investment and risk. Arrangements whereby the state government tries to collect most of the benefits create local opposition. On the other hand, arrangements with large subsidies for local users often attract considerable attention from politically powerful individuals. Even if the usurpation of rural resources can be controlled, highly subsidized projects are financially unsustainable and are rarely replicated.

Capacity development
Community forestry successes underline the advantages of strengthening the capacities of local groups and NGOs involved in forestry activities. Capacity development is needed for individual participation, communal management,

[86] For example, see C. Nesmith. 1990. *Gender, trees and fuel: social forestry in West Bengal.* Social Forestry Network. London, United Kingdom Overseas Development Institute.

[87] D.E. Rocheleau. 1987. The user perspective and the agroforestry research and action agenda. *In* H. Gholz, ed. *Agroforestry: realities, possibilities and potentials.* Dordrecht, the Netherlands, Martinus Nijhoff.

[88] M. Sarin. 1993. *From conflict to collaboration: local institutions in Joint Forest Management.* Joint Forest Management Working Paper No. 14. New Delhi, Ford Foundation.

BOX 25

CANADA'S FORESTS AND THE MODEL FOREST CONCEPT

Canada has an affluent society, a low population density and a forest cover of 454 million ha. However, the forest is remote to most Canadians – by far the majority of whom are urban. Furthermore, the forest is 94 percent publicly owned and most forested areas are managed by industrial firms distant from urban centres.

Nevertheless, over the past decade Canadians have become increasingly involved in forestry issues. Significant concern about how forests are managed has been raised by environmental groups, aboriginal and non-aboriginal communities and research scientists. Many of these groups agree on four issues: that forestry has focused on timber production at the expense of all other interests; that communities should be involved in forest decision-making; that there is too much reliance on single forest-based industries, which leads to economic instability in rural areas; and that forestry practices such as clear-felling, pesticide use and road construction are environmentally damaging.

Responding to these issues through public policy is a complex undertaking because there are many stakeholders with specific concerns. The government tends to have separate mandates for managing forests, wildlife, fisheries, aboriginal affairs, community and rural development and so on. As a result, a comprehensive policy is difficult to establish and trade-offs are made through legislation and regulations rather than discussion. Multiple legislative and policy constraints on timber management lead to conflicting requirements, onerous administrative efforts and disputes. It sometimes appears that the government has acted according to bureaucratic rules rather than using common sense.

These problems have forced provincial and federal forest agencies to seek new strategies and programmes that aim to integrate more public values into forest management. This new approach includes removing barriers between institutions with different mandates, moving to a forest management philosophy that includes all values and is not focused primarily on timber and pursuing cooperation among the various agencies and stakeholder groups so that they seek common goals.

The question, then, was how to translate this vision into a reality. Legislation, policies and guidelines were in place while licences, tenures and harvest rates were all strictly controlled. To attempt to change all these things at once was impossible, particularly since there was no clear idea of what would replace them. Therefore, it was proposed that Canada establish a series of working-scale projects aimed at effecting a transition from conventional forest management to sustainable development.

These projects were to be known as Model Forests. Each would be managed by a partnership of key stakeholders – industry, community groups, government agencies, environmental groups, academic and educational institutions, aboriginal groups and private landowners, among others, depending on geographic location; each would be a working-scale project (100 000 to 1 500 000 ha in size); each would demonstrate the integrated management of key values and would utilize state-of-the-art technology and ecologically sound forestry practices. Scientific research would be a key part of the programme of activities. Groups were invited to form partnerships and submit proposals. These proposals included a common "vision statement"; they described forest management goals and identified activities to achieve specific objectives. Ten projects were recommended to Canada's Minister of Forestry in June of 1992, and all were accepted.

Source: D.G. Brand and R.W. Roberts. 1993. *Canada's Model Forests.* Paper presented at the 14th Commonwealth Forestry Conference, Kuala Lumpur, Malaysia.

comanagement with government forest services or joint ventures with private sector groups. Local and provincial groups need expanded education, skill training and funding for national forest services.

Developing local and national capacity in forestry requires human resources with improved skills and capacities to formulate and implement policies, strategies and programmes; and improved institutional arrangement for economic development.

Evidence suggests that all countries need to improve their capacity to manage the growing demands on forest resources and increasing obligations to the international community. While it may be more urgent in some developing countries and those undergoing the transition from a centrally planned to a market-oriented economy, it is also necessary in the industrial countries. Although encouraging examples of organizational reforms and adjustments exist on a limited scale, every country faces challenges to achieve the kind of balance between development and the environment agreed to at UNCED.

Adjustment to more multisectoral activities is required by forestry sector organizations in all countries while forest services find more effective ways to collaborate with NGOs and people's organizations. These adjustments, along with increased demands for forest resources, require more personnel with professional and technical skills and a broader range of capabilities.

FAO identifies six specific areas that require special attention to capacity-building:[89]

- the ability to collect, analyse and use sectoral information for policy formulation, planning, priority-setting and programming;
- the capacity for dialogue and cooperation among sectors, institutions and the increased range of interest groups whose development strategies and programmes need to follow approaches to sustainability that are complementary to those for forestry;
- the capacity to promote sustained participation by rural communities and to provide them with adequate support, including extension;
- the capacity to identify, prepare, negotiate and secure funding for projects and programmes based on the demonstrable value of forest contributions;
- the capacity to adapt policies, laws, tenures, institutions and attitudes as well as to transform skills for effectiveness, especially in former centrally planned countries undergoing market-oriented reforms;
- research and technological development and research extension on the broad range of technical, socio-economic and policy issues relevant to forestry development.

[89] FAO. 1994. *The road from Rio: moving forward in forestry*. Rome.

BOX 26
**FORESTRY-RELATED
CONVENTIONS
AT UNCED**

In addition to significant roles for forestry in Chapter 11, Combating deforestation; Chapter 12, Combating desertification and drought; Chapter 13, Sustainable mountain development; Chapter 15, Conservation of biological diversity; and Chapter 10, Integrated approach to the planning and management of land resources, UNCED addressed forestry issues in three conventions.

• *The Framework Convention on Climate Change* focused on greenhouse gas emissions, the need to control further greenhouse gas increases, actions to sequester such gases, and response measures to climate change. The role of forests was considered particularly important from the viewpoint of being a greenhouse gas sink and store for carbon.

• Biodiversity is covered in Chapter 15 of Agenda 21 and the *Convention on Biological Diversity*. UNCED recognized the great value of diversity for ecological, genetic, socio-economic, educational-scientific, cultural and aesthetic reasons. The role of forests as a repository of much genetic wealth was underlined. UNCED called for action to assess the state of biodiversity, develop

strategies, conduct research, encourage appropriate methods of forestry and other land uses, share benefits equitably, protect and if necessary rehabilitate damaged habitats and ecosystems and develop and disseminate biotechnologies. Technology and funding transfers were proposed and equity in sharing the benefits was envisioned.

• *The International Convention to Combat Desertification in those Countries Experiencing Serious Drought and/or Desertification, particulary in Africa* (under negotiation through an intergovernmental negotiating committee) will supplement Chapter 12 of Agenda 21, Combating desertification and drought. It will provide for roles of forestry in national action plans to combat desertification and drought.

THE INTERNATIONAL DIMENSIONS

Evolving global interests in forest conditions (for carbon storage, biodiversity, wilderness, etc.) are increasing the level of international involvement in forest governance. International funding for forestry increased from $400 million per year in the mid-1980s to more than $1 billion in the early 1990s. During the last decade, a variety of new international arrangements emerged, including: international forest management protocols, debt-for-nature swaps and subsidized plantation programmes; tradable permits, quotas and quasi-market schemes for carbon storage; scientific, political, technical assistance and financial programmes to expand resource availability and increase national investments through capital and technology transfers; and freer trade and market liberalization.

UNCED devoted considerable attention to the world's forests. The conference drew up a non-legally binding authoritative statement of principles for a global consensus on the management, conservation and sustainable development of all types of forests, known as the "forest principles".

Chapter 11 of Agenda 21 focuses on deforestation, and forestry is an important element in other chapters dealing with desertification and drought, sustainable mountain development and the conservation of biodiversity (see Box 26).

The forest principles can be considered as a code of good stewardship applicable to all forests. They respect national sovereignty over forests and request all countries to adopt sustainable patterns of production and consumption. They also point out the multiple functions and uses of forests and the need for a balanced view of the issues and opportunities for their conservation and development.

Chapter 11 of Agenda 21 highlights four programme areas: sustaining the multiple roles and functions of all types of forests; strengthening capacities for planning assessments and systematic observations of forestry and related programmes, projects and activities; promoting efficient resource utilization and evaluation techniques that incorporate the entire range of values provided by forests, forest lands and woodlands; and enhancing, protecting, conserving and managing degraded areas. The UNCED Secretariat estimated the total annual cost of these programmes to be $30 billion.

The responsibility for implementing UNCED agreements rests with national governments, while the commitments made by NGOs, local communities and private sector groups in each country will determine the rate of progress.

FAO has identified several levels of action:[90]

- Establishing realistic targets in line with the financial and institutional capabilities of each country, taking into account that only modest flows of external assistance are likely to be available. The broad goals within which to set such targets are: i) promoting the conservation and use of forests in the context of contributing to

---

[90] FAO, op. cit., footnote 89, p. 342.

BOX 27
INTERNATIONAL ORGANIZATIONS AND FORESTS

FAO and UNEP are two of the UN agencies working on forestry-related projects. Since 1945, *FAO* has been mandated to deal with forestry and has cooperated with member countries in rural development, policy analysis, institutional strengthening, plantation forestry, community forestry, participatory forestry, sustainable forest management, education, training and the production of scientific education and global statistics on forestry. It provides an important forum for discussion on global and regional forestry matters, through meetings such as the biennial Committee on Forestry (COFO) and the Committee on Forest Development in the Tropics. *UNEP* seeks to promote environmentally sound, economically feasible and socially acceptable sustainable rural development through coordinated projects in desertification control, reforestation, energy resources and soil conservation.

In 1985, FAO, UNDP, the World Bank and WRI established a global forestry strategy aimed at increasing public awareness about the plight of tropical forests and at mobilizing human and financial resources with a view to halting tropical deforestation. Initially named the *Tropical Forestry Action Plan (TFAP)* and then renamed the *Tropical Forests Action Programme (TFAP)* in 1991, this strategy provides a framework for national programmes for sustainable forest utilization and for harmonizing and strengthening international donor cooperation. The TFAP placed emphasis on management and planning within the context of overall land-use development as well as the involvement of rural people. In many ways, this was a landmark agreement which explicitly recognized the importance of national leadership, multidisciplinary approaches and the involvement of forest-dependent people and NGOs. More recently, TFAP activities have led to a shift from donor coordination and project activity to a more long-term programme, emphasizing country capacity and policy advice on the conservation and sustainable development of forests.

The World Bank is the largest single multilateral forestry sector lender; up to 1991 it had provided nearly $2.5 billion in loans to a total of 94 forestry projects. Its new forestry policy document identified two main challenges: i) the prevention of excessive deforestation, especially in the tropical moist forests; and ii) action to meet increasing demands for forest products and services for the rural poor in developing countries through tree planting and the management of existing forest resources.

The World Bank's 1991 forestry policy paper pledged that future evaluations would distinguish between projects that are environmentally protective or small farmer-oriented and those that are purely commercial. It also promised that its lending in the forestry sector would be subject to commitments by governments to sustainable and conservation-oriented forestry. One condition laid down is that *"the World Bank will not under any circumstances finance commercial logging in primary moist forests"*.

The *ITTO*, whose members comprise the world's major tropical timber-producing and timber-consuming countries, commenced operations in 1986. It was established as a commodity organization with its main focus on the development of a sustainable trade in tropical timber. It was recognized that a sustainable trade would only be achieved if there was a sustainable resource, and thus the organization focused many of its efforts on the sustainable management of tropical forests. One of its efforts in this area consists in encouraging the achievement of the objective that all exports of tropical timber come from sustainably managed forest resources by the year 2000.

The *International Union of Forest Research Organizations (IUFRO)*. Founded in 1892, this institute links forestry research institutes into a global network of interest groups. Its Special Programme for Developing Countries (SPDC), begun in 1983, supports training and self-teaching programmes and information services and promotes interagency contacts.

The *Centre for International Forestry Research (CIFOR)*. Based in Bogor, Indonesia, CIFOR was established in February 1993 as a member of the Consultative Group on International Agricultural Research

(CGIAR). CIFOR's focus is on the conservation and improved productivity of tropical forest ecosystems, with programmes in natural forests, open woodlands, plantations and woodlots and degraded lands and important components for the strengthening of national forest research institutions in tropical countries.

The *International Center for Research in Agroforestry (ICRAF)*. Since its establishment in 1978, ICRAF has undertaken global agroforestry research and now collaborates closely with CIFOR. Based in Nairobi, Kenya, ICRAF is currently promoting "Alternatives to slash-and-burn" in Southeast Asia, Africa and Latin America.

The *International Plant Genetic Resources Institute (IPGRI)*. Formerly the International Board for Plant Genetic Resources, established as a separate body from FAO under the UN Conference on the Human Environment (Stockholm, 1972), the IPGRI is mandated to deal with the conservation of biodiversity and the germplasm of forestry species.

The *World Wide Fund for Nature (WWF)*. This international NGO is highly

concerned with forestry issues. It has a range of programmes on biodiversity, conservation and sustainable management as well as others in countries throughout the world.

The *World Conservation Union (IUCN)*. This international union has a mandate to promote action and to seek support for projects related to environmental protection and resource management. As in the case of WWF, the IUCN's activities are not directed by members in individual countries.

development, poverty alleviation and food security; and
ii) contributing to environmental stability.

- Encouraging action and policy improvement outside the forestry sector to contain external factors that threaten forests, especially rapid population growth, poverty, low agricultural productivity and unremunerative terms of agricultural trade.
- Establishing land-use planning capacity and mechanisms for better intersectoral dialogue on land matters and for enforcing sustainable practices.
- Strengthening public support for forestry, principally through improved information for political decision-makers, policy-makers and the general public. A primary objective should be to ensure that the value of forests and forestry is better appreciated and that forestry receives the visibility necessary to attract the share of funding and other resources it deserves.
- Enhancing the capacity of governments and non-governmental institutions for the implementation of forestry programmes. Given the long-term nature of forestry, the continuity of governmental and other institutions and their programmes is a prerequisite for success.
- Preparing forestry sector action plans and updating existing ones to serve as an appropriate framework for action based on the orientations provided by UNCED.
- Instituting appropriate incentives for action by non-governmental actors, including the commercial private sector.

Actions within the forestry sector alone cannot secure sustainable conservation and a wise use of forests. Success in the implementation of UNCED follow-up activities requires the promotion of follow-up actions in other sectors that influence forestry, especially agriculture which is the single largest cause of deforestation in the world.

Forest resources are in the forefront of national policy debate about how to restructure economic and political systems and how such structural changes can be made consistent with national interests in local action, social and sectoral distribution, international obligations and sovereignty. Perspectives and demands of politically diverse groups are proliferating, placing significant strain on current institutions and policies. However, this political mainstreaming of forestry issues has involved productive debates, leading to innovative responses to public concerns.

Redirecting public policies to achieve efficient and sustainable forest management requires significant changes. However, UNCED's consensus on forest principles represents the first-ever commitment of responsibilities beyond national boundaries. The formidable challenge ahead is to turn these principles into practice. The contributions of forests to national development will depend on how well this challenge is met.

Special chapters

In addition to the usual review of the recent world food and agricultural situation, each issue of this report since 1957 has included one or more special studies on problems of longer-term interest. Special chapters in earlier issues have covered the following subjects:

1957
Factors influencing the trend of food consumption
Postwar changes in some institutional factors affecting agriculture

1958
Food and agricultural developments in Africa south of the Sahara
The growth of forest industries and their impact on the world's forests

1959
Agricultural incomes and levels of living in countries at different stages of economic development
Some general problems of agricultural development in less-developed countries in the light of postwar experience

1960
Programming for agricultural development

1961
Land reform and institutional change
Agricultural extension, education and research in Africa, Asia and Latin America

1962
The role of forest industries in the attack on economic underdevelopment
The livestock industry in less-developed countries

1963
Basic factors affecting the growth of productivity in agriculture
Fertilizer use: spearhead of agricultural development

1964
Protein nutrition: needs and prospects
Synthetics and their effects on agricultural trade

1966
Agriculture and industrialization
Rice in the world food economy

1967
Incentives and disincentives for farmers in developing countries
The management of fishery resources

1968
Raising agricultural productivity in developing countries through technological improvement
Improved storage and its contribution to world food supplies

1969
Agricultural marketing improvement programmes: some lessons from recent experience
Modernizing institutions to promote forestry development

1970
Agriculture at the threshold of the Second Development Decade

1971
Water pollution and its effects on living aquatic resources and fisheries

1972
Education and training for development
Accelerating agricultural research in the developing countries

1973
Agricultural employment in developing countries

1974
Population, food supply and agricultural development

1975
The Second United Nations Development Decade: mid-term review and appraisal

1976
Energy and agriculture

1977
The state of natural resources
and the human environment for
food and agriculture

1978
Problems and strategies in
developing regions

1979
Forestry and rural development

1980
Marine fisheries in the new era
of national jurisdiction

1981
Rural poverty in developing
countries and means of poverty
alleviation

1982
Livestock production: a world
perspective

1983
Women in developing
agriculture

1984
Urbanization, agriculture and
food systems

1985
Energy use in agricultural
production
Environmental trends in food
and agriculture
Agricultural marketing and
development

1986
Financing agricultural
development

1987-88
Changing priorities for
agricultural science and
technology in developing
countries

1989
Sustainable development and
natural resource management

1990
Structural adjustment and
agriculture

1991
Agricultural policies and issues:
lessons from the 1980s and
prospects for the 1990s

1992
Marine fisheries and the law of
the sea: a decade of change

1993
Water policies and agriculture

FAO Economic and Social Development Papers

POLICY REFORM AND THE AGRICULTURAL SECTOR

65   Agricultural stabilization and structural adjustment policies in developing
      countries (1987)
66   Agricultural issues in structural adjustment programs (1987)
84   Measures of protection: methodology, economic interpretation and policy
      relevance (1989)
90   The impact of stabilization and structural adjustment policies on the rural sector –
      case-studies of Côte d'Ivoire, Senegal, Liberia, Zambia and Morocco (1991)
95   Guidelines for monitoring the impact of structural adjustment programmes on the
      agricultural sector (1990)
96   The effects of trade and exchange rate policies on production in agriculture (1990)
98   Institutional changes in agricultural product and input markets and their impact on
      agricultural performance (1991)
99   Agricultural labour markets and structural adjustment in sub-Saharan Africa (1991)
100   Structural adjustment and household welfare in rural areas – a micro-economic
      perspective (1991)
103   The impact of structural adjustment on smallholders (1992)
104   Structural adjustment policy sequencing in sub-Saharan Africa (1991)
105   The role of public and private agents in the agricultural sector of developing
      countries (1991)
115   Design of poverty alleviation strategy in rural areas (1993)
124   Structural adjustment and agriculture: African and Asian experiences (in press)

ENVIRONMENT AND SUSTAINABLE DEVELOPMENT STUDIES

107   Land reform and structural adjustment in sub-Saharan Africa: controversies and
      guidelines (1992)
110   Agricultural sustainability: definition and implications for agricultural and trade
      policy (1992)
121   Policies for sustainable development (1994)

In preparation

•   Agricultural taxation under structural adjustment, medium-term growth and
      the rural poor
•   Growth theories, old and new, and the role of agriculture in economic
      development
•   Analysing the effects of liberalization scenarios in North-South production and
      trade patterns using computable general equilibrium models
•   Transition and price stabilization policies in East European agriculture
•   The economics of international agreements for the protection of environmental
      and agricultural resources: an economics perspective

SELECTED

FAO forestry publications

UNASYLVA

- 46(180) – Common property
- 45(179) – Forestry in countries with economies in transition
- 45(178) – The changing role of forestry institutions
- 44(175) – Policy and legislation
- 44(174) – Forest resources assessment
- 43(169) – Sustainability

FAO FORESTRY PAPERS

92 Forestry policies in Europe – an analysis (1989)

111 Forestry policies in the Near East region – analysis and synthesis (1993)

112 Forest resources assessment 1990 – tropical countries (1993)

114 Assessing forestry project impacts: issues and strategies (1993)

115 Forestry policies of selected countries in Asia and the Pacific (1993)

122 Readings in sustainable forest management (in press)

TIME SERIES FOR SOFA '94 DISKETTE
Instructions for use

An experimental diskette was included in *The State of Food and Agriculture 1993*, with approximately 100 sets of time series data for about 150 countries. The data were accessible through TS-view software, incorporated in the diskette.

The response to this experimental diskette was overwhelmingly positive. Thus, *The State of Food and Agriculture 1994* includes a diskette containing an improved version of the software, renamed FAOSTAT TS, and almost twice as many data series. Since this year's special chapter deals with forestry, relevant forestry time series data are included on the diskette.

FAOSTAT TS

FAOSTAT TS software provides quick and easy access to structured annual time series databases. Even inexperienced computer users can use FAOSTAT TS. No spreadsheet, graphics or database program is required. FAOSTAT TS is fully menu-driven, so there are no commands to learn. Users can browse through and print graphs and tables, plot multiline graphs, fit trend lines and export data for use in other programs. FAOSTAT TS is trilingual (English, French, Spanish) and uses a standard menu format.

FAOSTAT TS software is in the public domain and may be freely distributed. The data files accompanying the software, however, are under FAO copyright and users must attribute FAO as the source. FAO can provide only very limited support to users of this software and the accompanying data and cannot assist users who modify the software or data files. FAO disclaims all warrants of fitness of the software or the data for a particular use.

Technical requirements

FAOSTAT TS software requires an IBM or compatible PC with a hard disk, DOS 3.0 or higher, 300 KB of available RAM and graphics capability. Graphics support is provided for all common graphics adapters (VGA, EGA, MCGA, CGA and Hercules monochrome).

FAOSTAT TS will print graphs on Epson dot matrix, Hewlett-Packard and compatible laser printers. To use FAOSTAT TS with other printers, users can enable their own graphics printing utility before starting the program. One such utility is GRAPHICS.COM in DOS 2.0 or later releases.

Because of its use of DOS graphics modes, if FAOSTAT TS is run under MS-Windows or OS/2, it should be set to run in a full screen DOS session.

Installation

Before running FAOSTAT TS you must install the software and data files on your hard disk. Installation is automated through the INSTALL.BAT utility on the diskette.
- To install from drive A: to drive C:
    - insert the diskette in drive A:
    - type *A:* and press ENTER
    - type *INSTALL C:* and press ENTER
    - press any key

A C:\SOFA94 directory is created and, after installation, you will already be in this directory.

Entering FAOSTAT TS

- To start the FAOSTAT TS software, if you are not already in the C:\SOFA94 directory (as after installation), change to this directory:
    - type *CD\SOFA94* and press ENTER
    - then, from the command prompt in the SOFA94 directory, type *SOFA94* and press ENTER

A graphics title screen will be displayed, followed by the main menu screen.

• If FAOSTAT TS does not start, graphs do not display correctly or the menus are difficult to read, your computer may not be compatible with the default functions of FAOSTAT TS.

The use of a command-line option may help. You may try to start FAOSTAT TS with the -E parameter to disable its use of expanded memory (type *SOFA94 -E*). You may also force the use of a particular graphics or text mode by typing its name as a parameter (for example, -EGA would force the use of EGA mode graphics).

Language choices
• The initial default language for FAOSTAT TS is English. To change the default language to French or Spanish:
- go to the FILE menu
- select LANGUAGE using the Arrow key (9) and pressing ENTER
- select your choice of language from those displayed and press ENTER

The language selected will remain the default language until another is selected.

Navigating the menus
The main menu bar consists of FILE, DATA, GRAPH, TABLE and HELP menus. Most menu options are disabled until you open a data file.
• Navigate the menus by using the Arrow keys (8 9 7 6) and make a selection by highlighting an item and pressing ENTER. To back out of a selection, press the ESC key.
• If you have a mouse, menu items can be selected with the mouse cursor. The left mouse button selects an item and the right mouse button acts as the ESC key.

After you have made a menu selection, the menu will redraw and highlight a possible next choice.
• Several short-cut keys are available throughout the program:

Key	Action
F1	- *Help:* Displays context-sensitive help text.

ESC	- *Escape:* Backs out of the current menu choice or exits the graph or table currently displayed.
ALT+N	- *Notes:* Displays text notes associated with the current data file, if the text file is available. This text may be edited. Notes will not appear while a graph is displayed.
ALT+X, ALT+Q	- *Exit:* Exits FAOSTAT TS immediately, without prompting.

Help
• You will see context-sensitive help displayed at the bottom of each screen. Press F1 for more extensive help on a highlighted option.
• Select HELP from the main menu to access the help information. Introductory information on the software, help topics and an "About" summary screen are available from the HELP menu.
• The HELP menu options call up the same Help windows obtained by pressing the F1 key at any of the menu screens:
- the FAOSTAT TS option displays the top-level help page
- the TOPICS option lists the help contents
- the ABOUT option shows summary program information

Opening a data file
• To display a list of FAOSTAT TS data files:
- go to the FILE menu
- select OPEN

All of the FAOSTAT TS data files in the current directory are displayed. Initially, only SOFA94 will be present. Other FAOSTAT PC data files, version 3.0, can be used with FAOSTAT TS.
• Use the Arrow keys to highlight the file you wish to view and press ENTER to select it. Files are shown with the date of their last revision. You can also highlight your choice by typing the first letters of the file's name. The current search string will appear in the lower left corner of the list.

• You can change the default data drive and directory from the file list by selecting the directory or drive of your choice.

If a current data file is open, loading in a new file will return FAOSTAT TS to its defaults (time trend, no trend line, no user-specified units or scalar). Only one file can be loaded at a time.

Once you have made a file selection, all the menu selections are activated.

Selecting a data series

• Use the DATA menu to select or modify a data series or to fit a statistical trend.

• Select a data series by choosing the name of a country and a data element from the scrolling menus. The first entry displays a list of country names, the second entry displays a list of data item names and the third displays a list of data element names.

If you type the first letters of a name in a list, the menu selection bar will jump to the matching name. For example:
- type *NEW* to skip to New Zealand
- press ENTER to select the highlighted name

Displaying graphs and graph options

The GRAPH menu allows you to view the data in chart form. You can display time trends and table or column profiles. Options under the GRAPH menu change the data series shown as well as its display.

For example, to show a plot of the data selected:
- go to the GRAPH menu
- select DISPLAY

Many options to modify, save or print a graph are available only while a graph is on screen. Remember to use the F1 help key for a reminder of your options.

Graph action keys. You have several options when a graph is displayed:

• Press ESC to exit the graph and return to the main menu.

• Press F1 for help on the graph action keys. The help box lists the choices available while a graph

is on the screen. You must exit the help box before making a selection.

• To change the series displayed, press the Arrow and PAGEUP or PAGEDOWN keys.

• The plus key (+) allows you to add up to three other series to the one displayed. Press the minus key (-) to remove a series. This is the way multiline charts are created:
- display an initial series
- press the + key to add subsequent series to the chart

• Press A to display a table of the axis data with statistics. Press T to show a table of the fitted trend data, the residuals and fit statistics (if a trend line is selected, see below).

• The INS key permits you to insert text directly on the graph. While inserting text, press F1 for help on your text options. You can type small or large, horizontal or vertical text.

• To print a graph, press P and select your printer from the menu. The print output is only a screen dump of the display, so the quality is limited.

• To save a graph for later printing or viewing, press S. The graph image will be saved in the common PCX bitmap format. You can use the PRINTPCX program or other software to view or print multiple images later. PRINTPCX also permits you to convert colour PCX images into black and white images suitable for inclusion in a word processing document.

Fitting trend lines

• To fit a statistical function to a data series, select FIT from the DATA menu. The options under FIT allow you to select the type of function, data year limits to include in the fit and a final projection year for a statistical forecast.

• By fitting a trend line (selecting the LINE option under FIT) with a projection (selecting PROJECTION under FIT), a statistical forecast can be plotted. Use the + key to add a new data series to the graph, which can be made with only a few key strokes.

Charting profiles

• The options under the GRAPH menu allow you

to change the year span or style of the graph display (options LIMITS and STYLE, respectively), or to switch from a time trend to a table or column data profile (VIEWPOINT). The VIEWPOINT option is an easy means to compare data for a particular year.

Viewpoint

• If you want to change from a time series display to a country or item profile display for a given year, select VIEWPOINT from the GRAPH menu. Select DISPLAY from the GRAPH menu, and the profile will be drawn.

The initial profile display is for the last year of historical data. To change the year, use the Arrow keys. Press F1 for help.

• For a tables profile (profile of data across countries), you can either choose the tables to be displayed or let FAOSTAT TS select the top members and array them in order. A limit of 50 items can appear in one profile.

By selecting TOP MEMBERS instead of SELECTED MEMBERS, FAOSTAT TS will sort the values in the file and display a ranking of table or column values.

Viewing tables

• The TABLE menu allows you to look at data in a tabular format and to define subset tables that may be saved and imported into other software packages:
  - go to the TABLE menu
  - select BROWSE DATA to view individual data tables from the current file
• When viewing tables, a help bar appears at the bottom of the screen. Press PAGEUP or PAGEDOWN to change the table displayed or press ALT+1 or ALT+2 to choose from a list of tables. Use the Arrow keys to scroll the columns and rows.

Series data

• The SERIES DATA option under the TABLE menu displays the last data series selected, including summary statistics. This is the data series used to plot a graph. To change the series,

you must make a new choice from the DATA menu.

• The SERIES DATA screen can also be displayed while you are in a graph by pressing the letter A. If more than one series has been plotted, only the last series is shown. The range of years used for the series and statistics can be adjusted through the LIMITS option under the GRAPH menu.

• To view country or item profile lists and statistics, select VIEWPOINT from the GRAPH menu. You can quickly see a list of the tables with the greatest values (for example, countries with the highest commodity consumption) by choosing a table profile from VIEWPOINT and selecting the TOP MEMBERS option. Then select SERIES DATA from the TABLE menu to view the list, or select DISPLAY from the GRAPH menu to plot a chart.

Trend data

• If the FIT option has been selected (from the DATA menu) for a time trend, then the values composing the trend can be displayed with the TREND DATA option. Summary statistics for the original series and for the trend as well as residual values are included. The list scrolls with the Arrow keys and you can toggle between the axis and trend data with the A and T keys.

Exporting data

• The EXPORT option under the FILE menu allows you to export FAOSTAT TS data into other file formats or to create custom tables for viewing or printing. By selecting EXPORT, you will jump into another set of menus.

• To select the tables and columns you want to view or save, go to the DATA menu. Select options with the + key. To undo all your selections quickly, select RESET MARKS.

• To arrange, view, save or print data, go to the options under EXPORT (in the FILE menu):
  - VIEW: displays a temporary text file of the data selected. It is a convenient way to view a subset of the tables and columns in a FAOSTAT TS file and can also be used to see the effects of the ORIENTATION or LAYOUT

selections before using the SAVE or PRINT option.

- SAVE: displays a list of file formats to let you save your data choices in a file. You will be prompted for a file name. If you need to export FAOSTAT TS data for use with other software, use this menu item. The WK1 and DBF file format selections are not affected by the LAYOUT option (see below).
- PRINT: prints your current table and column selections. Many printers cannot print more than five columns of FAOSTAT TS data. Select VIEW to check the table width before printing.
- LAYOUT: allows you to display years across rows or down columns. The default is down columns.

• To get back to the main FAOSTAT TS menu or to clear your selections and create more tables, go to the RETURN option.

Making notes

• To read or edit textual information on the current data file, select NOTES from the FILE menu. You also can call up the Notes box by pressing ALT+N at any of the menus. The option NOTES allows you to read or edit text associated with the data file.

DOS shell and exit

The DOS SHELL option under the FILE menu returns you to the DOS prompt temporarily but keeps FAOSTAT TS in memory. This is not the normal way to exit the program. It is useful if you need to execute a DOS command and would like to return to the same data file. The data file itself is dropped from memory and reloaded on return, so default values will be in effect.

Exiting FAOSTAT TS

• To exit FAOSTAT TS:
   - go to the FILE menu
   - select EXIT

The ALT+X or ALT+Q key combinations are short cuts to exit the program from almost any screen.